KB182780

Dictionary of the Mediterranean
Inter-Civilization Exchanges

This work was supported by the Ministry of Education of the Republic of Korea and
the National Research Foundation of Korea (NRF – 2018S1A6A3A02022221)

Institute for Mediterranean Studies
Humanities Publication Series

Dictionary of the Mediterranean Inter-Civilization Exchanges

General Editor Yong Soo YOON

Congratulations on the publication of the 2024 *Dictionary of Mediterranean Inter-Civilization Exchanges*, compiled by the IMS(Institute for Mediterranean Studies).

This English dictionary is second version of the one that has been prepared by IMS since 2007 and published in Korean in 2020. We hope that the publication of this dictionary will serve as an opportunity to lay a corner stone for the significant consequences of the collaborative work between domestic and international research networks that IMS has constructed and accumulated since their establishment in 1997 to be widely recognized and play a role of international academic source. We believe two main points are deserved to be noticed in this publication. One is the perspective and methodology of the collaborating researchers centered around IMS, that is, to go beyond the Euro-centric perspective and reveal the coexistence and hybridization of various civilizations around the Mediterranean and the 'Relation Balance Theory'(關係均衡論) between civilizations. The other is the hope that through this process, a new 'Mediterranean Civilization Exchange Studies'(地中海文明交流學) will born.

In other words, that new international cooperative research networks will unfold centered on Korea, a third-party country in East Asia that is neither European nor Islamic. With the publication of the Korean version of the dictionary in 2020 and the English version in 2024, I hope that this ambitious project improves and further be specified, and that 'Mediterranean Civilization Exchange Studies' become more recognized internationally and be developed into an opportunity for further verification and expansion. In this spirit, I would like to review the significance and expected value of the publication of the English version of the Mediterranean Civilization Exchange Dictionary and its future tasks in this congratulatory address.

Significance of the Compilation of an English-Language Dictionary of Mediterranean *Inter-Civilization Exchanges*

The Mediterranean has long been crossroads of civilizations, facilitating numerous cultural, economic, and political exchanges from ancient times to the present day. Despite its importance, access to the vast research and information related to Mediterranean civilization exchanges has had limited opportunities to be shared with public. This English edition of the dictionary aims to bridge the gap and provide both academia and the public a comprehensive resource on Mediterranean civilization interactions. I hope that this dictionary serves as a valuable source of knowledge for scholars and readers worldwide, offering an opportunity to explore the rich history of exchanges among the civilizations in the Mediterranean.

The compilation of an English-language dictionary on Mediterranean civilization exchanges carries notable academic, educational, and cultural value. The Mediterranean has been a focal point of exchange between Eastern and Western civilizations, and understanding these interactions extends beyond historical facts, shedding light on the contemporary value of multicultural cooperation and understanding.

The academic significance of the dictionary lies in its systematic compilation of diverse facets of Mediterranean civilization exchanges, providing a foundational resource for scholars. It covers the historical development of inter-civilization exchanges from ancient times to the modern era, marking itself as a critical reference across various academic disciplines.

The educational significance is evident in how this dictionary organizes academic achievements in a way that makes them easily accessible to students and researchers. As an English-language resource, this dictionary is a crucial tool for educational institutions and scholars across the world, deepening the global understanding of Mediterranean civilization exchanges and allowing students to delve deeper into the vital historical area.

Moreover, the cultural significance of this dictionary lies in reevaluation of the rich interactions among the different Mediterranean civilizations. As a region where diverse civilizations coexisted and mutually influenced, the Mediterranean would be an example on point to suggest a significant model for modern global inter-civilization cooperation and exchange.

Historical Development of Research Trends

Early research (19th century to early 20th century) primarily showed a Eurocentric approach, focusing on Greek and Roman civilizations. This period's research relied heavily on classical texts and treated other civilizations, such as Phoenician and Egyptian, as secondary in the Mediterranean narrative.

In the mid-20th century, archaeological discoveries remarkably expanded the understanding of the interactions among the civilizations, particularly with the uncovering of evidence of Phoenician, Egyptian, and Carthaginian trade and cultural exchange. Such findings emphasized the interdependence of Mediterranean civilizations.

The late 20th century witnessed the work of historian Fernand Braudel transforming Mediterranean studies. Braudel shifted the focus toward long-term structures and geographical factors, analyzing how economic, social, and environmental frameworks influenced the exchange among the Mediterranean civilizations over extended periods.

Recent Research Trends

Recent research on Mediterranean civilization exchanges adopts more global historical perspective. Scholars are examining how Mediterranean civilizations interacted not only with each other but also with regions beyond the Mediterranean by analyzing trade networks and tracing the clue of cultural exchanges in a global context. Additionally, with the development of field of digital humanities, Geographic Information Systems (GIS) and big data analysis are utilized to visually reconstruct ancient trade routes and interactions between civilizations.

Another emerging feature of recent research is the focus on environmental history and ecological studies. Researchers are exploring how climate change and natural environments influenced the development and interactions of civilizations in the Mediterranean, suggesting unnoticed insights into the relationship between nature and human activities.

Expected Value of the English-Language Dictionary

This dictionary is highly expected to contributes to facilitation of international collaboration and knowledge sharing among scholars by providing comprehensive information on Mediterranean civilization exchanges. Being authorized in English, it allows global researchers to access and delve into the complex networks of trade, culture, and diplomacy that shaped the Mediterranean world. Furthermore, the dictionary serves as a vital resource for promoting intercultural understanding and global cooperation, offering not only academic advantage but also broader public value.

Future Challenges

Continuous updates will be necessary to maintain the relevancy and consistency of the dictionary. As archaeological discoveries progress and new research findings emerge, it is crucial to incorporate such advancements into the dictionary to ensure the up-to-date information and understanding. Additionally, strengthening multidisciplinary approach is required, as collective work between historians, archaeologists, anthropologists, and others can provide deeper level of comprehensive understanding of Mediterranean civilization exchanges.

As living in the days of AI era, utilizing the AI technologies for research and dictionary management implies both opportunities and challenges. AI can process and analyze vast amounts of data promptly, letting more precise and faster research adopted into Mediterranean civilizations. However, careful consideration of ethical issues regarding AI-based interpretations and the imperative need for human scholars' role to provide nuanced judgments should not be forgotten to avoid oversimplification.

Conclusion

This English-language dictionary displays a comprehensive understanding of Mediterranean civilization exchanges and paves the way for further research and exploration. Observing daily evolution of AI and development of Digital Humanities, our hope for this dictionary to evolve and remain an indispensable academic resource is firm. It is also our expectation that this work encourages to activate global research and collaboration in Mediterranean civilization studies and inspire deeper inquiries into the rich history of inter-civilization exchanges. We wish that this dictionary to assist and guide scholars and readers alike, letting them explore the colorful history and significance of Mediterranean civilization exchanges.

Congratulations on Publication

I would like to express my respect and gratitude to the professors and researchers at IMS who showed their dedication to design and publish this dictionary, and to all the scholars and researchers from home and abroad who participated in authorship. I would especially like to express my respect and gratitude to Director Yong Soo Yoon, Professor Jung Ha Kim, and Emertus Professor Chun Sik Choi who devoted themselves to planning, compiling, and executing the English and Korean dictionaries. I wish this book contributes to academic journey of readers across the globe and inspire fostering in-depth exploration to the field of Mediterranean civilization exchanges.

September, 23rd. 2024.

Emertus Professor Young-gil Cha

Gyeongsang National University

The Mediterranean sea, as its name suggests, is a sea located between land masses. Covering an area of 2.5 million square kilometers with a width of approximately 4,000 km and a length of about 1,800 km, the Mediterranean sea appears the big ocean that divides continents. However, in reality, the Mediterranean serves as the joint connecting each continent, and has been a space for communication and exchange where human and material exchanges have continued.

Just as the circulation of blood is essential for life, uninterrupted cultural exchanges in the Mediterranean have been crucial for the advancement of human civilization. Ancient Phoenicians spread knowledge, technology, and writing from the eastern Mediterranean across to the western regions. The Roman Empire, which dominated the entire Mediterranean, referred to it as "Mare Internum," fostering cultural exchange and forming a unified cultural sphere.

In essence, the Mediterranean region is not a fragmented space but rather a vast organism where inter-connectedness prevails throughout.

From ancient times to the present day, various nations and peoples have dominated the Mediterranean, absorbing the scholarly and cultural nutrients of existing states to fuel their own growth. Existing states willingly became hosts to give birth to new nations, fading into history only to reemerge through cycles of revival. The Arabs who created the Orient civilization declined after giving birth to the Greek civilization, but were revived through Islamic civilization, and Latinos who formed the ancient Roman civilization stayed in the shadow of Islam for a long time, but were also revived through the Renaissance

The intellectual and cultural achievements of ancient Greece were facilitated by embracing Oriental civilization, while the glory of Islamic achievements was enabled by actively incorporating the accomplishments of Greece, Rome, Byzantium, and Persia. Thus, the history and civilization of the Mediterranean have continuously evolved in cycles, with new civilizations that embrace previous ones emerging in forms of higher advancement. The Mediterranean civilization has constantly developed over time, ultimately driven by communication and exchange.

The Institute for Mediterranean Studies at Busan University of Foreign Studies recognizes the Mediterranean as a space of civilization and communication, and has been studying the region. *The Dictionary of Mediterranean Civilization Exchange*, which was published in 2021 in Korean language, represents the institute's research achievements by tracking the creation, diffusion, transformation, and regeneration of Mediterranean civilizations to demonstrate that the achievements of the Mediterranean are deeply rooted in the history of exchanges.

The Korean version of *The Dictionary of Mediterranean Civilization Exchange* was selected as an 'Excellent Academic Publication' in 2021 by the Ministry of Education in Korea. The event prompted the publication of English version to further share the institute's research achievements. Scholars from diverse field in and out of the Korea have joined to the authorship of English version, focusing on entries not covered in the Korean edition.

While there are still many topics and areas to be covered, we hope that this dictionary become a cornerstone of Mediterranean civilization exchange studies. We deeply appreciate the domestic and international researchers who showed their deep contribution to authorship of the "Dictionary of Mediterranean Inter-Civilization Exchanges" on behalf of the Institute for Mediterranean Studies. We also would like to express deep gratitude to our members in the institute for their dedication to the publication of this dictionary.

October, 2024.

Director of the Institute for Mediterranean Studies

YongSoo Yoon

Publication Committee and Authors

Acquiring Editor : Yongsoo Yoon

Editorial Board : JungHa Kim

                       Younggil Cha

                       Sujung Kim

                       Minji Yang

                       Mona Farouk

                       Sebastian Müller

                       Jihoon Kang

                       Jisu Kim

Production Editor : Jisu Kim

Copy Editors : Motahare Mozafari

                 Jisu Kim

Authors

Byoung Joo Hah (Institute for Mediterranean Studies)

Chagyu Kim (Department of History, Myongji Univ.)

Chinsung Dury Chung (Korea Maritime & Ocean Univ.)

DongEun Lee (Dharma College, Dongguk Univ.)

Emiliano Pennisi (Sogang Univ.)

Eunsoon Choi (Division of Global Maritime Studies, Korea Maritime & Ocean Univ.)

HaeJo Chung (Division of Int'l and Area Studies, PKU)

Heejung Kim (Institute for Mediterranean Studies, BUFS)

Hyeyoung Choi (Jeonnam Univ.)

Inhyun Jung (Korea Maritime & Ocean Univ.)

Jaeyang Park (Department of Middle East Studies, BUFS)

Jeanam Park (Inha Univ.)

JeongHa Hwang (Seowon Univ.)

JiHoon Kang (Institute for Mediterranean Studies, BUFS)

JinHan Jung (HUFS)

John Chircop (Malta Univ.)

M.H. Mozafari (Institute for Mediterranean Studies)

Min Bae (Institute for Mediterranean Studies, BUFS)

Minji Yang (Institute for Mediterranean Studies, BUFS)

Mona Farouk M. Ahmed (Institute for Mediterranean Studies, BUFS)

NamMo Jung (Institute of Int'l Maritime Affairs, Korea Maritime & Ocean Univ.)

Nilly Kamal Elamir (Independent Researcher)

SangHo Moon (Department of Computer Engineering, BUFS)

Sebastian Müller (Institute for Mediterranean Studies, BUFS)

Soojeong Yi (Euro-Mena Institute, Sogang Univ.)

Sujung Kim (Department of Middle East Studies, BUFS)

Sunah Choi (The Institute for Eurasian Turk Studies, Dongduk Women's Univ.)

Yongsoo Yoon (Institute for Mediterranean Studies, BUFS)

*Abbreviation

BUFS : Busan University of Foreign Studies

HUFS : Hankook University of Foreign Studies

PKU : Pukyoung National University

Contents

▶ Laws and Regulations

▶ Trade Goods

▶ Science and Technologies

▼

Religions and Mythologies

01

Greek-Roman Mythology

Mythology is a collection of traditional stories that typically involve supernatural beings, gods, heroes, and various elements of the supernatural or divine. These stories are used to explain the origins of the world, natural phenomena, the customs and beliefs of a particular culture, and the moral and ethical values of that society. Mythology often serves as a means of conveying cultural and religious beliefs, as well as providing a framework for understanding the world and human existence. Myths can take various forms, including legends, folktales, creation stories, and heroic narratives, and they play an important role in shaping the cultural identity and shared heritage of a people. Since Greek and Roman mythology are closely related, the term Classical mythology, which refers to both of them as a unit, is also in use.

The oldest references to Greek mythology and the pantheon of the twelve Olympian gods and goddesses stems from the famous Homeric epics 'Iliad' and 'Odyssey' (ca. 8th century BC). The poet Hesiod, who lived around the same time as Homer, is the author of two other very important and detailed works, the 'Theogony' and 'Works and Days'. The 'Theogony' starts with the very beginnings of the world, namely Chaos, and describes the emergence of primary divine beings, including Gaia, Uranus, and the Titans. A recurring motif is that of father-against-son conflicts, such as Cronus overthrowing Uranus and Zeus overthrowing Cronus. 'Works and Days' also includes the myths of Prometheus, Pandora, and the Five Ages. In the huge body of classical literature references to mythology are omnipresent. The works from ancient Greek and Roman poets, e.g. Aeschylus and Sophocles; philosophers, e.g. Ovid and Seneca; historians, e.g. Herodotus and Diodorus Siculus; and geographers, e.g. Pausanias and Strabo, deal in one way or the other with matters related to mythology and the gods. Other sources are visual media such as sculptures or the famous Greek pottery paintings, which often feature episodes and references to mythological themes, adding details which are not represented in the surviving historical sources (figure 1 and 2).

Fig 1–1. Classical Greek red–figure terracotta bell–krater with depiction of Persephone's ascension from the underworld.[1]

---

1 Source: Metmuseum; Accession Number: 28,57,23; https://www.metmuseum.org/art/collection/

Fig 1–2. Roman statue of Dionysos leaning on Spes, a Roman personification of Hope.[2]

In Greek religion and daily life, stories from the myths took a central part. The heroic stories, for instance Hercules' tasks, Achilles' deeds, and Odysseus' adventures, served, among others, as entertainment, moral guidelines and as a means of identity construction. A key theme in Greek mythology is how the world began. Poems like Hesiod's 'Theogony' explain the birth of the universe, and stories like Prometheus and Pandora tell us how humans and their culture

search/252973.

2 Source: Metmuseum; Accession Number: 1990.247; https://www.metmuseum.org/art/collection/search/255973.

came into being.

The idea of fate is central in Greek mythology. There was a strong belief that destiny is predetermined. Trying to change fate typically leads to tragic outcomes, highlighting the limits of human control in the face of divine will. This divine will, represented by the works of the different gods and goddesses, was often imposed on the mortals. The gods and other spiritual beings were interested in the deeds of the people and not far away as they inhabited the environment or were present in their temples. Albeit divine, gods and goddesses displayed human emotions and they could be jealous, hostile or benevolent.

A common thread in mythological stories is the idea of hubris or excessive pride. Characters who display too much arrogance often incur the anger of the gods, resulting in their downfall or suffering. Transformation and change are other recurring themes in Greek myths. Gods, heroes, and ordinary people may change their form, reflecting on the evolving and interconnected nature of people's lives. Other strong themes are love and desire, as well as trickery and cleverness.

Greek mythology is populated by a huge variety of supernatural beings. The Olympian Gods and Goddesses, residing on the eponymous Mount Olympus, which is the highest mountain of Greece, located on the border between the northern regions of Thessaly and Macedonia, were the principal deities who ruled over different aspects of the world. Zeus, the king of the gods and ruler of the heavens, controlled thunder and lightning. He was the chief deity of Mount Olympus and the father of many gods and heroes. Hera, the queen of the gods and wife of Zeus, was associated with marriage and family. She protected married women and presided over the institution of matrimony. Poseidon, the god of the sea, was known for his control over the oceans and the creatures that inhabited them. He was often depicted with a trident. Demeter, the goddess of agriculture, governed the growth of crops and the changing of the seasons. She was closely linked to the fertility of the earth. Athena, born from the head of Zeus, was the goddess of wisdom and strategic warfare, known for her intelligence and courage. She was often depicted with an owl and a shield. Apollo, the god of the sun, music, and the arts, was a master archer and musician. He was associated with the pursuit of knowledge and artistic creativity. Artemis, Apollo's twin sister, was the goddess of the hunt and wilderness. She was also the protector of young girls and the moon. Ares, the god of war, represented the violent and chaotic aspects in battle. Hephaestus, the god of blacksmiths and craftsmen, was known for his exceptional skill in forging weapons and crafting intricate works of art. Aphrodite, the goddess of love and beauty, was often depicted as an enchanting and alluring figure. Hermes, the messenger god, was a swift and witty character. He was the divine herald and guide of souls to the afterlife, as well as the god of commerce and travelers. Dionysus, the god of wine and revelry, represented joy and ecstasy. He was associated with celebrations, theater, and the pleasures of life.

Aside from the 12 Olympians, there was a range of other spiritual beings with different meanings and abilities. There were, for instance, the Titans, powerful primordial beings who predated the Olympian gods and were often associated with cosmic forces and the passage of time. Cyclopes, one-eyed giants, were known for their craftsmanship, responsible for forging Zeus' thunderbolt. Gorgons, famously represented by Medusa, had snake-like hair and could turn onlookers into stone statues with their gaze. Famous are the Sirens, who lured sailors to their doom with their enchanting voices. The iconic Centaurs, creatures with human upper bodies and horse lower bodies, were often depicted as wild and unruly beings. A class of female natural spirits and guardians of their domains were the Nymphs, which can be further distinguished into dryads, naiads, and nereids. Satyrs, the companions of Dionysus, were known for their love of music, dance, and wine. Not bound to the realm of the earth were the Harpies, winged creatures with the bodies of birds and faces of women. This is also true for the Griffins, creatures with the body of a lion and the head of an eagle, symbolizing strength, majesty, and protection.

Mythological beings that occurred only as a single specimen were, for instance, the Minotaur with the body of a man and the head of a bull living in the labyrinth on Crete, or the Chimera, a fire-breathing monster with the body of a lion, the head of a goat, and the tail of a serpent, representing chaos and untamed nature. The mythological Sphinx, with the body of a lion, the wings of a bird, and the head of a human, who is a different entity from the famous Egyptian sphinxes, posed riddles to travelers and devoured those who could not solve them.

The close affiliation of Greek and Roman mythology has several roots. One of them is the seafaring activity and later the migration movement of Greek people from their homeland in the Aegean Sea to distant shores in the Mediterranean from the 8th century BCE. The earliest places of Greek settlement outside their own territories were located in southern Italy and Sicily. Sicily, for instance, became Hellenized over the course of the centuries to such a degree that its inhabitants spoke their own Greek dialect. Trade relations and the strong connectivity between communities that is inherent in the Mediterranean region contributed to the proliferation of mythological stories and religious practices. The archetypical character of many mythological narratives from the Greek world resonated well with the worldview of other communities in the Mediterranean region and beyond. The Etruscans, for instance, the northern neighbors of Rome, from whom the Romans borrowed many elements of their culture, had a particular favor for Greek customs and mythological stories, as can be seen in their famous tomb paintings and imported Greek pottery. Pottery from Greek workshops was favored all around the Mediterranean, but the Etruscans and other Italian communities had preferences for particular mythological scenes which were produced specifically for their taste.

The significance of Greek mythology and other aspects of Greek culture for the Romans becomes clear through the Roman foundation myth. The mythological ancestor of the Roman people, the hero Aeneas, escaped with his father and son from the city of Troy after the Achaeans managed to sack the city with the help of the wooden horse after 10 years of siege and warfare. After a classical hero's journey through the Mediterranean Sea, similar to the Odyssey of the hero Ulysses, he landed in Cumae, a site northwest of the modern town of Naples, and became the ancestor of the twin brothers

Romulus and Remus.

There are many other connections that link the Romans to the mythological past of the Greek communities and their gods. Thus it is not surprising that the 12 Olympian gods were syncretised with the Roman gods and goddesses. In Roman mythology, for instance, Zeus was equated with Jupiter, who held a similar role as the ruler of the gods and as the god of the sky and thunder. Hera corresponded to Juno, who had a parallel role as the goddess of marriage and women's well-being. Poseidon was matched with Neptune, who shared dominion over the seas and water. Demeter, the Greek goddess of agriculture, was linked to Ceres in Roman mythology, revered as the goddess of agriculture, fertility, and the harvest. Athena found her Roman counterpart in Minerva, being associated with wisdom and warfare but also crafts and medicine. Apollo retained his name in both Greek and Roman pantheons. Artemis corresponded to Diana, sharing roles and also being revered as the goddess of the moon. Ares, the Greek god of war, was matched with Mars, both representing war, courage, and military prowess. Hephaestus was akin to Vulcan in Roman mythology, the god of fire, metalworking, and the forge. Aphrodite corresponded to Venus, where she retained her role as the goddess of love, beauty, and desire. Hermes shared his role and attributes with Mercury, the god of commerce, travel, and messages. Dionysus found his Roman counterpart in Bacchus, who played a similar role in Roman culture.

The syncretism of Greek and Roman gods led to the addition of particular properties to some of the deities which were originally not associated with them in the Greek pantheon. Generally, there were slight differences in how the gods were perceived by Greeks and Romans. For the Greeks, the gods were divine beings with very similar sentiments and imperfections as human beings. The Romans saw their gods more as authoritative and flawless figures. The mythological stories played a more important role for the Greeks, whilst the Roman religious practice focused more on the performance of rituals and sacrifices.

Since Greek and Roman mythology had not the same origin, the Roman pantheon also included a number of deities who have no counterpart in Greek mythology. One of those is the god Janus, who stands out with his unique representation, possessing two faces that symbolize transitions, doorways, and beginnings. Another Roman deity without direct roots in the Greek tradition was Vesta, the goddess of the hearth and home. She was honored through the maintenance of a sacred fire tended by the Vestal Virgins, signifying the continuity of the Roman state. Quirinus, a god associated with the Roman people, was sometimes linked to Romulus, one of Rome's legendary founders. Fortuna, the goddess of luck, fate, and fortune, had the power to bestow both good and bad luck upon individuals.

As the territory of the Roman Republic and later the Empire expanded, the Romans came in contact with other gods. Those were either equalled with the gods of the Roman pantheon, in the process of cultural translation called 'Interpretatio Romana', or incorporated as new deities. One example is the god Mithras, associated with Persian and Eastern cults, who gained popularity through the Mithraic Mysteries, particularly among Roman soldiers from the late 1st century AD. The worship of Isis, an important Egyptian goddess, also found its place in Roman society, with her significance extending to motherhood, magic, and fertility. The acceptance of other deities was certainly one factor that was beneficial for the proliferation and growing popularity of the Christian religion. The Edict of Thessalonica in 380, issued by Emperor Theodosius I, declared Christianity the official state religion, which marked the end of relevance of Classical mythology for the Romans. Nevertheless, Greco-Roman mythology has inspired philosophers, psychoanalysts, various artists, architects and others up to modern times. The ancient stories of heroes and the deeds of the gods still play a huge role in popular culture and the entertainment industry.

Keywords

Ancient Greece, Ancient Rome, pantheon, religion, mythology

References

Dowden, Ken.1992. *The Uses of Greek Mythology*. London and New York: Routledge.

Gantz, Timothy. 1993. *Early Greek myth a guide to literary and artistic sources*. Baltimore and London: Johns Hopkins University Press.

Hard, Robin. 2004. *The Routledge Handbook Of Greek Mythology*. London and New York: Routledge.

Wiseman, T.P. 2004. *The Myths of Rome*. Exeter: University of Exeter Press.

written by Sebastian Müller (Busan University of Foreign Studies)

02

Egyptian Mythology

Egyptian Mythology and the Mediterranean

Egypt, one of the cradles of human civilization, gave birth to the Pharaonic civilization around 3000 BCE, which ranks among the oldest known civilizations. The Pharaonic civilization not only achieved academic advancements in mathematics, philosophy, and astronomy but also made significant progress in material culture, as evidenced by the construction of the pyramids and the Sphinx. This civilization extended beyond Egypt, spreading throughout the Mediterranean and leading the way in the development of global human civilization. As the earliest civilization to emerge in the ancient Mediterranean region, the Pharaonic civilization provided nourishment for subsequent cultures and laid the foundation for their progress. Notably, Egypt sublimated universal human curiosities about death, birth, and existence into myths that took the form of religion.

The existence of gods is central to mythology and religion. Myths, which tell the stories of these gods, are essential elements of early ancient faiths, where the worship of deities was a fundamental aspect. The ancient Egyptians addressed their questions about human birth, the creation of the universe, and the origin of life by creating the "Ennead," a group of 9 deities including 'Atum', 'Shu', and 'Tefnut'. Their curiosity and fear regarding death and the afterlife led to the creation of myths such as the Osiris myth and the composition of funerary texts like the Book of the Dead. Additionally, their belief in resurrection after death gave rise to elaborate funerary practices including mummification and the construction of pyramids.

Egyptian mythology is a mythological system that explains the gods and worldviews that ancient Egyptians believed in. It serves as a crucial source for understanding the various religious, philosophical, and social aspects of ancient Egyptian civilization, deeply rooted in its culture, literature, art, and religion.

However, the cultural development of ancient Egypt did not remain confined within its borders. It significantly influenced the worldview and philosophical systems of the Abrahamic religions-Judaism, Christianity, and Islam-which later emerged in the Mediterranean region, sharing common philosophies rooted in the figure of Abraham.

Origins and Development of Egyptian Mythology

Mythology is the product of human observation and interpretation of natural phenomena as well as creative expression of those interpretations. The ancient Egyptians viewed themselves as integral parts of the universe. They constantly pondered the supernatural forces behind the inexplicable phenomena around them such as day and night, the sun and the moon, the atmosphere, the birth and death of life, and other mysterious occurrences. As a result, they attributed these phenomena to the will or actions of gods, and these interpretations eventually took shape as myths. In essence, mythology can be seen as the outcome of human reasoning and creativity inspired by the observation of natural events.

The Nile River, which flowed through their lives, was considered a blessing by the ancient Egyptians. After the Nile's annual flooding, new sprouts emerged from the fertile soil, leading the Egyptians to develop agriculture. The food they produced was directly linked to human survival. Despite living in an arid desert region, the ancient Egyptians came to recognize the cycle of new life through the periodic flooding of the Nile. They also believed that the sun, which shone intensely over the Nile, was the force that provided energy for this life. These thoughts led to a broader contemplation of the forces of creation and the power to generate life. As a result, various gods appeared in various regions and eras, naturally imbued with the worldview of the ancient Egyptians.

Major Myths of Egypt: Creation Myths

All myths in ancient Egypt were formed through complex traditions and transmissions. There were approximately 2,000 gods in ancient Egypt, and the status of the chief deities shifted with the changes in dynasties. The Thebes Myth, Heliopolis Myth, Memphite Myth, and Hermopolis Myth are among the most prominent creation myths in ancient Egyptian mythology.

While creation myths varied by region and era, influenced by the prevailing powers of each time, they shared common themes centered on the creation and origin of the universe, as well as the birth of life.

Heliopolis Myth

The Heliopolis Creation Myth is one of the most well-known and representative myths of ancient Egypt. It was so influential that it was adapted and transformed into the creation myths of other cities.

According to this myth, in the beginning, there was no air, land, or water, only infinite waters of darkness, which the ancient Egyptians called as the god 'Nun'. They believed that this immeasurably deep and vast water was the source of all life. From Nun emerged 'Atum', who created the world. Atum self-created in the darkness, then brought forth light and imposed order on the world. Atum then generated the god of air, 'Shu', and the goddess of moisture, 'Tefnut', who together filled the world with air and moisture. These deities gave birth to 'Geb', the god of the earth, and 'Nut', the goddess of the sky, thereby shaping the world. Geb and Nut went on to give birth to 'Osiris', the god of death and resurrection; 'Isis', the goddess of love and fertility; 'Seth', the protector of the dead; and 'Nephthys', mistress of the castle. This creation myth, known as the Ennead (meaning "group of nine"), explains the structure of the universe and describes how the natural world and human society were formed by the gods, bringing order and life to the world.

Memphite Myth

The 'Memphite Creation Myth' emerged alongside the rise of Egypt's First Dynasty. As Memphis was established as the new capital, the Memphite theology was developed to legitimize the rule of the new regime, leading to the formation of the Memphite creation myth.

This myth centers on the creator god 'Ptah'. Initially Ptah was merely the god of a small town but the emergence of the Memphite myth aimed to justify the rule of the First Dynasty necessitating a reorganization of the gods' status in relation to those of Heliopolis. As a result Ptah was elevated to a position akin to Nun in the Heliopolis myth and he was endowed with creative powers.

According to the Memphite myth, Ptah created everything through the power of his will. He conceived all things in his heart and brought them into existence by speaking them into being with his tongue. Ptah created 'Horus', the symbol of the sun, and 'Thoth', the symbol of the moon. Additionally he brought forth the Ennead of Heliopolis, symbolizing them as the teeth and lips within his mouth.

Hermopolise Myth

In the Hermopolise tradition, creation is explained as the cooperative effort of eight deities known as the 'Ogdoad'. These 8 gods represented the primordial chaotic state of the universe, existing as 4 pairs of deities in a disordered and chaotic state before creation. The Ogdoad includes the gods of the chaotic waters Nun and 'Naunet', the gods of infinity and formlessness 'Huh' and 'Huhet', the gods of darkness 'Kuk' and 'Kauket', and the hidden gods 'Amun' and 'Amaunet'. The ancient Egyptians believed that the world was made of water and that the universe was created out of darkness.

Through their respective roles, these deities brought order out of chaos, causing the primordial mound to rise from the waters. Upon this mound, the sun god emerged, creating the world. This myth emphasizes the concept of cosmic balance and harmony, highlighting the importance of cooperation among the gods in the creation process.

Egyptian creation myths are not merely stories passed down through generations; they played a crucial role in shaping the social structure, political system, and religious beliefs of ancient Egyptian society. The Egyptian pharaoh was considered the son of the sun god, and as such, the creation and rule of the sun god were essential in legitimizing the pharaoh's authority. Maintaining the god's order was seen as a fundamental aspect of the pharaoh's reign.

Osiris Myth

The Osiris Myth is a significant narrative in ancient Egyptian mythology that vividly reflects religious beliefs related to death, resurrection, and the afterlife. This myth is essential for understanding the religious worldview of the ancient Egyptians, centering around key deities such as Osiris, Isis, Seth, Nephthys, and Horus. Through their interactions, the myth illustrates Egyptian beliefs about life and death, power, and justice.

The story of Osiris begins with him as the god of the earth and fertility. However, his brother Seth, driven by jealousy, murders Osiris and throws his body into the Nile River. Isis, who is both Osiris's wife and sister, finds his body and, through her magic, resurrects him, leading to the birth of their son, Horus. Seth, enraged, dismembers Osiris's body, but Isis gathers the pieces and revives Osiris once more. After his resurrection, Osiris becomes the king of the afterlife, overseeing the judgment of the dead, while Horus battles Seth, ultimately defeating him and becoming the rightful ruler of Egypt.

This myth plays a crucial role in the Egyptian religion, symbolizing the concepts of death, resurrection, and the afterlife. Osiris's death and resurrection are closely linked to the annual flooding of the Nile River which brought life to the land of Egypt. The river's cycles of flooding, retreat, and renewal represented the cycle of life itself with Osiris's resurrection symbolizing the promise of life after death. As a result, Osiris was revered as the god of the afterlife, resurrection, and eternal life.

Furthermore, the narrative of Horus reclaiming his father's throne from Seth served as a powerful symbol of the pharaoh's divine legitimacy. The pharaoh was seen as the living embodiment of Horus, and upon death, he was identified with Osiris. This divine connection provided a sacred foundation for the succession of kingship in Egypt. Isis's devotion and love also highlighted her roles as both a mother and a wife, leading to her veneration as the goddess of motherhood.

Cultural Exchange of Egyptian Mythology

The advanced civilization of the Pharaohs, which emerged in ancient Egypt, was not confined to the borders of the Nile but spread throughout the Mediterranean region, laying the groundwork for subsequent cultures. Geographically located on the eastern side of the Mediterranean, Egypt was a hub of continuous trade and cultural interaction with neighboring nations through both maritime and overland routes.

In this context of interaction, Egyptian mythology also exchanged influences with various Mediterranean cultures, leading to the formation of diverse mythological systems. By the time of the Greek and Roman empires, Egyptian religious symbols and myths had deeply influenced European culture. The Greeks and Romans adopted mystical elements and mythological symbols from Egypt, integrating them into their own religious practices. A prime example is the Osiris Myth, which was adapted into Greek mythology as the Dionysus myth and into Roman mythology as the Bacchus myth, becoming a prototype for Greco-Roman myths.

Moreover, Egyptian mythology is reflected in key episodes of the Abrahamic religions. Similar creation narratives appear, depicting the establishment of order and creation by a divine will from a state of nothingness and chaos. Elements from the Osiris Myth, such as sibling marriage, fraternal conflict and murder, virgin birth, revenge, judgment, the afterlife, resurrection, and eternal life, are mirrored in the stories of major prophets in the Abrahamic traditions. These include sibling marriage, fratricide, the virgin birth of Mary, and the resurrection and judgment of Jesus.

Thus, Egyptian mythology did not remain confined within Egypt but evolved and developed through its interactions with various Mediterranean cultures. The mythological elements of Egyptian mythology are found across a wide geographical area centered around the Mediterranean, illustrating the importance of cultural connectivity and interaction in the ancient Mediterranean world.

Keywords

Egyptian Mythology, Heliopolis, Memphite Myth, Hermopolise Myth, Osiris Myth

References

Kim Seong. 2001. "Geographical Background of Egyptian Creation Myths." *In World Creation Myths*, edited by Myth Academy, 123-150. Seoul: Dongbang Media Co.

Seo Gyu-Seok, ed. 2003. *The Egyptian Book of the Dead*. Seoul: Munhakdongne.

Yoo Seong-Hwan. 2016. "Memphis Creation Myth." *Religion and Literature* 31: 163-230. Institute for Religious Studies.

David Lorton.(Trans.) 2001. *The Search for God in Ancient Egypt. Assmann, Jan.* Cornell University Press.

Henri Frankfort, H. A. Frankfort, John A. Wilson, Thorkild Jacobsen, William A. Irwin. 1997. *The Intellectual Adventure of Ancient Man: Anessay of Speculative Thought in the Ancient Near East*. The University of Chicago Press.

written by Su Jung Kim (Busan Univesity of Foreign Studies)

▼

Letters and Literatures

03

Arabian Nights
(Alf Laylah wa Laylah)

'Alf Laylah wa Laylah' is not only an Arab folk tale but also a Middle Eastern folk tale including Persia and Turkey. The title of the work, "The Tales of Thousand and One Nights" means a book that encompasses all topics of human life. In the Middle East, the number '1,000' means 'complete', so '1,001' means 'definitely complete'.

The Origin and Transmission of the Work

There are 3 theories about the origin of this work. First, there is a theory of Indian origin, which is the theory that Indian folk tales came to the Arab world through Persia. The frame story structure of this work supports this theory. Second, there is a Persian origin theory that the Persian 'Hezar Afsane (a thousand stories)' transmitted to the Arab world. This is supported by the fact that the names of the main characters of the work, King Shahrayar and Queen Shahrazad, as well as their younger brothers, Shahzaman and Dunyazad, are Persian names. Third, it is a theory of Arab origin, which was written by an

Arab writer. Among these three theories, the Indian origin theory is most likely to be recognized.

In Arab world, Alf Laylah wa Laylah has been widely talked and enjoyed among the people for about 800 years (from the 9th to 16th century), and this work was transmitted to several countries in the Mediterranean region and translated into many languages including Spanish, Latin, and Hebrew.

The themes of the Work

The work contains numerous stories on various topics. The criteria and classification methods for classifying the topics of these stories differ from scholar to scholar. Richard F. Burton, who translated it into English, classified the stories into animal fables, fictive tales, and historical stories, while the Arab scholar Suhair al-Qalamāwi categorized it into extraordinary stories, religious stories, moral stories, animal stories, social stories, historical stories, and educational stories, and Western orientalist MIA I. Gerhardt classified it into love stories, crime stories, travel stories, fairy tales, and lessons.

The characteristics of love stories

Among the stories of Alf Laylah wa Laylah, love stories take the largest portion. The plot or motif of love relation is very often, and love issues are usually involved as main motives. In most of the stories, love and separation, jealousy and tricks between men and women are linked to the main themes. The formation period of love stories is divided into 4 stages depending on the forms and contents of the story: a small number of Persian origin stories, a very small number of early Arab stories, a relatively large number of Baghdad stories, and a large number of Egyptian stories.

First, in the stage of Persian origin stories, the main plot is the young man's passion and his plan to find an unknown lover and marry her. In the story of this stage, the male protagonist is active and the female protagonist is passive, and the two lovers meet by fate and inevitably marry.

Second, in the stage of early Arab stories, the lovers cannot achieve their love in this world and promise to meet and love in the next world. There are many relatively short stories compared to other stages of stories. In terms of fateful love, it can be seen in the same category as the Persian love stories. However, there is a difference in that fateful love in the early Arab stories meets a sad ending while fateful love in the Persian stories meets a happy ending.

Third, the stage of Baghdad stories is characterized by realistic and logical plots being developed through detailed descriptions and balanced narrative techniques. Fourth, the stage of Egyptian stories is characterized by a mixture of Persia style love stories, Baghdad style love stories, or traces of Hellenistic love stories, and includes endless disputes between Muslims and Franks. The setting of the story is often Cairo or Alexandria, but sometimes Baghdad or Basra. The characteristic of the Egyptian love stories is that the emergence and intervention of supernatural beings, magic, and fortune-telling take place in the plot.

Dual evaluation of the Arabs

The Arabs are not only proud of this work, they are also ashamed of it.

Their pride stems from its vast scale of literary works created by their rich imagination, and their shame stems from the obscene stories contained in the works. This two-sided evaluation is due to the conservative view of Arab literatures. Arabs value the writer's reputation and the work written in standard Arabic and instructive topics as factors that evaluate the literary works, especially in the case of prose literature. However, Alf Laylah wa Laylah is a folk tale and contains a number of obscene stories. Moreover, in the process of translating the work into Western languages such as English and French, obscene stories were expanded or added and spread around the world. Arabs felt anxious that the phenomenon may not only distort the originality of the work but also cause misleading the lives and thoughts of Arabs

Characters: Humans and Supernatural beings

In this work, there are far more stories in which humans and supernatural beings appear together to compete for strategy and make the plot of adventure and retribution than stories in which only humans appear. Furthermore, there are many stories in which the role of supernatural beings is more prominent than that of humans. In many stories, humans and the supernatural beings are recognized as the same rational beings, and the supernatural beings are regarded as important as humans in this world.

Various supernatural beings such as Jinn, Ifrīt, Mārid, Ghūl, and Iblīs appear in this work. They help and harm humans, have a great influence on the lives of the main characters, and play an important role in the development and ending of the plot. Jinn are freely transformable and powerful, and they are divided into good and evil beings. Ifrīt is a sort of Jinn and is referred to as a demon because it has rough, evil, and simple properties. Mārid, who is a sort of Jinn, has a large body, and is strong enough to prevent storms, so he plays a role as a gatekeeper in the human world and the world of Jinn. Ghūl is so evil and cruel that they are called evil spirits. Iblīs appears rarely and does not have a significant impact on humans.

Gender image: image of women and image of men

In Alf Laylah wa Laylah, the image of women and the image of men contrast. Women are generally wise, good, flexible and strong, so they lead matters to success. Men, on the other hand, are generally foolish, evil, violent and weak, so they lead matters to failure. Men's failures often turn into success with the help of women. The positive image of women and the negative image of men can be guessed that women who lived as subordinate beings in traditional patriarchal society used paradoxes, satire, and irony to find liberation in the imaginary world.

The Influence of Mediterranean Civilization Exchange: Frame Story Structure

Alf Laylah wa Laylah derives many inserted stories through the frame story structure and includes stories of various topics. The work consists of the introduction and 270 main stories - 88 big stories, 22 middle stories, 64 small stories - and the ending. The introduction explains the motivation and background of long storytelling during 1001 nights, and the main stories are what were told by Shahrajad to Shahrayar, and the ending explains the situation in which Sahrayar becomes good and Shahrajad is welcomed as a queen.

The motivation and function of the inserted stories are the expression of one's opinions and the persuasion of the other, and the derivative process is variant according to the occasion. When one story derives another, the former hints at the latter plot in advance, and the latter emphasizes the subject of the former.

The continuous derivation of the inserted stories is possible because of the dialogue narrative device. Such narrative device can add many stories continually, and allows the work to have an open structure. In addition, the multi-layered narrative structure provides a frame for stories of various topics. The frame story device had a circular structure in which the end of the story returns to its starting point. This represents the concept of cyclical time based

Fig 3-1. The King Sahrayar and The Queen Shahrajad

on India's belief of reincarnation, so it supports the view that the source of the work is Indian narrative.

The frame story structure originated from the East was spread in the process of translation into various languages in the Mediterranean region, and it was considered as an ideal narrative structure in the Middle Ages. Examples include Boccaccio's Decameron and Chaucer's Canterbury Story.

The Influence of Mediterranean Civilization Exchange: French Version by Antoine Galland (The first adapted version)

Alf Laylah wa Laylah was introduced to the world outside of Arab as a systematic version firstly when it was adapted into French language by French orientalist A. Galland. In 1703-1713, he completed a 12-volume translation titled "Mille et Uni Nuit" and it implied stories of about 200 nights. Galland translated the work based on Arabic manuscripts and the stories which were orally transmitted. The Arabic manuscripts he used were 4-volume complete collection and one more another manuscript which included the story of the boatman Sindbad. On the other hand, the 7 stories he heard from his Arab friend Hanna from Aleppo - "Aladin and Magic Lamp," "Khalifa's Midnight Adventure," "Ali Baba," "Ali Khawaja," "Black Horse," "Ahmad and Fairy Peribanu," and "Jealous Sisters." Galland abbreviated or expanded this work to suit the tastes of European readers. However, by not damaging the fundamental characteristics of the work, he left the achievement of introducing the true character of Alf Laylah wa Laylah to Europe for the first time.

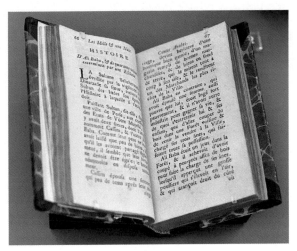

Fig 3–2. The first European edition of Arabian Nights, *Les Mille et une Nuits*, by Antoine Galland, 1730 AD, Paris

Arabic editions

The Arabic version was first created in 1814, about 100 years after Antoine Galland published the French version. The reason is due to the conservative and aristocratic view of the Arabs toward literature. They gave value to works written by authoritative writers and enjoyed among the upper classes while not paying attention to the folk tale that was shared among the ordinary people.

There are 4 types of early Arabic editions. First, Calcutta I edition was edited in 2 volumes from 1814 to 1818, and second, Breslau edition was edited in 8 volumes from 1825 to 1838 by a German, Habicht, and 4 more volumes were added by a German, Fleischer from 1842 to 1843, so it was consisted of 12 volumes. Third, the Bulak edition was edited in two volumes in 1835 and is also referred to as the "Cairo edition" because it was published

Fig 3–3. Arabic manuscript of *The Thousand and One Nights* dating back to the 14th century

in Cairo. Fourth, Calcutta II edition was edited in four volumes by a German, Macnaghten between 1839 and 1842, so it is also referred to as "Macnaghten Edition". This is evaluated as a very complete edition.

An Early Western Translations

A number of Western translations were published based on Antoine Galland's French adaptation and early Arabic editions. Among them, major Western translations are as follows. First, it is an English abbreviated translation of W. Lane. British orientalist W. Lane completed it as a title of 'New Translation of the Tales of a Thousand and a Nights' in 1839-1841. Second, it is Richard F. Burton' complete English translation. Burton, a British explorer and orientalist, published 10 complete English translations titled 'The Book of the Thousand Nights and a Night' in 1885-1886. Soon after, 6 supplementary volumes were presented in 1886-1888. Burton's translation

Fig 3–4. Cover of Richard Francis Burton's *The Book of the Thousand Nights and a Night*

represented English translation owing to its relatively good expression of the characteristics of the original Arabic text, especially for its excellence in poetry translation and for producing sentences that are good to read. Third, it is a French version of Mardrus. French physician, Mardrus, completed and published a 16-volume French adaptation in 1889-1904. He almost deleted religious stories and lessons from the original text while expanding sexual love stories. Fourth, it is a complete German translation of Litmann. German Orientalist Litman published a complete translation of 6 volumes in 1921-1928. His translation is the most complete translation of the original Arabic text in the translation history of Alf Laylah wa Laylah, and is evaluated as the first academic translation.

And Alf Laylah wa Laylah was adapted into Korean in 1895 under the title of "Yuokyeokjeon". This adaptation is evaluated as the first work in the history of Korean modern translation literature.

Arabian Nights (Alf Laylah wa Laylah)

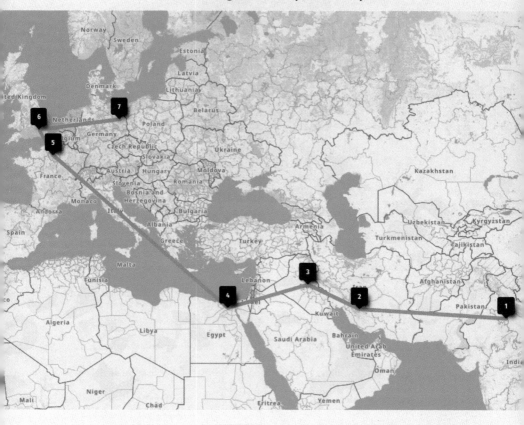

① India

② Persia

③ Iraq (8CE~12CE)

④ Egypt (12CE~16CE)

⑤ France (1713)

⑥ the United Kingdom (1840, 1885)

⑦ Germany (1928)

Scan the QR code
to view the map.

Keywords

Alf Laylah wa Laylah, Arabian Nights, Arab folk tale, Shahrazad, Frame Story Structure

References

Lee Dong-eun (2008). "The study of supernatural beings in Arab consciousness," *Journal of the Islamic Academy of Korea* 18-1st.

Alf Laylah wa Laylah(1999). Beirut, Dār Sādir.

Ghazoul, Forial J.(1996). *Nocturnal Poetics*, Cairo, AUC Press.

Muwayqin, al-Muṣṭafā(2005). *Bunyat al-Mukhayyl fi Naṣṣ Alf Laylah wa Laylah*, al-Lādhiqiyah, Dār al-Hiwār.

Pinault, David(1992). *Story-telling Techniques in the Arabian Nights*, Leiden, E.J. Brill.

Todorov, Tzvetan(2006). "Narrative-Man", *The Arabian Nights Reader*, Marzolph, Ulrich(Ed.), Detroit, Wayne state University Press, 233.

Image References

Picture1: The King Sahrayar and The Queen Shahrajad

https://search.daum.net/search?nil_suggest=btn&w=img&DA=SBC&q=%EC%B2%9C%EC%9D%BC%EC%95%BC%ED%99%94&vimg=61qGm-NlU5D UgFZ4Dg

Picture2: The first European edition of Arabian Nights, *Les Mille et une Nuits*, by Antoine Galland, 1730 AD, Paris

https://en.wikipedia.org/wiki/Antoine_Galland

Picture3: Arabic manuscript of The Thousand and One Nights dating back to the 14th century

https://en.wikipedia.org/wiki/One_Thousand_and_One_Nights

Picture4: Cover of Richard Francis Burton's *The Book of the Thousand Nights and a Night*

https://en.wikipedia.org/wiki/The_Book_of_the_Thousand_Nights_and_a_Night

written by Dong Eun Lee (Dongguk University)

04

Kalīlah wa Dimnah

'Kalīla wa Dimnah' is an Arab animal fable, and it has been considered one of the most important Arabic classical literature as well as one of the world-class classical literature. This work, which teaches the lessons of life interestingly and sharply accuses the political reality and social absurdity of those days through various animals, has become a milestone in satirical literature in the history of Arabic literature. The work, in which wisdom and philosophy are woven in harmony with political criticism and social reform ideas, has been translated into several languages in the Mediterranean region since the 10th century. These translations in Mediterranean languages were translated into other languages outside the Mediterranean region, either in those days or later. This work has high value as actual material for the transmission and exchange of literary works between civilizations in the cultural history of the world, including the Mediterranean region.

Its Origin and Transmission

Kalīlah wa Dimnah appeared in the Arab world in 750s, the early days of the Abbasid period (750-1258), which has been considered as a golden age in the history of Arabic literature. The origin of this work was 'Panchatantra', a Hindu fable in Sanskrit. The meaning of Panchatantra is 'Five books' or 'Five wisdom boxes'. The word 'Pancha' means five, and 'Tantra' means a book or a wisdom box. The preface of the book explains that a Brahmin sage named Vishnusharman tells five stories to educate the three princes, which indicates

Fig 4–1. The King Anushirwan and The Translator Bouzawaih

that the book is not only a didactic literature but also a strong political guide.

Panchatantra, which had been compiled between the 2nd and 5th centuries BC, was translated into Pehlevi (Medieval Persian) in 570 AD, which was translated to the classical Arabic language in the 750s by Ibn al Muqaffa'(724-759), an Arab writer of Persian descent. Taha Husein (1889-1973), a great Egyptian writer, evaluated this work as a masterpiece created by Hindu wisdom and Persian efforts and Arabic language. And many other scholars also evaluate it as a representative animal fable of the East.

Contents and Composition

This work consists of 4 preface chapters and 16 main chapters. The 4 chapters of the preface contain the motivation for writing the work, the background of translation, the biography of the translator (a person who translated from Sanskrit to Pahlevi), and the explanation of the work. The 16 main chapters of the text convey the wisdom and lessons of life through animal fables. The 16 main chapters open the story with the dialogue of King Dabshalim and the Sage Baidaba. When King Dabshalim asks the Sage Baidaba for a story on a specific subject, the Sage tells an animal fable corresponding to the subject. King Dabshalim and Sage Baidaba are fictional characters, but Baidaba is commonly referred to as the author of this work, which is unknown.

The 2 jackals 'Kalīlah' and 'Dimnah', which are referred to in the title of the book, appear only in Chapters 1 and 2 of the work. Most of the stories in the work are animal fables, but animals and people appear together in some stories. The examples of titles of the 16 main chapters are as follows. The Lion and The Ox (Chapter 1), Dimna's Defence (Chapter 2), The Ring-Dove (Chapter 3), The Owls and The Crows (Chapter 4), the Monkey and The Turtle (Chapter 5), the Monk and The Weasel (Chapter 6), the Big Mouse and the Cat (Chapter 7) and so forth.

Fig 4–2. Two jackals: Kalīlah and Dimnah

Narrative Device

The characteristic narrative device of Kalīlah wa Dimnah is a frame story technique which derives some inserted stories from an axis story, introducing legends and proverbs in order to emphasize lessons and topics. The multi-layered and recurring structure, which repeats the deepening and returning of the stories through various layers of narrative structures and eventually returns to the plot of the axis story and ends, might be seen as a reflection of the metempsychosis (Samsara) based on the Hindu concept of cyclical time.

Lessons and Religious Ideas

The lessons and religious ideas being contained in the multi-layered narrative structure are also multi-layered and complex. Kalīlah wa Dimnah is excellently harmonizing dual level themes - superficial themes and deep themes. The superficial themes are the principles and lessons of life that are interestingly dealt with through animals, and the deep themes are the political satire behind interest and lessons.

The lessons of this work do not teach the readers that a man must behave kindly and altruistically always. Rather, its lessons emphasize that a man must grasp the reality, which the law of the jungle is dominant and the boundary between good and evil is ambiguous, and ultimately stress overcoming the reality and living wisely.

Political satire allegorically deals with the principles of rulers, the qualities of bureaucrats, and the attributes of power, and in particular, traces targeting the ruler of that time, Khalifah al Manṣūr (r. 754-775). *Ibn al-Muqaffaʿ*, who translated this work into Arabic and recreated it, successfully realized the purpose of enlightening the ignorant people by criticizing Khalifah al Manṣūr's dictatorship and tyranny and presenting ideal reforms.

A dual characteristic also appears in religious thought. Since this work was born in Hindu society and completed in Islamic environments, Hindu ideas and Islamic ideas are naturally fused. Hindu elements include the principle of retribution based on reincarnation and karma, in addition to the customs of cremation and the frequent appearance of monks. As for Islamic elements, they include the al Qiṣāṣ, the effect of testimony in court, the principle of resurrection and final judgment, fatalism, and the emergence of Jinn (spirits).

Influence on the Exchange of Mediterranean Civilization

Kalīlah wa Dimnah was enjoyed by the aristocracy at the time of its emergence in the Arab world and gradually spread to the public. After being rooted as a valuable literary asset for Arabs, the work began to be translated into major languages in the 10th century. It was translated into the modern Syrian language in the 10th century, into Greek in the 11th century, into Persian in the 12th century, and into Hebrew and Latin and medieval Spanish in the middle 13th century, respectively. These early foreign language translations became the starting point of later work translations, resulting in translations of various languages. For example, the 11th century Greek version became the parent of the Italian version (1583), and the ancient Slavic version and the 12th century Persian version was translated into the Turkish version of the 16th century and the French version of the 18th century. The Hebrew version of the middle 13th century gave birth to the Latin version of the late 13th century. In addition, the translations of the work are still underway in modern times.

Known in the Western world as 'Bidpai Fables' or 'Pilpai Fables', the work has been widely spread and read as 'a book that has been read more frequently

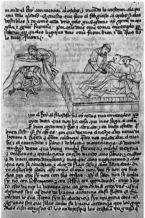

Fig 4–3. Latin manuscript of Kalīlah wa Dimnah

Fig 4–4. Spanish manuscript of Kalīlah wa Dimnah

among Western people than the Bible' or 'a book translated into many languages after the Bible'.

Literary Status

Kalīlah wa Dimnah has very important literary status as it has served as a bridge to transfer Eastern culture to the West based on the strong vitality of the work itself and the Arab's capabilities of cultural preservation. First, from the perspective of history of Arabic literature, this work was the beginning of satirical literature through animal fables and had a great influence on works and writers at those days as well as on the future generation of them. Ancient Arab writers were influenced by this work and created many animal fables, and modern Arab poets recreated them to suit their modern senses and expressed them as fable poems. This work provides literary inspiration and materials and essence of prose literature in all Arab countries. So various editions suitable for each level, from children to adults, have been published and read. Second, from the perspective of the history of Middle Eastern literature, Iranian (Persian) and Turkish writers have made efforts to translate this work into their languages over the years and they tried to establish this work as their own literary works. Third, from the perspective of the history of world literature, the narrative device of the frame story of this work transferred the technique of narrative form to the *Canterbury Tales* and *Decameron*, as well as the literary inspiration and theme of the animal fable played a fundamental role in the creation of *La Fontaine Fables*.

Common Stories with Korean Folktales

Panchatantra, the origin of Kalīlah wa Dimnah, has been transmitted to the Arab world via Persia in the western course, while it has been transmitted to Korea via China in the eastern course. Panchatantra, which has been transmitted to the East with the spread of Buddhism, had a great influence on Korean folktales. Therefore, due to the influence of Panchatantra, a common denominator, there are many common stories between Kalīlah wa Dimnah and Korean folktales in terms of content and themes. For example, the story of a monkey and a tortoise in Kalīlah wa Dimnah is similar to the story of a rabbit's liver in Korean folktales, and the story of a female mouse who chooses her bridegroom is similar to the story of a mouse's bridegroom in Korean folktales. In addition, similarities exist between Kalīlah wa Dimnah and the tales in Buddhist scriptures. For example, the story of a man in a well in the preface of Kalīlah wa Dimnah is consistent with the story of 'Ansu Jeong Deung' in Buddhist scripture 'Bul Seol Biyu Gyeong'. In addition, many of the stories of Kalīlah wa Dimnah are similar to those in the Buddhist scripture 'Baek Yu Gyeong'. For example, the story of a monkey and a bean in Kalīlah wa Dimnah is very similar to the story of a monkey and a bean in 'Baek yu gyeong', and the story of a pair of pigeons in Kalīlah wa Dimnah is consistent with the story of a male pigeon in 'Baek Yu Gyeong'.

Fig 4–5. The story of a man in a well in the preface of Kalīlah wa Dimnah

Fig 4–6. The story of 'Ansu Jeong Deung' in Buddhist scripture 'Bul Seol Biyu Gyeong'

Spread of Kalilah wa Dimnah

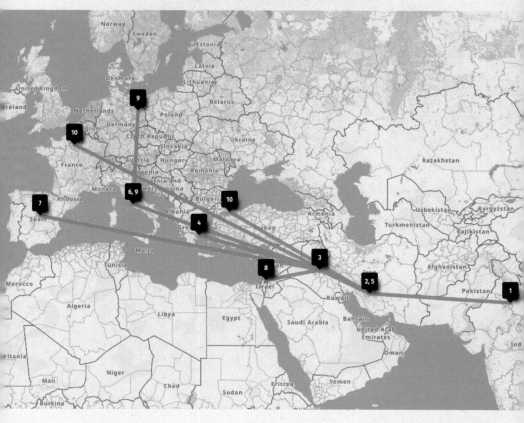

① India (5C BCE ~ 3C BCE)

② Persia (6CE)

③ Iraq (8CE)

④ Iraq → Greece (11CE)

⑤ Iraq → Persia (12CE)

⑥ Iraq → Latin-speaking regions (13CE)

⑦ Iraq → Spain (13CE)

⑧ Iraq → Hebrew-speaking regions (13CE)

⑨ Latin-speaking regions
　→ Germany(15CE), Italy (16CE)

⑩ Persia → Turkiye (16CE), France (18CE)

Scan the QR code
to view the map.

Keywords

Kalīlah wa Dimnah, Arab Animal Fable, Baidaba, Ibn al-Muqaffaʿ, Panchatantra

References

Baydabā.1987. *Kalīlah wa Dimnah*. Lee Dong Eun(trans.). 2008. *Kalila and Dimna*. Seoul: Kang Publishing. Lee Dong Eun. 2018. "A Comparative Study of Kalīlah wa Dimnah and a Korean Classic Novel -The Story of the Monkey and the Tortoise and Tokki Jeon -".

Journal of Middle Eastern Affairs,17-1. Institute of Middle Eastern Affairs. al-Fakhuri, Hanna. 1972. *Ibn al-Muqaffaʿ*. Cairo: Dār al-Maʿārif. Hamza, ʿAbd al-Latīf.1965. *Ibn al-Muqaffaʿ*. Cairo: Dār al-Fikr al-ʿArabī.

Ryder, Arthur W. 1973. *The Panchatantra*. Bombay: Jaico Publishing House. Saʿda al-Dīn, Laylā Ḥasan.1989. *Kalīlah wa Dimnah fī al-'Adab al-ʿArabī; Dirāsa Muqārana*. Amman: Dār al-Bashīr. Viṣṇu Śarma, Rajan. *The Pančatantra*. Chandra(trans.). 1993. London: Penguin Books.

Image References

Figure 4-1: The King Anushirwan and the Translator Bouzawaih

https://www.google.com/search?q=Kalilah+wa+Dimnah&sca_esv=e02c8f39a8b85 279&sca_upv=1&udm=2&ei=MAXAZsOmLcra1e8Pz_eG2AY&ved=0ahUKEwj D_sv59_qHAxVKbfUHHc-7AWsQ4dUDCBA&uact=5&oq=Kalilah+wa+Dimn ah&gs_lp=Egxnd3Mtd2l6LXNlcnAiEUthbGlsYWggd2EgRGltbmFoMgQQABge SJX9AVDZB1iY3gFwCHgAkAECmAGQAaAB-R6qAQUxMy4yNbgBA8gBAP gBAZgCH6AC6haoAgDCAgUQABiABMICBhAAGAcYHsICCBAAGIAEGIYD wgIHEAAYgAQYE8ICBhAAGBMYHsICCBAAGBMYHsICCBAAGBMYBRgemAMBiAYBkgcE OC4yM6AHgY4B&sclient=gws-wiz-serp#vhid=4HxNd2b2MLD6TM&vssid= mosaic

Figure 4-2: Two jackals: Kalīlah and Dimnah

https://en.wikipedia.org/wiki/Kal%C4%ABla_wa-Dimna

Figure 4-3: Latin manuscript of Kalīlah wa Dimnah

https://en.wikipedia.org/wiki/Kal%C4%ABla_wa-Dimna

Figure 4-4: Spanish manuscript of Kalīlah wa Dimnah, 1251-1261

https://en.wikipedia.org/wiki/Kal%C4%ABla_wa-Dimna

Figure 4-5: The story of a man in a well in the preface of Kalīlah wa Dimnah

https://en.wikipedia.org/wiki/Kal%C4%ABla_waDimna#/media/File:Kalila_wa
Dimna_Pococke_400_folio_36b.png

Figure 4-6: The story of 'Ansu Jeong Deung' in Buddhist scripture

'Bul Seol Biyu Gyeong'

https://search.naver.com/search.naver?sm=tab_hty.top&where=nexearch&ssc=tab.
nx.all&query=%ED%95%B4%EC%9D%B8%EC%82%AC+%EC%95%88%EC
%88%98%EC%A0%95%EB%93%B1&oquery=%EC%95%88%EC%88%98%E
C%A0%95%EB%93%B1+%EB%B6%88%EC%84%A4%EB%B9%84%EC%9C
%A0%EA%B2%BD&tqi=iVTgKdpzLiwssUkU5LRsssstSV-491600#imgSlot=slo
t1&imgId=image_sas%3Ablog_a8e51cfdbd04bbcc3ace290ce8dde53e

written by Dong Eun Lee (Dongguk University)

▼

Architectures and Arts

05

Construction and Architecture of Ancient Rome

All roads lead to Rome

The Cambridge dictionary defines the abovementioned expression as follows: all methods of doing something will achieve the same result in the end. As a historical fact, all roads of the ancient Roman era stretched like a spider web throughout the Roman Empire and centered on Rome.

Ancient Rome was established in 753 BC. It started as a small village on the Palatine Hill in the middle of the present-day Italian peninsula. At that time, the territory of Etruria in the north and Magna Graecia in the south had already been settled. As the years went by, Rome gradually grew stronger and conquered the Italian peninsula. Eventually, by winning the war against Carthage, Rome gained control of the Mediterranean Sea and completed the Roman Empire, including the entire Mediterranean and a significant part of present-day Europe. One of the most important pieces of infrastructure that made this possible was the network of roads that connected the entire Roman Empire, which was one of the most remarkable aspects of this accomplishment.

Roman legions swiftly moved through a network of paved roads that could be driven by two-horse chariots, expanding the territory of Rome. A network of paved roads was necessary to facilitate the transportation of the supplies needed for Roman troops to conquer the surrounding territories and quickly deploy them to areas they needed to conquer. The road network constructed for military purposes was useful in controlling the conquered lands that allowed the smooth movement of goods and proper delivery of taxes collected from conquered lands to Rome. It served to convey the sovereignty of the Roman Emperor to the end of the vast conquered land. The Roman Empire, which conquered all regions surrounding the Mediterranean Sea, Gaul, Britain, Asia Minor, and North Africa, was the first state to unify the Mediterranean Region. Numerous human and material exchanges occurred through the road network that spread like a spider web across this integrated and vast territory; Even the post office was developed to facilitate correspondence. Additionally, there were numerous civilizational exchanges between various peoples.

In the process of building a road network, various technologies were used construct roads, such as surveying, masonry, concrete, and pavement. The Romans seem to have inherited and used road construction techniques from various peoples, including the Etruscans, Carthaginians, Egyptians, Greeks, and Phoenicians. Using a surveying tool called Groma, the pavement was kept as horizontal as possible, and the slope was reduced. To construct the straight road, mountains were flattened, tunnels were drilled, and bridges or embankments were built.

The road's foundation was then built higher than the drainage ditches and surrounding land, using earth excavated from the drainage ditches. A layer of dry sand was frequently laid on top of this foundation. Roman roads typically consisted of 4 layers. The first was the 'Statumen', which is a layer of large stones. On top of this layer was the 'Rudus', or a layer of grave in concrete. Followed by the nucleus, a layer of sand, and smaller gravel in concrete. The top layer was called the 'Summum Dorsum'; this layer consisted of large, flat stones that were used by travelers to walk or ride on. The materials used off or constructing these layers occasionally varied according to the location of the road and the availability of materials. The layers of sand and gravel promoted drainage; part of the goal was to build highways that would not get muddy or flooded when it rained.

Fig 5-1. Minturno Via–Appia
https://it.m.wikipedia.org/wiki/File:Minturno_Via–Appia.jpg

The constructed road network in Rome was approximately 50,000 miles, enabling rapid and efficient military movement and the replenishment of supplies. It was used for various purposes, such as trade, travel, and migration, in addition to military and governmental purposes, and became a channel for active cultural exchange among multiethnic peoples.

The road network of ancient Rome was used for the movement of military chariots and troops throughout the Roman Empire, collecting supplies for the army, taxes, transporting goods, exchanging cultural relics of various ethnic groups, and exchanging letters.

Aqueduct of the ancient Rome

A system of aqueducts that were built during the era of ancient Rome supplied water to the important cities of the Roman Empire. In all the territories conquered by ancient Rome, one can see the great ruins of Roman aqueducts. The Pont du Gard, located outside Nimes in France, the aqueduct of Segovia in Spain, and the Gadara Aqueduct in Syria and Jordan have become popular tourist destinations.

The aqueduct was not an original invention of the Romans. The Greeks built an aqueduct in the 6th century BC. In Greece, records reveal that water was supplied through an aqueduct in Athens, and a long tunnel aqueduct was discovered in Samos, although it was not as extensive as that of ancient Rome. The ancient city of Nineveh was also connected to water by the Jerwan aqueduct, which was built deep in the desert.

The Roman aqueduct was built in 312 BC and continued to supply water to the city for approximately 500 years. Water was supplied to Rome through 11 aqueducts. Along with this network, the city of Rome was equipped with water supply facilities using wells and cisterns. The water supplied through the aqueduct was used for baths and fountains instead of drinking. Except for the remains of the great Roman aqueducts which are now tourist attractions, most aqueducts were built underground. To prevent the evaporation of the water from sunlight and to protect it from various contaminants, the lid was covered to prevent exposure to the outside. These canals created ramps that did not use any power and relied solely on gravity. The slopes, which are typically 5 to 10 feet per mile, were constructed using tools such as dioptra and chorobates and remarkable manpower.

Fig 5–2. Roman Aqueduct in Sergovia, Spain
https://commons.wikimedia.org/wiki/File:Aqueduct_of_Segovia_01.jpg

Among the 11 aqueducts that supplied water to the city of Rome, the Aqua Virgo, which was built by Agrippa, continues to supply water to the most beautiful fountain in the city, the Trevi Fountain. The Roman aqueduct, still in use today after 2500 years, is a wonder of ancient Rome. Along with the flow of water throughout the Mediterranean, civil engineering and the exchange of people must have been active.

Sewer system of ancient Rome: Cloaca Maxima

The ancient Roman sewer system, along with roads and aqueducts, is one of the legacies of Roman civil engineering. In the 6th century BC, the Romans built the Cloaca Maxima in the Roman Forum. Rainwater was drained from the center of Rome to the Tiber River. The open drain was then covered with a vault. The Etruscans were mobilized to build it. The ancient Romans did not purify wastewater, however, dumped it into the Tiber. The main purpose of the Roman sewers was to pump surface water. People's excrement was dumped in the streets or hauled away for agriculture use.

The Cloaca Maxima starts from the Forum Augustum and passes through the main areas of Rome, including the Forum Romanum, and flows into the Tiber River through an outlet near the Ponte Rotto and the Ponte Palatino. In the process, the city's waste was swept away.

The Cloaca Maxima was built to such a size that it was said to be "large enough for a wagon loaded with hay to pass through." It was so solidly built that some are still in use today.

Fig 5–3. Cloaca Maxima
https://www.researchgate.net/publication/322185243_A_History_of_the_Urban_
Underground_Tunnel_4000_BCE_−_1900_CE/figures?lo=1

Pantheon

"The most beautiful relic of ancient Rome, a temple so well preserved that it appears as the Romans must have seen it in their times," said the 18th century French writer Stendhal when he first saw the Pantheon.

The Pantheon consists of 3 parts, namely, a portico with granite columns, a huge domed rotunda, and a rectangular area connecting the 2 other parts. It features a domed ceiling with a diameter of 142 ft and a 27 ft-wide oculus at the top of the dome. It was built to draw a circle with a diameter of 142 ft from the domed ceiling to the floor. The beauty of the Pantheon has inspired Renaissance and modern architecture. Sunlight shines into the dome through an uncovered oculus and when it rains, rainwater flows down into the dome as well. And drainage holes are situated at the bottom of the dome to drain rainwater.

After 2000, the Pantheon now is the crowning glory of most of Rome's architectural wonders. It is derived from the Greek words 'Pan', meaning "all", and 'Theos', meaning "god." Marcus Agrippa built it circa 25 BC as a temple to the Roman god. It was destroyed by fire circa 80 AD and rebuilt by Hadrian circa 126-128 AD. It is considered to have had the original inscription by Agrippa.

Fig 5–4. Interior of the Pantheon, Giovanni Paolo Panini, circa 1734
https://artsandculture.google.com/asset/1AHJFNF8OkfG9Q

In 608, Pope Boniface IV moved the remains of many martyrs from the Christian catacombs and placed them in the Pantheon, where they were converted to Christianity. The temple was named 'St. Maria ad Martyres', and Catholic masses continue to be celebrated to this day.

Colosseum

The Colosseum, also known as the Flavian Amphitheater, is a building that stands as a symbol of Rome. It is called the Flavian Amphitheater. Scholars mention that the construction of the Colosseum began during the reign of Emperor Vespasian between 70 and 72 AD, which was renovated during the reign of Emperor Titus to hold gladiator fights for 100 days.

Measuring approximately 189 m x 156 m (620 ft x 513 ft), this enormous structure was 4 stories high and had 80 entrances to the amphitheater. It could hold more than 50,000 spectators. The Colosseum is located at the golden palace of Emperor Nero, with an artificial lake and a garden. However, Nero was killed in a rebellion against Emperor Nero. Afterward, Emperor Vespasian, who ascended the throne, began the construction of a huge amphitheater on the spot.

Common people attended the Colosseum. There was a separate aisle reserved for the entrance of nobles and separate seats for members of the royal family. Many common people gathered and enjoyed the gladiator fights. In addition, simulated naval battles, wild animal hunts, and executions of criminals were conducted.

After the fall of the Western Roman Empire, the Colosseum declined. An

Fig 5–5. Colosseum (photo taken by the author)

earthquake in the 5th century AD destroyed the structure of the Colosseum. A great earthquake in Rome in the 14th century destroyed the southern wall of the Colosseum. The Colosseum, which was remained in a state of disrepair until the 19th century, was restored several times during the 20th century to achieve its current appearance.

Keywords

Road network, Aqueduct, Cloaca Maxima, Pantheon, Colosseum

References

Andrews, Evan (2021), "8 Ways Roads Helped Rome Rule the Ancient World," 8 Ways Roads Helped Rome Rule the Ancient World | HISTORY

"Basilica of Santa Maria ad Martyres", https://www.pantheonroma.com/home-eng/

Betz, Eric (2020), "Aqueducts: How Ancient Rome Brought Water to Its People", Discover, 27 Oct.2020. https://www.discovermagazine.com/planet-earth/aqueducts-how-ancient-rome-brought-water-to-its-people

Britannica, The Editors of Encyclopaedia. "Pantheon". *Encyclopedia Britannica*, 19 May. 2023, https://www.britannica.com/topic/Pantheon-building-Rome-Italy.

Cambridge Dictionary, https://dictionary.cambridge.org/dictionary/english/aqueduct.

Deming, David (2019), "The Aqueducts and Water Supply of Ancient Rome", Groundwater Vol.58, Issue 1, 2020, pp. 152-161.

Dresser, Sophie (2022), "Ancient Roman Roads", https://study.com/learn/lesson/ancient-roman-roads-facts-construction-history.html.

History.com Editors (2023), "Pantheon", Pantheon (history.com)

Muench, Stephen T. (2017), "An Ancient Network: The Roads of Rome", https://brewminate.com/an-ancient-network-the-roads-of-rome/

Kuo, James (jimkuo2) (2004), "The Colosseum: Power, Brilliance, and Brutality", https://depts.washington.edu/hrome/Authors/jimkuo2/IlColosseo/pub_zbarticle_view_printable.html

Puiu, Tibi (2023), "How the ancient Romans built roads to last thousands of years", https://www.zmescience.com/feature-post/history-and-humanities/history/how-roman-roads-were-built/.

Olson, Katrina (2006), "Wastewater and the Tiber", Engineeringrome, http://engineeringrome.org/wastewater-and-the-tiber/

Omrania (2019), "Urban Water Systems: The Great Sewer of Ancient Rome", Urban Water Systems: The Great Sewer of Ancient Rome - Omrania

Uy, Joaquin I. (2023), "Cesspools and Cholera: The Development of the Modern Sewer", Greywater Action, History of Sewers - Greywater Action.

Price, Miachael (2017), "Origeins of ancient Rome's famed pipe plumbing system revealed in soil samples", https://www.science.org/content/article/origins-ancient-rome-s-famed-pipe-plumbing-system-revealed-soil-samples.

Water Science School (2023), "Ancient Roman aqueducts are still standing today", https://www.usgs.gov/media/images/ancient-roman-aqueducts-are-still-standing-today

written by HaeJo Chung (Pukyong National University)

06

Islamic Architecture
Rise and Development of Arab Islamic Civilization

The development of a civilization does not occur in isolation but rather through interaction with neighboring civilizations, leading to the creation of a new civilization. In the mid-7th century, the Islamic civilization emerged in the arid Arabian Peninsula. Regionally, the Islamic civilization developed in the presence of Judaism, Christianity, and indigenous beliefs. Geographically, it was by the Sassanid Empire, which was affected by the Mesopotamia and Persian Civilizations, to the east, and the Byzantine Empire, which was affected by Ancient Syria, Egypt, Maghreb, and Hellenistic Civilizations, to the west. The Arabian Peninsula, particularly the Mecca region, served as an intermediary region where these 2 civilizations influenced and gave birth to the Islamic civilization while contending for dominance.

The advanced cultures of the Sassanid Empire and the Byzantine Empire had an impact on the overall way of life of the nomadic people of the Arabian Peninsula. Religiously, the monotheistic religions of Judaism, Christianity, and Zoroastrianism mixed with the indigenous beliefs of the Arabian Peninsula.

In the midst of this complex blend of cultures, the Islamic civilization was born with the decline of these 2 civilizations : the Sassanid Empire and the Byzantine Empire. The Islamic civilization, which originated from the commercial cities of Mecca and Medina on the Arabian Peninsula, unified the nomadic people of the Arabian Peninsula. Then, it expanded westward, conquering Damascus, the center of the Byzantine civilization in the western Mediterranean. This expansion led to the establishment of the Umayyad Dynasty, an Islamic dynasty. During the Umayyad Dynasty (661-750), the Damascus region, which was a center for ancient Syrian and Byzantine civilizations, played a crucial role in influencing the sophisticated Byzantine civilization to blend with the desert civilization of the Arabian Peninsula, giving rise to a new Islamic culture.

Following this period, the Abbasid Dynasty (750-1258) emerged in the eastern region and established its capital in Baghdad, which was influenced by ancient Mesopotamia, Persia, and India. The Abbasid Dynasty blended the Umayyad civilization in the west, which was developed based on the foundations of Byzantine civilization, with the Persian Sassanid in Baghdad, adding elements from Indian civilization. This fusion resulted in improving cultural maturity in Islamic civilization.

When the Abbasid dynasty flourished, the Western world was in the midst of the medieval Dark Ages. The Abbasid dynasty translated various fields of knowledge from the West into Arabic, fostering the development of scholars. With the translated works, Arabic scholars integrated knowledge acquired from regions like Persia and India, leading to advancements in a wide range of fields such as chemistry, astronomy, medicine, and philosophy. Such advanced scholarship was transmitted to Europe through regions such as Al-Andalusia in the Iberian Peninsula and the island of Sicily during the later Umayyad dynasty. Europe's highly developed knowledge was re-translated into Latin, leading to its transmission back to Europe. The cultural exchange between the Arab-Islamic civilization, which was in its Golden Age, and Europe, which was in the Dark Ages, across the Mediterranean played a pivotal role in Europe's Renaissance. Across the Mediterranean, the Arab-Islamic civilization and European civilization engaged in cultural exchange during the later Umayyad dynasty, which established itself in Spain on the Iberian Peninsula, leading to interactions with the existing Christian civilization. Additionally, in the 9th century, the North African Islamic Kingdom of the Aghlabid Dynasty conquered Sicily, establishing the Emirate of Sicily (831-1091). The Islamic Emirate on the Italian island of Sicily was influenced by the Abbasid and Fatimid dynasties and experienced significant development. However, it was subsequently conquered and finally fell in 1901 due to the consistent invasion of the Norman forces. During that time, both Christian and Islamic kingdoms, including the Emirate of Sicily, implemented religious and cultural tolerance policies towards the conquered population, which led to a cultural renaissance and development. Palermo, the capital of the Emirate, became one of the largest cities in Europe with a population of 350,000, attracting intellectuals and scholars from both Europe and the Arab world. This environment fostered a rich exchange of knowledge and scholarship between the East and West. The Islamic civilization of Sicily and the Iberian Peninsula played a pivotal role as bridges for transmitting the advanced civilization of the Abbasid Dynasty in Baghdad to the Dark Ages of Europe. This transmission occurred through the North African Fatimid Dynasty and the Maghreb region.

The emergence of Islamic architecture in the Mediterranean region of Europe

The Arab-Islamic and European civilizations, separated by the Mediterranean, engaged in diverse exchange across various fields. The 'House of Wisdom' established by the Abbasid dynasty served as a hub for scholars from across the Islamic world, fostering vibrant intellectual activities. These scholars translated European works into Arabic, integrating them with existing Persian and Indian knowledge, leading to advancement in various fields. This new body of knowledge spread to Europe through the Iberian Peninsula and Sicily. The exchange served as a driving force for the advancement of various fields in Europe, including medicine, chemistry, mathematics, philosophy, agriculture, and architecture. In this context, this paper aims to explore how European and Arab-Islamic civilizations across the Mediterranean influenced and developed the field of Islamic architecture, particularly e mosque architecture. Mosques have been places of worship dedicated to Allah since the early days of Islam, and rulers have paid great attention to their construction. The decoration, both inside and outside mosques, adhered to unified principles from a religious perspective. In Islamic tradition, it is forbidden to depict humans or living animals in decorative art due to the prohibition of idol worship. Therefore, mosque ornaments have developed using geometric patterns of

Arabic calligraphy and vine motifs. This style of ornamentation also includes Arabesque. In terms of architectural structure, mosques in the early Islamic period followed the design of the Prophet's Mosque in Medina. They featured a central courtyard that receives sunlight, surrounded by shaded arcades. During the Umayyad Dynasty, the arcades around the central courtyard were expanded and widened by installing arch-shaped columns. Common architectural features found in mosques across Islamic-conquered regions include 'Mihrab (indicating the direction of Mecca)', 'Minbar (a pulpit)', 'Wodu area (where worshippers can perform ablution or ritual washing before prayer)', and 'Minarate (where the call to prayer is made)'. These common architectural elements transcend geographical boundaries and time, making them characteristic features of mosque architecture across Islamic regions. Indeed, various Islamic dynasties placed great emphasis on decorating mosques as a means of expressing their identity and faith. They often employed highly skilled artisans, regardless of their place of origin, to construct these mosques. Rulers aimed to inspire awe and reverence among the people through these mosques, which served as places of communion with Allah. The distinctive mosques served as a way to enhance the legitimacy of their ruling authority.

With the expansion of the Umayyad Dynasty into the Iberian Peninsula and Sicily, the construction of mosques in the European region began. New mosque architecture evolved through a fusion of architectural styles from the Umayyad and Abbasid periods, integrating with the existing architectural traditions of Christian areas such as the Iberian Peninsula and Sicily, where cathedral architecture was prevalent. In the construction of mosques, common elements such as central courtyards, arch-shaped columns, Arabic calligraphy, and geometric plant motifs were indeed applied to the existing framework of Christian cathedrals. However, apart from the fundamental structural and decorative aspects that are common to Islamic architecture, local building materials, and regional architectural traditions were often utilized, resulting in a diverse range of architectural forms.

Distinctive features of Islamic architecture in Mediterranean Europe

The Islamic kingdom of the Iberian Peninsula was founded by the descendants of the Umayyad dynasty (711-1492), who sought refuge and established their rule concurrently with the Abbasid dynasty. When the Abbasid dynasty in Baghdad was in decline, the Islamic Empire had 3 caliphates in different regions. The Abbasid dynasty in Baghdad, the Fatimid dynasty in Cairo, and the Umayyad dynasty in Iberia each ruled over significant portions of the Islamic Empire. The Umayyad dynasty, situated between the Mediterranean, blended the local culture with the influx of Islamic civilization from North Africa and the Maghreb region, leading to the resurgence of Islamic culture in the European Mediterranean region. Cordova, the capital of the Islamic dynasty on the Iberian Peninsula, was once a thriving city where tens of thousands of people, including envoys from Europe and North Africa, resided. The mosques constructed by the Islamic dynasty of Cordova showcased the beauty of Islamic architecture. They were influenced by the architectural styles of the Abbasid dynasty and the Fatimid dynasty, which mixed elements of ancient Christianity and Byzantine styles with Persian architectural influences. Skilled artisans from various regions of the Islamic empire were recruited for the construction of these mosques, using materials from the Iberian Peninsula and incorporating architectural forms from the subjugated regions. The rounded arch style within mosques originated from the Umayyad Mosque in Damascus. This rounded arch style, which began in ancient Christian buildings in the region of Great Syria (present-day Levant), spread through North Africa and the Maghreb before making its way to the Iberian Peninsula. From there, it continued to spread into Europe.

The Great Mosque of Cordoba, originally constructed in 784, was initially a building that had been used as a temple during the Roman era and later converted into a cathedral. Skilled artisans of Persian origin utilized existing materials, such as stone, in the construction of the mosque. Its unique features include a double-tiered horseshoe arch structure, Arabic script, and geometric plant motifs carved into the arches and ceiling as well as Mihrab indicating the direction of prayer. Later, it was converted into a cathedral in 1236, preserving Islamic architectural elements like arches and decorations while incorporating Christian architectural styles into the renovation process. The Great Mosque of Cordoba has witnessed various architectural transformations throughout the ages, reflecting the different rulers and civilizations that controlled the Iberian Peninsula, including ancient Rome, Byzantium, Islam, and Christianity. Today, the existing architecture of the mosque in Cordoba showcases the exchange of various cultures, with the utilization of local building materials to create a structure that embodies the influences of different civilizations.

The Alhambra Palace in Granada, built between 1238 and 1358, also exhibits influences from Persian Sassanid architecture, particularly in the use of arch-shaped columns and other decorative elements like Muqarnas. Furthermore, the Alhambra Palace was influenced by the structure and arch-based decorations of the Ibn Tulun Mosque in Cairo, constructed between 876 and 879. The Ibn Tulum Mosque is renowned in Islamic architecture and is often considered a masterpiece of the genre.

Sicily has a rich history that includes periods of ancient Roman, Byzantine, Norman, Islamic, and then back to the Norman rule. These different dynasties coexisted and often integrated their respective cultures and influences rather than being exclusive or antagonistic. The arrival of Islam in Sicily in 902 was followed by the Islamic rule on the island from 965 to 1061. During this time, existing Eastern Orthodox cathedrals were converted into mosques, not through destruction and reconstruction but by decorating them with Islamic architectural features both inside and outside. Subsequently, the Norman dynasty, after the Islamic period, further modified these structures back into cathedrals. The coexistence and mutual accommodation of Islamic and Christian civilizations in Sicily resulted in a rich exchange of influences, which is evident in many of the existing cathedrals on the island today.

Exchange of Islamic architectural elements around the Mediterranean: Qubba, Qbla, Mihrab, Muqarnas, Horseshoe arches, Arabesque

The use of the half-dome or Qubba-shaped roofs in European cathedrals and other structures was influenced by artisans under the Umayyad dynasty who drew inspiration from the Byzantine civilization. They adopted the half-done roof form, notably seen in the 'Dome of the Rock' in Jerusalem, into their architecture. Subsequently, during the Abbasid dynasty, this architectural style spread to regions in Central Asia and Persia. The Qubba-shaped half-dome roof form was later transmitted to Europe through the Umayyad dynasty's influence on the Iberian Peninsula.

The 'Qibla', which indicates the direction of Mecca, began to be installed during the Umayyad dynasty when reconstructing the Prophet's Mosque in Medina. Over time, this practice extended to include all mosques in the Islamic Empire, including those in the Iberian Peninsula. The Mihrabis a niche on a wall that signifies the Qibla direction, featured by Arabic calligraphy, intricate Arabesque patterns, and other decorative elements.

The Muqarnas decorations on the ceilings of the Alhambra Palace were inspired by architectural elements from the Abbasid era, particularly in regions like Iraq, Iran, and Central Asia. These designs made their way to the Iberian Peninsula through North Africa, the Fatimid dynasty, and the Maghreb, where they were used in the construction of mosques. The architectural influences of the Alhambra Palace also encompassed elements such as horseshoe arches, geometric and floral Arabesque patterns, columnar arcades, and central courtyards, which reflect the characteristic features of Arab-Islamic architectural forms. The Iberian Peninsula and the island of Sicily were regions where Arab-Islamic civilization interacted with European Christian civilization during the medieval period. These areas played a crucial role in the flourishing of Islamic civilization and the transmission of its influence to Europe.

In particular, the leaders of the Norman dynasty, who conquered the Islamic rulers in Sicily, implemented a policy of religious tolerance. This approach encouraged intellectuals, artists, and scholars from various backgrounds to gather in Sicily. The rulers of the Norman dynasty adorned themselves with cloaks featured by Arabic script and allowed the construction of mosques in the Islamic architectural style. Additionally, during the medieval period in Sicily, the Islamic sciences and philosophy, which had been advanced and translated into Arabic during the Abbasid era, were further translated into Latin. Sicily was also a hub where Muslim and Christian scholars who were exchanging new knowledge. Built in the early 12th century, the Palatine Chapel in Sicily is a medieval architecture that reflects the characteristics of various ruling dynasties in Sicily. The chapel features Norman-style candlesticks and pulpits, Byzantine-style domes and mosaics, and Islamic-style arches and ceilings. Notably, the ceiling is adorned with Muqarnas decorations, Arabesque patterns, and Arabic calligraphy.

Spread of Islamic Architecture

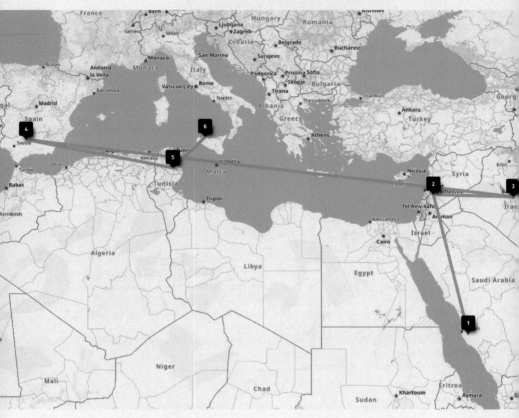

① the Arabian Peninsula (Mecca)   ④ the Iberian Peninsula (Al-Andalusia)

② the Umayyad Dynasty (Damascus)   ⑤ the Aghlabid Dynasty*

③ the Abbasid Dynasty (Baghdad)   ⑥ the Emirate of Sicily

* The North African Islamic Kingdom (Fatimid & Maghreb regions)

Scan the QR code
to view the map.

Keywords

Cultural Exchange, Islamic Civilization, Islamic Architecture, Iberian Peninsula, Sicily, Interaction,

written by Jaeyang Park (Busan University of Foreign Studies)

89

07

Andalusian Architecture
Architecture of Andalusia

The architecture of Andalusia refers to the architectural styles that developed in and around the region of Andalusia, located in southern Spain. In terms of the interaction between the Islamic and Catholic worlds, it mainly refers to the architecture that developed during the period between 711 and 1492, when Islamic and Catholic populations coexisted in the Iberian Peninsula.

The term Andalusian architecture can be used to refer specifically to the architecture of Andalusia. It can be called for the geographical category can be broadened to include the architecture of Morocco, Algeria, and Tunisia, and the term Moorish architecture can be used to refer to the architecture of the region.

The architecture of Andalusia is a mixture of Roman, Byzantine, and Visigothic architectural styles that influenced the Iberian Peninsula before the arrival of Islam, as well as the architecture of Islamic cultures. Major cities where Andalusian architecture is well represented include Córdoba, Granada, and Sevilla.

The types of architecture can be categorized into two groups: religious architecture and secular architecture. One of the most prominent examples of religious architecture is the Great Mosque and Cathedral of Córdoba, while secular architecture includes the Alhambra Palace.

In 711, Islamic troops first entered the Iberian Peninsula, where the Kingdom of the Visigoths was situated. In 750, the Umayyad Dynasty in Damascus, Syria, was overthrown by the Abbasid Dynasty. Abd al Rahman I, a member of the Umayyad Dynasty royal family, founded the Cordoba

Fig 7–1. Cathedral in the great mosque in Cordoba

Fig 7-2. Inside of the great mosque

Umayyad Dynasty in Córdoba in 756, making the city its capital. In 785, he built The Great Mosque of Córdoba, which still stands today. In 1236, after the city was recaptured by Catholic conquerors during the Reconquista, it was converted into a cathedral. More recently, it has been renamed the Great Mosque-Cathedral and is known for its architecture that incorporates both Islamic and Catholic identities.

The Alhambra showcases a variety of Andalusian architectural styles. There's the hypostyle structure, the presence of the courtyard, and the Horseshoe Arch. The walls are decorated with geometric, vegetal, and floral patterns. In addition, Arabic inscriptions were used to decorate the walls. Especially the Muqarnas on the ceilings of the Ambassador's Room and the two sisters' rooms, which represent the essence of architectural decoration in the Islamic world.

These examples illustrate that Andalusian architecture continuously incorporates features of early Islamic architecture. Jonathan Bloom, a scholar of Islamic art, notes that the architecture of Andalusia is much more conservative than that of other regions. In contrast to the Ottoman and Safavid empires, which incorporated massive domes and Iwan, Andalusian architecture persisted in using elements typical of early Islamic architecture, such as hypostyle and arch structures. It also followed the tradition of simplifying the exterior decoration of buildings and focusing on the interior.

Even after Muslims had left the Iberian Peninsula, the architectural tradition of the Andalusian style persisted under the name of the Mudejar style Especially in the Moroccan region, the Hispano-Maghreb style continues to this day. In the modern world, Andalusian architecture has become a symbol of cultural exchange and development between Islam and Catholics.

Keywords

Andalusia, the Great Mosque in Cordoba, Alhambra, Islam, Catholic

written by Soojeong Yi (The Sogang Euro-MENA Institute)

08

Mosaic

An art technique that combines small fragments to express a certain shape. Patterns or paintings are formed by joining pieces of various colored stones, glass, metal, seashells, tiles, etc. This technique, which originated in ancient Mesopotamia, was adopted in Rome through Greece and was popular during the Byzantine period. In ancient Central America, the mosaic technique was developed early on, and many artifacts from the Mayan culture and the Aztecs were decorated with mosaics. It was also used as decoration for walls and ceilings in the Ancient Orient and Classical Greece, and was especially developed after the Hellenistic period. Representative examples include the mosaics excavated in Pompeii and the mosaics of Ravenna Cathedral. Mosaics, which were produced sparingly, were revived along with stained glass at the end of the 19th century and are now widely used in the decoration of public and religious buildings.

Typically, the tesserae mosaic is an art form that originated in the Hellenistic civilization and spread throughout the Mediterranean. Influential people who lived through the Hellenistic and Roman periods gained satisfaction from life by showing off luxurious decorations, tastes, and vanity. Mosaics are the pinnacle of it. However, there is some confusion in the aspect of art being a result of the exploitation of slaves and colonists. Of course, pouring legitimately accumulated wealth into culture and arts would have a great positive effect in expanding diversity and improving the quality of life. In any case, if you look for mosaics without forgetting that they were not the culture of the people who struggled to support the bottom of Roman society, but the culture of the highest class, and that they are relics made with the blood and sweat of helpless people, you will have a balanced historical awareness and sense of art. How many citizens during the Roman era installed mosaics in their homes for architectural or artistic purposes? To conclude, it does not seem that the installation of mosaics was widespread during the Roman era. Let's look at Pompeii, which was briefly buried under volcanic ash and then came back to life. As a result of the survey, the proportion of building floors paved with mosaics in Pompeii was only 2.5% of the total floor area. Additionally, 75% of the discovered mosaics are concentrated in 3 specific houses. It is not difficult to recognize that it is a product of architecture and art enjoyed only by a few wealthy people. However, it is difficult to judge the Hellenistic world simply by using Pompeii as an example. In the case of Delos Island in the Aegean Sea, excavations revealed that mosaics were used in many houses. In the Hellenistic world, the home of color tesserae mosaics, mosaics appear to have been more common than on the Italian peninsula, the heart of the Roman Empire.

In which building and where are the tesserae mosaics mainly installed? These are luxurious homes such as the Domus, a mansion for the wealthy, and manor villas, and public facilities such as public baths. The places in the house that were most expensively decorated were the Tablinum (Oecus), a living room where guests were welcomed, the Triclinium (dining room), and the Exedra (corridor), an outdoor summer restaurant. There is a long bench-shaped dining room at the back, a bathhouse (Terme), a bedroom (cubiculum), and a corridor (*peristilium*). Unless they were in the highest class, they used public bathhouses rather than individual bathhouses, so they did not put effort into installing mosaics in the bathhouses of their houses. What did they do with the parts of the house where furniture like beds and tables were placed? The mosaic was not installed, and the space was left empty. Or, it was laid with a simple geometric pattern or a monochromatic black and white mosaic.

The mosaic artists appear to have taken great pride in their work. Even during the Hellenistic period, the name of 'Musearius', the creator, was left on some works, but during the Roman period, his name appeared in quite a few works. The artist's name is engraved in the corner of the mosaic screen, which is similar to writing a name in the corner of a painting. It seems that the treatment was not that good compared to the pride. According to records from the time of Emperor Diocletian in 301AD, the emperor accounted for only about 75% of the painters who painted frescoes. Moreover, compared to portrait painters, it was less than a half. This shows that they belong to the second class of the artisan class that creates culture and art. As is the case in any field, there were some people who had amassed considerable wealth.

Additionally, Aelius Proclus followed in his father's footsteps and made a name for himself as a mosaic artist. He became wealthy enough to use his wealth to build and donate a temple to Tyche, the goddess of fate. Thanks to this achievement, he gained popularity among the public and rose to public office through election.

Emblema means 'inserted,' which refers to the method of pre-creating a specific topic into a panel within a square frame. Emblems were inserted into specific parts of the overall floor mosaic, which was decorated with geometric patterns or other flora and fauna. This is a technique derived from painting and is a characteristic feature of mosaics in the Hellenistic region. During the Hellenistic period, frescoes hung on walls were often painted using the Emblema technique, and the principle was taken from this. Mosaics from the Italian peninsula, the mainland of the Roman Empire, widely used the method of incorporating a single theme across the entire screen rather than the Hellenistic style emblem technique. For reference, cities such as Alexandria and Samos served as supply points for making Emblema panels and exporting them throughout the Mediterranean.

Mosaic patterns remain at the ruins of Mesopotamia, one of the world's 4 great civilizations. Ziggurat, a temple made of bricks, is a representative Mesopotamian ruin. Here, on the stairs, is a mosaic made by baking clay into a cone shape, coloring it, and stacking it closely to create a pattern. This is called a 'Cone mosaic'. The mosaic at this time was a pattern of repeated geometric abstract patterns, and concrete shapes began to appear only during the ancient Greek period. Though the Hellenistic and Roman periods, the aesthetic perfection of mosaics increased to the point where they depicted people's facial expressions, muscles, and wrinkles on clothes in detail.

As Christianity began to flourish in the Roman Empire, people began to think that there should be a medium to effectively spread the doctrines of the Bible. At the same time, they felt that there was a need for a space that would allow one to experience the image of heaven in detail. The means to satisfy this was church architecture and mosaics.

What is the difference between Greek and Roman architecture and Christian architecture? Famous ancient buildings such as the Parthenon, the Arc de Triomphe, the Colosseum, and the Aqueduct placed more emphasis on the exterior than the interior. The interior is faithful to the basic functions of the building, with only a few decorations, and most of the focus is on beautifying the exterior. The shapes of pillars and arches, as well as the sculptures decorated on the exterior walls and roofs, look much more realistic as they are directly exposed to the strong sunlight of the Mediterranean, adding a shadow effect.

On the other hand, Christian architecture focused on creating a feeling of unreality by splendidly decorating the interior space rather than decorating the exterior. Rather than using strong light directly, the light flows into the room through arch-shaped windows in the ceiling dome and pendant. This light is reflected by the mosaic decorated on the wall and scatters in all directions, creating an atmosphere so mysterious that one cannot tell exactly where the light is coming from, making one feel ecstatic as if one were in another world than this one. The ceiling of the place with the highest dome is filled with images symbolizing heaven, and like the Basilica of San Vitale, there is also a lamb representing Jesus.

The background of light being drawn into the interior and creating a mysterious atmosphere is the philosophy of Neoplatonism, which played a major role in the formation of Christian doctrine. It is the school of philosophy that represents best the ideological tendency of late Roman mysticism, which desperately wanted salvation in the afterlife. It can be understood as a further refinement of the dichotomy between the ideal world and the real world mentioned by the ancient Greek philosopher Plato.

Plotinus (c. 205-270), a philosopher active in Alexandria, represents Neoplatonism. He developed the outflow theory that this world is the light that flows down from the absolute being in the heavens and reaches the material beings on earth through several stages. Light flows from the 'One', the most fundamental being, and 'Nus (Spirit)' is created. Therefore, it is said that by looking at the Nus, you can see how the one reveals itself. 'Nus (Spirit)' contains all the true things called 'Idea'. In Nus, the 'soul' flows out, and the soul can be seen as the principle that creates specific movements or forms. The 'substance' flowing out from the soul is the final stage and refers to the world we live in. The One-Nus-Soul-Matter form a hierarchy that becomes increasingly incomplete and diversified as it goes down. You can think of the heavenly light flowing down and spreading out here and there, becoming increasingly blurred. Therefore, the core of Neoplatonist philosophy is that we, who are material, should strive to ascend toward the soul, toward Nus, and ultimately aim to meet and become one with the One. Neoplatonism directly influenced the Christian goal that humans with original sin should become one with Jesus through salvation and atonement. It is said that in order to reach this goal, one must discipline oneself through moral restraint, abstinence, and diligence, as well as receive the grace of God and experience ecstasy. So, how can ecstasy be experienced? It involves experiencing the feeling of being close to heaven in a cathedral filled with the mystery of light. Therefore, Christian architecture made every effort to create an atmosphere of heaven by decorating the interior space with high windows and mosaics. The production of a mosaic itself requires a huge amount of labor and cost, and the generous use of gold to decorate the church shows that it was well supported by wealth and power.

Influence of these Byzantine mosaics spread widely throughout Europe, but during the Renaissance era, which pursued realism, there was a backlash against the decorative qualities of Byzantine art, and it gradually lost popularity.

In the 19th century, mosaics regained popularity as many public buildings were decorated with mosaics, and tiles and glass tesserae were reproduced in factories. Pre-Columbian American Indians had a particular fondness for mosaics of semi-precious stones such as garnets, turquoises, and mother-of-pearl, which were commonly used to decorate the surfaces of small objects such as shields, masks, and statues of gods. Mexican writers of the 20th century preferred mosaic decoration, and many of Mexico's modern buildings were decorated with mosaics using natural stones.

Fig 8–1. Mosaic from the Galla Placidia Mausoleum in Ravenna, Italy, 5th century.

Fig 8–2. Floor mosaic from Paphos, Cyprus, 3rd–5th century

Keywords

ancient Mesopotamia, Rome, Greece, the Byzantine period. the Mayan culture, the Aztecs, the Hellenistic period, Pompeii, the mosaics of Ravenna Cathedral, the tesserae mosaic, the Mediterranean, public facilities, the Tablinum (Oecus), the Triclinium (dining room), and the Exedra (corridor), a bathhouse (Terme), a bedroom (cubiculum), a corridor (*peristilium*), Musearius, Aelius Proclus, a temple to Tyche, Emblema, Cone mosaic, Christianity architecture, the Basilica of San Vitale.

References

Erminio Fonzo, Hilary A. Haakenson (2019), Mediterranean Mosaic. History and Art. ICSR Mediterranean Knowledge

Anita Benarde, Benarde (1984). Mediterranean Mosaic Designs. Stemmer House Byzantine Art in the Making

Ernst Kitzinger (1977). Main Lines of Stylistic Development in Mediterranean Art, 3rd-7th Century, Harvard University Press

Joshua J. Thomas (2021). Art, Science, and the Natural World in the Ancient Mediterranean, 300 BC to AD 100. Oxford University Press

Umberto Pappalardo, Rosario Ciardiello (2006). Stories in Stone Conserving Mosaics of Roman Africa : Masterpieces from the National Museums of Tunisia. Greek and Roman Mosaics. WW Norton

Image References

www.wikipedia.org

https://ko.wikipedia.org/wiki/%EB%AA%A8%EC%9E%90%EC%9D%B4%ED%81%AC

written by Hee jung Kim (Busan University of Foreign Studies)

09

Fresco

Definition

Fresco is a wall painting technique performed on freshly laid lime plaster. Water is used as a vehicle for the fusion of the dry-powdered pigment with the plaster and with the hardening of the plaster itself the painting with its colors becomes an integral part of the wall, remaining for an unlimited time.

It is an ancient pictorial technique which is achieved by painting with pigments generally of mineral origin diluted in water on fresh plaster: in this way, once the carbonation process has been completed, the color will be completely incorporated in the plaster, thus acquiring considerable resistance over time.

The word *fresco* ('Affresco' in Italian) is derived from the Italian adjective 'Fresco' meaning *fresh* and may thus be contrasted with 'Fresco-secco' mural painting technique ('Colore a Tempera' in Italian), which is applied to dried plaster to supplement painting in fresco. The fresco technique is closely associated with Italian Renaissance painting.

Fresco pigment is mixed with room temperature water and is used on a thin layer of wet, fresh plaster, or 'Intonaco' in Italian, which is composed of a mixture of fine river sand, marble powder or sifted pozzolana, lime and water. Due to the chemical composition of the plaster, the pigment mixed only with water will sink by being absorbed into it; the plaster itself becomes the medium that holds the pigment, and after some hours, the intonaco dries in reaction to air: it is this chemical reaction which fixes the pigment particles in the intonaco itself.

The color must necessarily be spread on the still damp plaster, hence the Italian term *a fresco* and it must belong to the category of oxides, given that it does not have to interact with the carbonation of the lime.

In painting frescoes, a rough underlayer called 'Arriccio' is added to the whole area to be painted and allowed to dry for some days. Many artists in the Middle Ages and then in the Renaissance sketched their compositions on this underlayer, which would never be seen, in a dark reddish-brown natural earth pigment called 'Sinopia', which they often used on the rough initial layer of intonaco for the preparatory drawing for a *fresco*. With the development of modern techniques for transferring paper drawings to the wall, the main lines of a drawing made on paper were pricked over with a point, the paper was held against the wall, and a bag of soot ('Spolvero') banged on the lines to produce black dots along them.

If the painting was to be done on an existing fresco, the surface would be roughened to provide better adhesion. On the day of painting, a thinner, smooth layer of intonaco was added to the amount of wall that was expected to be completed that day, sometimes matching the contours of the figures or the landscape, but more often just starting from the top of the composition. This area is called the 'Giornata (day's work)', and the different day stages can usually be seen in a large fresco by a faint seam that separates one from the next.

Frescoes are difficult to create because of the deadline associated with the drying plaster. Generally, a layer of it will require ten to 12 hours before the drying time, giving seven to 9 hours of working time. Once a giornata is dried, no more fresco can be done, and the unpainted intonaco must be removed with a tool before starting again the next day. If mistakes have been made, it may also be necessary to remove the whole intonaco for that area or to change them later with a secco technique.

Another problem consists in understanding what the effective tone of the color will be: wet plaster, in fact, makes the colors darker, while lime tends to whiten colors. One of the remedies used by the artists was to carry out tests on a pumice stone. An indispensable component of this process, therefore, is the 'Carbonatation' of the lime, which fixes the color in the Intonaco, ensuring the durability of the fresco for future generations.

History and Background

The earliest known frescoes come from the ancient world.

The oldest Egyptian fresco, a mural with painted decoration on its plaster walls, is thought to date to circa 3500~3200 BCE, and it was found in the current city of Nekhen, formerly known as Hierankopolis, "the city of the falcon", a reference to Horus, one of the most significant Egyptian deities. Several of the themes and designs visible in the fresco are otherwise known from other objects belonging to the culture of Gerzeh, a prehistoric Egyptian cemetery located along the west bank of the Nile River. It shows the scene of a "Master of Animals", a man fighting against two lions, individual fighting scenes, and Egyptian and foreign boats.

An old fresco from Mesopotamia is the 'Investiture of Zimri-Lim', a large colorful mural discovered between 1935 and 1936 at the Royal Palace of the ancient city-state of Mari in eastern Syria. This fresco, which dates to the 18th century BCE, depicts 'Zimri-Lin', king of Mari, receiving the rod-and-ring symbol (a ring and a staff, symbols of rule) from the goddess Ishtar, and it was discovered "in situ" on its original wall located opposite the grand doorway to the podium which leads to the throne room of the palace. The 'Investiture of Zimri-Lim' is distinguished in part by its wide range of colors, including green and blue, and it is painted on a thin layer of mud plaster applied directly to the palace's brick wall.

The oldest frescoes made using the day's work technique, known in Italian as 'giornata' or 'buon fresco', date from the first half of the second millennium BCE during the Bronze Age, and are to be found among Aegean Civilizations, more precisely Minoan art from the island of Crete and other islands of the Aegean Sea. The most famous of these frescoes is the 'Bull-Leaping' fresco, the most completely restored of several 'stucco' panels originally sited on the upper-story portion of the east wall of the palace of Knossos in Crete. It depicts a sacred ceremony in which some people jump over the backs of a large bull.

Fig 9–1. The Fisherman, Minoan Bronze Age Fresco (circa 1640~1600 BC).

Although they were frescoes, they were painted on stucco relief scenes and were difficult to produce. Artists had to manage not only the altitude of the panel but also the simultaneous molding and painting of fresh stucco. In Minoan chronology, given their polychrome hues, white, pale red, dark red, blue, and black, these frescoed panels are dated around 1700~1600 BCE.

The Etruscan paintings that have survived are almost all wall frescoes from tombs mainly located in the old town of Tarquinia, located in the Lazio region, Central Italy, and dating from roughly 670 to 200 BCE.

Fig 9–2. The *Tomb of the Leopards* (circa 470~450 BC), an Etruscan burial chamber with frescoes depicting two confronted leopards above a banquet scene. Monterozzi Necropolis, nearby the town of Tarquinia, Lazio region, Italy.

Fig 9–3. The Tomb of the Diver. Paestum, Italy. 480~470 BC.

The Greeks very rarely painted their tombs in the same period, with rare exceptions such as the *Tomb of the Diver* in Paestum, southern Italy, dating to 470 BCE.

These frescoes depict scenes of the life and society of ancient Greece: one shows a group of men reclining at a *symposium*, while another one shows a young man diving into the sea. The whole tradition of Greek painting on walls and panels is almost entirely lost, giving the Etruscan tradition, which undoubtedly drew much from Greek examples, an added importance, even if it does not approach the sophistication of the best Greek masters.

The Etruscan tombs were apparently sites for recurrent family rituals, and the subjects of paintings probably have a more religious character than might at first appear. Frescoes in these tombs are created by applying paint on top of fresh plaster so that when the plaster itself dries, the paintings become part of it, and consequently, part of the wall. Colors were created from ground-up minerals and then mixed into the paint. In the so-called 'Tomb of the Leopards' (around 470~450 BCE), women are depicted as fair-skinned, while men as dark red-skinned, in keeping with the gender conventions established in Archaic Greece, Ancient Near East and Ancient Egypt.

Roman wall paintings, such as those at the magnificent 'Villa dei Misteri '(1ˢᵗ century BCE) in the ruins of Pompeii and others in Herculaneum and Stabia, were made using the 'Buon fresco' technique. The knowledge of Roman painting is mainly due to the good conditions of preservation of the three famous Vesuvian cities, where large quantities of paintings have been found, especially wall frescoes. Pompeian paintings can be dated between the

Fig 9–4. A fresco from the Roman period. Pompeii, Villa of the Mysteries (I century AD)

II century BCE and the great eruption of Vesuvius in 79 CE. Frescoes were typically painted on plaster while it was drying.

Roman (Christian) frescoes from the I to II century CE were found in catacombs beneath Rome. They were done by the artist painting the artwork on the still damp plaster of the wall so that the painting became part of the wall itself, colored plaster. Both in early Christian and early medieval times, the preparation of the wall to be frescoed took place quickly: the figuration was carried out directly on the preparation: first, the outlines in ocher and then the filling up to the shadows. The execution of the various parts was determined by the development of the scaffolding on the construction site: the different phases of the realization of a fresco can be determined by the pictorial joints created by the movement of the scaffolding itself.

Early Christian or Paleochristian art is the term that refers to the art produced by Christians or under Christian patronage from the earliest period of Christianity to, depending on the definition used, sometime between 260 and 525 CE. Basically, identifiably, Christian art only survived from the 2nd century CE onwards, while after 550 CE at the latest, Christian art was classified as Byzantine or of some other regional type.

Early Christian art is placed in the orbit of imperial Rome and would have had its maximum development between the first decades of the 4th century and the beginning of the 6th century, possibly even up to 604, the year of the death of Pope Gregory I, so that the Christian ideal in its beginning assumed the forms of late antiquity.

Even the fresco painting of the first centuries of the Christian era took its cue from artistic currents already in progress and linked to paganism, attributing different meanings to their representations. An emblematic example is that of the image of the banquet, already used for centuries in ancient art, especially in the funerary field: it became the representation of the Last Supper, a symbol of the celebration of the Eucharist, the fundamental liturgy of the new Christian religion. Other symbolic images in these frescoes are those that do not describe events but express a concept, such as the 'Good Shepherd', which symbolizes Jesus Christ's philanthropy. Until the 3rd century CE, it was not allowed to depict God, and therefore, symbols were used such as the lamb.

The ban on depicting Jesus Christ was lifted following the first Council of Nicaea, 325 CE, when the dual divine and human nature of Christ was sanctioned, thus arguing that He possessed representable human features. Initially, Jesus was depicted beardless, as in the frescoes of the catacombs of Domitilla, but later, he began to be depicted with beard and royal insignia, which assimilated Him to the emperor, according to the Roman imperial iconography of the 'Traditio Legis', the Delivery of the Law, as can be seen in the catacombs of Commodilla.

It is worth mentioning as a further example the Castelseprio frescoes, a cycle of paintings dating from between the 6th and the 9th century located in the church of Santa Maria Foris Portas in Castelseprio, a town in the Italian region of Lombardy. Made by an anonymous painter known as 'Master of Castelseprio', a probably Byzantine artist who worked for Greek, Lombard or Carolingian patrons, these frescoes represent scenes of Jesus's childhood inspired, it would seem, by the apocryphal Gospels and they were made at the same time as the church was built, given that the painted plaster is above a curl (*arriccio*) on which the painter traced the essential lines of the figures.

These purple lines were painted in buon fresco, i.e., on the still fresh plaster, and the most used colors are carbonaceous black for the shading, lime white for the clothes of the characters, red, yellow, and blue.

Romanesque painting includes the artistic forms that developed in Western and Central Europe from the early 11th to the mid-12th century, with significant differences from one region to another. In the Romanesque era, the work of fresco artists was still carried out considering the working days on the scaffolding, but the technique began to be refined: the use of straw, shards and fabric was introduced in the mixture of curl and plaster to keep it moist and allow a longer time for pictorial drafting. Figures are still spread out with red, ocher outlines, but we begin to see the use of glue for colors (melted wax, albumen, animal glue). Furthermore, in some cases, it is possible to detect the presence of guidelines for the figuration traced on the fresh plaster.

During this period, Europe grew steadily more prosperous, and art of the highest quality was no longer confined, as it largely was in the Carolingian and Ottonian periods, to the royal court and to monasteries. City churches, those of pilgrimage routes, and many churches in small towns were elaborately decorated to a very high standard. Among the most significant frescoes, those of the last part of the XI century in Novalesa Abbey in Piedmont, Italy, depicting Saint Nicholas and Saint Eldrado with a range of colors employed that is limited to light blue-green, yellow ochre, reddish brown and black.

Between 14th and 15th century, fresco techniques spread considerably throughout Europe, and the craftsmen of the time introduced, as previously mentioned, an important innovation: the sinopia, a preparatory drawing for the application of color, made before on the 'Arriccio' and then on the plaster, which precisely reproduced the figures on the fresco. The craftsmen meticulously plan the development of the fresco by deciding, before applying the plaster, how much of it they will be able to paint in a day's work time (Giornata). The techniques used for the retouching, which take place dry, make it often possible to identify the artist who executed the fresco. Giotto (Scrovegni Chapel), Masaccio (Brancacci Chapel), Ambrogio Lorenzetti (Palazzo Pubblico of Siena), Piero della Francesca, Domenico Ghirlandaio (Tornabuoni Chapel), Leonardo da Vinci (*The Last Supper*), Sandro Botticelli, Luca Signorelli, Pietro Perugino (Sistine

Fig 9–5. Scrovegni Chapel, with a fresco cycle by Giotto, completed around 1305. Padua, Veneto region, Italy.

Chapel) are some of the great artists who made frescoes in this period.

With the Renaissance, fresco knows its maximum diffusion. In the Italian peninsula, the technique of sinopia was abandoned in favor of the use of preparatory cardboards, and pouncing, a technique used for transferring an image from one surface to another by using a fine powder called 'Pounce', was introduced.

The whole preparatory drawing was brought to life-size on the cardboard, and the lines that made up the figures were perforated. Once the cardboard was placed on the fresh plaster, it was dusted with a pad soaked in fine charcoal powder which, passing through the small holes, left a trace to be followed for the application of the fresco with the brush.

The Renaissance painting was the culmination of the varied means of expression and various advances in painting techniques such as linear perspective, the realistic depiction of both physical and psychological features, and the manipulation of light and darkness, including tone contrast, 'Sfumato (softening the transition between colors)' and 'Chiaroscuro (contrast between light and dark)', in a single unifying style which expressed total compositional order, balance, and harmony.

Fig 9–6. The Allegory of Good and Bad Government, a series of three frescoes painted by Ambrogio Lorenzetti between 1338 and 1339. Palazzo Pubblico of Siena. Tuscany region, Italy

The Renaissance painting is the absolute zenith of western painting and achieved the balancing and reconciliation, in harmony, of contradictory and seemingly mutually exclusive artistic positions, such as real versus ideal, movement versus rest, freedom versus law, space versus plane, and line versus color. The Renaissance was viewed as a great explosion of creative genius, following a model of art history first proposed by Giorgio Vasari.

Fig 9–7. *The Last Judgment*, a fresco painted by Michelangelo between 1536 and 1541, covering the whole altar wall of the Sistine Chapel in Vatican City.

The paintings in the Vatican (including the fresco cycles) by Michelangelo and Raphael are said by various scholars to represent the culmination of the Renaissance style in painting because of the ambitious scale of these works, coupled with the complexity of their composition, closely observed human figures, and pointed iconographic and decorative references to classical antiquity, can be viewed as emblematic of the Renaissance.

Even relatively minor painters of this period, such as Fra Bartolomeo and Mariotto Albertinelli, produced works that are still lauded for the harmony of their design and techniques. The elongated proportions and exaggerated poses in the late works of Michelangelo, Andrea del Sarto, and Correggio prefigure Mannerism, a style in European art that emerged in the later years of the Italian Renaissance around 1520, spreading by about 1530 and lasting about the end of 16th century in Italy, when the Baroque style largely replaced it. The serene mood and luminous colors of paintings by Giorgione and early Titian exemplified the Renaissance style as practiced in Venice. Great recognizable works of the period include Leonardo da Vinci's 'Monna Lisa' and Raphael's 'The School of Athens': Raphael's fresco, set beneath an arch, is a virtuous work of perspective, composition, and design.

Other significant works of this same era include the Sistine Chapel ceiling, painted in fresco by Michelangelo between 1508 and 1512; the 4 'Raphael's Rooms' frescoes in the Apostolic Palace, now part of the Vatican Museums, in Vatican City; Raphael's frescoes in the Villa Farnesina, a Renaissance suburban villa in Rome; Giulio Romano's frescoes in the Palazzo Te, Padua, Italy; the 'Camera degli Sposi', a room frescoed with illusionistic paintings by Andrea

Mantegna in the Ducal Palace in Mantua, Italy; 'The Loves of Gods', a monumental fresco cycle completed by the Bolognese artist Annibale Carracci in the Farnese Palace, Rome, currently the French Embassy in Italy and the 'Allegory of Divine Providence and Barberini Power', a fresco by the Italian painter Pietro da Cortona in the Barberini Palace, Rome.

Keywords

Fresco; Ancient Egypt; Pompeii; Giotto; Piero della Francesca

References

Vincent Cronin, *The Renaissance*. 1992

Frederick Hartt, *A History of Italian Renaissance Art*. 1970, Thames and Hudson

Michael Baxandall, *Painting and Experience in Fifteenth Century Italy*. 1974, Oxford University Press

John Boardman, *The Oxford History of Classical Art*. 1993, Oxford University Press

Giorgio Vasari, *Lives of the Most Excellent Painters, Sculptors and Architects*. English edition translated by George Bull. Penguin 1965

Peter Burke, *The Italian Renaissance: Culture and Society in Italy*. Princeton University Press, 1999

Keith Christiansen, *Italian Painting*. Hugh Lauter / Lavin Macmillan, 1992

Gino Piva, *Manuale Pratico di Tecnica Pittorica*. Hoepli 1989

Otto J. Brendel, *Etruscan Art*. Yale University Press, 1995

Image References

www.wikipedia.org

https://www.worldhistory.org/image/2442/fisherman-fresco-akrotiri/

https://en.wikipedia.org/wiki/Tomb_of_the_Leopards

https://en.wikipedia.org/wiki/Tomb_of_the_Diver

https://en.wikipedia.org/wiki/Villa_of_the_Mysteries

https://en.wikipedia.org/wiki/Scrovegni_Chapel

https://en.wikipedia.org/wiki/The_Allegory_of_Good_and_Bad_Government

https://en.wikipedia.org/wiki/The_Last_Judgment_(Michelangelo)

written by Emiliano Pennisi (Sogang University)

10

Miniature
Book illustration

The term "miniature" encompasses 3 distinct meanings. Firstly, it refers to a meticulous technique used in producing miniature paintings, which can depict medallion portraits or images on cards. Secondly, it describes a craft that is scaled down in size, such as a miniature scale model. Lastly, it pertains to the illustrations found within manuscripts. In this text, miniatures refer to the pictures inserted into manuscripts.

The etymology of the word "miniature" can be traced back to the Latin term "Miniare," meaning "to color with Minium." Minium refers to a red pigment made from lead. Initially, the term was used to describe the technique of decorating the first letter of early manuscripts with red, known as "Miniatura." Etymologically, it does not directly imply "small," but due to the nature of decorative paintings in manuscripts, it has acquired the additional meaning of "small paintings" or "miniature paintings." In non-Western languages, miniatures are simply referred to as "pictures" or "descriptions." However, due to the influence of Westernization, the term "miniature" is also frequently adopted in these languages. For instance, in Türkiye since 19th-century, illustrations of manuscripts have been labeled as "Minyatür." It's worth noting that beyond the academic definition of miniatures, there is often a misconception that they exclusively exist in the Islamic world. Nevertheless, this discussion also encompasses the exchange aspects of Islamic manuscript illustrations.

The early miniature can be traced back to ancient Egyptian papyrus manuscripts from the 2nd century BC. Subsequently, miniatures evolved during the Greek, Roman, and Byzantine eras. Particularly, with the rise of Christianity, biblical stories and motifs became the primary subjects for miniatures. Byzantine miniatures were crafted across the empire, encompassing not only religious works but also illustrations in medical books, chronicles, and tales of legendary figures like Alexander the Great. While many works were lost during the Iconoclastic period, remnants found in Palestine and Italy provide glimpses into the miniatures of that time. These miniatures were characterized by the use of thick, black brush, with no clear boundary between the text and the images.

In European culture between the 9th and 12th centuries, miniatures began to be depicted on parchment, either encompassing the entire manuscript or occupying only a small portion of it. The area surrounding the initial letter was adorned with decorative pictures. Notably, decorative elements from Islamic culture started to influence European miniatures during this period.

Following the advent of Islam, miniatures also thrived in the Arab-Persian-Turkic peoples' cultural sphere. Early miniature painting in this context developed through a mutual exchange of influences from Hellenistic and Roman painting traditions, ancient Persian culture, and Central Asian and Far Eastern cultures.

The miniature artworks that have survived from the early Islamic culture date back to the 12th and 13th centuries. Unfortunately, very little is known about miniature works immediately following the birth of Islam.

Determining the exact region or timeframe of the miniature works from the 12th and 13th centuries is challenging. Manuscript illustrations were frequently reproduced and copied for many centuries, as manuscripts lacked artist signatures. While the style of painting can provide clues to estimate the era and region, it is crucial not to overlook the characteristics of the period and region marked by constant exchange and interaction.

The miniature paintings of 12th and 13th-century Islamic culture draw their foundations from various regional factors. Specifically, they are influenced by the Byzantine manuscript tradition, Persian regional art, and Central Asian manuscripts. In Persia, the influence of the wall painting tradition from the Parthian and Sassanian periods, predating Islam, is evident. Additionally, the development of Manichaeism played a significant role, as its founder, Mani (216-274), was known as a painter. The spread of Manichaeism to Central Asian Uyghurs led to the development of Central Asian murals and miniatures. During the 8th century, Turkish cities such as Hocho, Turpan, Bezeklik, and Kyzyl saw the emergence of Buddhist and Manichaean mural paintings and illustrations, which were subsequently transmitted as the Turks advanced westward.

As a result of these influences, the characteristics of miniature paintings underwent numerous transformations in response to the rise and fall of new dynasties and the arrival of new peoples. The coexistence of small countries alongside the Abbasids, the establishment of the Seljuks, their expansion into Anatolia, the assimilation of other small kingdoms, the interactions and conflicts with the Byzantine Empire, the Mongol invasions, and the subsequent founding of various states all naturally influenced the evolution of miniatures.

Various instances can be found where different cultural elements are amalgamated in miniature paintings. One such example is the 'Kitab al-Diryaq', with the oldest edition being the French National Library edition (Bibliothèque Nationale de France, Arabe 2964/Nur al-Din Arslan Shah I of the Janggi Dynasty, reign: 1193-1210), produced in January 1199 in Baghdad. The depiction of the figures, characterized by round faces and slightly slanted eyes, demonstrates the influence of Seljuk and Central Asian Uyghur art. However, the style of drawing without frames reflects the Byzantine tradition.

'Nasir al-Din's Daqa'iq al-haqa'iq' (Bibliothèque Nationale de France, Persan 174), created in 1271 in Kayseri and Aksaray, Anatolia, is a book containing various magic and illusions. It is believed to have been influenced by Byzantine cave paintings in the nearby region of Göreme, as well as the Uyghur Turk legacy, as evidently observed in the depiction of characters, clothing, and astronomical information.

The 13th-century Mongol invasion and the establishment of the Ilhan Empire (1259-1336) brought about a new trend in miniatures. Chinese painting, particularly the style of the Tang Dynasty, began to be incorporated into miniatures. This new style showcased flat compositions adorned with decorative elements, distinctive brushwork, character portrayals, clothing depictions, and the use of light-colored paint. It also introduced new features like Chinese-style background representations. Additionally, the separation between the text and the pictorial realm became more distinct compared to the previous century.

The 13th-century edition of Maqamat al-Hariri in the National Library of France (Bibliothèque Nationale de France Arabe 5847, made by Yahya ibn Mahmud al-Wasiti in 1236/37) is painted in the Baghdad style. The figures are depicted with long noses, black beards, and bulging eyes. Another copy from the collection of the National Library of Vienna, which was produced in Mamluk Egypt (Österreichische Nationalbibliothek, Chart. Ar. 25612), exemplifies a shift from the Baghdad painting style. In Mamluk's works, one can observe the influence of Mongol-Turkic portraiture. Even on the first page of the Vienna National Library collection, an Amir is depicted sitting on a throne with a cup of wine, surrounded by musicians, entertainers, and court ladies wearing Seljuk-style costumes over gold leaf. Notably being different from Arab influences, one can see Uyghur and Seljuk influences, such as exotic shapes with slanted eyes.

An early 13th-century Seljuk work in Anatolia, titled Varaka and Gülshah (Topkapı Sarayı Müzesi Kütüphanesi, Hazine 841), not only portrays figures in the Seljuk style but also employs horizontal frames to depict each scene in the narrative, revealing the influence of Chinese painting.

Miniatures created in the Tabriz style, which was the center of the

Ilkhanate, display the new style more prominently. Examples include Jami at-tavari (University of Edinburgh, Rare Books Collections: Or.Ms.20), Sahahname (Topkapı Sarayı Müzsesi, H.1479), Kalila and Dimna (İstabul Üniversitesi Kütüphanesi, F1422), characterized by diverse backgrounds, vibrant colors, and dynamic descriptions.

A similar trend can be observed in the miniature paintings of the North African Mamluks. During the early period, spanning from the mid-13th century to the 14th century, miniatures primarily served as narrative illustrations. Frames were minimal, and compositions were flat. The figures were portrayed in a simple and schematic manner, with clothing maintaining a two-dimensional pattern. Notable changes emerged in manuscripts from the mid-14th century onwards. Gold leaf decorations became prevalent, and influences from Chinese painting, such as lotus and peony motifs, tree depictions, and dragons, started to appear. Additionally, the characters began to resemble Asians, which can be attributed to the influence of the Ilkhanate.

In the first half of the 15th century, the Mamluk style gradually came under Turkmen influence. The depiction of landscapes and costumes, including lush lands adorned with invisible grass and flowers, began to reflect the influence of Iranian Turkmen art. By the late 15th century, the early Mamluk style had largely vanished, making way for a new painting style. However, following the Ottoman conquest of the Mamluks, numerous painters and manuscripts were transported to Istanbul.

There are limited surviving miniatures manuscripts from the Islamic period in Spain, making it challenging to establish a comprehensive overview. During the reign of al-Hakam II (961-976) of the Umayyads, a significant number of manuscripts were produced. However, under the rule of Hisham II (976-1013), manuscripts were intentionally destroyed to appease orthodox beliefs. Despite the scarcity of surviving manuscripts, we can gain insights into the Spanish style through the examination of extant Jewish and Christian texts.

For instance, the Biblia Hispalense (988; Madrid, Bib. N., Cod. Vit. 13-1) or the First Kennicott Bible (1476; Oxford, Bodleian Lib., Ken. MS. One) and a Hispano-Moresque Haggadah from Castile (1300; London, BL, Or. MS. 2737) offer glimpses into the form of Spanish miniatures. These miniatures often feature decorative palmettes, abstract designs, and turbaned prophets. These stylistic elements reflect the natural process of cultural exchange among diverse communities coexisting in the same region.

Following the decline of the Ilkhanate, Persian miniature painting during the Timurid era flourished in cities like Herat and Shiraz. The Shiraz style of miniature painting sought to revive the original Persian aesthetic, distancing itself from Chinese influences. Meanwhile, Herat emerged as a prominent center for miniature art under the patronage of Baysunghur (1397-1433) and Sultan Husayn Bayqara (1438-1506). The miniatures showcased stylized figures with long hair and pointed beards, characterized by their tall and slender stature. These figures were brought to life through dynamic poses and intricate detailing. One of the notable artists from Herat was Kamāl ud-Dīn Behzād (1455?-1536?), known for his realistic depictions. Behzād's paintings featured dynamic characters and geometrically rendered architectural elements, enhancing the narrative quality of the artwork. One of his renowned works is "Yusuf and Zulaikha" [Cairo, National Library, MS. Arab Farsi 908] (fig1). Behzād's innovative style not only influenced future painters during the Safavid era but also had an impact on the development of miniature painting in the Mughal Empire of India.

After the decline of Timur's empire, Tabriz, Shiraz, and Herat became influential centers for miniature painting, serving as the foundation for the miniatures of the Aq Qoyunlu dynasty. Turkmen miniatures associated with the Qara Qoyunlu and Aq Qoyunlu dynasties thrived in Eastern Anatolia, Azerbaijan, Iran, and Iraq during the 14th and 15th centuries. The distinctive Turkmen style, particularly seen in Qara Qoyunlu miniatures, featured figures with large heads and robust builds. The natural elements depicted were often simple plants, rocky horizons, and vibrant colors. These artistic developments were prominent in the regions around Shiraz and Baghdad. Various editions of Nizami's "Khamsa" [Berlin Staatsbibliothek, nr. Diez, A. Fol. 7; London Royal Asiatic Society, Morley, nr. 246; Chester Beatty Library, nr. 137] serve as examples of this style. Meanwhile, Aq Qoyunlu miniatures thrived around Tabriz. The Tabriz Aq Qoyunlu style had an influence on notable works like the Safavid "Shahname" [New York The Metropolitan Museum of Art, nr. 1970. 301.36].

In India, one can observe the presence of stylized wrinkle patterns reminiscent of Mamluk miniatures, as well as the depiction of plants and the sky. This influence is highly likely due to trade interactions between India, particularly the Gujarat port and the west coast, and the Mamluk Empire. Furthermore, the presence of imported manuscripts and immigrated illustrators from Timurid territories, coupled with Timur's growing interest in India, which eventually led to his invasion, contributed to the infusion of Persian influences into Indian miniatures. Consequently, unique Persian style emerged and combined with indigenous Indian artistic traditions.

During the Indo-Islamic period of miniature painting, Humayun (1508-1556) returned from the Safavid Empire to the Mughals, bringing along artists from Tabriz. These Tabrizi artists incorporated their unique style into the miniatures, blending it with the techniques of local artists. Humayun commissioned various manuscripts, including the "Baburnama" and "Akbarnama," which were written for Babur and later Mughal emperors, respectively. These manuscripts served as platforms for intricate miniature paintings alongside the textual content.

In the case of the Ottoman Empire, which can be considered the western region of the Islamic world, influences from Timur and Europe can be observed during the early and middle periods. Given the tense relationship between the Ottomans and Timur over dominance in the eastern part of the Anatolian Peninsula during the 14th and 15th centuries, it is not surprising that cultural exchanges took place. Additionally, the return of Selim I and his sons, who were captured during the Battle of Ankara, introduced Eastern influences to Ottoman painting. These influences may have come from early 16th-century Iranian paintings that were acquired as trophies or gifts, such as Amir Khusraw Dihlavi's Khamsa ("Five poems"; 1493; Istanbul, Topkapı Pal. Lib., H. 799). The late 14th-century Dilsûznâme [Bodleian Library, Quseley, nr. 133] or Ahmedî's İskendernâme [Biblioteca Nazionale Marciana Cod. Or., nr. XC] demonstrates the influence of Shiraz in Edirne.

Ottoman miniature painting was not only influenced by Iran but also by Europe. The portrait of Mehmed II (1432-1481) by Gentile Bellini, who was invited from Italy after Sultan Mehmed II's conquest of Istanbul, as well as the bronze medallion made by Costanzo da Ferrara, had an impact. Ottoman painters Sinan Bey and Şiblîzâde Ahmed, who painted portraits of Mehmed II during the same period, were also influenced by these European works (Fig.2). The Ottoman tradition of portraiture, characterized by a realistic depiction with remnants of the 15th-century Renaissance, continued into the following centuries. Furthermore, it's important to note that the European painters in the Ottoman Empire were not limited to portraying only the Sultan. It is assumed that painters who worked in Istanbul, such as Gentile Bellini and

Fig 10–1. Yusuf and Zulaikha (Yusuf pursued by Potiphar's wife), miniature by Behzād, 1488

Costanzo Ferrara, interacted with or mentored local artists. This interaction with European artists had a partial influence from the Renaissance on the paintings of the Ottoman Empire. Nevertheless, Ottoman painters were still hesitant to fully embrace realistic depictions, such as the use of perspective, unlike their European counterparts. The flatness of the painting style retained Islamic influences.

The presence of Western influences does not mean that the Ottoman Empire completely detached itself from the East. The fusion of Eastern and Western elements gave rise to a unique style of Ottoman miniature painting. During the reign of Bayezid II (1447-1512), the Ottoman style developed by incorporating Western influences along with the 15th century Turkmen miniature painting style that focused on literary subjects. Works like Kalila and Dimna [Bursa İnebey Kütüphanesi, Hüseyin Çelebi, nr. 763; Bombay Prince Wales Museum, nr. 51.34] or Hüsrev ü Şîrîn [Uppsala University Library, Vet., nr. 86; New York The Metropolitan Museum, nr. 69.27] serve as typical examples.

The numerous wars and cultural developments during the reigns of Selim I (1470-1520) and Suleiman I (1494-1566) led to further advancements in Ottoman miniature painting. The painters brought to Istanbul by Selim I from Iran and Egypt amalgamated various artistic traditions, creating a painting style that reflected the Ottoman character while showcasing decorative techniques reminiscent of the Herat region. Works such as Mantiq-ut-Tayr [Topkapı Sarayı Müzesi Kütüphanesi, Emanet Hazinesi, nr. 1512], Divan-i Neva'i [Topkapı Sarayı Müzesi Kütüphanesi, Revan Köşkü, nr. 804, 806], Hamsetül-Mütehayyirin [Topkapı Sarayı Müzesi Kütüphanesi, Hazine, nr. 802], and

Selimnâme [Topkapı Sarayı Müzesi Kütphanesi, Hazine, nr. 1597-98]

In addition to the portrait tradition mentioned earlier, the Ottoman Empire also produced topographic paintings without figures. A notable artist in this genre is Matrakçı Nasuh. Nakkaş Osman, a representative artist of the classical style born in the late 16th century, broke away from the decorative approach of Suleiman I and embraced simpler backgrounds. Furthermore, miniatures depicting Ottoman history and the Turkic version of Shahnama were created, and genealogical records of the Ottoman dynasty (silsilanama) were illustrated. In other words, these artworks showcased the empire's history, landscapes, and daily life, as well as providing visual support to literary genres. From the late 17th century to the 18th century, during the Westernization movement, Ottoman miniature paintings once again experienced European influences. The style of miniature painting was influenced not only by the subject matter but also by the adoption of new perspectives. For foreign visitors to Istanbul, depictions of individuals dressed in traditional Ottoman costumes (reflecting ethnic characteristics) were created. By the 18th century, works such as Surnâme-i Vehbi [Topkapı Sarayı Müzesi III. Ahmet Kütüphanesi, Hazine 3593] showcased the early use of perspective through the layering of architecture and figures.

However, the introduction of new painting styles from other regions did not always lead to development alone. After the 18th century, the acceptance of oil painting on canvas marked the decline of traditional Ottoman miniature painting.

Fig 10–2. Left– Sultan Mehmed II, 1480; oil on canvas; National Gallery, London by Gentile Bellini. Right– Sultan Mehmed II, end of 15th century, Sinan Bey, from Sarai Albums

Miniature painting in the Mediterranean region, particularly within the Islamic world, has evolved uniquely over time and across various cultures. It combines painting traditions from the Far East, Central Asia, and Europe with the local painting traditions of the region. This highlights the importance of not hastily categorizing it solely under the label of 'Islamic miniatures.' Such a perception can lead to misconceptions, assuming that the figures, including human beings, are flat and solely depict Islamic themes. However, in reality, miniature painting has undergone its own development, incorporating elements from other religions and cultures to suit its distinct characteristics. It is Just as miniature paintings and artworks outside the Islamic culture have evolved by incorporating some aspects of Islamic culture.

Keywords

Miniature, Book illustration, Illuminated manuscript, Middle east, Islamic Miniature

References

Başkan, S. (2009). Başlangıcından Cumhuriyet Dönemine Kadar Türklerde Resim, Ankara: Atatürk Kültür Merkezi.

Bloom, J.,& Blair, S.(Eds).(2009). The Grove encyclopedia of Islamic art and architecture(ebook). Oxford:Oxford University Press.

Grabar, O. (2000) Mostly Miniatures: An Introduction to Persian Painting, New Jersey: Princeton.

Grabar, O.& Robinson C. (Eds). (2001) Islamic Art and Literature, New Jersey: Princeton.

Mahir. F.B. (2020), Minyatür, *TDV İslâm Ansiklopedisi*, cilt 30, Ankara: Türkiye Diyanet Vakfı, 118-123.

Thompson, E. M. & Williamson, G.C. (1911), MINIATURE, *Encyclopædia Britannica*, Volume 18, Cambridge: Cambridge University Press, 523-528.

https://archives.collections.ed.ac.uk/repositories/2/archival_objects/145535

https://islamicart.museumwnf.org/database_item.php?id=object;EPM;at;Mus24;27;en

Image References

https://upload.wikimedia.org/wikipedia/commons/thumb/6/6c/Yusef_Zuleykha. jpg/800px-Yusef_Zuleykha.jpg

https://en.wikipedia.org/wiki/Gentile_Bellini#/media/File:Gentile_Bellini_003.jpg

http://www.ee.bilkent.edu.tr/~history/Pictures1/im39.jpg

written by Sunah Choi (Dongduk Women's University)

▼

Laws and Regulations

11

Code of Hammurabi

The Code of Hammurabi

Significance of the Code of Hammurabi

The Code of Hammurabi, dating back to 1754 BC, is the law of the ancient Babylonian Empire in Mesopotamia and was once known as the oldest written law in existence. However, in 1952, the 'Code of Ur-Nammu' from around 2050 BC was discovered, and now the 'Code of Urukagina' created between 2380 and 2360 BC, is recognized as the oldest code of law.

In 1901, an archaeological team led by Gustav Jequier and Jacques de Morgan discovered a stele inscribed with the entire content of the Code of Hammurabi in the ancient city of Susa. It was then translated and published by Jean-Vincent Scheil in 1902.

The Code of Hammurabi covers a vast and varied range of issues, including theft, assault, bodily injury, fraud, medical malpractice, divorce, children's rights, obligations of building contractors, norms of weights and measures, fees and penalties for professional negligence, and property. It provides insights not only into the legal system of ancient Mesopotamia but also into the socioeconomic conditions of the time.

Along with the Codex Justinianus(533) enacted by Eastern Roman Emperor Justinian and the Napoleonic Code(1804) established by Napoleon, it is one of the 3 great legal codes of the world and can be considered a compilation of ancient laws.

Form of the Code of Hammurabi

The stele on which the Code of Hammurabi is inscribed is a monumental finger-shaped piece of diorite rock, 2.25 meters high and 2 meters wide. It is composed of 282 articles. Some parts of the stele were damaged by the Elamite king in 12th century BC, and the content of 35 articles has been erased and cannot be deciphered. The Code was recorded in cuneiform, which was invented by the Sumerians.

Structure of the Code of Hammurabi

When examining the legal provisions, the Code covers criminal law, property law, family law, commercial law, and social law. On the top 65cm, there's a bas-relief of King Hammurabi receiving the code of laws from the sun god and the guardian deity of justice, Shamash. The lower 160cm is divided into a prologue, legal provisions, and an epilogue. Both the prologue and epilogue emphasize Hammurabi's legitimacy as the conqueror and ruler of the entire world under the protection of various city deities in Mesopotamia.

On the corner of the stele, there's an image of a man carefully receiving a tablet from Shamash, the god of the sun and justice. In the preamble,

Hammurabi says, "Anu and Bel called me, Hammurabi, the exalted prince who worships the gods, to establish justice in the land, to banish the wicked and the evil, to prevent the strong from oppressing the weak. I will walk like Shamash to give light to the land, rule the black-haired people, and promote the welfare of humanity like Anu and Bel."

Legislative methods of the Code of Hammurabi

Firstly, there is the well-known Lex Talionis, often referred to as 'an eye for an eye, a tooth for a tooth.' Given the context of the time when the Hammurabi Code, which is considered the law of the jungle, was enacted, King Hammurabi's proclamation of 'only returning as much as received' is evaluated as being in line with a primitive notion of justice. There are legal provisions that stipulate the same amount of punishment or fines as the damage or injury that the offender caused to the victim. For instance, "If a man causes a pregnant woman to have a miscarriage and die, the daughter of the offender is executed." "If a doctor causes the loss of a slave's eye during a procedure, the doctor's hand is cut off."

Secondly, the Code adopted the method of setting individual regulations for individual legal issues. For instance, Article 8 of the Hammurabi Code states, "If someone steals a cow, sheep, donkey, pig, or goat… they will be punished." This is different from the way modern laws generally establish general provisions for certain legal issues. For instance, Article 329 of the South Korean Penal Code states, "Anyone who steals the property of another shall be punished by imprisonment for not more than 6 years or by a fine of not more than 10 million won."

Lastly, all legal provisions begin with 'if' and are composed of a conditional clause and a consequent clause, stating "if you do ~, then ~ will happen." This is because the notion that punishment for human actions is administered by a god dominated the ideas of ancient people.

Contents of the Code of Hammurabi

The Code of Hammurabi can be broadly divided into 3 areas. It consists of procedural laws(Articles 1~5), laws regarding property(Articles 6~126), and laws about people(Articles 127~282).

Procedural laws cover false accusations, false testimonies, and wrongful judgments.

The laws regarding property(Articles 6~126) are subdivided into property ownership(Articles 6~52), property rights and rights of the owner(Articles 53~99),

Fig 11-1. Code of Hammurabi carved on the pillar. 1760 BC.

and methods of acquiring property and forms of commerce(Articles 100~126). In the case of property ownership, it is divided into illegal possession and legal possession. The rights of property and the owner involve protection from damage caused by water, livestock, people, and various lease agreements. Methods of acquiring property and forms of commerce cover partnerships in trade, selling wine, circulation of goods, debt, storage of grain, and deposit of valuables.

Laws about people(Articles 127~282) can be split into family(Articles 127~193) and responsibilities(Articles 194~282). Law of Family is divided further into marriage(Articles 127~161), inheritance(Articles 162~184), and adoption(Articles 185~193). Marriage law includes articles about injury to a wife, marriage contracts, divorce, domestic restrictions(for instance, restrictions on taking a concubine, restrictions on debt seizures), crimes related to marriage, and breach of promises. Inheritance law includes provisions on a wife's property and inheritors as well as a husband's property and inheritors. Adoption law covers the possibility of disownment, passing on property to an adopted child, and punishments for an ungrateful adopted child. Law of Responsibility is divided into responsibility arising from illegal activities(Articles 194~227) and responsibility arising from contracts (Articles 228~282). Law of Responsibilities for illegal activities include accidental death by a nursemaid, physical injury or death, and monetary compensation and punishment for professional negligence. Law of Responsibilities arising from contracts are divided majorly into employment of workers and purchasing of slaves.

Civilizational Exchange of the Code of Hammurabi

The Code of Hammurabi had a significant influence on the development of legal systems in the Near East. For instance, its traces can be found in the

Assyrian laws and the Laws of Moses. It also laid the foundations for Roman law and Islamic law. This legal tradition permeated worldwide, influencing and interacting with each other, and significantly affecting neighboring civilizations.

Fig 11–2. Upper part of the code of Hammurabi.

Keywords

the Code of Hammurabi ; King Hammurabi ; Babylonian Empire in Mesopotamia ; Lex Talionis ; legal systems in the Near East.

References

노세영 · 박종수, 『고대 근동의 역사와 종교』, 대한기독교서회, 2010

서울대학교 역사연구소, 역사용어사전, 서울대학교 출판문화원, 2015

Amelie Kuhurt, The Ancient Near East, Routledge, 1995

Bryant, T., The Life & Times of Hammurabi, Mitchell Lane Publishers. 2005.

Driver, G. R, and J. C. Miles, The Babylonian Laws, 2 vols. (Oxford, 1952). Meek, Th. J.(trans.), "The Code of Hammurabi", in J. Pritchard(ed.), Ancient Near Eastern Texts (Princeton University Press, 1955)

Image References

https://collections.louvre.fr/ark:/53355/cl010174436

written by Ihn Hyun Jung (KOREA MARITIME & OCEAN UNIVERSITY)

12

Islamic Law

An Overview of Principles and Applications

I. Introduction

Islamic law, also referred to as Sharia Law, constitutes a comprehensive legal framework that originates from its primary sources, The Quran and the Sunnah, coupled with jurisprudential principles, rules, and methods. Islamic jurisprudence and Islamic law have been foundational disciplines within the realm of Islamic knowledge, continuously explored and imparted from the very inception of Islam up to the present day.[1] In this exploration, we delve into Islamic law, tracing its historical evolution, clarifying its core system of belief, and delving into its sources and methodology. It encompasses major domains of Islamic law, such as personal, criminal, commercial, and constitutional law. Furthermore, it examines the ongoing contemporary discourse surrounding the interpretation and enactment of Islamic law in a variety of contexts.

The influence of Islamic laws extends far and wide, profoundly impacting

---

1 The Holy Quran 9: 122: "It is not for the believers to go forth totally; but why should not a party of every section of them go forth, to become learned in religion, and to warn their people when they return to them, that haply they may beware?" (Arberry (Translated by) n.d., 206)

various aspects of Muslim life and significantly contributing to the development and advancement of Islamic civilization. This legal system, in turn, has been shaped by historical, religious, and cultural influences, propagating its reach globally, with a promising prospect of enduring influence in the future. According to select Quranic verses, the ultimate objective of divine teachings, directives, and mandates is nothing short of establishing justice and fostering the growth and progress of humanity.[2]

The Quran was revealed to Prophet Muhammad through divine revelation from God and is Allah's direct word. The second source encompasses the teachings of Prophet Muhammad, including his sayings, actions, and approval, collectively referred to as the Sunna.[3] Unlike modern legal codes, Islamic law has not been categorized or classified into a single legal codex during the time Prophet of Islam. The legal teachings and regulations of the Quran and Hadith have been progressively revealed over time, adapting to various circumstances and conditions. Prophet Mohammad introduced the concept of monotheism and carried forward the legacy of previous prophets within the primitive Arabian society prior to the advent of Islam. The monotheistic teachings of Islam and the leadership of the Prophet Muhammad unified the scattered tribes of the Arabian Peninsula, shaping them into a single nation and community (Alidoust 2014).

---

2 The Holy Quran: "He (Allah) manifested the path to growth and error." (2: 256), and "Certainly We sent Our apostles with manifest proofs, and We sent down with them the Book and the Balance, so that mankind may maintain justice" (57: 25).

3 From the Shia point of view, the words, deeds and approval of the infallible imams are also considered Sunnah.

Before the advent of Islam, the Arabian Peninsula was inhabited by Bedouin tribes, characterized by a nomadic lifestyle. These tribes had their own customary rules and practices that governed various aspects of life, including family, property, and conflict resolution. However, there was no uniform set of laws, and the diverse tribal customs coexisted. The emergence of Islam brought about significant changes to this fragmented legal landscape.

II. Historical Development of Islamic Law:

The evolution of Islamic Law, or Sharia, spans various historical periods and is rooted in the social, cultural, and religious context of the Muslim world. From the early period of Islam to the establishment of major schools of jurisprudence and Sharia law, the development of Islamic Law can be traced through several distinct phases:

1. The Divine Disclosures Era

The final 23 years of Muhammad bin Abdullah's life mark the period of divine revelation, the revelation of the Qur'an, and the establishment of his Tradition (Sunnah). In 610 CE, the Prophet Muhammad experienced his initial divine revelation. This significant moment, often referred to as Muhammad's first revelation, occurred while he was in meditation inside a cave on Mount Hira, near Mecca. It was during this period that he received a visitation from the Angel Jibril (Gabriel), who began revealing the verses that would eventually form the Qur'an. This divine communication unfolded over a span of time, lasting from 609 to 632 CE.

Revelation is a celestial form of communication and divine inspiration that transcends human sensory perception, reasoning, and intellect. It constitutes a unique mode of understanding and insight, granted exclusively to God's selected emissaries, the prophets, and messengers. This divine bestowal enables them to receive hidden instructions in the form of divine verses and convey them to humanity[4] (Tabatabai 1978, 30-32)

While the Qur'an unquestionably serves as the word of God and remains the most authoritative source of Islamic jurisprudence and law, its role primarily entails providing fundamental principles and ethical guidelines, both for individual conduct and societal norms. It elaborates upon the specifics of various aspects of Islamic knowledge and entrusts its interpretation to the Prophet. The Qur'an presents the Prophet as an exemplary figure for Muslims, implying that his words, behaviors, and actions can serve as a correct and acceptable standard for all.[5] Furthermore, in numerous verses, the Holy Qur'an emphasizes obedience to Allah and the Prophet, underscoring that the Prophet's words and actions essentially represent divine commands.[6]

---

4 The Holy Quran 53: 2-11: "Your companion has neither gone astray, nor amiss. Nor does he speak out of [his own] desire: it is just a revelation that is revealed [to him], taught him by one of great powers, ⋯ whereat He revealed to His servant whatever He revealed. The heart did not deny what it saw." (Qarai (Translated) n.d., 526), in another verse, 10: 1-2 stated: "These are the verses of the Book of wisdom. Why should it seem strange to mankind that We sent revelations to a mortal among them, who would warn others and give to the believers the glad news of their high rank in the sight of God." (Sarwar (Translated by) n.d., 208)

5 The Holy Quran 33: 21 "The Messenger of God is certainly a good example for those of you who have hope in God and in the Day of Judgment and who remember God very often." (Sarwar (Translated by) n.d., 420)

6 The Holy Quran 33: 132 "Obey God and the Messenger so that you may receive mercy." (Sarwar (Translated by) n.d., 66)

Therefore, the Sunnah of the Prophet (his words, behaviors, and actions) is the second source of Islamic teachings and laws and Sharia. The prophet's tradition complements the Quran and provides practical guidance on various issues.

Research indicates that during the era of the Prophet of Islam, literacy rates in the Arabian Peninsula were relatively low. In response to this, the Prophet of Islam placed significant emphasis on memorizing the Quran and Hadith. He encouraged his companions and the wider community to commit these teachings to memory.[7] This approach represented one of the key methods employed by the Prophet to ensure the permanency of the Quran and Sunnah. It can be deduced from this information that the Prophet of Islam, taking into account the prevailing societal conditions of his time, provided pragmatic solutions for the preservation and transmission of the Quran and the Sunnah.

In the early days of Islam, during the time of the Prophet, he employed various methods to impart the teachings of the faith to the people, both directly and indirectly. Prophet Mohammad actively encouraged newly converted tribes and individuals to dispatch representatives to Medina to learn about Islamic principles. The idea behind this initiative was to equip these individuals with a comprehensive understanding of Islam, allowing them to subsequently return to their communities and disseminate the teachings and rules of the religion.[8] Furthermore, he also dispatched some of his companions,

---

7 Sunan Ibn Majah, Chapter: The virtue of one who learns the Qur'an, H. 216; It is narrated that Ali bin Abu Talib reported the Messenger of Allah as saying: "Whoever reads the Qur'an and memorizes it, Allah will admit him to Paradise and allow him to intercede for ten of his family members who all deserved to enter Hell." (Ibn Majah al-Qazwini 2007)

8 The Holy Quran 9: 122 "Not all believers have to become specialists in religious learning. Why do

who possessed a solid understanding of the Quranic teachings and his tradition, to various regions. Their primary mission entailed the dissemination of Islamic beliefs and religious practical orders, as well as the resolution of daily disputes by drawing upon the guidance of the Quran and Sunnah.

In their efforts to address the religious needs of the people and mediate disputes, these companions relied on their knowledge of the Quran and the Prophet's tradition. However, when faced with situations for which they could not find explicit answers in the Quran and Sunnah, they resorted to the practice of interpretation and reasoning to offer solutions, both for their own benefit and that of the community. This method of problem-solving persisted beyond the lifetime of the Prophet (peace be upon him) and during the era of his Companions (Sahaba). People sought guidance on religious matters and rulings from the notable Companions such as Omar (the second Caliph), Aisha (the Prophet's wife), Ibn Abbas, and, notably, Imam Ali (the Prophet's son-in-law). They turned to these respected figures for clarity and wisdom in understanding their religious questions and concerns. It is consistently narrated by Aisha that she used to say, "Indeed, Ali is the most knowledgeable among the people about the Sunnah; he has the most profound understanding of the traditions of the Messenger of God." (Al-Nimri, 1989, 206). Meanwhile, disputes in the interpretation of the Quran and the Sunnah gradually emerged among the Companions, either through personal opinion or adherence to apparent texts.

---

not some people from each group of believers seek to become specialists in religious learning and, after completing their studies, guide their group so that they will have fear of God." (Sarwar (Translated by) n.d., 206)

These divergences continued during the second and third generations of Muslims.

In the initial century of Islamic history, a wide range of individuals, including Qur'an and hadith reciters and memorizers, interpreters, and judges, actively engaged with the evolving religious needs of the burgeoning Islamic society. This collaboration gradually laid the groundwork for the emergence of Islamic scholars and jurists, who went on to establish the various schools of Islamic jurisprudence.

By the end of the first century and the beginning of the second century, a generation of jurists emerged, embarking on the formulation of jurisprudence and the expansion of its branches. These jurists, commonly referred to as "Fuqaha", embarked on the systematic interpretation and extrapolation of legal principles derived from the primary sources of Islamic law. Various jurisprudential schools flourished, with each city boasting its own eminent jurist whose opinions held sway over those of other jurists in that region. Furthermore, scholars adopted distinctive methodologies for deriving legal rulings. It has been said that during that era, the number of jurisprudential schools had reached well over 100 (Makarem Shirazi 2006, 137). This pivotal intellectual endeavor was instrumental in shaping and solidifying the bedrock of Islamic jurisprudence schools, that continue to guide and govern various aspects of the Islamic legal system in various parts of the Muslim world.

These early Islamic jurists, while contributing significantly to the development of Islamic jurisprudence, engaged in a meticulous process of deducing legal rulings from the foundational sources of Islamic law. Their collective efforts provided a comprehensive framework for understanding and implementing the tenets of Islam, thus fostering an enduring legacy that remains a crucial element of Islamic legal tradition. Over time, these jurists' rigorous intellectual pursuits and scholarly insights ensured the continuity and adaptability of the schools of Islamic jurisprudence to meet the evolving religious and societal needs of the Muslim community.

Muslims share numerous commonalities, ranging from their core beliefs and values to their understanding of jurisprudence and rights. Central to their faith are the fundamental principles of Monotheism, Prophet-hood, and Resurrection, which serve as unifying pillars of their religious convictions. Moreover, Muslims universally recognize the Qur'an and Sunnah as the primary founts of their religious teachings, forging a bond through these sacred sources. Nonetheless, despite these strong bonds, variations exist among Muslims, primarily revolving around issues related to jurisprudence and law. These discrepancies are chiefly rooted in variations in foundational principles and interpretative methodologies.

Within the diverse of the Muslim community, primary groupings emerge: Sunni and Shia. The Sunni branch encompasses several major schools of thought and jurisprudence, including the Hanafi, Maliki, Shafi'i, and Hanbali sects, each with its distinct beliefs and jurisprudential interpretations. On the other hand, the Shia[9] branch of Islam also comprises various sects like the

---

9 According to Shia, the main founder of the Shia school of Islam is Allah and His messenger, Mohammad the Prophet of Islam. When the Prophet of Islam was sent, he secretly invited people to Islam for 3 years, until the verse of the Quran was revealed to the Prophet: "O Prophet, warn your close relatives and spread your wings for the believers who have followed you, and if they disobey

Zaidi, Ismaili, and Alavi, which diverge in terms of their theological perspectives and jurisprudential approaches. Thus, while Muslims share a foundational unity, the rich tapestry of Islamic tradition is woven with a variety of threads, reflecting the vibrant diversity within this global faith community.

2. Schools of Islamic Jurisprudence

The most important schools of Islamic jurisprudence are:

a. Hanafi School:

The founder of this jurisprudential school was Abu Hanifa (Nu'man ibn Thabit, 699-767). He was born in Kufa (Today's Iraq), where he spent his formative years

---

you, say, "I hate what you are doing." So according to God's order, the Prophet invited his relatives to monotheism, to Islam and added whoever helps and supports me in spreading the message of Islam will be my brother, guardian, and caliph among you." Though the Prophet repeated this sentence 3 times, none was ready to support except Ali ibn Abi Talib. Ali who had never worshiped idols and never lived in disbelief, stood up and said: "O! the Prophet of God, I support you.

Then the Prophet put his hand on the shoulder of Ali ibn Abi Talib and said: "This is my brother, my guardian, and my successor, so listen to him and obey him."

Therefore, according to Shia, at the first stage, when Mohammad, the messenger of Allah, publicly declared his mission he appointed his caliph in the same meeting! Many Sunni historians and commentators consider this hadith to be reliable (sahih al-sand), it is the beginning of Ali's succession (Caliphate) of the prophet. It was the beginning of the Shia school. Some sources of the aforementioned hadith are: 1. Tarikh al-Tabari, vol. 2, pp. 319 to 321, published by Al-Maarif Egypt; 2. Al-Kamil fi al-Tarikh, Ibn Athir, vol. 2, p. 62 and p. 63; 3. Al-Sirah al-Halabiyyah, Halabi Vol. 1, p. 311, Egyptian. The Musnad of Ahmad ibn Hanbal.

From the first public invitation meeting with his relatives to publicize the invitation to Islam (Yum al-Andhar) until the last year of his life and his last Hajj (Hajj al-Widaa), the Prophet repeatedly introduced Ali Ibn Abi Talib to the people as his successor, the Imam and the leader of Muslims. During the last Hajj in his lifetime, when the pilgrims were returning from Hajj, in a large gathering in the Ghadir Khom region, the prophet once again introduced Ali Ibn Abi Talib as his successor. Shia has provided many reasons for this claim. Many documentations of the Shia narrative and rational reasons are also mentioned in the sources of the Sunnis, which include: Tarikh Ibn Asaker, vol. 1, p. 85; Mostadrak Hakim, vol. 3, p. 35; Imam Ahmed, Kitab al-Fath al-Rabani, vol. 23, p. 122; Kanz al-Ummal, vol. 5, p. 15.

and received his education. Hammad, Ibrahim Nakha'i, Zaid ibn Ali, Imam Mohammad Baqir, and Imam Jafar Sadiq were his teachers, and among his illustrious disciples were Ya'qub ibn Ibrahim al-Kufi, who held the position of Chief Judge during the rule of Harun al-Rashid and Muhammad ibn Hasan Shaybani. Abu Hanifa's approach to issuing legal opinions tended to emphasize the Quran and personal opinions (Ra'y) and analogical reasoning (Qiyas) over the tradition (Sunnah), a stance that frequently brought criticism from traditionalists (Ahl al-Hadith) (Makarem Shirazi 2006, 139).

b. Maliki School:

Imam Malik ibn Anas is one of the 4 Sunni jurists, and the Maliki school of jurisprudence is attributed to him. He was born in the year 711–795 CE (93–179 AH) in "Dhu al-Marwah" located approximately 32 miles north of Medina (Today's S. Arabia). His jurisprudential approach is characterized by a strong reliance on the traditions of the Prophet Muhammad and a cautious approach to avoid excessive reliance on personal opinions (Ra'y) and analogical reasoning (Qiyas).

He benefited from many teachers and also had about 300 direct students and many who studied under his direct students. Due to his long life, Malik had a significant influence on large parts of the Islamic world. His students spread his teachings in Hijaz, Yemen, Iraq, Syria, Egypt, and Africa (Shanechi 2010), (Editors n.d.).

c. Shafi'i School:

Imam Shafi'i was one of the founders of the Shafi'i School of Jurisprudence. He studied Arabic language, interpretation, jurisprudence, and hadith under various scholars in Mecca, Medina, Iraq, Yemen, and Egypt. Drawing upon his scholarly knowledge and practical experiences, he established his jurisprudential school based on established principles, adopting a unique and distinct approach from the schools of Ahl al-Hadith (people of tradition) and Ahl al-Ra'y (people of opinion).

Prominent teachers of Imam Shafi'i include Malik ibn Anas, Muslim ibn Khalid al-Makhzumi, Muhammad ibn al-Hasan, and Yahya ibn Hassan. Some of the most famous students of Imam Shafi'i are Yusuf ibn Yahya al-Buwayti, Ishaq ibn Rahwayh, and Ahmad ibn Hanbal.

Imam Shafi'i's jurisprudential method was characterized by the formulation of rules that he established himself. He derived secondary rulings from the Quran, Sunnah, consensus (ijma'), and the practices of the companions, and he employed analogical reasoning (qiyas) uniquely. He also provided some arguments in favor of public interest (Maslahah) and the judgment of the common intellect while rejecting the notion of 'Urf (customary practice) and Masalih Mursalah (unrestricted public interest), (Zargarinejad, Gholamhossein & Yousefi, Osman 2010), (Editors, Mohammad ibn Idris Shafi'i n.d.)

d. Hanbali School:

Imam Ahmad ibn Hanbal (781-855 CE / 164-241 AH) was a renowned scholar of Hadith in Baghdad, originally from Khorasan. He laid the foundation for the Hanbali jurisprudential school. Initially, this school did not have an independent identity separate from the general Ahl al-Hadith tradition until scholars like Abu Bakr Khallal (d. 311 AH) made efforts to establish its independence, ultimately forming the distinct Hanbali school attributed to Ahmad ibn Hanbal. Ahmad ibn Hanbal studied under various scholars, with one of the most significant being Shafi'i. He was known for his strict examination of Hadiths and their narrators. He authored the Musnad, a compilation of over 30,000 Hadiths.

Imam Hanbal's jurisprudential approach was rooted in the reliance on Hadiths, reports, and the practices of the early Muslim generations (Salaf). He based his legal rulings on the tradition of the Prophet and his judgments, as well as the Fatwas of the Companions, giving preference to their positions in cases where there was no opposing evidence. He prioritized the views of the Tabi'un (followers of the Companions) or other scholars known for their expertise in narrations and well-known traditions when formulating his own Fatwasd (Sabouri 2013).

Many people may believe that the followers of Abu Hanifa, Malik ibn Anas, Idris ibn Shafi'i, and Ahmad ibn Hanbal continue to adhere to them and make no effort to address contemporary issues such as financial matters, banking, insurance, international relations, and laws. However, this perception is incorrect. Among the Sunni scholars, jurists, and religious authorities, there are 4 categories of jurists (Mujtahids):

- A group like Abu Hanifa, Malik ibn Anas, Shafi'i, and Ahmad ibn Hanbal are considered "absolute Mujtahids" who have established their own unique foundations, principles, rules, and independent methods of deriving Islamic legal rulings from primary sources. This group does not follow anyone in their legal deductions (Isa-zadeh (translated by) and Siyuti 2013, 117-123).

- Another group, known as "affiliated Mujtahids", gives Fatwas based on the school and method of the "absolute Mujtahids". They follow the foundations, principles, rules, and methods of the absolute mujtahids in their jurisprudential reasoning but have some degree of independence in issuing fatwas and adapting subsidiary issues to the principles and results of jurisprudential studies.

- The third group, "Mujtahids within the school", possesses the ability to engage in Ijtihad in specific jurisprudential matters. They can compare specific issues with established rulings and provide fresh insights (Shah Waliullah 1994, 23-24), (Emami 2014, 123-125)

- The last group, "Mujtahids in fatwa and preference" only has the ability to issue Fatwas and make preferences among different opinions within a particular school of jurisprudence.

Sunni Muslims believe that for centuries there have been no "absolute Mujtahids" or "affiliated Mujtahids," and in the present age, even "Mujtahids within the school" do not exist. This is because, firstly, access to the primary texts that were available to the Imams is no longer possible. Secondly, meeting the requirement of a full understanding of the principles and subsidiary issues of the school is also unattainable at present. As a result, Ijtihad in the field of Islamic jurisprudence is not permissible. However, the possibility of Ijtihad in issuing Fatwas always exists. People can refer to a "Mujtahid in fatwa and preference" in matters and contemporary issues to seek Islamic legal rulings (Mohiti 2017).

However, the Wahhabi sect, as a distinct group within Sunni Islam, does not adhere to any of the established schools of Islamic jurisprudence. They claim to follow the Salaf al-Saleh (righteous predecessors) in theological and jurisprudential matters and consider the four major schools of thought and jurisprudence as innovations in religion (Bida).

e. Shia Jurisprudential School:

Shi'a Islam (Shi'ite) stands as the second-largest denomination within Islam. As mentioned, Shi'a believe that the prophet Muhammad appointed Ali ibn Abi Talib as his successor, most notably during the event at Ghadir Khumm, in the last year of his life and after performing his last Hajj ceremony. This perspective fundamentally differs from that of Sunni Islam, whose followers maintain that the prophet Muhammad did not appoint a successor before his passing. Shi'a Muslims assert that after the prophet the leadership should have passed directly to Ali bin Abu Talib, who was Muhammad's cousin and son-in-law, and then to the rightful rulers or Imams certain descendants of the prophet, known as the Ahl al-Bayt. These Imams, according to Shia Muslims, possess unique spiritual and political authority over the Muslim community. After the Sunni majority, the Shi'a Muslims (Twelver Shia) stand as the largest and most influential in the Muslim world. Other subsects encompass the Ismailis and Zaydis. (Tabatabai and Chittik 1980, 10- 45).

From the very beginning of Islam, Shia jurisprudence has existed as an integral and naturally born part of the Islamic tradition. The origin and emergence of Shia jurisprudence have been debated in historical and theological sources for a long time, and in contemporary times, it has become a major focus of study for Shia scholars. According to Shia scholars the application of the Jurisprudential principles, even at a basic level, was customary and widely recognized in the early days of Islam.[10] However, the formalization and establishment of these Jurisprudential principles (Usul al-Fiqh) as a discipline is attributed to Imam Baqir and Imam Sadiq (World Assembly of Shia Studies 2011).

Shia jurisprudence is characterized by an evidential approach to expressing legal rulings, where, in addition to issuing a verdict (fatwa), all the evidence and indications for that verdict are also provided. In this method, jurists examine and critique different opinions and clarify their verdicts by presenting the supporting reasons. Shia jurisprudential styles encompass Akhbari Jurisprudence, the Traditional Jurisprudence, and Dynamic Jurisprudence. (Al-Shia (Editors) n.d.)

Traditional scholars (Usuli) derive legal rulings per detailed evidence from the Quran, Sunnah, reason, and consensus of the early prominent jurists. They

---

10 The name "Usuli" derives from the term Usul al-fiqh, which translates to "principles of jurisprudence". In Usuli thought, the Quran, hadith, ijma' (consensus), and 'aql (intellect) are 4 valid sources of Islamic law. When the Quran, hadith, ijma' are not available to drive the rulings, 'aql (Reason) refer to one of the 4 practical principles: bara'at (immunity), ihtiyat (recommended precautions), takhyir (selection), and istishab (the presumption of continuity in the previous state). Usulis differ from their now much smaller rival, the Akhbari School. They rely and trust on narrations more than the Usulis.

utilize the science and methodology of Jurisprudence (Usul al-Fiqh) in their Ijtihad to deduct the legal rulings. Akhbari jurists are also a group of Islamic scholars who derive legal rulings based on detailed evidence from the Quran, Sunnah, reason, and consensus but comparatively emphasize more on Sunnah. Dynamic jurisprudence, as articulated in the thought of Imam Khomeini, involves Ijtihad (independent reasoning) based on the foundations of traditional jurisprudence.[11] It takes into account a broader understanding of issues, avoids narrow-mindedness, and carefully discerns public interests (Janati 2000). These diverse approaches within Shia jurisprudence reflect the rich tradition and different methodologies employed by scholars to derive legal rulings. However, since the late 18th century, the traditional school (Usuli) has been the dominant school of Twelver Shia Islam and now forms an overwhelming majority within the Twelver Shia denomination.

In contrast to the Sunni schools of jurisprudence, distinguished by the names of their esteemed founders such as Imam Abu Hanifa, Imam Malik, Imam Shafi'i, and Imam Hanbal, the Shia tradition does not bear the label of any specific jurist. This distinct characteristic is deeply rooted in the fundamental principles of Shia jurisprudence.

In Shia Islam, Mujtahids are considered independent scholars who possess the expertise and authority to derive legal rulings through the process of ijtihad, independent reasoning. The Shia approach emphasizes the autonomy of individual jurists in interpreting and deriving legal rulings from the primary

---

11 The traditional reasoning method is a method used by Mohammad Hassan Najafi in writing his famous work, Jawahir al-Kalam fi Sharḥ shara'ia al-islam.

sources of Islamic law, namely the Quran and the traditions of the Prophet Muhammad and his family (Ahl al-Bayt). This emphasis on the independence of Mujtahids in the Shia tradition underscores the dynamic nature of Shia jurisprudence, wherein legal interpretations can adapt to contemporary contexts while remaining rooted in the foundational principles of Islam.

3. Shia and Sunni Jurisprudential Differences:

a. As mentioned, both Sunni and Shia recognize the Quran and the Sunnah of the Prophet as primary sources of Islamic teachings. Shia Muslims, alongside primary sources, regard the words and actions of Ahl al-Bayt as an additional source of Islamic legal rulings.[12] The Ahl al-Bayt possessed a comprehensive knowledge of the Quran and Sunnah and demonstrated a steadfast and practical commitment to these principles.

b. Shia jurisprudence, influenced by historical and political factors, has predominantly retained a more distinct and specialized character due to its historical absence in official state affairs. In contrast, Sunni jurisprudence, having historically held a close connection and the support of the caliphs, has ventured more into public arenas. It is crucial to remember that Islamic jurisprudence and its legal rulings encompass a wide range of personal, social, and governmental matters, where private

---

12 The Holy Quran, 33:33, refers to the Ahl al-Bayt (People of the House) of the Prophet of Islam, Imam Ali, Fatima (the Prophet's daughter), their sons Hasan and Hossain. This verse shows that God has purified these people from any impurity and sin and made them a model for Muslims. This verse is known as part of the Hadith of the Cloak, in which the Prophet of Islam covered these people under a cloak and prayed for them.

and public domains are inseparable. Jurists have organized their legal texts into comprehensive chapters and topics, addressing various private and public issues, from matters of purity and impurity, prayer, fasting, pilgrimage, almsgiving, marriage and divorce, employment, commerce, rent, enjoining the good and forbidding the evil, jihad, judicial decisions, and punishments. These laws, however, lack executive authority without the establishment of an Islamic government. Consequently, Islam fundamentally is not a secular religion, and its jurisprudential reasoning (ijtihad) obligates itself to respond to a diverse array of societal issues and major concerns, actively participating in public spheres (Rahdar 2020).

c. In Sunni jurisprudence, consensus (Ijma), analogy (Qiyas), juristic preference (Istihsan), the sayings and actions of the Companions of prophet Muhammad (Saḥāba) and the generation of Muslims who followed the companions (Tabi'een), public interest (Maslaha), and blocking the means (Sadd al-dhara'i) are also recognized as sources of legal rulings. In contrast, Shia jurisprudence does not accept most of these methods as sources of Islamic jurisprudence, except for the consensus of the first generation of Shia jurists. The unique aspect of this consensus is that it is not based on any narration or reason. Therefore, it shows that the early jurists had access to a certain narration that was the basis for issuing a consensus verdict, but that narration has been lost for any reason and has not reached us. But if the consensus is based on a specific and acceptable argument, the validity of that consensus is due to the strength of the argument and its validity has nothing to do with the consensus.

Therefore, if the argument is weak and is criticized and rejected, such a consensus is not valid. The role of reason (aql) in Islamic jurisprudence is generally acknowledged by both Sunni and Shia schools as a tool for deriving legal rulings. However, they differ in the extent and conditions of the authority of reason. Shia jurisprudence considers reason as an independent and primary source of Islamic jurisprudence. They believe that reason can independently understand many aspects of morality, such as distinguishing between justice and oppression, even without the guidance of Islamic teachings. This contrasts with the Sunni perspective, which considers reason as a secondary source and relies more on textual evidence for moral judgments.

Another significant difference lies in the concept of Ijtihad (independent juristic reasoning). Followers of the Hanafi, Shafi'i, Maliki, and Hanbali schools have restricted absolute Ijtihad to their great jurists based on specific criteria since 665. Each scholar within their respective school operates within the framework of their school's principles and rules. In contrast, Shia jurists engage in Ijtihad based on the Quran, Sunnah, consensus, and reason. They view Ijtihad as a right and duty for different generations and do not impose any restrictions on it beyond the requirements of Islamic evidence. Therefore, over the centuries, Shia jurisprudence has strived to adapt and respond to the evolving religious needs of the people without imposing rigid limitations.

The period of jurisprudential debates and discussions from the late 3rd century of Islam until the Mongol invasion and the fall of the Abbasid rule in Baghdad witnessed significant differences between Sunni and Shia jurisprudential approaches in terms of sources of legal rulings, the role of reason, and the concept of Ijtihad. These differences continue to shape the distinctive features of both branches of Islamic jurisprudence.

Keywords

Islamic jurisprudence, Hanafi, Shafi'i, Maliki, Hanbali, Shia.

References

Alidoust, Abolqasem. 2014. "Jurisprudence and purposes of Sharia." *Journal of Ahl al-Bayt jurisprudence* (*14*) 118-137. http://ensani.ir/fa/article/93277/%D9%81% D9%82%D9%87-%D9%88-%D9%85%D9%82%D8%A7%D8%B5%D8%AF-%D8%B4%D8%B1%DB%8C%D8%B9%D8%AA.

Al-Nimri, Yusuf bin Abdullah. 1989. *Al-Istiab fi Marifat al-Ashab*. Cairo: Dar Ibn Al-Jawzi.

Al-Shia (Editors). n.d. *Historical periods of principles of jurisprudence*. Accessed 11 24, 2023. https://fa.al-shia.org/%D8%A7%D8%AF%D9%88%D8%A7% D8%B1-%D8%AA%D8%A7%D8%B1%DB%8C%D8%AE%DB%8C- %D8%A7%D8%B5%D9%88%D9%84-%D9%81%D9%82%D9%87/.

Arberry (Translated by). n.d. *The Holy Quran*. Accessed 10 25, 2023. https://tanzil.net/.

Editors. n.d. *Hadith*. Accessed 11 2, 2023. https://hadith.net/post/68043/%D9%8 5%D8%A7%D9%84%DA%A9-%D8%A8%D9%86-%D8%A7-%D9%86- %D8%B3/.

-. n.d. *Mohammad ibn Idris Shafi'i*. Accessed 11 3, 2023. https://fa.wikishia.net/view/ %D9%85%D8%AD%D9%85%D8%AF_%D8%A8%D9%86_%D8%A7%D8%A F%D8%B1%DB%8C%D8%B3_%D8%B4%D8%A7%D9%81%D8%B9%DB% 8C.

Emami, Abd al-Salam, Saberi, Hossein, Ghabouli, Seyyed Mohammad Taghi. 2014.

"The Closing the Door of Ijtihad in Sunni Jurisprudence." *The Journal of Civil Jurisprudence* Razavi University of Islamic Sciences.

Ibn Majah al-Qazwini, Mohammad. 2007. *Sunan Ibn Majah*. Saudi Arabia: Darussalam Publishers & Distributors.

Isa-zadeh (translated by), Abdolbasit, and Abd al-Rahman ibn Abu Bakr Siyuti. 2013. *The necessity of ijtihad in all eras from the Sunnis point of view*. Tehran: Ehsan Publishing House.

Janati, Mohammad Ibrahim. 2000. "Jurisprudence: general methods of inference in jurisprudence." *Andisheh Hawza* 65-79. Accessed 10 15, 2023. http://ensani.ir/fa/article/96041/%D9%81%D9%82%D9%87-%D8%B4%DB%8C%D9%88%D9%87-%D9%87%D8%A7%DB%8C-%DA%A9%D9%84%DB%8C-%D8%A7%D8%B3%D8%AA%D9%86%D8%A8%D8%A7%D8%B7-%D8%AF%D8%B1-%D9%81%D9%82%D9%87.

Makarem Shirazi, Nasser. 2006. *Encyclopedia of Contemporary Jurisprudence*. Qom: Madresa Amir al-Mumenin .

Mohiti, Mojtaba. 2017. *Ijtihad from the point of view of Sunnis*. 2 1. Accessed 11 3, 2023. https://www.adyannet.com/fa/news/22040.

Qarai (Translated). n.d. *Tanzil*. Accessed 10 31, 2023. https://tanzil.net.

Rahdar, Ahmad. 2020. "The Nature, Rationale, and Mechanism of Islamic State Jurisprudence." *Journal of Jurisprudence and Islamic State, Baqer Al-Ulum University* 5-18.

Sabouri, Mojtabi. 2013. "Creed of Ahmad Bin Hanbal." *Journal of Baqir Al-Uloom Research Institute* 56. Accessed 10 29, 2023. http://pajoohe.ir/%D8%A7%D8%B9%D8%AA%D9%82%D8%A7%D8%AF%D9%86%D8%A7%D9%85%D9%87-%D8%A7%D8%AD%D9%85%D8%AF-%D8%A8%D9%86-%D8%AD%D9%86%D8%A8%D9%84_a-45424.aspx.

Sarwar (Translated by). n.d. *Tanzil*. Accessed 10 31, 2023. https://tanzil.net.

Shah Waliullah, Halabi, Muhammad Ali (edited by). 1994. *Ahkam al-Ijtihad wal-Taqlid*. Sharjah: Dar Al-Fath.

Shanechi, Kazem. 2010. *History of Jurisprudence of Islamic Religions*. Qom: Bostan

Kitab Institute.

Tabatabai, Mohammad Hussain. 1978. *Al-Mizan fi Tafsir al-Qur'an*. Qom: Ismailian.

Tabatabai, Sayyid Muhammad Husayn, and William (Translated by) Chittik. 1980. *Shi'ite Anthology*. London: Muhammadi Trust of Great Britain.

World Assembly of Shia Studies. 2011. *History of Shi'ism*. Accessed 10 22, 2023. https://shiastudies.com/fa/%D8%AA%D8%A7%D8%B1%DB%8C %D8%AE-%D9%BE%DB%8C%D8%AF%D8%A7%DB%8C%D8%B4- %D8%AA%D8%B4%DB%8C%D8%B9/.

Zargarinejad, Gholamhossein & Yousefi,Osman. 2010. "The Development of the Scientific and Religious Jurisprudential Personality of Imam Shafi'i." *Journal of Cultural History Studie* 34.

written by Mohammad Hassan Mozafari (Institute for Mediterranean Studies)

13

Halal and Kosher

The Islamic dietary law called "Halal" has many similar features to the Jewish dietary law called "Kosher." This is understandable referring to the common roots of both Islam and Judaism as Abrahamic religions. The word 'halal' is an Arabic word that means allowed or permitted. Thus, halal food is the permitted food for Muslims according to Islamic law and based on the Islamic holy book of the Quran. Similarly, the word 'kosher' is a Hebrew word that means proper or fit, and accordingly, kosher food is also related to Jewish dietary law, deciding what is permitted to be eaten by Jews based on their holy book of Torah.

When comparing the dietary restrictions of halal and Kosher, it can be noted that kosher regulations are more extensive and complex. While all Halal restrictions except for the prohibition of alcohol are covered by kosher restrictions, Kosher has additional and more complex requirements. This means that Muslims can consume any kosher food that does not contain alcohol, while Jews may not be able to consume certain halal foods due to the additional restrictions of kosher regulations. Moreover, Jewish dietary laws require that the food is prepared or the animal is slaughtered by someone who follows Judaism, while in Islam, Jews are considered "People of the Book" referring to their status as followers of a divine scripture, and thus their food and slaughtered animals are permissible for Muslims to consume.

Kosher Rules:

Kosher regulations mainly focus on restrictions related to meat, but they also have certain restrictions related to the consumption of plants prohibiting planting various plant species together. Other restrictions include those regarding grape juice or wines as it must be prepared under strict Orthodox Rabbinic supervision. There are also some restrictions concerning dairy products as it is forbidden to cook meat and milk together in any form, or to eat such cooked products, or to derive benefit from them.[1] Therefore, the Jewish Rabbis prohibit even eating meat and dairy products at the same meal or using the same utensils for cooking or preparing them. Furthermore, there is a period of time, determined by various traditions, during which dairy products cannot be consumed after eating meat, with a recommended waiting period of six hours. Thus, one can eat meat after consuming dairy products, except in the case of hard cheese aged 6 months or more, which requires the same waiting period as dairy after meat. Before consuming meat after dairy, it is necessary to eat solid food, drink a liquid, or rinse one's mouth thoroughly,

---

1 This is based on the Torah verses: Exodus 23:19; Exodus 34:26; Deuteronomy 14:21 stating: "Do not cook a young goat in its mother's milk."

and also ensure that hands are clean.

According to the Jewish rules of Kosher, while meat and dairy products have restrictions to be consumed together, there are certain neutral foods that can be consumed without any restrictions and can be eaten with either meat or dairy products. Those neutral foods are called "pareve" by Jews. The pareve concept includes fruits and vegetables as they can be consumed with either meat or dairy unless they have been processed or cooked in a way that changes that status. Cakes and similar foods are also classified as pareve, provided they are prepared with vegetable oil and "neutral" liquids instead of butter and milk. Fish, eggs, and plant-based foods are considered pareve as well.

As for Grains and bread, they are basically considered kosher if they are not processed by methods that may deem them to be non-kosher. For example, processing grain products using non-kosher ingredients or processing them in the same equipment that processes non-kosher products. Thus, the bread may be considered non-kosher if it was cooked with an animal-based shortening. Furthermore, the product would also be non-kosher if animal-based fats were used for greasing the baking pans or if any equipment of the cooking process was used for making other dishes that used meat or dairy.

The same thing is applied to Nuts, seeds, fruits, and vegetables as they are also kosher in their unprocessed form, but processing can change their status to turn non-kosher, similar to grains and bread. Additionally, as insects are prohibited according to the rules of kosher, the presence of insects or larvae in fruits and vegetables turns their status to non-kosher.

Generally, we can say that any food may become non-kosher if it is prepared using equipment contaminated by either dairy or meat products, or if it is processed by equipment that has been used for both dairy and meat products. The same rule is applied on any plant- based food as well, such as vegetable oil.

As for the kosher regulation regarding meats, the Torah specifies which mammals are considered kosher for consumption, and these are only the ones that chew their cud and have cloven hooves, including cows, sheep, goats, deer, and bison. Special preparation is required for kosher meat, including a specific method of slaughtering called 'shechita', which can only be performed by a trained kosher slaughterer. Following slaughter, the internal organs of the animal must be inspected by a trained inspector to ensure that there are no physiological abnormalities, particularly in the lungs. Moreover, certain sections of the animal are deemed kosher, while others are not. The kosher applies solely to the front portion of the cow, as most of an animal's prohibited

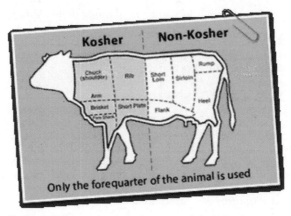

Fig 13–1. Kosher and non–kosher parts of the animal

fats, known as chailev (cheley), are located in the rear portion of the animal, behind the diaphragm. In order to prevent the consumption of chailev (cheley), it is a common practice to divide the animal between the 12th and 13th ribs and sell the entire hindquarters as non-kosher. The specific parts of the cow where kosher meat is derived include the shoulder, rib, leg, area beneath the rib, and hind leg.

When it comes to poultry, there are no specific guidelines provided in the Torah to differentiate between permitted and forbidden birds. Instead, the Torah lists 24 species of birds that are not allowed, while all other birds are considered kosher. Kashrut organizations in the United States, adhering to mainstream practices, exclusively recognize chicken, turkey, duck, and goose as acceptable kosher poultry options. Similar to meat, kosher poultry must undergo the "shechita" slaughter and must be "koshered" or prepared for consumption by removing the blood through either salting or broiling.

In certain Jewish communities or for some individuals, only meat from animals with completely smooth lungs is considered to be kosher, which is referred to as 'glatt kosher'. In the case of certain kosher animal species, numerous blood vessels, fat lobes, and nerves are prohibited and need to be eliminated using a specific cutting procedure known as 'nikkur'. After the animal has been correctly slaughtered and inspected, the meat must be "koshered", removing the blood. There are two accepted methods to extract blood from meat, which are salting and broiling. To salt meat, it must first be soaked in cool water for 30 minutes in a utensil reserved solely for that purpose. After removing excess water, the meat is salted with coarse salt so that the entire surface is covered. Before the koshering process, it is necessary to salt all sides of the meat or poultry and remove any loose internal sections of poultry. In the event that the meat or poultry is sliced while being salted, the newly exposed surfaces must be soaked and salted once more. The salted meat is then left for an hour on an inclined or perforated surface to allow the blood to flow down freely. The poultry's cavity should be positioned in an open and downward direction. After salting, the meat must be soaked and then washed thoroughly to remove all the salt applied.

As per the previously stated kosher regulations, a variety of meat and meat products are deemed non-kosher, including those sourced from pigs, rabbits, squirrels, camels, kangaroos, and horses, as well as predator or scavenger birds like eagles, owls, gulls, and hawks, and specific cuts of beef from the hindquarters.

To be considered kosher, dairy products such as milk, cheese, butter, and yogurt must adhere to specific rules. These include being derived from a kosher animal, being free from any meat-based derivatives like gelatin or rennet, and being prepared using utensils and equipment that have not been previously used for any meat-based products.

Fish is considered kosher if it has both fins and easily removable scales, with shellfish being prohibited. In contrast to meat and poultry, fish does not require any specific preparation. However, to determine its kosher status, it is important that the scales of the fish are visible. To ensure the kosher status of filleted or ground fish, it should not be consumed unless there is appropriate supervision or if the fillet contains a visible skin tab with scales still attached to the flesh. Processed and smoked fish products also require reliable rabbinic supervision, as do all processed foods.

While it is not allowed to eat fish and meat together, one can consume them one after the other in the same meal. To prevent mixing them, it is necessary to use different dishes and utensils for each course and to clean them thoroughly between each one. Additionally, it is recommended to eat some solid food and drink water or a beverage in between to cleanse the mouth and avoid any remaining residue.

The eggs or any other derivatives that come from non-kosher birds or fish are considered non-kosher. Hence, to ensure that caviar is kosher, it must come from a kosher fish. Moreover, any eggs from kosher birds with blood spots must be thrown away, so it is vital for Jews to inspect eggs before using them.

Halal rules:

Compared to kosher rules, halal rules are much simpler. Briefly, all eatable plants are permitted as halal food for Muslims except for intoxicating plants. Different from kosher, for halal food, all Alcoholic drinks are prohibited and all food or drinks that cause intoxication are prohibited as well. As for meats, basically, according to the Quran[2] and Hadith,[3] non-halal animals

---

2 Specifically, verse 3 of chapter 5: "Forbidden to you are carrion, blood, and swine; what is slaughtered in the name of any other than Allah; what is killed by strangling, beating, a fall, or by being gored to death; what is partly eaten by a predator unless you slaughter it; and what is sacrificed on altars. You are also forbidden to draw lots for decisions" (Quran, 5:3).

3 Hadiths that report the sayings or actions of the prophet Mohamed regarding the halal diet include:

include dead animals, pigs, all animals slaughtered without the name of Allah pronounced on them, animals with long pointed teeth or tusks, donkeys, and mules. According to halal rules, animal blood or products made with blood are also prohibited.

Although the fundamental guidelines of halal are rooted in the primary Islamic sources of the Quran and Hadith, it is noteworthy that the interpretation and comprehension of halal can vary across different schools of Islamic jurisprudence. Presently, the overwhelming majority of Muslims worldwide adhere to the Sunni branch, which comprises four major schools of jurisprudence: Hanafi, Maliki, Shafi, and Hanbali. Other Muslim sects include Shi'a, Ibadi, and others. Throughout history, these various Islamic branches and schools have individually interpreted the concept of halal in their own distinct ways. Although all agree on the prohibition of pork, Islamic law does not impose punishment for its consumption. Although it is clearly stated in the Quran that intoxicants are prohibited[4], there exist divergent viewpoints among prominent Muslim scholars, such as Abu Hanifa, who established one of the four major Sunni schools of jurisprudence. Some scholars, including Abu Hanifa , permitted the consumption of certain alcoholic beverages as long as they were not consumed in quantities that caused intoxication.

"Jabir ibn 'Abd-Allah said: On the day of Khaybar, the Prophet (peace and blessings of Allah be upon him) forbade the meat of domesticated donkeys, but he granted us a concession allowing us to eat the meat of horses" (Al-Bukhari: 5520).

4 This can be seen in the following Quranic verse: ≪O believers! Intoxicants, gambling, idols, and drawing lots for decisions are all evil of Satan's handiwork. So shun them so you may be successful≫ (Quran, 5:90).

Moreover, the Hanafi School, like the Shia'a School, has specific regulations regarding seafood, sharing some similarities with the rules of kosher dietary laws. Conversely, non-Hanafi Sunni Muslims consider fish and seafood to be inherently permissible (halal) without any specific restrictions. This is based on the Quranic verse 96 of chapter 5, states that "It is lawful for you to hunt and eat seafood, as a provision for you and for travelers." Hence, ritual slaughter is not required for any marine creatures, and all parts of these creatures can be consumed without restrictions. Nevertheless, the Shi'a sect and the Hanafi Sunni School differ in their interpretation, as they limit their consumption exclusively to sea fish, similar to kosher dietary laws, allowing only fish with fins and scales. They classify shellfish and other seafood as prohibited. It is worth noting that the Shi'a sect has a distinct perspective on halal seafood, as they permit the consumption of shrimp.

Regarding the method of slaughtering animals for halal meat, it bears similarities to the kosher method. The animal's throat is cut in a single stroke, specifically severing the carotid artery, jugular vein, and windpipe. This process is carried out to fulfill the requirement of draining the blood from the carcass. However, there is a distinction from kosher requirements, as halal permits any adult Muslim to perform the slaughter, whereas kosher slaughtering necessitates a trained kosher slaughterer certified by Jewish rabbis. Furthermore, in halal slaughtering, an additional guideline entails pronouncing the name of Allah before the act of slaughter. According to the Sunni sect, it is also preferable to perform the slaughter in the direction of the Muslim prayers (Qibla), which aligns with the direction of the Kaaba in Mecca.

This is considered an additional condition for halal slaughter according to the Shi'a sect.

Among other rules for halal slaughtering, the animal should be healthy, and a sharp knife should be used to ensure a swift and less painful process. It is also important to avoid sharpening the knife in front of the animal to prevent that stress. Additionally, according to the Quran, Sunni Muslims are allowed to consume meat that has been slaughtered by Christians or Jews since they are recognized as "People of the Book."[5] However, for Shi'a Muslims, it is prohibited to consume meat that has been slaughtered by non-Muslims, including Christians and Jews. According to the Shi'a sect, halal meat is only slaughtered by a Muslim who is facing the Qibla during the slaughter.

Differences and similarities between halal and kosher:

Both the kosher and halal diets follow strict guidelines that determine which foods are permissible based on Jewish and Islamic laws, respectively. Both diets have specific regulations regarding the method of animal slaughter, and they also impose restrictions on certain types of meat. The similarities between halal and kosher guidelines allow many Muslims to comfortably consume kosher food, as almost all the rules of halal can be found within the kosher guidelines. In fact, kosher rules include additional regulations beyond those of halal.

The primary similarity lies in the religious origins of both dietary guidelines, which stem from the shared belief in the same God within the Abrahamic religions encompassing Judaism and Islam. Halal dietary laws are based on

---

5 The Quranic verse states this: "The food of those who were given the Scripture is lawful for you, and your food is lawful for them" (Quran, 5:5).

Islamic teachings found in the Quran and Hadith, while kosher dietary laws are derived from Jewish religious texts, primarily the Torah.

Halal and kosher share several commonalities, beginning with the prohibition of certain types of food. Both halal and kosher diets strictly forbid the consumption of pork and its by-products. Additionally, they prohibit the consumption of certain predatory animals and birds of prey. Another similarity is the development of certification systems. Halal and kosher food products can undergo certification processes by respective religious authorities to guarantee adherence to their dietary laws.

Fig 13-2. Halal and Kosher Logos for certifying products

Another shared aspect can be observed in the method of animal slaughter. Both halal and kosher dietary practices require a specific slaughter method that ensures the thorough removal of blood from the animal. However, there are distinctions in the execution of this process. In halal, it is necessary for the animal to be slaughtered by a Muslim, reciting the name of Allah and facing the Qibla. Nevertheless, many Muslims also accept meat slaughtered by Christians or Jews. Conversely, kosher dictates that the animal must be slaughtered by a trained Jewish ritual slaughterer (shochet) who adheres to specific ritual requirements. Both halal and kosher regulations prioritize the humane treatment of animals. Both dietary systems emphasize the significance of treating animals with compassion throughout their lives, articularly during the process of slaughter.

Kosher regulations include additional requirements that are not mandatory for halal food. These include the separation of meat and dairy, which is strictly prohibited by kosher rules, extending to the cooking and consumption of these items together. In contrast, halal does not have such stringent separation requirements, allowing the consumption of meat and dairy together. Furthermore, kosher guidelines specify the permitted animals, parts of the animals, and their specific characteristics, such as having split hooves and chewing their cud. In contrast, halal guidelines do not have such intricate restrictions and allow for the consumption of a broader range of animals.

In conclusion, while kosher and halal diets exhibit certain similarities, they diverge significantly when it comes to the specific additional rules and restrictions imposed by kosher dietary practices. Kosher regulations tend to be more rigorous in comparison to the relatively more flexible nature of halal guidelines.

Keywords

Kosher, Halal, Restrictions, Muslims, Jews

References

Ajmera, Rachael, "What's the Difference Between Kosher and Halal Diets?", 5 Feb. 2021. https://www.healthline.com/nutrition/different-types-of-salt

Al-Mongid, Muhammad Saleh, "Buying foods made according to the Jewish religion," Islam Question & Answer, https://islamqa.info/ar/answers/103701/شراء-الماكولات-التي-صنعت-حسب-الديانة-اليهودية

Al-Mongid, Muhammad Saleh, "Permissibility of eating meat slaughtered by Christians and Jews", Islam Question & Answer, https://islamqa.info/en/answers/103/permissibility-of-eating-meat-slaughtered-by-christians-and-jews

Almissiri, Abd Alwahhab (1999) *Encyclopedia Of Jews - Judaism And Zionism: Judaism Concepts and sects*, Cairo: Dar AlSherouk, 1st edition, Vol. 5, pp. 209-211.

Al-Sistani, Question and answer: Food Sistani.org, [Online]. www.sistani.org/english/qa/01187.

Al-Sistani, Question and answer: Meat Sistani.org, [Online]. www.sistani.org/english/qa/search/8714.

Al-Sistani, Question and answer: Meat, Sistani.org, [Online]. https://www.sistani.org/english/qa/01251/

Cohen, Rabbi Dovid. Identifying Meat That Was Not Properly Menukar, Chicago Rabbinical Council. Dec. 2007. https://www.crcweb.org/kosher_articles/identifying_meat.php

Kosher Food: Everything You Need to Know, 15 March 2023, https://www.healthline.com/nutrition/what-is-kosher#passover

Kosher Food: The Kosher Primer, U-Kosher, https://oukosher.org/the-kosher-primer/

Soon, J. M., Chandia, M., & Joe, M. R. (2017). Halal integrity in the food supply chain. British Food Journal, 119 (1), 39-51.

Twaigery, Saud and Spillman, Diana, "An Introduction to Moslem Dietary Laws", Food Technology, February, 1989.

Zer Farber, Rabbi, "Prohibition of Meat and Milk: Its Origins in the Text", TheTorah.

com, https://www.thetorah.com/article/prohibition-of-meat-and-milk-its-origins-in-the-text

Image References

Roger Horowitz, April 2016.
  http://www.rogerhorowitz.com/uploads/4/0/8/8/40882439/6946217.gif?314
Institute for Freedom of Faith & Security in Europe, Halal & Kosher Food.
  https://www.iffse.eu/religious-freedom/kosher-halal/

written by Mona Farouk M. Ahmed (Busan University of Foreign Studies)

▼

Trade Goods

14

Spice

Spices, from origins to spread and global impact

1. Origin and meaning of spices

Spices are the parts of the roots, bark, and seeds of tropical plants, such as chili peppers, black pepper, and cinnamon, that spice up or aromatize food. The main spices used worldwide and historically at the center of exploration and trade are chili pepper, black pepper, cinnamon, clove, and nutmeg, and we'll focus on these spices to explore their origins, spread, and impact.

The origins of spices can be traced back to human history. Early humans would have known that the taste of food could be enhanced by accidentally eating the meat they hunted with the fruit or shell of a plant. Evidence of plants and herbs being used to spice up food has been found in Neolithic tombs and caves in the Near East. The use of certain plants eased the pain of wounds and also enhanced the flavor of food with a pleasant aroma. Around 3,000 BC, the Sumerians of Mesopotamia recorded spices and foods on clay tablets, and by 1700 BC, spices were used in religious and funerary ceremonies.

Biblical accounts say that in 1,000 BC the Queen of Sheba visited King Solomon in Jerusalem and offered him spices. In ancient Egypt, spices were used as an ingredient in perfumes, there are records of onions and garlic being given to workers to keep them healthy as they mobilised to build the pyramids, and spices such as garlic and cloves were found in the tomb of King Tutankhamun.

Spices also played an important role in Greek medicine, with Hippocrates writing about the benefits of spices and herbs, and the Romans adding spices to wine for consumption. The East is no exception. In China, the 'Běncǎo Gāngmù(本草綱目)', which is estimated to be written around 2,700 BC, mentions over 100 spices and medicinal plants including cinnamon. In India in particular, peppers and cloves have been used since 3,000 BC to prevent food from spoiling or to burn incense to ward off disease. Thus, spices have been used in India for thousands of years to flavor dishes and for medicinal purposes.

The use and significance of spices has changed over time. Until the early modern period, spices were used to cleanse the body or treat certain illnesses. For example, pepper was considered an effective remedy for coughs and asthma, cinnamon was used to reduce fever, nutmeg was used for flatulence, and ginger was used as an aphrodisiac. In the Middle Ages, when the Black Death broke out across Europe, people burned longan incense to ward off the disease. Today, spices are still used as medicines, but mainly as ingredients to remove bad odors and enhance the flavor of food. And Conflicts and wars over the hegemony of spices have led to the development or collapse of countries and changed the course of world history.

2. Origin and main growing regions of spices

The origin of spices is mainly in the tropical and equatorial regions. They have expanded to Southeast Asia, the Indian Ocean, and South America, and are grown in various parts of the world. The most important regions are Asia, where black pepper, nutmeg, cinnamon, and cloves are produced; the Middle East and North Africa, where coriander and paprika are grown; Latin America, where chili, vanilla, anato, and ginger are grown; and the Mediterranean, where basil, rosemary, and other herbs are grown. Here's a look at the main spices, where they come from, and how much they produce.

1) Chilli Pepper

Chili peppers (scientific name 'Capsicum annuum L.') are native to Central and South America and the West Indies. Chili peppers come in many varieties, shapes, and colors, so it's hard to define them as a singular spice. The Spanish first introduced chili peppers to Europe, and the Portuguese likely introduced them to South and East Asia. Today, East Asia is the world's largest consumer of chili peppers, and India is both the largest producer and largest consumer.

Today, sweet and spicy peppers are produced in the following countries in order of production : India, China, Thailand, Pakistan, Myanmar, Ethiopia, and Bangladesh, accounting for 67% of the world's total production, of which India produces 40%.

2) Black Pepper

Black pepper (scientific name 'Piper nigrum') is a vine in the pepper family whose berries are used for aroma and flavor. It is native to the Malabar Coast of southwestern India. Europeans were particularly fond of pepper because it removed fishy odours from meat, preserved meat and acted as a preservative. So for millennia, ships traveling to and from destinations and the Indian Ocean sought out and imported pepper to meet European demand. Pepper comes from Indonesia, Brazil, Vietnam, and Malaysia. Indian peppers from Malabar are some of the best in the world, with a fruity, spicy flavor.

Today, Vietnam, Indonesia, India, Brazil, Sri Lanka, Malaysia produce 85% of the world's total, of which Vietnam produces 22%.

3) Cinnamon

Cinnamon is the dried, peeled bark of a tree in the Lauraceae family. It is native to Sri Lanka (Ceylon), but has been cultivated in India and Bangladesh. By the end of the 18th century, it had been successfully cultivated in northern India, eastern Java and the Seychelles in the Indian Ocean, east of Zanzibar. The largest consumers are the United Kingdom, the United States, and Spain, and cinnamon is also used in a variety of foods, confectionery, baking, and beverages.

Today, in order of cultivation and production, Indonesia, China, Sri Lanka, and Vietnam produce 99% of the world's total, of which Indonesia produces 45%.

4) Clove

Cloves are the flower buds of cloves (Syzygi um aromaticum Merrill et Perry) in the clove family. Picked and dried before the buds open, the shape of this bud resembles the shape of a nail, hence the name clove. It is native to the Moluccas Islands, which are part of Indonesia and is used in China for five-spice stewed meat and in the West for a variety of uses in beverages, desserts, pickles, and sauces. Indonesia consumes most of the cloves it produces. Today's production is grown in Madagascar, Zanzibar, and PembaIsland (part of modern-day Tanzania), north of Zanzibar.

Today, clove is grown and produced in Indonesia, Madagascar, Tanzania, and Sri Lanka. The Comoros produces 98% of the world's total, with Indonesia producing 70%.

5) Nutmeg

Nutmeg (scientific name 'Myristica fragrans') is a type of walnut with a musky aroma and is native to the Banda Islands of Indonesia. Nutmeg was used in food and also as a medicine because it removed the odour and fishy smell from meat and fish. In general, nutmeg was a more expensive and valuable spice than pepper.

Today, in terms of nutmeg and cardamom plantings and production, Guatemala, Indonesia, India, and Nepal produce 92% of the world's total, with Guatemala producing 40%.

Anise, star anise, fennel, coriander: Growing 83% in India, Mexico, China, Syria, Iran, Bulgaria (in India 58%), Dry garlic: Growing 90% in China, India,

Korea, Egypt, Russia, Bangladesh, Myanmar (in China 79%), Ginger: Growing 79% in India, China, Nepal, Indonesia, Nigeria (in India 32%), Herbs and other spices: Growing 91% in India, Bangladesh, Turkey, China, Pakistan (in India 70%), Vanilla: Growing 90% in Indonesia, Madagascar, Mexico, Papua New Guinea, China (in Indonesia 38% and in Madagascar 37%).

3. Spice Spread and Key Events

Spices from Asia came to Europe via the Silk Road, which existed since the Bronze Age, but it wasn't until Alexander the Great's conquest of Persia and Rome's hegemony over the Mediterranean that spices began to spread across Europe, with Rome importing pepper directly from the source. Here are the key events that led to the global spread of spices chronologically.

1) Alexander's Eastern Expeditions and the Roman Conquest of Egypt

The first major event that brought spices to Europe was Alexander the Great's conquest of Persia around 330 BC, which brought many types of spices to Europe. Many of these spices, including black pepper, were used as therapeutic or detoxifying agents. In the 4th century BC, the leading maritime power in the pepper trade was the Austronesians from Southeast Asia, who established maritime trade routes from Southeast Asia to India and the Arabian Peninsula, bringing spices to Europeans. From ancient times until the end of the Middle Ages, there were 2 main trade routes connecting Europe and Asia: the northern route by land (via the Black Sea and Asia Minor) and the southern route by sea (via Syria and Egypt). Of these, the southern route by sea was much more economical and hence, the volume of trade was much bigger.

Later, spices were imported and used in earnest after the Roman conquest of Egypt, around 30 B.C. The spice trade flourished as routes were developed from India to Egypt via the Indian Ocean and Red Sea. In the case of pepper, which was produced on the Malabar coast of India and then shipped to Rome via Alexandria via Hormuz or Aden, pepper accounted for half of Europe's imports in the first century.

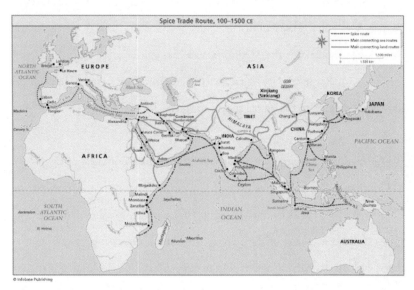

Fig 14–1. Trade routes of spices (100-1500)[1]

2) Fall of the Roman Empire and rise of Islamic power

The rise of Islamic power in the Mediterranean and the Islamic era (641-

---

1 http://fyumul.blogspot.com/2012/11/spice-sa-kasaysayan-ng-pilipinas.html

1798) in Egypt led to major changes in the spice trade. Spices were important to Mohammed (570-632 AD), who was a spice trader, co-owned spice shops and developed distillation techniques to extract floral scents. Muslim merchants bought spices exclusively from Asia and sold them to Venetian merchants at high prices. At the time, Venice, a trading center for both Islamic and European merchants, grew immensely wealthy from its trade with the East, as this trading environment provided them the support of the Venetian government and customers. They bought spices from India, pepper, ginger, and turmeric from the port of Malabar, and cinnamon, mace, and nutmeg from Sri Lanka. The Muslims kept the origin and importation of spices a closely guarded secret. The Muslims sold spices at high prices with high tariffs; for example, 500 grams of saffron cost the price of a horse.

In the 14th century, as the Ottoman Empire grew in power and cut off trade routes between Europe and Asia, spice prices skyrocketed. Especially for Portugal and Spain on the western end of the Mediterranean, long distances made spices more expensive to purchase, so Portugal sought a new route to Asia, sailing around the Cape of Good Hope in Africa, to purchase spices directly from the East, rather than the traditional Red Sea-centered trade routes.

3) The Age of Sail and the East India Company

The Age of Exploration began in the early 15th century when Prince Enrique of Portugal opened a route to Africa via the Atlantic Ocean. The 16th and 17th centuries were the time of spice wars and colonization for the Asians, with Portugal and Spain bisecting the New World and being challenged by the Dutch and English.

In 1497, Vasco da Gama of Portugal sailed from Lisbon, rounding the Cape of Good Hope in Africa, and arrived in Calicut on the west coast of India in 10 months. Carrying a cargo of pepper and other spices, he returned to Lisbon the following year with an estimated 60-fold profit. From then on, the Portuguese chose to use force with guns and artillery instead of peaceful trade to gain a monopoly on the spice trade. This marked the beginning of the Age of Exploration and the colonization of the East. Meanwhile, Spain believed in Christopher Columbus, who claimed he could reach India by sailing west across the Atlantic, and he set sail in 1492, bringing back gold and silver as well as new spices such as pepper and vanilla from the Americas. The Portuguese and Spanish opened 2 separate spice routes, and the age of sailing began in earnest. The Portuguese colonized Goa in western India, captured Hormuz in 1515, controlled the Indian Ocean, captured Malacca, and expanded their East Asian trade routes (Guangzhou-Nagashima), adding new goods like tea and ceramics. Spain's expansion into the Americas led to gold mining, the introduction of new spices, and control of the Atlantic Ocean with its largest fleet, which also shipped pepper from the Indonesian Moluccas. Later, Magellan, a Portuguese native, also became obsessed with spices and planned to sail to the Americas, but when he could not find sponsorship in his homeland, he was sponsored by the Spanish crown and sailed from Spain in 1519, passing through Brazil and Argentina before reaching the Philippines. However, a clash with natives in Mactan left Magellan dead, and the crew barely survived, arriving back in Spain with 26 tons of spices.

At the end of the 16th century, the invincible Spanish Armada was defeated by the combined forces of England and the Netherlands. This marked the beginning of a new spice trade centered on England and the Netherlands. In 1602, the Dutch established the Dutch East India Company, and war broke out between England and Spain over the establishment of the English East India Company. The East India Company was armed with guns and prisoners of war and had the authority to make treaties, declare war, and establish colonies, which is the authority of a state. In order to avoid the problems that could arise from direct state intervention, the company delegated state powers to private companies, which took the lead in colonizing the East, including the exploitation of spices.

In the early 17th century, the Dutch East India Company, based in Batavi, Jakarta, Indonesia, took control of Asia by driving out the Portuguese, and in 1658, seized the cinnamon trade in Ceylon and the pepper ports on the Malabar and Java coasts. By the end of the 18th century, the British had driven the Dutch out of India, and London became the center of the spice market. Although not as influential as the Dutch and British in the 17th and 18th centuries, Denmark and France also entered the spice wars, making Asia a European battleground for spices. Later, American merchants, having gained independence from Britain, entered the spice trade and became influential in the 19th century.

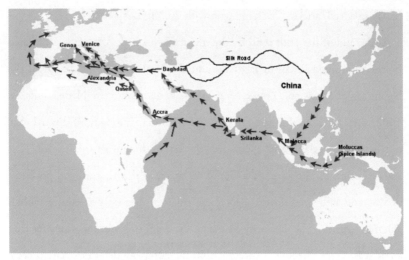

Fig 14–2. The global spread of Spice[2]

4. The geographic spread of spices and their impact on human history

Even today, spices are used extensively around the world in cooking, medicine, and cosmetology. In particular, spices are considered an important element of flavor and the creation of new tastes in food. They have had a profound impact on the cuisines of people around the world and will continue to do so in the future. We can summarize the impact of spices on humanity in 3 ways.

First, spices have influenced humanity as therapeutic agents. Medieval medical texts mention the use of spices like black pepper and cinnamon in medical prescriptions. Spices were used primarily for their anti-inflammatory, antioxidant, and antibacterial properties. Even today, spices and herbs are used for medical treatment and health. Recent data from the United States shows that 5-10% of adults in the United States use botanicals like spices for health.

---

2 https://www.*linkedin*.com/pulse/spice-route-ceylon-especias-agro

Spices also have antioxidant properties and are effective in preventing the modern diseases of obesity and diabetes. Many studies have also shown that spices promote the growth of good bacteria, improve gut health, and boost cognition.

Second, spices have had a profound impact on cooking. They have influenced the taste, aroma, and appearance of food. Through spices, humans have created and developed new flavors. As the world's chefs have developed new cuisines using more and more different spices, spices have become more versatile and more widely used. There are also many studies that show that using spices in food can create a higher quality diet that reduces sugar, saturated fat, and sodium while increasing food flavor. As a result of these spices, spice consumption in the United States has grown exponentially over the past half-century, especially for spices like ginger and chili peppers, according to the U.S. Department of Agriculture (USDA).

Finally, it has had a significant impact on trade and economies in the East and West. Spices have been an important commodity in trade from ancient times to modern times and have had a profound impact on the economy, and this economic impact continues today. Pepper, for example, is an important global industry, grown in countries such as India, Indonesia, and Vietnam and transported around the world. Today, advances in transportation and communication technology have made spices easier and faster to transport and more affordable, so their use continues to grow. Today, spices are used in many industries beyond medicine and cooking, for example, in perfumes, scented candles, cosmetics, shower gels, and other products, creating new demand.

Spread of Spice (Black Pepper)

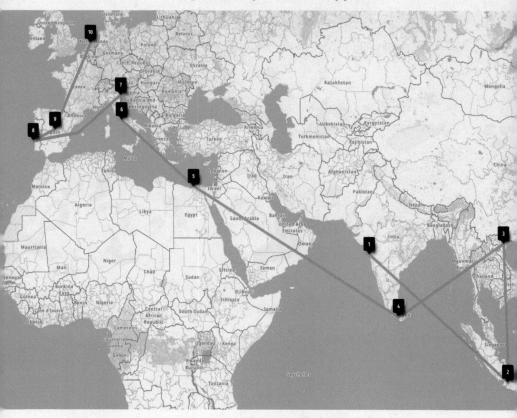

① India (Malabar Coast)　　⑥ Rome

② Indonesia　　　　　　　　⑦ Venice

③ Vietnam　　　　　　　　　⑧ Portugal

④ Sri Lanka　　　　　　　　⑨ Spain

⑤ Egypt (Alexandria)　　　　⑩ Netherlands

Scan the QR code
to view the map.

Keywords

Spice, origins, spread, Chilli Pepper, Cinnamon, Clove, Nutmeg

References

프레드 차라(저), 강경이(역), 〈향신료의 지구사 A Global History of Spices〉, ㈜휴머니
　　스트 출판그룹, 2014.
장-마리 펠트(저), 진중현(역), 〈향신료의 역사 Les épices〉, 좋은 책 만들기, 2005.
남종국, 〈1395년 베네치아 향신료 무역〉, 동국사학 54집, 2013, p.364.

Online References

World Spice Production
　　https://www.jardinsdefrance.org/wp-content/uploads/2018/01/JdF639_1_G.pdf
History Through Spices
　　https://www.youtube.com/watch?v=57QXKmPlmSg
"Spice Trade" in the Philippines
　　http://fyumul.blogspot.com/2012/11/spice-sa-kasaysayan-ng-pilipinas.html

written by NamMo Jung (Korea Maritime & Ocean University)

15

Cotton

Cotton is considered one of the most important crops associated with the development of humanity, as it is a plant that is transformed into a fabric, then into clothes, and then a fashion. This chain of developments undoubtedly represents an integral part of learning about people's culture and life.

Cotton, in other words, remains one of the evidences of the development witnessed by the inhabitants of the Mediterranean region, south and north, and the development of cotton continues to be traced as well. Cotton harvesting is, in fact, a reflection of the evolving levels of interaction and interdependence between the two sides of the Mediterranean. It is one of the axes of explaining the state of mutual dependence between the two parties throughout history.

History, specifically regarding cultural and economic interaction between the two sides of the Mediterranean, is full of many situations and examples in which Egyptian cotton was present. For example, Egypt buys Greek cotton, England waits for Egyptian cotton, and France wears Egyptian cotton textiles.

No one knows specifically how cotton was grown in the past, but the first discovery of cotton harvesting dates back to the caves of Mexico, where scientists found some remains of cotton bolls and pieces of cotton clothing dating back to about 7,000 years ago. The shape of the cotton they found was very similar to the cotton grown in the American continent to this day. About 5,000 years ago, in the area of what is now called Pakistan, people practiced cotton cultivation. Some remnants of cotton textiles found in the Indus River Valley in Pakistan, dating back to 3 thousand years ago. Approximately during the same period, the people of the Nile Valley region in Egypt were making cotton clothes.

The Greek historian Herodotus wrote about a tree in Asia that bore cotton (its quality and beauty exceeding the wool of any sheep). It is also mentioned that the army of Alexander the Great first brought cotton to Europe in 300 BC. Cotton fabrics were so expensive at that time that they could only be purchased by the rich.

It is certain that cotton has always played a developmental role from ancient times until today, locally, regionally, and internationally. The development of modern Egypt was also linked to the introduction of cotton cultivation over large areas. During the past few years, when Egypt planned to develop the industrial sector, cotton was one of its most important goals. We will not exaggerate if we tell that cotton is an indicator of the development of life and human development, as cotton has been a witness to the development of social, cultural, economic, commercial, political, and even environmental life. We will find that cotton is a reflection of a climate that had an impact on culture, and cotton has specific uses with specific specifications depending on holidays and ceremonies, whether in design or the colors used. Cotton was also one of the crops that responded to environmental changes, which reflects the changes in development policies locally and internationally.

Cotton has appeared several times in the series of cultural, commercial, and social exchanges between the two sides of the Mediterranean. We will find, for example, that when the Arabs began cultivating cotton and after learning about the richness of that plant, they paid great attention to it, and its cultivation was one of the channels of communication between the two sides of the Mediterranean. The Arabs grew more cotton, and they transferred this cultivation to the islands of Sicily and Andalusia. And from there, it spread to all parts of Europe. Therefore, it was not surprising to find similarities between the Arabic and English pronunciation of the word cotton, which was originally taken from the Arabic language, the source of much knowledge in Europe, including cotton cultivation, as explained above.

Let us first learn about cotton as a plant and where its filament is extracted from, which turns into fabric, then into cloth, and then into a product. The cotton filament is the most important part of the cotton plant and is in the form of a flat tube wrapped around itself, composed of cellulose deposits. Geographically, it is mentioned that the Indians were the first people to use cotton in their clothes, and then after that, cotton cultivation spread from India to the world, but not all regions of the world, at least in the beginning. We will find, for example, that the inhabitants of the Arabian Peninsula had wool spinning extracted from camel hair, and they focused their agriculture on producing foodstuffs for food consumption and fulfilling their basic needs. In other words, the cultivation of cotton expresses a state of human development in which man began to master agriculture and diversify his skills related to it until he began to cultivate non-food varieties, such as aromatic or wild textile varieties, led by cotton, of course. From cotton cultivation, people began to know another level of progress in which they were able to transform it into fabric using manual tools, then simple machines, and then giant factories for ginning, spinning, and weaving.

Cotton has always influenced the image creation of Mediterranean countries, recently. When the Egyptian state searched for areas to launch an Egyptian name or brand, cotton was also present, and the textile sector was chosen to market the products of the Mahalla Spinning Company globally and locally, and the brand name came after the ancient Egyptian goddess of spinning and weaving. This is because the textile industry is one of the most important vital industries in Egypt, and during the recent period, the state has paid great attention to it because it is a source of national income.

Cotton was situated in the center of government policy when the Egyptian government tried to reduce the bill for importing textiles from abroad and also provided a good product of high quality, explaining that it would help the country obtain hard currency as a result of exporting the surplus. The textile industry is one of the vital sectors in the Egyptian economy, as it contributes greatly to Egyptian exports as the sector represents one of the largest industries to local production. In addition, the sector ranks fifth in supplying Egypt with foreign currencies, after oil and expatriate remittances. The factors for the success of the textile and spinning industry sector in Egypt lie first in the availability of raw materials, the most important of which is Egyptian cotton. Quantities of it are even exported to several countries such as Turkey and India to produce products made entirely of Egyptian cotton to meet the global demand for it, as Egypt is the largest producer of long-staple cotton in the world.

We will find in Egypt that the government is already providing several ongoing training programs in order to develop and raise the level of workforce skills and is keen to give them stable and competitive wages, many of which were conducted in cooperation with Mediterranean countries. The Egyptian market represents a good and promising consumer market, and Egypt is also distinguished by its proximity to the Mediterranean markets, where, thanks to its location, it is able to export goods easily and quickly to several countries. The Egyptian government pays great attention to the textile sector. This interest emerged through the endeavor to establish the largest spinning and weaving factory in the world in Egypt.

The beginning of the renaissance of cotton cultivation in the southern Mediterranean was the beginning of an exceptional historical era in terms of shaping economic, political, and social relations between the two sides. When the governor of Egypt, Muhammad Ali Pasha, planned to formulate renaissance development policies in the early nineteenth century, he introduced cotton cultivation in Egypt, and it was the beginning of global leadership for it that led to attracting the colonial attention that came and occupied Egypt for many reasons, one of which was control of the raw materials.

The English began the process of weaving cotton in the seventeenth century. They imported raw cotton from countries bordering the eastern borders of the Mediterranean Sea, and after that, they imported it from the southern colonies in America. In the eighteenth century, English textile factories developed machines that made it possible to spin threads and weave clothes in large quantities. Then, they started exporting cotton clothes. On the other hand, since the ninth century, the process of extracting oil from cotton seeds began after its economic and nutritional value was confirmed. Today, cotton is ranked second globally in edible oils after soybean oil. Cotton oil has a mild nutty flavour.

Back to cotton cultivation, it began in Egypt in 1820 when the ruler of Egypt, Muhammad Ali Pasha, began introducing long-staple cotton, which was successfully cultivated in 1821 after experiments. Industries were established for the manufacture of cotton ginning and pressing machines. Factories started to staple processing for dyeing, oil production, and manufacturing chemical materials.

In the same context, records of the history of cotton in the Agricultural Library of the Ministry of Agriculture confirm that Muhammad Ali Pasha was the first to grow cotton in Egypt and expand the areas cultivated with the crop, and he was the first to realize its value as a strategic crop that served the national economy and was its backbone in establishing modern Egypt.

According to another report prepared by the Cotton Research Institute, the second decade of the nineteenth century can be identified as the real beginning of Egyptian cotton, when Muhammad Ali Pasha summoned the French engineer Louis Jumel to supervise the organization of cotton cultivation in Egypt, where it was no longer just a crop produced by Egyptian land but turned into a necessary agricultural commodity. After Muhammad Ali Pasha, Egyptian cotton became strategically important for textile factories in England, after the occupation of Egypt in 1882 and later after the First World War, the need arose to establish a research center concerned with studying the serious problems facing cotton as its quality declined.

Here, the Cotton Investigation Authority was formed in 1919, which is the Cotton Research Institute. Two types of cotton were being developed: Al-Sakal in the Delta and Al-Ashmouni in Upper Egypt, and its area reached one million acres during the period from 1916 to 1925. It is reported that the production of one ton of cotton provides job opportunities throughout the year for 5 people on average.

Given that the cotton weaving field is part of the heritage in southern Mediterranean countries such as Egypt, weaving generally began thousands of years ago. Egyptian textiles were extremely famous throughout the world. It was also the subject of appreciation and proverbs for its precision, splendor, and beauty. Centuries ago, the Arabs recognized this and worked to benefit from and encourage this artistic heritage until the textile industry flourished throughout the Islamic countries in general and in Egypt in particular.

Until now, we will find makers and craftsmen in the southern Mediterranean, specifically in Egypt, who produce all handmade products from pure raw material of cotton, which contains no fibers, starting with coverlets, curtains, bed sheets, etc., and they are often exported to the northern part of the Mediterranean. In view of this, the scene of attention to the importance of cotton in the development of the southern Mediterranean has recently been repeated, and after exactly 200 years, Egyptian President Sisi has returned interest in cotton cultivation, but this time in short-staple cotton, with great success equal to the success rates of its cultivation in the countries that produce it, through its cultivation in the East.

Nevertheless, cotton cultivation and its products face multi-faceted competition. Firstly, it faces competition from synthetic fiber industries that have dominated the global market since the mid-1990s. It is known that both types of textiles are mainly used in clothing. While wool and cotton are considered biologically degradable materials, it is therefore important to focus on understanding the environmental impacts and rates of biological degradation of natural fibers such as cotton and synthetic fibres. In addition to technological competition, although it is supposed to support cotton in the process of processing it or recycling its waste, there is economic competition, where some voices are raised, attacking cotton as responsible for environmental pollution.

There is also a social dimension to cotton, as the textile industry was also a way for some village women to earn a living or help their husbands. In any case, qualitative shifts have occurred since the beginning of history with regard to cotton in the Mediterranean countries or its European surroundings. Therefore, we will find that the textile "industry" is one of the oldest industries known to humanity and the peoples of the Mediterranean, and like other ancient industries, it has witnessed great development since its inception as a result of scientific and technological progress, especially since the era of the Industrial Revolution in Europe, which changed many aspects of life in the world.

In the southern Mediterranean, specifically in Egypt, some ancient Egyptian drawings were found depicting two or more individuals using a primitive loom. Ancient fibers dating back to that era were also found. The ancient Egyptians are among the oldest ancient peoples who have known the textile industry since 5000 years BC. Ancient Egyptian drawings illustrate the ancient Egyptians' use of a machine similar to a loom. The methods used in weaving in the past have changed throughout history, and technology and its progress have changed production rates so that the textile industry not only aims to meet local needs but has gone further than that to become a profitable export and trade industry. After many centuries, the Englishman Edmund Cartwright was the first to mechanize the textile industry in 1785, as he developed a steam-powered loom for weaving cotton, which later led to the creation of more efficient looms.

Cotton, as a central representative for textile industry, was and still a reflection of a development and interdependency between the two sides of the Mediterranean, witnessing times of competition, conflict, and cooperation.

Keywords

Egypt, Nile, agriculture, cotton, textile

References

دراسة اقتصادية لمحصول القطن العضوي فى مصر د/ خالد السيد عبدالمولى محمدالمجلة المصرية للاقتصاد
الزراعى– المجلد الثامن والعشرون– العدد الثانى – يونيو ٢٠١٨

https://www.almrsal.com/post/584553

https://www.almrsal.com/post/584553

https://arab-ency.com.sy/ency/details/7135/12

https://arab-ency.com.sy/ency/details/7135/12

https://www.hindawi.org/books/52829692/4/

https://www.hindawi.org/books/52829692/4/

https://msna1.wordpress.com/2013/08/27/%D8%AA%D8%A7%D8%B1%
D9%8A%D8%AE-%D9%88%D8%AA%D8%B7%D9%88%D8%B1-
%D8%B5%D9%86%D8%A7%D8%B9%D8%A9-%D8%A7%D9%84%D9%86
%D8%B3%D9%8A%D8%AC/

https://msna1.wordpress.com/2013/08/27/%D8%AA%D8%A7%D8%B1%
D9%8A%D8%AE-%D9%88%D8%AA%D8%B7%D9%88%D8%B1-
%D8%B5%D9%86%D8%A7%D8%B9%D8%A9-%D8%A7%D9%84%D9%86
%D8%B3%D9%8A%D8%AC/

https://msna1.wordpress.com/2013/08/27/%D8%AA%D8%A7%D8%B1%
D9%8A%D8%AE-%D9%88%D8%AA%D8%B7%D9%88%D8%B1-
%D8%B5%D9%86%D8%A7%D8%B9%D8%A9-%D8%A7%D9%84%D9%86
%D8%B3%D9%8A%D8%AC/

written by Nilly Kamal Elamir (Independent Researcher)

16

Tea

The Odyssey of Tea: Its Journey to the Mediterranean and European Realms Through Civilizational Exchange

In the annals of history, few commodities have evoked as much passion, war, and diplomacy in the annals of history as the humble leaf of the tea plant. The tale of tea's journey to the Mediterranean and the broader European tapestry is one imbued with the complex interplay of geopolitics, commerce, and cultural exchange.

Origins in the East

Tea's origins are rooted in the verdant landscapes of ancient China, with legends attributing its discovery to Emperor Shen Nong around 2737 BCE. By the time of the Tang Dynasty (618-907 AD), tea had become an integral part of the Chinese socio-cultural fabric, immortalized in treatises like Lu Yu's "The Classic of Tea."

Silk Road: The Gateway

The renowned Silk Road played a pivotal role in transporting tea and its allure westward. As merchants plied their routes, carrying silk, porcelain, and other prized items, tea inevitably found its way into the hands and hearts of people in Central Asia and eventually, the Middle East. The Arab traders, discerning the potential of this new beverage, facilitated its spread throughout the region.

Anatolia and the Middle Eastern Tapestry

By the medieval period, tea had begun to leave its mark in the Middle East. The Ottoman Empire, with its vast territories and influence, was instrumental in propagating tea culture in Anatolia and beyond. By the 16th century, tea was a recognized import in Constantinople (modern-day Istanbul), serving as a luxurious counterpart to the more commonly consumed coffee.

Europe's Tryst with Tea

Europe's initial encounter with tea was largely through its interactions with the Portuguese and Dutch traders in the 16th century. The maritime expeditions of these nations to the East not only brought back exotic goods but also tales of a captivating brew. Portugal's Catherine of Braganza, upon her marriage to England's King Charles II, is credited with popularizing tea among the English aristocracy.

By the 18th century, Britain had become the epicenter of a global tea trade, a narrative not without its dark chapters, such as the Opium Wars with China. The British passion for tea was so profound that it precipitated the establishment of tea plantations in its colonies, notably India.

The trajectory of tea from the valleys of China to the salons of Europe is a testament to the inexorable force of civilizational exchange. It underscores how a simple beverage can become a nexus of cultures, forging connections, and shaping histories across continents. As we sip our brew today, we are not just partaking in a ritual but also in a story that spans millennia and civilizations.

Tea in the Mediterranean: Symbolism and Influence

The narrative of tea, while predominantly associated with East Asia, finds fascinating chapters written in the tapestry of the Mediterranean. As the liquid embodiment of cultural exchange, tea has navigated the crossroads of civilizations, binding societies with shared rituals and understandings. Its arrival and assimilation in the Mediterranean provide a deep insight into the subtleties of cultural diffusion and appropriation.

The Mediterranean Prelude

The Mediterranean region, a mélange of cultures, has historically been receptive to foreign influences, whether through conquests, trade, or diplomacy. Its storied shores have witnessed the ebb and flow of empires, each leaving an indelible mark. Into this milieu came tea, not as a conqueror, but as an ambassador of a distant land's ethos.

Trade and Transmission

Though the Silk Road's primary purpose was the westward movement of silk, it unwittingly became the conveyor of tea. Arab traders, with their established networks across Asia, were pivotal in introducing tea to the

Middle Eastern territories, which played a role as a geographical bridge to the Mediterranean. These traders didn't merely transport tea but interwove it with local customs, getting the Eastern tradition of tea-drinking merged with regional flavors and nuances.

Cultural Assimilation in the Mediterranean World

In the Mediterranean, tea's arrival could not meet with universal acceptance. Here, it was juxtaposed against well-established beverages like wine in the West and coffee in the East. However, the adaptability of tea - its capacity to be infused with local herbs, spices, and traditions - made it a versatile drink, finding resonance in various Mediterranean societies.

Countries like Turkey embraced tea with unparalleled fervor. The famous Turkish çay, a variant of black tea, became an integral part of the daily routine and social interactions. In a society known for its coffee houses and intricate rituals around coffee, tea carved a space for itself, evolving into a symbol of hospitality and warmth.

Tea as a Socio-Political Tool

In the Mediterranean's political tapestry, tea also found significance. As in Britain, where tea became a symbol of empire and colonial ambition, Mediterranean nations used tea as a tool of diplomacy and a reflection of their cosmopolitan ethos. Inviting someone for tea in many of these cultures became an act of trust, an offer of friendship, and a gesture of goodwill.

Tea's journey in the Mediterranean is emblematic of how a foreign element can weave itself into the fabric of an established culture. Far from its Chinese origins, through the Mediterranean's azure waters and golden sands, tea found a new home, a testament to the region's adaptability, and the universality of shared human experiences over a comforting brew.

Spread of Cha & Tea*

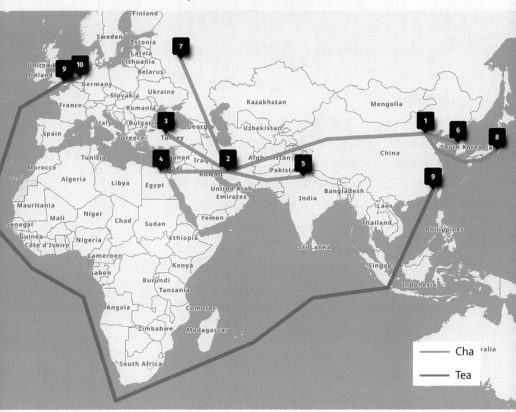

〈Cha〉

① Madarin — cha   ⑤ Hindi — chai

② Persian — chay   ⑥ Korean — cha

③ Turkish — chay   ⑦ Russian — chay

④ Arabic — shay   ⑧ Japanese — ocha

〈Tea〉

⑨ English — tea**   ⑩ Dutch — thee

* This map explains the regions that serve as reference points for the spread based on
  language and cultural areas rather than place names. Also, the numbers preceding each
  language and cultural area are for convenience in explanation and do not indicate the
  order of spread.

** Enter the United Kingdom from the Minnan, China through the sea

Scan the QR code
to view the map.

Keywords

Silkroad, China, Central Asia, Medicine, Türkiye

References

Aladin Goushegir, "Safevîlerden Günümüze İran'da Kahve Kahvehaneler", Doğu'da Kahve ve Kahvehaneler, İstanbul 1999, s. 155-193.

Ali Nazîmâ, Çay, İstanbul 1309.

Ali Rıza Saklı, Türk Çayının Dünü ve Bugünü, İstanbul 2008.

Asım Zihnioğlu, Bir Yeşilin Peşinde, Ankara 1998.

Burhan Kacar, Yapraktan Bardağa Çay, Ankara 1980.

Deniz Gürsoy, Demlikten Süzülen Kültür: Çay, İstanbul 2005.

Ebülhayr Ahmed, Çay Risâlesi, Bulak 1300.

Kemalettin Kuzucu, Bin Yılın Çayı: Osmanlı'da Çay ve Çayhane Kültürü, İstanbul 2012.

Mehmed Arif, Çay Hakkında Mâlûmat, İstanbul 1318.

Mehmed İzzet, Çay Risâlesi, İstanbul 1295.

Mustafa Duman, Çay Kitabı, İstanbul 2005.

O. Kakuzo, Çayname (trc. Ali Sühâ Delilbaşı), İstanbul 1944.

S. Reimertz, Çayın Kültür Tarihi, Ankara 1999.

V. Khokhlachov, Çay Alemi (trc. N. Hasanaliyev), Bakü 1990.

written by Minji Yang (Busan University of Foreign Studies)

17

Glass

Glass in the Mediterranean

Glass, as a material for the creation of aesthetic and functional objects, has a long history in the wider Mediterranean region. Although the raw materials for making glass, which are basically sand (silicon dioxide), soda or alternatively ash (alkali oxide), and lime are widely available, the actual production of glass, however, requires a few crafts that were originally not known to all the people in the ancient Mediterranean. The most important thing is reaching the necessary temperatures for initiating the transformation process of the mentioned raw materials. This requires more than 1300°C, which can only be done with specialized ovens and the right fuel (charcoal). As the techniques of glass production evolved, the knowledge of which substances may be added in order to achieve different colorings increased. Naturally, glass possesses a faint greenish tinge, which arises inadvertently from the existence of iron or aluminum within the unprocessed components. Completely transparent and colorless glass required the addition of a specific quantity of manganese oxide to the raw materials. In varying ratios, manganese oxide can also color the glass with a deep shade of aubergine purple. Alternatively, cobalt, copper, and iron oxides were used as colorants, while tin oxide served the purpose of making the glass less translucent. The unique properties of glass, specifically its translucence and color but also its plasticity in the process of production, offered interesting options for creating works of art, containers, jewelery, elements for mosaics and inlays, and later, from around 100 AD, also windows.

Natural glass, also known as obsidian, which is a possible byproduct of volcanic eruptions, had been already used in the Paleolithic for the production of tools and weapons. There are several places with obsidian deposits in the Mediterranean, each with their own chemical spectrum which allows for the reconstruction of the mobility of communities as well as for the detection of exchange networks in early prehistoric times.

The origins of glass-making date back to ancient Mesopotamia around 2500 BCE. The earliest glass artifacts were carved glass beads, pendants, and inlays formed from molds. Over time, glass production evolved to create vessels, initially limited to elite clientele before becoming common household items. The popularity and value of glass objects were closely tied to advancements in manufacturing techniques.

The earliest technique for crafting hot glass vessels involved wrapping molten glass around a core made from materials like sand, clay, or other substances, resulting in small bottles or jugs (figure 1). Glass-makers later discovered that they could create beautifully contoured open vessel forms, such as bowls, cups, or plates, by placing cut sections of glass cane into molds and fusing them with heat. These methods gave rise to colorful variations like mosaic (or *millefiori*) and marbled glass, which used multiple colors to produce patterns.

Fig 17–1. Glass alabastron (perfume bottle), late 4th – early 3rd century BCE.[1]

1 Metmuseum n.d. "Glass alabastron (perfume bottle)."

In the late Bronze Age (ca. 14th and 13th century BCE), there was already a clear division of the production of glass as a raw material and the end products, as impressively demonstrated by the glass ingots found among the cargo of the famous Uluburun shipwreck (ca. 14th century BCE). A significant breakthrough in ancient glass-making occurred during the 2nd to 1st centuries BCE with the invention of free-blown glass. In this technique, glass artisans used a hollow tube to inflate molten glass, enabling them to shape it into various forms and experiment with different colors. This innovation made glass production more cost-effective and efficient, leading to a wider range of glass vessels that became available to a growing market. The mold-blown technique emerged later and allowed glass-makers to expand hot glass into multipart molds, resulting in vessels with added features like feet and handles.

In antiquity, a number of decorative techniques were developed and refined by the glass-makers, such as adding minerals to create different colors. The mentioned core-forming technique that involved rolling heated vessels on a slab produced patterns such as stripes and zigzags. Cast glass was used as a component for the creation of mosaics. Free-blown glass and related methods offered more creative possibilities with colorful bands or unique patterns. Mold-blown glass vessels exhibited a wide range of raised decorations, from simple geometric motifs to complex figurative scenes (figure 2). Decorations were often used to appeal to specific audiences, such as the use of religious symbols like the cross on pilgrim flasks. The relief patterns on some mold-blown vessels could even hint at their origins in specific workshops. Facet cutting, achieved with abrasive wheels, created geometric patterns on clear free-blown vessels.

Fig 17–2. Roman glass beaker, blown in a dip mold.[2]

The production of every ancient glass vessel took place within a glass-maker's workshop, although the exact locations of many of these workshops remain unknown. However, excavations have uncovered glass-making furnaces at specific sites in Israel. Clues to the origins of certain glass vessels can sometimes be found in the vessel shapes and decorative styles of the artisans, as well as occasional artist signatures.

Roman glass production relied heavily on natron, a mineral soda primarily obtained from Egypt. The use of natron set Roman glass apart from other

2 Metmuseum n.d. "Glass beaker."

glass types. Glass-making workshops expanded from the eastern regions of the Roman Empire, especially along the Levantine coast, to the western provinces. Like other artisans in the Hellenistic and Roman eras, glass-makers were mobile, seeking new opportunities and markets, which renders it difficult and quite complex to understand the ancient glass industry. Modern methods for differentiating between various glass compositions are trace element analysis and isotopic analysis, which allow, for instance, a distinction between Middle Eastern and Roman glasses. These analyses provide support for the existence of both centralized and decentralized glass production systems during the Roman period. In the 9th century, there was a transition in the raw materials used for glass production. The industry moved away from relying on natron and began using quartz pebbles and plant ash. This transformation came along with a more centralized glass production and reflects the evolving nature of glass-making throughout history.

When Islam expanded in the 7th century AD along the eastern and southern coast of the Mediterranean, the two most innovative glass manufacturing places, the cities of Tyre and Sidon, came under Muslim control. These cities continued their production and evolved their repertoire of shapes, ornaments, and techniques. Those eastern Mediterranean workshops were crucial for the origin of Venetian glass production, which became the foundation of European glass-making.

Keywords

glass-making, workshops, natron, antiquity, eastern Mediterranean

References

Al-Bashaireh, Khaled, Elham Alama and Abdul Qader Al-Housan. "Analytical and Technological Study of Roman, Byzantine and Early Islamic (Umayyad) Glasses from Al-Fudein Archaeological Site, Jordan." *Mediterranean Archaeology and Archaeometry* 16, No 1: 257–268.

Caron, Beaudoin and Eléni P. Zoitopoúlou. 2008. *Montreal Museum of Fine Arts, Collection of Mediterranean Antiquities. Volume 1 The Ancient Glass.* Leiden, Boston: Brill.

Jackson, C.M. and P.T. Nicholson. 2010. "The provenance of some glass ingots from the Uluburun shipwreck." *Journal of Archaeological Science* 37 (2): 295–301.

Jenkins, Marilyn. 1986. "Islamic Glass: A Brief History." *The Metropolitan Museum of Art Bulletin*, v. 44, no. 2.

McClung Museum. 2014. *Glass of the Ancient Mediterranean.* Exhibition brochure of the McClung Museum of Natural History and Culture.

Metmuseum. n.d. "Glass alabastron (perfume bottle)." https://www.metmuseum.org/art/collection/search/245446

Metmuseum. n.d. "Glass beaker." https://www.metmuseum.org/art/collection/search/245247

Rosenow, Daniela, Matt Phelps, Andrew Meek and Ian Freestone (eds). 2018. *Things that Travelled. Mediterranean Glass in the First Millennium CE.* London: UCL Press.

written by Sebastian Müller (Institute for Mediterranean Studies)

18

Coffee

Coffee Chronicles:
From the Ottoman Majesty to European Elegance

In the vast canvas of human history, the discovery and subsequent spread of coffee paints a rich tapestry of cultural exchange, myth, and evolution, shimmering like the intricate patterns on a Byzantine mosaic.

As the old Mediterranean tales would have it, the discovery of coffee is cloaked in more legends than facts. Among the myriad stories that waft through the ages like the aroma of freshly brewed coffee, two stand out distinctly.

The Root of All Beans: Ethiopia

Picture a 9th-century Ethiopian shepherd named Kaldi, whose goats became unusually spirited after feasting on the cherries of a peculiar tree. Overcome by curiosity, Kaldi sampled these cherries himself and was filled with a joyous energy, akin to the exuberance his goats displayed. Sharing his discovery with local monks led to a serendipitous twist; when one monk threw the cherries into a fire, disliking the bitter taste, the roasted beans filled the air with an intoxicating aroma. This heralded the birth of the coffee beverage we know today.

A Resonant Aroma through Arabia

Yet, another fable tells of a dervish named Shazeli, exiled and wandering in starvation, who stumbled upon the same miraculous cherries. The drink made from these cherries brought rejuvenation, and soon, tales of the "magical fruit" spread like wildfire.

Whichever story holds the kernel of truth, one thing is certain: coffee began its relentless march across continents, starting with its journey to the Arab Peninsula.

Coffee's Dance with Destiny: The Ottoman Empire

With the expansion of the Ottoman Empire, coffee graced the courts and homes of the Turkish elite. By the late 15th century, the Yemeni Governor Özdemir Pasha introduced its delectable taste to the Ottoman Palace in Istanbul, laying the foundations for a thriving coffee trade. The brew soon became an imperial favorite, with entire teams dedicated to its preparation and even a special rank titled "Chief Coffee Maker." Coffee also permeated the public sphere, with coffeehouses, or "qahveh khaneh," sprouting up. These establishments became centers for intellectual discourse and societal gatherings.

Coffee's European Sojourn

From the grandeur of Istanbul, coffee embarked on a new voyage to Europe. Its first European stop was Venice in 1615, courtesy of Venetian traders. While initially met with skepticism, and even termed a "devil's invention" by some clerics, the intervention of Pope Clement VIII cemented coffee's status in Europe. From the first coffeehouses in Poland, which brewed coffee from beans left behind after the Siege of Vienna, to the thriving coffee culture in England, France, and Germany, coffee's reputation evolved. In England, coffeehouses earned the epithet "Penny Universities" for the intellectual exchanges that could be had for the price of a coffee.

By the 17th century, with coffee's popularity burgeoning, its cultivation couldn't remain confined to the Arabian Peninsula. Efforts to grow coffee were initiated in the Dutch colonies, with successful plantations established in the Indonesian island of Java. A single coffee plant, a gift to King Louis XIV of France, would, in time, lead to the proliferation of coffee cultivation in the Americas.

Tracing coffee's odyssey from Yemen to Makkah, Medinah, Iran, Egypt, and Turkey, and further afield, one witnesses the beautiful dance of cultural exchange, a testament to humanity's shared history and mutual enrichment. Whether introduced to Turkey by Syrian traders in 1554 or through another route, what's undeniable is coffee's intoxicating influence on the tapestry of civilization.

From the vivid landscapes of Ethiopia to the bustling qahveh khanehs of Istanbul, from the grandeur of Venetian trading houses to the intellectual hubs of London, the story of coffee is a tale of exploration, discovery, and shared human experience. A tale that, much like a cup of freshly brewed coffee, invigorates and unites.

Spread of Coffee

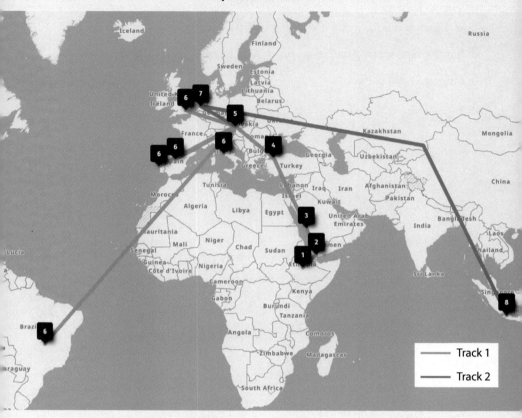

〈Track 1〉

① Ethiopia

② Yemen (Mocha)

③ Saudi Arabia (Mecca)

④ Ottoman Empire (Istanbul)

⑤ Austria

⑥ Italy, the United Kingdom, Spain, Portugal, Brazil

〈Track 2〉

⑤ Austria

⑦ Netherlands

⑧ Indonesia

Scan the QR code
to view the map.

Keywords

Ottoman Empire, Interaction, Coffee House, Trade, Ethiopia, Yemen

References

Çekirdekten Fincana Kahve, Jonathan Morris, Mona, 2021.

Kahve: Topraktan Fincana, Cenk R. Girginol, A7 Kitap, 2017.

Kahvenin Hikayesi: Bir Fincan Kahvenin İzinde Dünya Yolculuğu, Stewart Lee Allen, Mayakitap, 2018.

The World Atlas of Coffee: From Beans to Brewing, James Hoffmann, Firefly Books, 2014.

written by Minji Yang (Busan University of Foreign Studies)

19

Wine

Wine, from origins to spread and global impact

1. The Origin and Meaning of Wine

Wine has become a beverage enjoyed by people all over the world, including Europe, America, Africa, and Asia, due to its delicious flavor and aroma. It has also been used for therapeutic purposes since the time of the ancient Greeks and Egyptians, and the polyphenols in wine have been shown to have antioxidant and anticancer properties, as well as preventing cardiovascular disease. So, let's take a look at how and when wine originated and how it spread throughout Europe and the rest of the world.

The grape, a member of the Vitaceae family, first appeared about 140 million years ago (during the Cretaceous period) and was largely extinct during the Glacial Period. Since then, it has survived in only a few regions: the indigenous species in the East is called Vitis Amurensis, in North America Vitis Labrusca, and in Western Asia Vitis Vinifera. Currently, the main variety of oenological grapes are wines made from variety of Vitis Vinifera, which are strongly associated with Mediterranean and European cultures.

The spontaneous generation theory of wine's origin is probably the most convincing, suggesting that the sugars in the grapes would have come into contact with the many species of wild yeasts on the skins and spontaneously fermented. Then, for thousands of years, people made wine by spontaneous fermentation, crushing the grapes to bring them into contact with the yeasts on the skins.

However, in the 19th century, Louis Pasteur's discovery of the activity of microorganisms (yeast) led to the production of wine in the modern sense of controlled yeast. In this context, "modern wine" refers to the method of brewing wine by controlling the yeast through the use of sulfur dioxide (SO2) and temperature (30-35°C).

The earliest traces of wine-making from variety of Vitis vinifera can be found in Armenia and Georgia during the Mesopotamian Civilization around 6000 BC, where large clay jars were buried and fermented in the ground. In addition, the Syrian capital of Damascus has unearthed presses that are believed to have been used to press fruit and grapes at the time. Later, around 4,000 BC, wine spread throughout Mesopotamia, including Babylonia, Sumeria, and Assyria, where The Epic of Gilgamesh describes workers drinking white and red wine while building ships. By 3,000 BC, wine was being made in Minoan tombs in Crete, the center of the Aegean Civilization, and there are murals in Egypt showing the cultivation of grapes and the production of wine. Later, through the Phoenician, Greek, and Roman periods, vines and wine spread to all parts of Europe, including Italy, France, and Spain.

During the Ancient period, wine was divinized and was a beverage for kings and nobles. In ancient times, wine spread rapidly from Asia Minor to Europe because it was enjoyed by the aristocracy and was often used in religious ceremonies. Evidence of wine brewing has been found in cave burials in Armenia, Minoan tombs in Crete, and the pyramids of the pharaohs in Egypt. Noah was also a grape grower and winemaker by today's standards, as Genesis records that Noah began to farm and plant vines, and he drank wine and became drunk[...]. The red color of wine signified blood, which was symbolic of life or resurrection, and was used in religious ceremonies, burial rites, and for medical purposes. The Greeks worshiped Dionysus, the god of wine, viticulture, fruit, and vegetation, and held rituals and festivals in his honor. Great Greek philosophers and artists such as Platon, Socrates, and Aristotleles loved wine and were inspired by it. The use of wine in religious ceremonies was seen as a way of approaching the gods, and the Greek tradition carried over into the Roman period, where wine was used in religious ceremonies and festivals. By the 4th century, it was part of the Christian citadel ritual.

As we've seen, wine is strongly associated with Hellenistic and Hebraic cultures. France is called the "wine capital of the world" because, from medieval Catholic monks to the present day, the country has continued to develop grape cultivation and vinification methods, selecting and developing many of the world's most popular variety, including Cabernet Sauvignon, Merlot, Pinot Noir, Chardonnay, and Sauvignon Blanc to make quality wine.

2. The origin of wine and its main growing regions

In ancient times, the spread of wine was linked to Mediterranean exchanges, the centerpiece of which was the Phoenicians, who established a maritime kingdom in the Mediterranean. From their colonies around 1,200 BC, they exported a great deal of wine, especially to North Africa, such as Egypt and Algeria, and to southern Europe, such as Italy, France, and Spain, where they also transmitted viticulture and brewing methods.

The Greeks transplanted the Vitis vinifera grape variety to their colonies, spreading viticulture and winemaking to Italy, Germany, France, Spain, Portugal, and into the Balkans and Central Europe. Primarily, vines were grown in areas where Roman soldiers were stationed to fulfill their wine needs. In ancient Greece and Rome, 900-100 BC, clay jars called 'Amphorae' were used to store and transport wine. In particular, large Amphorae were loaded onto Roman merchant ships and traded across the Mediterranean to Africa, India, and China.

Ancient Greek and Roman viticulture and brewing techniques were passed on to Italy and France, especially in the Middle Ages, where they were developed and taught in French monasteries. In France, the Roman Empire introduced grapes to the French region between the 1st and 4th centuries AD, and in the 8th century, Emperor Charlemagne encouraged the production of wine.

In modern times, France established the Bordeaux wine classification in 1855 and the INAO in 1935 (which created the AOC) to improve quality by controlling wine's origin. France currently has a cultivation area of 840,000 ha, the world's 1st to 2nd largest production along with Italy. The main growing regions in France are Bordeaux and Bourgogne. On the left coast of

Bordeaux, the main growing region is Haut-Médoc, and the main variety is Cabernet Sauvignon, which has aromas of black fruits such as black currants and plums and oak, and the wines are dark in color and have strong tannins. On the right bank, the main regions are Pomerol and Saint-Emilion, where the main varietal, Merlot, has ripe plum and oud flavors and soft tannins. In Burgundy(Bourgonge), the main growing region is the Côte de Nuits, where the main varietal, Pinot Noir, has raspberry flavors, light tannins, and a lighter color. The Côte de Beaune also grows more Chardonnay than Pinot Noir. In addition to the above regions, France produces a variety of white wines, including the Syrah variety in the Rhône, Cabernet Franc in the Loire, Sparkling Wine in Champagne, and Riesling in Alsace.

Italy now produces wine in all 20 provinces. Of the three major regions, Toscana, the most prolific, produces wines primarily from the Sangiovese grape; Pimonte, the most DOCG-rated, produces Nebbiolo; Veneto produces Corvina. Other regions include Valle D'Aosta, Lombardia, Trentino-Alto Adige, and Friuli-Venezia-Giulia. And most countries in Europe produce quality wines from a variety of regions. For example, Germany makes wines from the Riesling and Spaetburgunder variety, with the main regions being Mosel, Pfalz, and Baden. Spain's main regions include Rioja, La Mancha, and Penedes. Portugal's regions include Verde, Douro, and Madeira, while Germany produces primarily white wines from a number of regions, including Mosel-Saar-Ruwer, Rheingau, and Rheinhessen. Austria produces a variety of wines from its eastern border region, Hungary from Tokaj, Slovenia from Podravje, and Greece from Mavrodaphne.

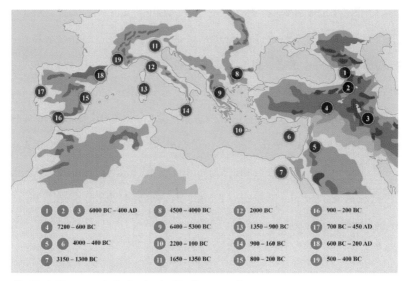

Fig 19–1. The spread of wine in the Mediterranean[1]

❶ ❷ ❸ 6000 BC – 400 AD	❽ 4500 – 4000 BC	⓬ 2000 BC	⓰ 900 – 200 BC
❹ 7200 – 600 BC	❾ 6400 – 5300 BC	⓭ 1350 – 900 BC	⓱ 700 BC – 450 AD
❺ ❻ 4000 – 400 BC	❿ 2200 – 100 BC	⓮ 900 – 160 BC	⓲ 600 BC – 200 AD
❼ 3150 – 1300 BC	⓫ 1650 – 1350 BC	⓯ 800 – 200 BC	⓳ 500 – 400 BC

3. The Spread of Wine and Key Events

The two main events that led to the spread of wine around the world were the expansion of Christianity and the influence of the Age of Exploration. After the ancient Greek and Roman periods, wine continued to develop and spread in the Middle Ages, and the reason for this was the expansion of Christianity.

1) The expansion of Christianity and wine

In 312 AC, Christianity became an official religion under Emperor Constantinus I, and in 380 it became the state religion. Christ's first miracle

---

1 https://www.mdpi.com/2571-9408/5/2/43

was turning 6 jars of water into wine at a wedding, and wine was served by Christ at the Last Supper. In the Christian Eucharist, the wine symbolizes Christ's blood and the bread symbolizes his body. "This wine is my blood, which will be poured out to forgive the sins of many and begin the new agreement from God to his people." -Gospel of Matthew 26:28-30-. As wine was used in key rituals, both Catholic and Orthodox churches focused on wine growing and production. For this reason, in the 4th and 5th centuries, monks in Italy, France, and the Byzantine Empire also worked hard to develop the art of growing grapes and brewing.

2) The Age of Sail and Wine

During the Age of Exploration, Christianity spreads across the globe, and wine became a centerpiece of trade between nations. With wine's strong association with Christianity, it was natural for it to expand during the Age of Exploration. From 1492 to the 16th century, it spreads to the New World in South and North America. Spanish conquistadors crossed the Atlantic, bringing viticulture to Mexico and Brazil, and wine spread throughout South America, with Spanish missionaries establishing the first wineries in Chile.

Wine in North America was also influenced by the Age of Exploration, with Europeans planting grapes beginning in the 16th century. In California, Spanish missionary Junipero Serra first planted grapes at his mission in San Diego in the late 18th century, and the Spanish established the first winery in Sonoma in 1805. California's Mediterranean climate and lack of phylloxera made grape cultivation a success, but it failed in places like Virginia and

Canterbury to the east. In the 17th century, grape cultivation began in South Africa, and in the 18th and 19th centuries, it spread to Australia and New Zealand. In Australia, Captain Arthur Phillip first cultivated it in the Hunter Valley of New South Wales in 1788 and succeeded in 1820, and in the early 19th century, Scottish-born James Busby brought grape seedlings from Europe and cultivated them in Australia and planted some in New Zealand, establishing the first winery in New Zealand in 1836.

3) The wine crisis and the rise of New World wines

There was an event that put European wine at great risk: the Phylloxera outbreak in England in 1863. Phylloxera is a type of aphid that parasitizes on the roots of vines and sucks the sap out of them, eventually killing the tree. The pest was brought over from the United States when vine seedlings were imported to the United Kingdom, and has nearly devastated vineyards in Europe, including 70% of vineyards in France that were not resistant to Phylloxera. Fortunately, Thomas Volney Munson of Texas devised a method of grafting European Vitis Vinifera scions onto American Vitis Labrusca vine rootstocks, which were resistant to phylloxera, and phylloxera was eradicated from Europe.

New World wines toppled European wines at a wine tasting that New York Times journalist George Taber called "The Judgment of Paris". Held on May 24, 1976, at the Intercontinental Hotel in Paris, the blind tasting resulted in an upset, with an American wine that was considered inferior to its European counterparts taking first place, beating out the established European wines. In the white wine category, a number of California wineries beat out Bordeaux and Burgundy wines for top 10 honors, with California's Château Montelena and Stag's Leap Wine Cellars, also in California, taking first place in the red wine category. This was not only a victory for California wines, but also a call to action for New World wines and their potential for success.

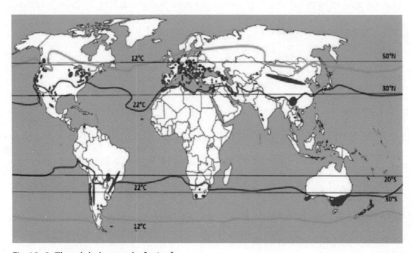

Fig 19–2. The global spread of wine[2]

4. The geographic spread of wine and its impact on human history

Today, wine is grown all over the world, including the Americas, Asia, Africa, Australia, and New Zealand, and has become a global beverage due to the growth of international trade and transportation networks. These wines spread to Europe during the Greek and Roman periods, and then to the New World during the Age of Sail, where wineries settled and developed as the New

2 www.researchgate.net/figure/Wine-producing-regions-of-the-world-Source_fig1_268328620

World was colonized. Let's take a look at some of the major growing regions, variety, and wines that were created as a result of this geographic spread.

Bordeaux's Cabernet Sauvignon and Merlot variety were brought to the United States, where they produce quality wines primarily in Napa Valley and Sonoma Valley. The style of wine here is dark in color, tannic, and weighty, an ideal environment for the Bordeaux variety. In Chile, these Bordeaux variety are also used alone and in blends to produce premium wines, typically with ripe black fruit flavors such as black cherry and blackberry. Key regions include the Maipo Valley, Colchagua, and Cachapoal.

The main Pinot Noir growing regions in the New World are Oregon and California in the United States, Central Otago and Marlborough in New Zealand, and Australia, where the variety produces light red wines with flavors of raspberries and cherries. Sauvignon Blanc, especially in New Zealand, produces fresh white wines with green fruit and gooseberry flavors. Syrah, the main varietal in the Rhone region of France, is a dark-colored, tannic wine, which is also used in Australia to produce Shiraz wines with violet and mint flavors. Other regions include Argentina, where the Malbec varietal produces wines with black fruits, and South Africa, which produces a unique red wine with coffee flavors from the Pinotage variety. Similarly, the wines of the New World use the Vitis vinifera variety, but differences in geography and terroir give each region a distinctive flavor. In addition to the above regions, wine is also produced in Eastern Europe, North Africa, and Asia (Korea, Japan, etc.) Today, wine is produced in many countries around the world, each with its own unique growing environment (climate, soil), wine-making methods, and different styles of wine.

From ancient times to the present day, wine has had a profound impact on cultural exchanges between the West and the East, and on industries and economies. Even today, wine is a global beverage that is commonly consumed for communion, although it is sometimes used for ceremonial purposes in religious events. The impact that wine has had and continues to have on humanity is ongoing and immense. In ancient times, grape cultivation and wine-making techniques were brought to the Greek and Roman colonies, and during the Age of Sail, wine expanded beyond Europe to the continents of the world, making it more than a trade but an industry. The globalization of the wine industry has created diverse and competitive markets, increased consumer choice, and spread the culture of wine drinking by creating jobs and economic growth in rural areas where grapes are grown and wineries are located. This spread of culture has led to cultural exchange and communication between different regions and communities. There are also numerous studies showing that wine has antioxidant and anti-cancer benefits, as well as preventing and treating certain diseases, such as heart disease. Wine is also used directly in cooking to change the flavor and style of food, and as a way to complete the palate through wine and food pairings.

However, the future of wine is not all rosy. Since the 2000s, there has been a global oversupply of wine, which has led to price competition and a decline in wine prices. This oversupply has also had a negative impact on the environment, including the use of pesticides and other chemicals and the depletion of water resources. To solve these problems, it will be necessary to change to increase the quality of wine rather than the quantity and to grow and vinify organic grapes sustainably. In addition, due to climate change, it is possible to grow grapes in Antarctica, so traditional production areas are in crisis, and it is difficult to find new production areas.

Spread of Wine

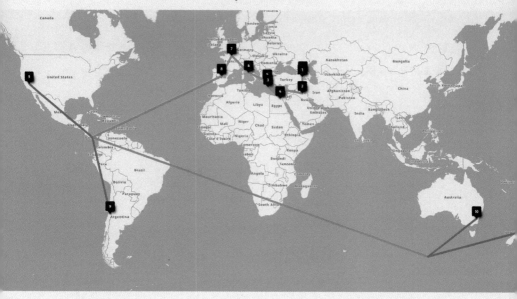

① Armenia & Georgia

② Mesopotamia (Babylonia, Sumeria)

③ Crete

④ Egypt

⑤ Greece & Rome

⑥ Italy

⑦ France

⑧ Spain

⑨ California & Chile

⑩ Australia & New Zealand

Scan the QR code
to view the map.

Keywords

Wine, Grape, origins, spread, impact, Vitis Vinifera, viticulture, winemaking, Bordeaux, Bourgogne

References

김대철, 『와인과 포도』, 한올출판사, 2009.

케빈즈랠리, 『와인 바이블』, 정미나 옮김, 한스미디어, 2008.

휴 존슨 · 잰시스 로빈슨, 『와인 아틀라스』, 세종서적 편집부 · 인트랜스 번역원 옮김, 세종서적, 2009.

박교선 외 5명 「포도학 개론」, RAD Interrobanbang (77집), 2012.

ONAGLIA Frédérick, Le Secret des cépages, Roman, 2004.

RETOURNARD Denis, La vigne, Rustica, 2010.

REYNIER Alain, Manuel de viticulture, Lavoisier, 2007.

Online References

Mkrtich Harutyunyan, 〈The Rise of Wine among Ancient Civilizations across the Mediterranean Basin〉, Heritage 5(2), 2022, pp.788-812.

https://doi.org/10.3390/heritage5020043

https://www.mdpi.com/2571-9408/5/2/43

www.researchgate.net/figure/Wine-producing-regions-of-the-world-Source_fig1_268328620

written by NamMo Jung (Korea Maritime & Ocean University)

20

Paper

Paper Exchange and Paper Road

Paper is one of mankind's most monumental inventions. When writing met paper, the writing culture began, and the history of mankind began to be recorded.

We know from history that wherever paper has reached, learning and culture have developed without exception. Therefore, the transmission and exchange of paper is consistent with the development of human civilizations, the transmission and the exchange. In other words, the exchange and spread of paper is another manifestation of the exchange and development of human culture.

Paper, made in China, spread eastward to the Korean Peninsula and Japan and westward to Central Asia, India, Persia, the Arab-Islamic world, Europe, and the Americas.

It is also interesting to note that the eastward spread of paper was relatively peaceful, either through commercial trade (China→Korean Peninsula, 4th century CE) or the introduction of advanced civilizations (Korean Peninsula→Japan, 7th century

CE), whereas the westward spread was primarily through wars, such as Thales War (China→Arab Islamic World, 751 CE), the Arab conquest of Andalusia and Sicily, and Crusade War(Arab Islamic World→European Christian World, 8th-12th century CE). In other words, paper represents all the main phenomena that lead to the exchange of civilizations.

The Chinese, Central Asians, Persians, Arabs, and Latins participated in the paper road. They were the protagonists of human civilization in their periods, and it is no exaggeration to say that their history is the history of human civilization. Therefore paper road is the process of the development of human civilization through contact and exchanges.

The Origin and Development of Paper

In Mesopotamia around 3,000 BCE, during the Neolithic period, the Sumerians created the first writing system(cuneiform), but the writing mediums were primitive, such as clay tablets and animal skins. Although writing was created, it wasn't enough for a writing culture to develop.

In the 3rd century BCE, the Ptolemaeos Dynasty(305-30 BCE) in Egypt built the largest library on earth in the city of Alexandria, recording and preserving knowledge from around the world. The material used for writing was primarily papyrus. Later, Eumenes II (ruled 197-159 BCE) of the Anatolian kingdom of Pergamon built a large library with a capacity of 200,000 volumes. But as papyrus was not readily available, he used parchment from sheep, cow, and deer skins as a recording medium. In India, palm leaf was used as a recording material.

Under these circumstances, the invention of paper was a land-marking event in the history of human civilization. It ushered in an era of written culture and dramatically improved the dissemination of learning and knowledge. The invention of paper was a revolutionary event comparable to the invention of computers and the Internet in the 20th century.

It is commonly believed that paper was created by Chae Lun (estimated 50-121 CE), an eunuch of Emperor He of Han (79-106 CE) of the Eastern Han dynasty (25-220 CE) in China. In the Eastern Han dynasty, records were mainly written on silk, bamboo, and wooden tablets, but these materials were either expensive or less convenient. Chae Lun became aware of the inefficiencies and inconveniences of these written media and sought ways to improve them, so he created a paper made from vegetable fibres such as bark, burlap, and fishing nets and presented it to the emperor, which is believed to be the first paper in human history. Chae Lun had discovered the art of paper making.

However, archaeological research and discoveries have shown that paper was already being made and used during the Han Dynasty (BCE202 - CE8), and Chae Lun made improvements to it.

In the 4th century CE, it seems that paper made significant advancements in quality, although not yet in mass production. Materials were diversified, the quality of paper improved, and paper began to be used in the Korean Peninsula. In the 6th century CE, paper was made with added sap to prevent insects from gnawing on it, and in the 7th century CE, the world's first colored paper was made on the Korean peninsula (Dard Hunter. 1936).

This improved-quality paper was traded at a high price and was exported via the Silk Road from the Korean Peninsula to the Central Asia, and the Arab Islamic world. Naturally, manufacturing methods were strictly controlled. It can be argued that paper plays a major role in China's status as the birthplace of human civilization.

The Spread of Paper

It was not until the mid-8th century CE that paper reached the outside world, particularly the Arabs. In the 7th century CE, the Tang dynasty was expanding its territory to the west, while the Arab Islamic states of the Umayyad Dynasty (660-750 CE) and Abbasid Dynasty (750-1458 CE) were expanding to the east.

Finally the Tang Dynasty and Islamic kingdoms clashed at Talas, in present-day Kyrgyzstan, in 751 CE. The Tang army was led by Gao Xianzhi(? - 755), a native of Goguryeo, and the Arab Islamic army was led by Abu Muslim(718 - 755), a native of Persia. The war, as the first war in history between Chinese and Arab muslim forces, ended in victory for the Arab Islamic forces.

War is a military confrontation, but in a civilizational implications, it is also a major factor in the exchange of civilizations. In other words, war is an important opportunity for civilizations to come into contact with each other, not only in terms of weapons and military technology but also in terms of systems, cultural and academic achievements, and customs.

Through the Battle of Thales, the achievements of the Tang Dynasty, which was culturally and academically advanced at the time, were transmitted to the Arab muslim forces. Among the Tang soldiers taken prisoner by the muslim force were paper-makers, and with their help, the first paper factory was built in Samarkand in 757 CE.

The Arab Islamic world had the opportunity to utilize captured paper-makers from the Battle of Talas to produce paper. Furthermore, Samarkand in Uzbekistan was at the center of the Silk Road and had an ample supply of plant fibres, such as mulberry trees, suitable for paper-making. In other words, the Arab muslim powers had won the war and gained access to both paper-making technology and a suitable location for a paper factory.

The paper factory in Samarkand was the first paper factory in history to be built outside of China. Paper had finally crossed the Pamirs, the border between the Tang dynasty and the Arab Islamic world. Samarkand paper produced by the factory spread throughout the Islamic world, quickly replacing parchment and papyrus. Samarkand paper signalled the globalisation of paper.

The importation of paper into the Islamic world brought about major changes in the Islamic world. The 3rd orthodox caliph, Uthman(576-656 CE), was the first to write Quran on deerskin attached paper.

Paper was not widespread in Islamic society by the mid-7th century. Since Uthman's Quran predated the full-scale production of Samarkand paper, it is likely that the paper used in Umar's Quran was partly imported from the Tang dynasty.

Caliph Harun al-Rashid(763-809 CE), the 5th caliph of the Abbasid Dynasty, established a paper factory in Baghdad, capital of the Abbasid Dynasty, in 795 CE. Caliph Al-Mamun (786-833 CE), Caliph Harun Rashid's son, founded the 'Bayt Al-Hikmah(House of Wisdom)', a national research and translation institute,

242

where numerous Greek and Roman works were studied and translated.

This process required a convenient recording medium, and paper factories were built to provide for such need. These state policies and an environment that encouraged learning led to the rapid spread of paper throughout the southeastern Mediterranean and Iberian Peninsula, which were under Arab Islamic influence.

In Egypt, the African outpost of Arab Islamic power, paper factories were established around 900 CE. In the 10th century CE, the Fatimid Dynasty (909-1171 CE), an Islamic dynasty in North Africa, founded the 'Dar Al-Hikmah', the Cairo version of the House of Wisdom, which ushered in an era of widespread learning and knowledge.

This process also brought the spread and popularisation of paper, and Egyptian paper-making spread to North Africa via Kairouan in Tunisia and Fes in Morocco.

The spread of paper did not stop in North Africa, but reached the European continent. There were 2 main routes for Arab Islamic forces to reach Europe. The first was crossing the Strait of Gibraltar to the Iberian Peninsula, and the second was through Sicily to the Italian peninsula.

Paper spread to the Islamized Iberian Peninsula, and finally, in 1150, a paper mill was built in Xativa in the eastern Iberian Peninsula. Xativa has traditionally been an area of early development of the textile industry including linen, so it had the good environment for a paper factory. This is the moment when paper spreads to Europe.

When the Arabs conquered Sicily, they brought advanced agricultural techniques with them, including Arab crops, irrigation, and paper. Paper crossed the strait of Messina and spread to the Italian peninsula, where paper factories were built all over the peninsular. Paper factories were established in Fabriano(1276), Montefano(1276), and Bologna(1295).

From the Italian peninsula, paper-making continued to move north and spread to Germany. In Germany, Paper factories were built in Mainz(1320), Cologne(1320), and Nuremberg(1336). In France, paper factories were built in Troyes(1348), and in England, built in Hertfordshire(1498).

Paper made in China around the 2nd century CE finally arrived in Europe after long trip through Central Asia, Persia, and the Arab world for 1,200 years.

Gutenberg(Johannes Gutenberg, 1398~1468) developed the technology of metal movable type, which led to the popularisation and widespread of printing, and thus the demand for paper grew rapidly. This was the beginning of the Renaissance in the East and Europe, a period of revival of learning and culture, and it was paper that laid the foundation.

The Civilizational Importance of Paper

The history of mankind can be divided into prehistoric and historic periods, and the historic period began with record. Recording requires characters and writing materials, and when these 2 elements come together, the age of writing begins.

Paper is not just a recording material, but a medium for culture, learning, and knowledge systems. Wherever culture and learning flourished, paper was needed for recording, and the spread of paper meant the development of learning and knowledge. In other words, paper is the record and witness of human civilization. The paper shows all the various forms of civilizational exchange. Chinese paper illustrates the phenomenon of civilizational exchange, which involves both peaceful trade and war. No matter what form it took, paper was an essential commodity in the universal human culture and knowledge system, so it was accepted without resistance in the receiving country and continued to develop in the second and third stages. In the case of trade through warfare, the traded goods would be resisted for a period of time in the host country, but paper assimilated quickly enough to cause voluntary acceptance and continued to develop in the process of exchange and diffusion.

Chinese paper evolved into dyed paper on the Korean peninsula, and in the Arab world and Europe, it contributed to the invention of metal type as well as mass production through paper factories. In other words, paper is a living reminder that civilizations advance through exchange.

It is also encouraging to note that Koreans made a significant contribution to the development of paper in China and its spread to neighbouring regions. Koreans played an important role in the spread of paper. Paper was introduced to the Korean Peninsula around the 4th century CE, and was brought to Japan by Dam Jing, a Korean Buddhist priest in the 7th century CE, and the commander of Tang Dynasty force at the Battle of Thales, who brought paper from China to the Arab world, was Gao Xianzhi from Goguryeo. In addition, Koreans also invented the world's first dyed paper by improving on paper imported from China. Namely, Korea played an important role and contribution in the development and exchange of paper.

Spread of Paper

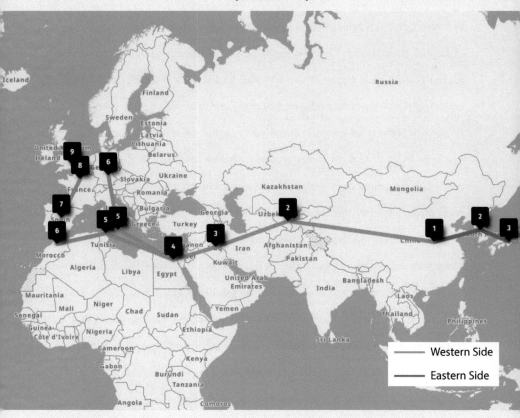

〈Western Side〉

① China (Luoyang)

② Uzbekistan (Samarkand)

③ Iraq (Baghdad)

④ Egypt

⑤ Tunisia / Italy (Sicily)

⑥ Morocco (Fez) / Germany (Nuremberg)

⑦ Spain

⑧ France

⑨ the United Kingdom

〈Eastern Side〉

① China (Luoyang)

② the Korean Peninsula

③ Japan (Heijo–kyo)

Scan the QR code
to view the map.

Keywords

Paper, Chae Lun, Thales, Crusades

References

Cho, Hyung-gyun (ed.). 2002. 『Paper Road』. Yedam. Chin Shunshin. 1997. Paper
    Road. Japan. Shueisha.

Dard Hunter. 1936. *A Papermaking Pilgrimage to Japan, Korea and China*. Pynson
    Printers.

Jung, Soo-il. 2001. 2001. 『Silk Road Studies』. Seoul. Creation and Critical History.

https://www.strathmoreartist.com/blog-reader/the-history-of-paper-how-paper-is-
    made.html

https://pbs.twimg.com/media/D8psZsQVUAE47BA?format=jpg&name=medium

written by YongSoo Yoon (Busan University of Foreign Studies)

21

Potato

The Potato in the Mediterranean

The potato, scientifically known as 'Solanum tuberosum', is native to the Andes Mountains in South America. Indigenous peoples in this region had cultivated and consumed potatoes for thousands of years. The potato plant was highly adaptable to the harsh mountainous terrain and became a staple crop for these communities. The Inca Empire, in particular, is often credited with promoting potato cultivation and developing various potato varieties.

The "discovery" of the New World by Christopher Columbus in 1492 opened the way for the introduction of a wide range of formerly unknown plants to Europe. When the Spaniards entered the Andes in1532, they got in contact with the potato plant. The first written record of the potato dates to 1537 in a region that belongs today to Columbia. It remains unclear when the potato arrived first in Europe. It is often assumed that the Spaniards brought it back to their homeland, where it was introduced to other European and Mediterranean countries. However, based on the available information, which is very limited, this is only speculation. Evidenced is the cultivation of potatoes in the second half of the 16th century in Gran Canaria and Tenerife, both part of the Canary Islands archipelago, and the export of potatoes from both islands to the city of Rouen in France and the city of Antwerp in Belgium. Therefore, it seems that the potato was not introduced to Europe through the Spanish mainland but via the Canary Islands.

The plant spread across the entire European continent over the next few decades, but not for providing staples to the population. The plant was rather seen as an exotic specimen, often grown for ornamental purposes. Even after it was understood that the tubers were the edible part of the plant, they were initially only consumed in times of shortages to prevent starvation. The frequent wars in late Medieval and early modern Europe had a huge impact on the population of the warring countries. Grain storages on the countryside were easy targets for the acquisition of food for the military whilst potatoes, if kept in the ground, were more difficult to obtain in large numbers. The chance that some of the tubers were left was much bigger and thus the basis of existence for the farmers was not completely destroyed. It is this circumstance and the high nutrition of the potato that led to an increase of the population in North-European countries. In some cases, the cultivation of the plant was even promoted and carried out under royal order, as famously known from the kingdom of Prussia.

Today, potatoes are an important crop in the Mediterranean region, where they can be cultivated throughout the year. However, yields are generally lower than in Northern European countries due to different environmental and agro-economic conditions. Water is important for the growth of the tubers, and some Mediterranean regions, due to the scarcity of this resource, are not suitable for growing the plant. Additionally, the storage of the potato in warmer regions can be a problem, as slight warm weather conditions spur the fast growth of new shoots from the tuber. Generally, even under good conditions, potatoes cannot be stored for a longer period in contrast to grains.

Despite these limitations, potatoes are an integral part of different Mediterranean cuisines, each with its unique flavors and ingredients, appearing as the main or a side ingredient. In Lebanon, for instance, 'Potato Kibbeh' is an iconic dish made from mashed potatoes, bulgur, a blend of spices, and fresh coriander. Crossing over to Syria, potatoes may be stuffed with ground lamb, a drizzle of pomegranate syrup, pine nuts, sumac - a red spice with a lemony taste -, and mint. Greek cuisine, too, makes use of the versatility of potatoes, often filling them with savory sausages. An essential Greek potato-based speciality is 'Skordalia', a garlic-and-potato sauce with the consistency of mayonnaise. A version of the famous Greek 'Moussaka' contains layers of potatoes in combination with ground meat and aubergines fused with a tomato and a bechamel sauce. In Turkey, 'Patates Silkmesi', or "shaken" potatoes, emerged as a remarkable dish. Thinly sliced potatoes are combined with lamb, onions, and tomatoes seasoned with a blend of cumin, red pepper, and black pepper. The dish earns its name from the occasional pan shaking to prevent sticking. In Sicily, 'Patate a sfincione', is a typical dish of potatoes with sweet red onions, tomatoes, and oregano. Gnocchi, a potato-based pasta, is eaten all over Italy, but its origin is probably in the north of the country (figure 1).

Fig 21–1. Gnocchi with tomato sauce, a popular Italian dish.[1]

Spain, whose people were responsible for bringing the potato across the Atlantic Ocean, developed its own recipes as well. Notably, 'Atascaburras' which is a simple combination of salt cod and potatoes, simmered with garlic and walnuts. 'Patatas en salsa verde', originally a dish from the Basque Country, involves cooking potatoes with garlic and parsley, often served alongside grilled fish. For those observing Lent, the traditional annual fasting period in Christendom, there is 'Patatas viudas', or "widowed" potatoes, a meatless dish with tomatoes, green bell peppers, garlic, onion, oregano, paprika, cayenne pepper, and parsley. A famous and well-known tapas dish is 'Patatas bravas', crispy fried potatoes with a spicy sauce of paprika and sometimes tomatoes (figure 2). Many more dishes could be mentioned, but this short, incomplete enumeration indicates that the potato is an integral part of many different Mediterranean cuisines. It has been combined with local spices

1 Foto by MaximusTG 2011

and ingredients, which led to the emergence of new and exciting creations, exactly as can be seen in all the other manifold cultural influences in the Mediterranean region.

Fig 21–2. Patatas Bravas: Fried potatoes with a spicy sauce, a common Spanish dish.[2]

The journey of the potato through the Mediterranean is one of several examples for the interconnection between humans, crops, and the environment. From its initial introduction as an exotic plant to its integration as a staple food source, the potato's story underlines the impact of a crop plant on society and how it influenced the course of history. Although the Mediterranean faces new environmental challenges, the cultivation and use of the potato will remain an integral part of the region's food culture.

---

2 Foto by Lobo 2010.

Keywords

Mediterranean cuisine, Andes, Spain, potato dishes, staple food

References

Frusciante, L., Amalia Barone, D. Carputo and P. Ranalli. 1999. "Breeding and physiological aspects of potato cultivation in the Mediterranean region." *Potato Research* 42: 265-277.

Hawkes, J.G. and J. Francisco-Ortega. 1993. "The early history of the potato in Europe," *Euphytica* 70: 1-7.

Lobo. 2010. "Plato de patatas bravas con salsa picante." Wikimedia Commons, https://commons.wikimedia.org/wiki/File:Patatas_bravas_madrid.jpg

MaximusTG. 2011. "A bowl of "gnocchi di patate" with a tomato-chorizo sauce, with red bell pepper. Seasoned with some seasalt, pepper and basil." Wikimedia Commons, https://commons.wikimedia.org/wiki/File:Gnocchidipatate.jpg

McNeill, William H. 1999. "How the Potato Changed the World's History," *Social Research* 66, No. 1: 67-83.

Salaman, Redcliffe N. 1949. *The History and Social Influence of the Potato*. Cambridge: Cambridge University Press.

Wright, Clifford A. 2001. *Mediterranean vegetables: a cook's compendium of all the vegetables from the world's healthiest cuisine*. Boston: The Harvard Common Press.

written by Sebastian Müller (Busan University of Foreign Studies)

253

▼

Science and Technologies

22

Wheel

Before the 1850s, the steam engine was considered one of the greatest inventions in the world. But by 1950, an even older invention, the wheel, was getting more attention than the steam engine.[1] Historically, the wheel has always been regarded as one of mankind's greatest inventions. Many people consider the wheel as the most important object in human history. Wheels have created a variety of means of transportation and made it possible for people to travel farther and faster. As a result, roads connecting villages were created, markets were formed, and cities were built. In addition, roads connecting cities and cities were created, and trade routes for exchanges between countries were created.[2] The wheel is a great tool and invention that builds new civilizations and enables exchanges between civilizations through communication between civilizations, and connects modern civilized societies.

There have been several great migrations since the advent of mankind.

---

1 『바퀴, 세계를 굴리다(The Wheel: Inventions & Reinventions)』. MID. Richard W. Bulliet. (2016)
2 『모든 움직이는 것들의 과학(The Science of All Moving Things)』. 사과나무(apple tree). 한근우 (Keun-Woo Han). (2018)

Movement itself is not an exchange between civilizations. However, historically, it is true that the result of this great movement has led to exchanges. Large-scale movement is bound to have limitations due to environmental or technological problems. The 'wheel' is a device that helps overcome these problematic factors. The wheel made it possible to overcome physical limitations in the great migration of mankind. And it is safe to say that exchanges between civilizations through the first great migration of mankind began with the invention of the wheel.

Around 4000 BC, the Sumerians built one of the world's four major civilizations and the first human civilization in Mesopotamia, known as the Fertile Crescent between the Tigris and Euphrates rivers in the Arabian Peninsula. At this time, traces of wheeled vehicles have been discovered by archaeologists in the civilized areas of Mesopotamia and Central Europe. The wheel appeared with the first human civilization. In fact, it is known that even before Mesopotamian civilization, logs or trees were cut wide to carry loads in the form of planks. Also, around 5000 B.C., it is said that a wheel in the form of a round disk, like the present wheel, was used.

Relatedly, the ancient Indo-Europeans, who are known to be the ancestors of modern Europeans, are known to be the most prominent nomads of early humans. Unlike humans in ancient Egypt, the Indus, and the Huanghe(黃河) civilization, this people did not develop agricultural cultivation technology, so they lived mainly by hunting. Hunting was their first goal and strategy for survival. For a stable food supply that could replace agriculture, they had to constantly move, and for this, a groundbreaking technology or tool, that is, a wheel, would have been needed.[3]

Around 4000 B.C., they began to domesticate animals using wheels, and were able to lead a nomadic life without difficulty by creating a means of transportation that combined livestock and wheels. Their great movement began with horses loading luggage, livestock, and people and pulling wheeled carts. The invention of the wheel made long-distance movement and large-scale transportation of goods possible, and exchanges between civilizations gained momentum. Many scholars agree that the wheel is one of the greatest man-made tools. Wheels contributed to the construction of great civilizations such as architecture, warfare, trade and transport, transportation and industry, and it is also true that the exchange of civilizations was facilitated by means of wheeled vehicles.

Tools of Civilization Building

Around 6,000 B.C., before the advent of the wheel, people in the north of Europe found it inefficient to move things with human physical power, so they moved things with animal power instead of people. For example, by having a cow pull a wooden sled. In ancient Egypt, before wheels, rollers were used to move objects or move on uneven floors. It was made in the form of a wooden sled by supporting a round log-shaped support at the bottom of the wooden sled, so it could be effectively used on slopes or muddy roads. Ancient Egypt was able to move huge marble in this way, and through this, it was

---

3 『역사를 뒤흔든 7가지 대이동(7 great migrations that shook history)』. 현암사(hyeonamsa). 北京大陸橋文化傳媒. (2010)

possible to build the pyramids, which can be called the symbol of Egyptian civilization. The ancient Egyptians built huge pyramids with great precision and without major errors through their own scientific and technical methods, and the technology used here was weights and measures measure of the size and volume of stones and the distance of the pyramids. It is indeed surprising that the pyramid was built with only knowledge and labor, such as setting units based on the human body and using logs as leverage, without any tools for measurement. An example of using a log-shaped rolling table to move huge objects can also be found in Stonehenge in England. If you refer to the description of the construction of the pyramid civilization mentioned above, you can guess how the huge stones in [Figure 1, Figure 2] were transported.

Fig 22–1. pyramid   Fig 22–2. Stonehenge ww.pixabay.com

A megalithic temples refers to a temples in which a huge stone is carved and elaborately processed. The last of these megalithic temples can be found on the Mediterranean islands of Marta, Gozo, and Sarnena. Research suggests that the most recent date to around 1500 B.C., and the oldest to around 4000 B.C. In the construction of these temples megaliths weighing 20 tons each and stone pillars measuring 6 meters per pillar were used. This leads us to guess that the wheel was used in the process of moving the megalith through the wheel marks remaining around the temples.[4] As such, it can be assumed that the wheel was directly used in ancient civilizations, especially in architecture, and that the wheel was used as a tool for constructing civilization.

Civilization exchange seen through wheels

Archaeologist Stuart Ernest Piggott says that the wheel was invented in Mesopotamia. This is because images that can be seen as means of transportation with wheels were found in Mesopotamian paintings and textiles. However, it is known that there are no archaeological data for wheeled transportation in the ancient Egyptian civilization, which flourished at the same time.[5] It is already known that the two civilizations came into contact through trade, but was there no exchange about the wheel? It can be assumed that the use of the wheel was different due to the circumstances of the times, although the necessity was not fully recognized politically and socially, or the necessity was recognized. Richard W. Bulliet, an American historian and author of "The Wheel Turns the World," believes that Mesopotamian wheels were used to show off the dignity of kings and priests, not as a popular means of transport or carrying loads. . Also, he says, the wheels weren't very effective

---

4 『세상에서 가장 재미있는 문명지도(The most interesting civilization map in the world)』. Book Story. Susumu Shimazaki (2010)

5 Author of 『바퀴, 세계를 굴리다(The Wheel: Inventions & Reinventions)』

due to their geography, so they probably weren't widely used in practice.[6] This can be confirmed through the remains of a statue of a god being transported by a sled-type mobile tool on an Egyptian mural dating from around 1300 B.C.

Fig 22-3. medieval cart

Ancient Egypt is said to have introduced wheeled chariots as a means of transportation for the pharaohs around 1600 BC. Given that the first wheels originated in Mesopotamia, this is very surprising.[7] As such, there are not few cases of civilizations that did not actively introduce the wheel even after knowing the existence of the wheel. Representative traces of wheels appearing in archaeological relics excavated from various areas of ancient civilizations were used as toys or ornaments rather than as means of movement or transportation.

---

6 In areas where sandy beaches or roads are uneven, transportation using livestock was probably more
   convenient than wheels.

7 『모든 시작의 역사(The history of all beginnings)』, 김영사(Gimmyoungsa). Jurgen Kaube. (2019)

Without the war, it seems that the wheel could have developed more slowly than expected. In places where there are no properly maintained roads, wheels are not a good means of transporting or carrying loads. Rather, livestock may be a better means. However, as conquest activities such as wars became frequent, the wheels used for chariots needed to be faster, stronger, and simpler. This was the most important factor in the technological development of the wheel.

Exchanges between civilizations may or may not occur depending on the extent to which the goals pursued by the society and the way of life coincide. There are exchanges by necessity, but there are also forced exchanges caused by war and conquest, and there are various forms of exchange. Among the Sumerians, Akkadians, Babylonians, and Assyrians known to have built the Mesopotamian civilization, the Sumerians used both disc-shaped four-wheeled carts and two-wheeled carts.[8] In particular, relatively light two-wheeled carts were used in warfare, but disc-shaped wheels were thick and heavy and were not suitable for maneuverability, so they were not effective on the battlefield. Around 3000 B.C., ancient Indo-Europeans entered the Anatolian Peninsula, which is now Asia Minor, and established the Anatolian civilization. Later they were called Hittites. The Hittites, the first people of the iron age, developed bronze technology (metallurgy) by utilizing the abundant mineral resources of Anatolia. Looking at the iron weapons they left behind and the chariots equipped with spokes, it can be seen that metallurgy in handling bronze and

---

8 It appears that horses could not be tamed during the time when the Sumerians were active.

iron was excellent. In particular, a spoke chariots were excellent in mobility and played a large role in their conquest activities. Later, wheel civilization equipped with spokes quickly spread to the surrounding areas, influencing chariots of the Egyptian kingdom and Greco-Roman times. Considering that ancient conquest activities were mainly made up of war, the development of spoked chariots and wheel technology was one of the most important factors that led to victory in war. Later, in the the Greek-Roman period, chariots were used for various means of transportation in everyday life as well as for war purposes. Spokes wheel were further developed by the Celts in England around 100 BC. The Celts greatly increased the lifespan and durability of wooden wheels by putting iron plates around the rims of spokes. As a result, the Hittite wheeled chariot can be seen as the beginning of modern wheel technology. Spokes Since the birth of the wheel, the wheel has not been simply a tool of war or a means of transportation. It was used in various ways in everyday life, such as the water wheel or gear wheel, and these phenomena can be collectively defined as wheel civilization.

Fig 22–4. Hittite chariot

Fig 22–5. Sumerian chariots

Greatest invention in history

The wheel is the most historical, mathematical, and scientific tool created by mankind. With the advent of the wheel, could move more, farther, and faster. As a result, a road connecting with other regions was created and a place of exchange where people and people, culture and culture met. The wheel is a means of movement and exchange of civilization. The movement of people was an exchange between civilizations. The knowledge, information, ideas, habits and ways of thinking that a person possesses represent an era. Any area that someone has traveled through on a wheeled cart can become an area where that person's civilization (knowledge, information, way of thinking, etc.) is disseminated. The opposite situation also occurs. In this way, the wheel was the greatest invention to exchange and move civilization. Could the current world map have been completed if the wheel had not been invented?

Keywords

wheel, chariot, civilization, exchange, movement

References

• Book

『바퀴, 세계를 굴리다(The Wheel: Inventions & Reinventions)』. MID. Richard W. Bulliet. (2016)

『세상에서 가장 재미있는 문명지도(The most interesting civilization map in the world)』. Book Story. Susumu Shimazaki (2010)

『역사를 뒤흔든 7가지 대이동(7 great migrations that shook history)』. 현암사

(hyeonamsa). 北京大陸橋文化傳媒. (2010)

『모든 움직이는 것들의 과학(The Science of All Moving Things)』. 사과나무(apple tree). 한근우(Keun-Woo Han). (2018)

『모든 시작의 역사(The history of all beginnings)』. 김영사(Gimmyoungsa). Jurgen Kaube. (2019)

『지도에서 사라진 사람들 : 사라진 민족 사라진 나라의 살아 숨 쉬는 역사(People who disappeared from the map: The living history of a vanished nation and a vanished nation)』. 서해문집(Seohae Literature Collection). 도현신(Do hyun sin). (2014)

Online References

https://terms.naver.com/entry.nhn?docId=3574486&cid=58941&categoryId=58960

Image References

www.pixabay.com
https://commons.wikimedia.org/wiki/File:Hittite_Chariot.jpg
https://commons.wikimedia.org/wiki/File:Standard_of_Ur_-_War.jpg

written by JiHoon Kang (Busan University of Foreign Studies)

23

Metal Type & Printing

Printing as a medium of communication

Humanity's medium of communication has been developed in 4 stages. The first stage was to communicate through gestures and sounds with promised meanings; the second was to create and record various symbols and letters. The third was the publication of books by metal type, and the last was electronic media, which led to the invention of the computer. Metal type has been considered the greatest technical revolution of all invention, since it allowed publication and distribution of books, letting knowledge be transmitted massively.

Printing is a technology that uses ink to reproduce texts, pictures, symbols, etc. drawn on the surface of a plate and print them on paper or other objects. It began in the East with woodblock printing in the early 8th century. The oldest surviving woodblock print is the 'Darani Sutra(無垢淨光大陀羅尼經)', which was printed in Korea in the mid-8th century.

Woodblock printing saved a lot of labor and time compared to the previous handwritten transcription. In addition, it also revolutionized the production of books and the transmission of knowledge. However, printing a book using woodblocks meant that each page had to be engraved, which required a lot of time and wood, as well as space to store the woodblocks, which was a huge financial burden. Metal type printing, which was invented based on the foundation of woodblock printing, resolved these contradictions and greatly improved the efficiency of printing. Type is categorized into earthen type, wood type, and metal type according to its material. Metal calligraphy is further subdivided into bronze, lead, and iron calligraphy, depending on the composition of the metal. In Korea, the bronze type was mainly cast, whereas the lead type was mainly used in Europe, including Gutenberg, Germany.

Metal type printing began in Korea in the early 13th century and spread throughout Europe by the mid-15th century. It is a method of printing by casting a single typeface and typesetting the required characters according to the manuscript. After the book is printed, the printing plates can be dismantled, and the type can be reused until its abrasion to print different types of books. This method was commonly used until the 20th century. It was the primary method of printing books, magazines, newspapers, etc. published worldwide.

Metal type printing has been an important pillar in the development of modern civilization and is often hailed by Westerners as the "mother of civilization." Countries in Europe fought long and hard to claim the honor of inventing the metal type, but in the end, the credit went to Gutenberg, Germany.

From woodblock printing to metal type through the development of photography, the invention of printing presses, the rise of computers, and the widespread use of the internet, printing has evolved to the point today where we can print on everything around us except water and air. The development of printing has had a significant impact on the breakthrough of human civilization and social change through the popularization of information.

As a source of knowledge and information, printing plays a very important role in spreading and inheriting knowledge and technology that are necessary for cultural development. It also plays a major role in preserving and transmitting a country's culture and is a measure of the level of culture and education.

Development of metal type printing

The evolution of printing from handwriting to xylograph printing began with the creation of earthenware-type(膠泥活字) by the Chinese printer Bi Sheng(畢昇) around 1041. It was difficult to succeed due to the difficulties in typesetting and repeated use, such as crumbling by the pressure of rubbing when printing, so it was considered impractical technology as a letterpress, but it is significant that it created the idea of the principle of letterpress, which is printed by making individual letters and typesetting them, unlike woodblock printing. According to Wang Zhen's(王禎) 'Nongseo(農書)' written in 1313, in the 14th century, the types were made from tin, but from the struggle to develop proper ink for the metal types, they eventually printed with wood type. Therefore, China did not improve its printing technology and continued to rely on woodblocks, and metal type printing was limited to print the 'Song Jesin Juui(宋諸臣奏議)' in the Huaxi Huitong Guan(華氏會通館) in 1490. To shorten, China created the principle of metal type printing but did not practicalize and develop letterpress printing technology.

Korea invented metal type printing in the early 13th century and began printing books. It can be confirmed by the historical printing of the 'Nammyeong Cheon Hwasang Song Jeungdoga(南明泉和尙頌證道歌)' before 1239 and the 'Sangjeong Yemun(詳定禮文)' between 1234 and 1241. In addition, the actual copy of the 'Baegun Hwasang Cholog Buljo Jikji Simche Yojeol(白雲和尙抄錄佛祖直指心體要節, abbreviated Jikji)', published in July 1377 in metal type, is now in the Bibliothèque nationale de France(BNF). The book was listed on the UNESCO Memory of the World in 2001.

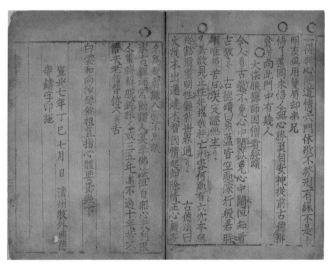

Fig 23-1. Jikji, published in metal type in July 1377 by Heungdeoksa Temple in Cheongju Bibliothèque nationale de France collection

The method of casting metal type in Korea is well documented in 'Yongjae Chonghwa(慵齋叢話)', written by Sung Hyun(成俔). The patrix was made of box tree(黃楊木) wood, and the matrix was made by placing the box tree in a mold, made by fine-grained sand and making marks on it. And then, bronze was melted and poured at 1200°C to cast the type. The printing method consisted of selecting type according to the manuscript, typesetting it, painting it with ink, placing Korean paper(韓紙) made of mulberry on top of the letters and rubbing it with Inche(印髢), a solid beeswax mixed with human hair. Metal type printing in Korea began in 1403, when the king established the Jujaso(鑄字所), a national printing center to cast type. The first typeface produced by the office was the 'Gyemi font(癸未字, 1403)'. During the reign of King Sejong, the casting method was improved and the 'Gyeongja font(庚子字, 1420)' and 'Gabin font(甲寅字, 1434)' were created. After that, about 6 to 70 types of fonts were created during the Joseon Dynasty, and they were used to print more than 14,000 books on agriculture, medicine, astronomy, mathematics, and medicine, including Confucian books, and influenced China and Japan.

In the 14th century, Europe's contact with the Arab world allowed Chinese paper production techniques to spread beyond the Spanish and Italian gateways. The first paper mill in Central Europe was built in Nuremberg in 1390 by Ullmann Stromer, who had a large manufacturing business. Around the same time, woodblock printing was introduced from China. In Europe, woodblocks were used to print sacred pictures and playing cards. Soon, woodblocks with biblical verses as well as pictures began to appear. Most of the books of the 15th century were produced in this way. They were richly illustrated and included secular and religious texts. Woodblock printing remained in use for about 50 years until Gutenberg's metal type printing was improved and spread.

In the mid-15th century, the German Johannes Gutenberg popularized the use of metal type in Europe. Gutenberg printed 148 to 180 copies of the 42-line Bible in his hometown of Mainz between 1453 and 1455. It was a breakthrough change compared to the 3 years it took one scribe to transcribe the Bible at that time. However, Gutenberg's 42 line-bible printing method is still veiled because the lack of record.

Reconstructed and refined from sources more than a century after his death, European metal type printing was based on the use of mould-casting to cast the type. An imprint is punched into a copper plate to form a matrix, and metal is melted into a hand mold. The metal is an alloy of 65% lead, 23% antimony, and 12% tin. The melting temperature is 232°C. Printing is done by typesetting with a galley and applying ink. A parchment or thick paper was placed on top and printed on both sides, front and back, using a printing press. The casting of metal type and typesetting and the use of manual printing presses were new technologies in Europe. The use of typesetting and manual printing presses was an adaptation of parchment and thick paper, which were hard to be folded in half. In Korea, metal type printing was done by hand because the paper was thin whereas in the West, where parchment and paper were thicker, made the printing press indispensable and valuable. It tells that difference of printing paper and bookbinding between the East and West resulted technical difference in bookbinding culture and tradition.

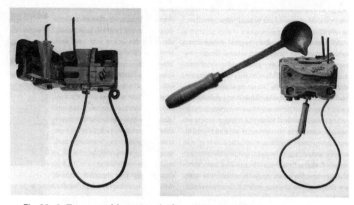

Fig 23–2. Type mould casting, before 1850, Munich Museum collection

Fig 23–3. Printing press, restored 1925, Gutenberg Museum collection

Spread and impact of metal type printing

Metal type was created by the principle of letterpress printing, which started with the idea of Bi Sheng in China, and started the publishing revolution by printing various books in Korea by utilizing metal type printing. Although it is not clear from the history of world printing culture, there may have been an exchange of information on metal type printing between Korea and Gutenberg of Germany. Just as paper and woodblock printing spread to Europe from China, we can spare the possibility of a "Type Road," or the spread of metal type printing to the West through the Silk Road, which was a transportation route for East-West trade at that time. Metal type printing spread spread through the Mediterranean and was improved by Gutenberg in Europe, where it spread rapidly, leading to the swift development of book printing and distribution. It was encouraged by the flow of the Renaissance in Europe, where classics were translated and published, universities were established, and the demand for books exploded. The spread of printing was personal and independent event of any particular state, church, or guild. For this reason, the art of printing spread rapidly throughout Europe through the apprentices of Gutenberg. By the 1500s, printing was already taking place in 260 European cities. Around 30,000 different types of books were produced and sold in 10 million copies, including religious texts, classics from the Hebrew and Roman languages, scientific texts, and reports of Columbus's discoveries in the New World. It was the first byproduct of Gutenberg's printing that accelerated the Renaissance. After Gutenberg, the widespread availability of books through metal type printing facilitated the circulation of knowledge and information, leading to the Reformation, the Civil Revolution, the Scientific Revolution, the Industrial Revolution, and Capitalism.

European metal type printing, which began with Gutenberg, was able to be mechanized and commercialized. The system has not changed much in the 350 years since it spread around the world, but its fame has now shifted to computerized printing.

Spread of metal type printing around the world after Gutenberg are such below

1453~55 Mainz(Germany)

1460 Strasburg (Germany)

1464 Rome(Italy)

1465 Cologne(Germany)

1466 Basel(Switzerland)

1468 Augsburg(Germany)

     Pilsen(Czechoslovakia)

1470 Nuremberg(Germany)

     Paris(France)

1473 Utrecht(Netherlands)

     Lyon(France)

1474 Valencia(Spain)

1475 Lübeck(Germany)

     Breslau(Poland)

1476 Brussels(Belgium)

Pilsen(Czech Republic)

Krakow(Poland)

Westminster(England)

1477 London(England)

1482 Odense(Denmark)

Vienna(Austria)

1483 Stockholm(Sweden)

1487 Lisbon(Portugal)

1503 Istanbul(Turkey)

1515 Saloniki(Greece)

1539 Mexico(first attempt at printing outside of Europe)

1553 Moscow(Russia)

1556 Goa(India)

1584 Peru

1590 Kyushu(Japan)

1602 Philippines

1610 Bolivia

1638 Massachusetts(USA)

1640 Isfahan(Iran)

Spread of metal type printing around the world after Gutenberg

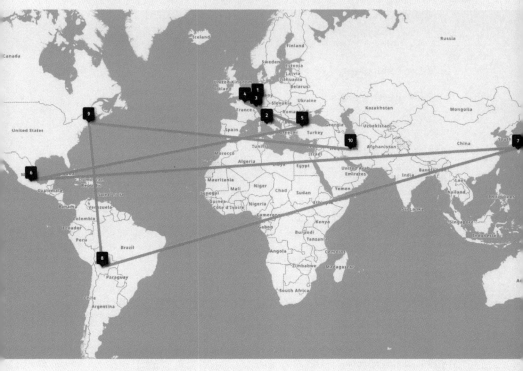

① Germany (Mainz) (1453~1455)

② Italy (Rome) (1464)

③ Switzerland (Basel) (1466)

④ France (Paris) (1470)

⑤ Turkiye (Istanbul) (1503)

⑥ Mexico (1539)*

⑦ Japan (Kyushu)

⑧ Bolivia

⑨ The United States of America (Massachusetts) (1638)

⑩ Iran (Isfahan)

* First attempt at printing outside of Europe

Scan the QR code
to view the map.

Keywords

printing, paper, woodblock printing, xylograph, typography, movable type, movable metal type, Jikji, Gutenberg 42-line Bible, type-casting mould, press

References

Albert Kapr. 1996. *Johannes Gutenberg, The Man and His Invention*, Scolar.

André Blum. 1935. *Les origines du papier, de l'imprimerie et de la gravure*, La Tournelle.

Elizabeth L. Eisenstein. 2005. *The Printing Revolution in early Modern Europe*, Cambridge University.

Eva Hanebutt Benz. 1997. Features of *Gutenberg Printing Process, International Symposium on the Printing History in East and West*, Korea National Commission for UNESCO/German Commission for UNESCO/Ch'ongju City.

Eva-Maria Hanebutt Benz. 2000. *Gutenberg's Inventions, Gutenberg. Man of the Millennium. -From a secret enterprise to the first media revolution-*, The City of Mainz.

Hwang Jeong Ha. 2013. *Movable Metal-Type Printing in Europe: Gutenberg's Inventions, The journal of the Humanities vol. 97*, Institute of the Humanities, Yousei University.

Hwang Jeong Ha. 2021. *A Comparative Analysis of Eastern and Western Movable Metal Type Printing Technique -Focused on Korea and Germany Gutenberg-, Jikji International Forum 2021*, World Jikji Culture Association.

Hwang Jeong Ha. 2021. *It's time to talk about Jikji*, World Jikji Culture Association.

John M. Hobson. 2004. *The Eastern Origins of Western Civilization*, Cambridge University.

Geoffrey F. Hudson. 1961. *Europe and China, A Survey of their Relations from the Earliest Time to 1800*, Beacon.

Olivier Deloignon. 2015. *Double-layered "printing incident" experienced via phototypography in the West, Jikji International Conference Report*, Cheongju

Early Printing Museum.

Pan Jixing. 2001. *A History of Movable Metal-Type Printing Technique in China*, Liaoning Science and Technology Publishing House.

Stephan Füssel. 1997. *Gutenberg and Printing in the Western Culture, International Symposium on the Printing History in East and West*, Korea National Commission for UNESCO/German Commission for UNESCO/Ch'ongju City.

Stephan Füssel. 1999. *Gutenberg und seine Wirkung*, Frankfurt am Main und Leipzig.

Tai-youn Hwang. 2022. *The Silk Roads of Korean Metal Typography, A Criticism on the Fabricating Gutenberg's Invention of Movable Metal Type and Printing Revolution*, Solgwahag.

Thomas. F. Carter. 1955. *Invention of printing in China and its spread Westward*, rev. by Goodrich. 2nd ed. New York.

Time Inc. 1998. *The Life Millennium, The 100 most Important Events & People of the Past 1,000 Years*, New York.

Timorthy H. Barrett. 2008. *The Woman who Discovered Printing*, Yale University.

written by JeongHa Hwang (Seowon University)

24

Gunpowder

Gunpowder refers to a chemical compound that causes instantaneous combustion or decomposition reaction by light stimulation such as heat, electricity, or shock and generates gas with high-temperature heat and pressure to destroy and propel. This is one of China's four great inventions, along with the compass, paper, and printing, and has had a significant impact on human history and technological development, playing a key role in military and industrial fields. Gunpowder is an important technology that was invented in China and spread throughout the world. The process of its spread from China to the West is an important historical event. It is used in fireworks, gunpowder, artillery shells, and a variety of military and civilian applications and has transformed traditional military strategies and the way weapons are used. The invention of gunpowder and the emergence of gunpowder weapons have had the most significant impact on warfare and the evolution of human civilization, becoming pivotal factors that altered the course of world history. Developed in China and transmitted through Asia and the Islamic world to the West, it profoundly influenced the advancement of global industrial and scientific civilization.

Invention of Gunpowder Changed Human History

Gunpowder was first invented in China in the mid-9th century, and initially, the Chinese created black powder using ingredients like saltpeter, sulfur, and charcoal powder. The name 'black powder' is given because it is typically produced as a black-colored powder. Initially, it was mainly used to start fires or for medical and artistic purposes, but from the 11th century, the use of gunpowder spread within China and was used for a variety of purposes, including explosives, artillery, and fire guns. It appears that the initial military use began in the late 'Tang Dynasty', and substantial military applications are presumed to have occurred during the 'Song Dynasty'.

During the Song Dynasty, gunpowder manufacturing methods were extensively developed, including gunpowder for artillery used in weapons, gunpowder for smoke bombs containing poison, and gunpowder containing iron fragments. During the Song Dynasty, as the performance of gunpowder increased day by day, weapons used in large quantities, and the emergence of these weapons brought about a great change in the military. Subsequently, during the Song and Yuan Dynasties, it was extensively employed for military purposes, and the main use of gunpowder was for rockets or smoke barrels, such as slash-and-burn guns or fire spears, as shown in Figure 1. There are records of the Mongol army's use of gunpowder in 1232 during their war with the 'Jin Dynasty'. The earliest chemical formula for gunpowder appeared in the 11th century Song dynasty text, 'Wujing Zongyao' (Complete Essentials from the Military Classics), as shown in Figure 2, written by 'Zeng Gongliang' between 1040 and 1044.[1]

Afterwards, gunpowder began to be systematically utilized for military purposes in China, and gunpowder-based explosives incredibly advanced military technology, finding applications in weaponry and artillery, thus contributing to significant developments in Chinese military capabilities. Various gunpowder weapons such as bombs, fire lances, and gun appeared in China.[2] Explosive weapons such as bombs have been discovered in a shipwreck off the shore of Japan dated from 1281, during the Mongol invasions of Japan.[3]

Fig 24-1. Chinese gunpowder weapon

Fig 24-2. Earliest known written formula for gunpowder

1 Chase, Kenneth (2003), Firearms: A Global History to 1700, Cambridge University Press, ISBN 978-0-521-82274-9.

2 Buchanan, Brenda J., ed. (2006), Gunpowder, Explosives and the State: A Technological History, Aldershot: Ashgate, ISBN 978-0-7546-5259-5.

3 Delgado, James (2003), "Relics of the Kamikaze", Archaeology, 56 (1).

The black powder, initially invented in China, spread through Asia and the Islamic world before reaching Europe. In Europe, the gunpowder technology was refined and developed, eventually returning to the East in a cyclical process of knowledge transfer. The reason for the spread of gunpowder technology, initially invented in China, to various parts of the world, including the Middle East and Europe, was due to the active utilization of gunpowder weaponry by the Mongol Empire, which was engaged in wars across the world during its territorial expansion at the time.

As the Mongol Empire conquered regions in Western Asia, the Middle East, and beyond, global cultural exchange accelerated, naturally leading to the transmission of gunpowder technology to Europe. Gunpowder that reached Europe played a pivotal role in various wars on the continent and led to significant advancements, resulting in the development of superior firearms and weaponry. Due to the active acceptance and innovation of gunpowder technology in Europe, gunpowder is now widely used worldwide and continues to play an important role in various fields, even in modern times.

Global Spread of Gunpowder

The gunpowder technology has developed continuously over a long period of time in China and spread to the regions of Asia and the Islamic world. The dissemination of gunpowder from China to Asian and Islamic civilizations was primarily associated with warfare, political circumstances, and commercial trade. Gunpowder and artillery technology were spread to the Arab world in the 13th century when the Mongolian 'Yuan Dynasty' sent military expeditions to West Asia and were brought to Europe by Arabs. The Mongol Army's first use of gunpowder weaponry in the Arab region took place during the 1219 Western Campaign led by 'Genghis Khan', when they attacked the Khwarazm Empire in Central Asia. Subsequently, in 1221, during the siege of Nessa, they began to extensively employ gunpowder-based weapons such as rockets and firearms expensively. Also, Gunpowder and gunpowder weapons were transmitted to India through the Mongol invasions of India and were introduced to Southeast Asia when Kublai Khan's Chinese army invaded Java.[4] After learning about the powerful gunpowder weapons of the Mongolian army, the Arab and Islamic world learned how to manufacture gunpowder and began producing various firearms in imitation of China.

Through this process, gunpowder technology spread from China to the Middle East and the Islamic world in the 13th century. According to Iqtidar Alam Khan, it was invading Mongols who introduced gunpowder to the Islamic world, and the Muslims acquired knowledge of gunpowder sometime between 1240 and 1280.[5] This diffusion occurred through trade and cultural exchanges between China and Arabia, with gunpowder being employed in the Islamic world for the manufacture of firearms and fireworks. The transmission of China's gunpowder technology to the Islamic world historically resulted from cultural, economic, and technological exchanges. In the 14th century,

---

4 Iqtidar Alam Khan (2004). Gunpowder and Firearms: Warfare in Medieval India. Oxford University Press. ISBN 978-0-19-566526-0.

5 Khan, Iqtidar Alam (1996), "Coming of Gunpowder to the Islamic World and North India: Spotlight on the Role of the Mongols", Journal of Asian History, 30: 41–45

the Islamic world began using gunpowder for weapons and explosives, leading to significant advancements both in military aspects and engineering and technology. Gunpowder evolved for various military purposes, including fireworks, firearms, and artillery shells. This period saw technological innovations that involved the study and utilization of the chemical properties of gunpowder.

'Hasan al-Rammah' included 107 gunpowder recipes in his text 'al-Furusiyyah wa al-Manasib al-Harbiyya'(The Book of Military Horsemanship and Ingenious War Devices), 22 of which are for rockets. Al-Hassan claims that in the Battle of 'Ain Jalut' of 1260, the Mamluks used against the Mongolsin "the first cannon in history", a formula with near-identical ideal composition ratios for explosive gunpowder as shown in Figure 3.[6] In the Islamic world, gunpowder technology played a significant role in the fields of chemistry and technology, and knowledge related to gunpowder advanced in the Middle East. This technology contributed to military and technological innovation

Fig 24–3. Two illustrations from an Arabic military treatise showing the first use of explosive gunpowder and cannon.

---

6 Hassan, Ahmad Y. "Transfer of Islamic Technology to the West: Part III". History of Science and Technology in Islam.

in various Islamic empires, including the Islamic Republic and the Ottoman Empire.

Flourishing of Gunpowder Technology in the West

Gunpowder technology, which continued to develop in the Islamic world, began to spread to Europe after the 14th century. The earliest Western accounts of gunpowder appear in texts written by English philosopher 'Roger Bacon' in 1267 called 'Opus Majus' and 'Opus Tertium'.[7] "In Europe, there were early experiments conducted with gunpowder, leading to the development of various types of gunpowder. Subsequently, gunpowder became a crucial component of Europe's military revolution and scientific innovation. In late 14th century Europe, gunpowder was improved by corning, the practice of drying it into small clumps to enhance combustion and consistency.[8]

The introduction of gunpowder technology to Europe had a significant impact on European military and navigational capabilities. In particular, the emergence of gunpowder transformed in the traditional medieval military tactics, leading to the active use of firearms and artillery. In the mid-14th century, firearms were developed in China and Europe almost simultaneously. However, in the subsequent years, while gunpowder technology in China did not progress significantly, Europe saw rapid development and continuous

---

7 Needham, Joseph (1986), Science & Civilisation in China, vol. 7: The Gunpowder Epic, Cambridge University Press, ISBN 978-0-521-30358-3.

8 Kelly, Jack (2004), Gunpowder: Alchemy, Bombards, & Pyrotechnics: The History of the Explosive that Changed the World, Basic Books, ISBN 978-0-465-03718-6.

improvement of firearms for military purposes. In Europe, field artillery and muskets utilizing gunpowder, as shown in Figures 4 and 5, were developed and widely used. There were improvements in firearms, such as breech-loading rifles and cannons, featuring smokeless powder and stronger barrels. As the 17th century approached, gunpowder, primarily used for military purposes, began to be utilized for industrial applications. Around 1627, the mining entrepreneur 'Kasper Weindle' conducted mining explosions using black powder in Hungary.

Fig 24–4. Field artillery   Fig 24–5. Muskets www.namu.wiki

From the 17th to the 19th century, Europe witnessed the pioneering of modern chemistry theories and the discovery of the structures of new organic compounds. During this period, various types of gunpowder were invented, and gunpowder became widely used in mining and civil engineering. After the 19th century, gunpowder technology further advanced, leading to the development of various types of gunpowder, such as black powder and smokeless powder, which were mass-produced alongside the Industrial Revolution. As a result, gunpowder had a significant impact on modern warfare and industry. It became one of the driving forces behind the Industrial Revolution that originated in the West. Before the Industrial Revolution, various manufacturing processes that were previously done manually were automated, greatly increasing productivity. In modern times, gunpowder technology continues to advance, developing even more advanced explosives. Gunpowder plays a crucial role not only in the military but also in various fields such as industry, transportation, and agriculture.

Impact of Gunpowder on Western Civilization

Gunpowder, as a revolutionary invention from China, had a profound impact on Western civilization, bringing about significant changes in various aspects. Firstly, the introduction of gunpowder led to a revolutionary transformation in Western military strategies and combat methods. Weapons like firearms, artillery, and cannons, which were actively used during the medieval era, became prominent. This resulted in shifts in military strategies and tactics, leading to a remarkable enhancement in military power. Furthermore, the advancement of gunpowder technology spurred European nations to enhance their maritime navigation and continental exploration. Ships equipped with cannons and gunpowder provided a military advantage, facilitating the discovery of new continents and accelerating colonial expansion.

Moreover, the invention of gunpowder served as a catalyst for technological innovation. Gunpowder played a pivotal role in the development of technologies such as bullets, cannons, and various explosive weapons, which, in turn, became the driving force behind the Industrial Revolution. From an economic perspective, the demand for gunpowder and its production stimulated the manufacturing and trade of items like bullets, artillery shells, and cannons. This led to increased economic competition and commercial activity among nations, contributing to the advancement of industries.

The invention of gunpowder is considered one of the pivotal turning points in human history. Its introduction brought about innovations in medieval military strategies and weapon usage, exerting a profound influence on various fields, including military, economy, and technology. Therefore, gunpowder stands as a revolutionary invention that had a significant impact on Western civilization and played a crucial role in the development of world history and civilizations.

Spread of Gunpowder

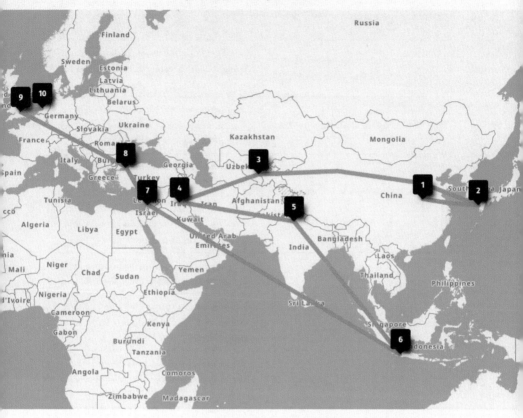

① Xuchang regions : Sambongsan (Henan Province, China) (1232)

② Nagasaki Coast (Japan) (1281)

③ the Khwarazmian Empire (Samarkand, Uzbekistan) (1219)

④ the Abbasid Caliphate (Baghdad, Iraq) (1258)

⑤ India (Delhi)

⑥ the Singhasari Kingdom (Java, Indonesia)

⑦ Israel (around Jerusalem : Ain Jalut) (1260)

⑧ the Byzantine Empire : Constantinople (Istanbul, Trkiye) (1453)

⑨ England (Oxford)

⑩ Netherlands

Scan the QR code to view the map.

No.	Mark	Description
1	Xuchang area : Sambongsan (Henan Province, China) (1232)	Assumed to be the first use of gunpowder weapon during the war between the Mongol and Jin Dynasty in 1232
2	Nagasaki Coast (Japan) (1281)	Explosive weapons were found in shipwreck on Japanese coast, assumed to wrecked during the invasion of Mongolians to Japan in 1281.
3	the Khwarazmian Empire (Samarkand, Uzbekistan) (1219)	First used by Mongolian armies in Arab region during the 1st invasion of Khwarazmian Empire in 1219
4	the Abbasid Caliphate (Baghdad, Iraq) (1258)	Yuan Dynasty uses bomb shells named 'Cheol-Byoung(Iron-Jar)' in Baghdad invasion in 1258
5	India (Delhi)	Gunpowder techniques were spread in India through the battle of Mongol invading India
6	the Singhasari Kingdom (Java, Indonesia)	Gunpowder techniques were planted in Southeastern Asia when the Kublai Khan of Mongol invaded Java, Indonesia
7	Israel (Jerusalem : Ain Jalut) (1260)	First use of explosive cannon in the battle of Ain Jalut by the Mamluks resisting Mongol invasion in 1260
8	the Byzantine Empire : Constantinople (Istanbul, Turkiye) (1453)	Ottomans produced cannon from gunsmiths to invade Constantinople in 1453
9	England (Oxford)	The oldest record in Europe about gunpowder, written by the English philosopher Roger Bacon in Oxford University, is found.
10	Netherlands	Netherlands achieved independence from the war with the new gunpowder weapon, letting UK and France join the competition developing powder weapons.

Keywords

gunpowder, fireworks, artillery shells, military war, industrial revolution

References

Chase, Kenneth(2003), Firearms: A Global History to 1700, Cambridge University Press.

Buchanan, Brenda J., ed.(2006), Gunpowder, Explosives and the State: A Technological History, Aldershot: Ashgate.

Delgado, James(2003), "Relics of the Kamikaze", Archaeology, 56 (1).

Iqtidar Alam Khan(2004), Gunpowder And Firearms: Warfare in Medieval India. Oxford University Press.

Khan, Iqtidar Alam (1996), "Coming of Gunpowder to the Islamic World and North India: Spotlight on the Role of the Mongols", Journal of Asian History, 30: 41 −45.

Hassan, Ahmad Y. "Transfer of Islamic Technology to the West: Part III". History of Science and Technology in Islam.

Needham, Joseph(1986), Science & Civilisation in China, vol. 7: The Gunpowder Epic, Cambridge University Press.

Kelly, Jack (2004), Gunpowder: Alchemy, Bombards, & Pyrotechnics: The History of the Explosive that Changed the World, Basic Books.

Image References

https://yoosi0211.tistory.com/186

www.namu.wiki

written by Sang-Ho Moon (Busan University of Foreign Studies)

25

Calendar

Calendars in the Ancient Mediterranean Region

Basic Information

Since the early stages of civilization, humankind has been accumulating knowledge about the changes in the sun, moon, and stars. Units of time measurement included hours, days, months, and years. Calendars were essential for practical and religious purposes, such as determining agricultural activities, irrigation operations, and selecting specific days for gatherings, market days, and ceremonial occasions. Calendars regulated daily life.

The specific measurement of time varied among different civilizations. For example, the ancient Egyptians considered sunrise as the beginning of a day, while the Jews considered sunset as the start of a day. The Babylonians divided a day into 12 parts, while the Egyptians divided it into 24 parts. Some cultures had weeks consisting of 5 days, 7 days, or even 10 days. The start of a year varied as well, with some cultures, like Babylon, considering the vernal equinox as the beginning, others, like ancient Athens, considering midsummer, and some, like the Roman Empire, considering winter. The Jews took the month of their escape from Egypt as the beginning of their year (Exodus 12:2).

Seasons also varied by region. Mesopotamia had two seasons, summer and winter, while Anatolia had four. Egypt classified its seasons based on the flooding level of the Nile River: the flooding season (July-October), the sowing or sprouting season (November-March), and the harvest or drought season (March-June). The number and names of months also differed among cities. Around 1800 BC, the city of Mari in the middle of the Euphrates River had six months. Even within the same area, each city had different names for the months. Rome initially had ten months but later expanded to twelve, while Athens used both a democratic calendar with 10 months and a festival calendar with 12 months simultaneously. It was not uncommon for multiple calendar systems to be used within the same region. Thus, historian 'Diodoros Siculus' said that to reckon the year was different from place to place: for example, in some places, the year consisted of 30 days, while in other places, the year was composed of 4 months, which comprised the seasons of each year.

However, in most regions, a month was generally set to approximately 30 days, taking into account the cycle of the moon's phases, and the length of a year was determined based on the changing seasons corresponding to the sun's movements. When creating calendars, the emphasis was placed on either the sun or the moon's movements, leading to the use of solar calendars, lunar calendars, or lunisolar calendars. Generally, the movement of the sun was important for agriculture. However, some regions preferred to base their calendars on the distinct movements of the moon. Some regions used a lunisolar calendar, attempting to synchronize the movements of both the moon and the sun.

Occurrence

The Mediterranean region has long been a cradle of civilization, witnessing the rise and fall of numerous empires and cultures. Among the remarkable aspects of these ancient civilizations were their calendars, which played a crucial role in organizing social, religious, and agricultural activities. In the Mesopotamian region, such as in the Babylonian civilization, they preferred the lunar calendar, which was determined by the shape and movement of the moon. In these regions, where the moon god held a higher position than the sun god, the lunar calendar continued to be used. The calendar of the Sumerian civilization consisted of 5 days in a week and 12 months, each consisting of 30 days. The Babylonian kingdom, which unified this region, established a unified legal code and standardized the calendar around 2000

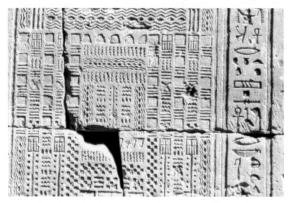

Fig 25–1. Ancient Egyptian Calendar

BC. At that time, the system of 12 months per year and 7 days per week was established. Certain days were considered unlucky. In the 7th century BC, the unlucky days were the 7th, 14th, 21st, and 28th of each month, coinciding with the appearance of the crescent.

On the other hand, the ancient Egyptians devised the solar calendar by observing the periodic flooding of the Nile River and the appearance of the star 'Sirius'. The Greek historian 'Herodotus' claimed that the Egyptians were the first to observe the stars and calculate the year, dividing it into 12 months. For administrative and economic purposes, Egypt's civic calendar consisted of 365 days, namely twelve 30-day months and an additional 5 special days at the end of the year. The last 5 days were known as the 'epagomenal days' and were considered the birth dates of the gods Osiris, Horus, Seth, Isis, and Nephthys. A month was divided into 3 weeks of 10 days each. 'Decans' were groups of stars in ancient Egyptian astronomy, and each decan consisted of 10 days, resulting in 36 decans, which accounted for a 360-day year. Although the Solar calendar was not predominant in Ancient Egypt, it was the only calendar used. It was run according to 3 different calendars, including the lunar calendar.

Process and Development

The calendars of Egypt, and Mesopotamia spread throughout the Mediterranean region through multiple pathways. Each region, while influenced by these advanced calendars, adapted and applied them according to their own social, political, religious, and economic conditions.

1) Phoenicians, Jews, and Etruscans

The Phoenicians, who were at the forefront of Mediterranean civilization exchange, developed a calendar closely related to maritime activities. They based their calendar on the lunar system but also incorporated the solar calendar. The Phoenicians, renowned for their navigational abilities and extensive trade networks, utilized calendars to obtain information necessary for determining favorable sailing times and trade expeditions, in addition to crop cultivation and religious ceremonies.

The longest-surviving Jewish calendar is the 'Gezer Calendar' during the reign of King Solomon. Considering using the word 'Yereah', which is the foundation of the term 'Gezer', meaning moon. In reference to the calendar, it is inferred that it was a lunar calendar. In the *Books of Kings*, three month names are mentioned, two of which also appear in the Phoenician calendar,

Fig 25–2. Gezer Calendar

indicating mutual influence between these civilizations. Regardless of who first created the seven-day week, it was the Judeo-Christian civilization that had a decisive influence on the later seven-day week. After Roman Emperor Constantine adopted the 7-day week system, it became widely used in Western civilization and is still used worldwide today.

The calendar of the 'Etruscans', who migrated from Lydia in Anatolia to the Italian Peninsula had a significant influence on the Roman calendar. The Etruscan calendar is believed to have influenced the structure of the Roman calendar with its 12-month system.

2) Ancient Greek Calendar

The calendar of ancient Greece can generally be regarded as learned from the East. However, unlike the centralized calendar systems based on unified monarchies such as Egypt and Babylon, Greece did not have a unified calendar system. Each city-state had its own calendar, resulting in a time difference of about 2 weeks between cities. The names of the months also varied depending on the region. Even within Athens, multiple calendar systems coexisted. These included the "agricultural calendar" based on the positions of stars, the "festival calendar" based on the lunar cycle, and the "democratic calendar" that divided the year into ten months after a reform by Cleisthenes to align with the administration of ten tribes. Various certificates and legal obligations were calculated based on this democratic calendar. However, religious ceremonies and offerings were performed according to the 12-month festival calendar, which followed the lunar cycle. Gradually, the calculation of the Greek year became based on the Olympic Games.

In 433 BC, the Greek astronomer 'Meton' developed the 'Metonic cycle', which was close to the Babylonian calendar system. In 330 BC, 'Kallipos' introduced the 'Kallipos cycle', which adopted the Egyptian calendar system and considered a year to be 365.25 days. Overall, the time calculation methods in ancient Greece can be said that they were mostly learned from the East.

3) Ancient Roman Calendar

The Roman calendar, influenced by the 'Etruscan calendar', developed complex variations in its calculation methods due to political and religious considerations. The term "calendar," which refers to the modern-day calendar, originated from the Latin word 'Kalendae,' which indicated the first day of each month. The Romans used the words kalendae, 'nonae,' and 'idus' to designate dates. This had a connection to the changing appearance of the moon, where nonae referred to the half-moon (first quarter) and fell on the 7th or 9th day of each month, while idus referred to the full moon and fell on the 15th or 13th day of each month. The word kalendae derived from 'Kalare,' meaning "to call," and had a ceremonial origin, signifying the days called from the observation of the new moon until nonae.

The early Roman calendar was a mix of lunar and solar reckoning which created confusion. This confusion strengthened the authority of the magistrates during the late Republic since they had the power to decide the introduction of leap years at the appropriate time. With this authority, they could either lengthen or shorten a year, exerting significant influence in political matters.

Fig 25–3. 'Fasti Amiterni'[1]

It is said that during the reign of 'Romulus', the first legendary king of Rome, the calendar consisted of 10 months, and then it was expanded to 12 months during the second reign of 'King Numa Pompilius'. Originally, the year began in March (Martius), but around the 2nd century BC, January was changed to the beginning of the year. In the Roman Empire, the new year varied by region and could change. For example, the day the Roman emperor visited a city could be designated as the new year for that place. Alternatively, the emperor's accession or birthday could be celebrated as the new year. In this, the Roman calendar was highly sensitive to political, judicial, and military purposes, leading to frequent changes.

In Latin, the word for calendar was 'fasti,'" which derived from the word 'fas.' 'Fas' meant permission, indicating a favorable day for political assemblies, commercial activities, or legal proceedings. Thus, fas represented days suitable

---

1 Julius Caesar' adopted the Egyptian solar calendar and made marbles engraved with it and circulated them.

for legal actions, while unfavorable or unlucky days were called nefas.' The concepts of auspicious and inauspicious days from the Mesopotamian region, seem to have been seamlessly integrated into the Roman calendar. The calendar had important functions not only in religious contexts but also in political and judicial matters. Eventually, Julius Caesar proclaimed a new calendar based on the solar system in 45 BC, following the advice of the Alexandrian astronomer 'Sosigenes'. This new solar calendar rapidly spread throughout the Roman Empire, leveraging Rome's military power.

Influences

The formation and development of calendars have been influenced by various factors. The solar calendar in Egypt and the lunar calendar in Mesopotamia evolved differently, reflecting the geographical and cultural conditions of its own, and had a great influence on the calendar system in each region of the Mediterranean. These regions did not apply the solar or lunar calendar as it was but transformed it into various applied forms according to their respective geographic and cultural environments and customs. The Phoenicians developed a calendar suitable for sea voyages. Though heavily influenced by the calendar of the Orient, The Athenians developed a democratic calendar and used it along with a religious calendar based on the lunar calendar. The Roman calendar, which developed under the influence of the 'Etruscan calendar', underwent complex variations in its calculation methods due to political and religious reasons. With the introduction of the new Julian calendar by Julius Caesar, based on the Egyptian solar calendar, a more convenient standard calendar came into use. This system became the prototype for the calendar we use today. However, the 'Julian calendar' initially did not have a concept of a week. And it was during the reign of Emperor Constantine, when a seven-day official calendar week was introduced, heavily influenced by Christianity. Similarly, the Islamic calendar is a prominent example of a calendar shaped by religious considerations. In the 7[th]century, IslamicauthorityproclaimedtheimplementationofapurelunarcalendarfortheIslamicworld.This decision was based on the teachings of the Quran. Asaresult, tothisday, mostIslamiccountriescelebratefestivalsandevents, suchas 'Ramadan', based on the lunar calendar. This connection seems to be reflected in the inclusion of crescent moons on the flags of Islamic countries. It is interesting to note that the Islamic region, which continues the tradition of a pure lunar calendar to this day, was a region where the lunar-based lunar calendar tradition continued from a very long time ago (and where the moon god was more important than the sun god).

Spread of Calendar

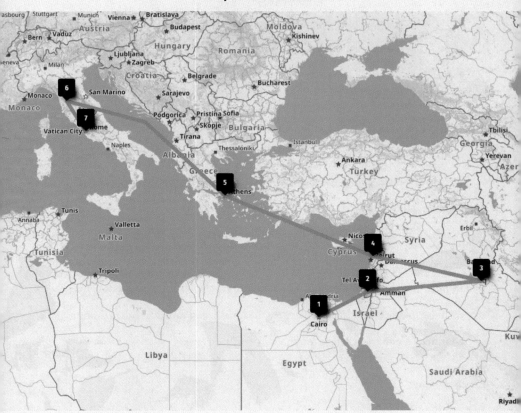

① Egypt

② Israel

③ Mesopotamia / Babylonia

④ Phenicia

⑤ Greece

⑥ Etruria

⑦ Rome

Keywords

Calendar, Lunar calendar, Solar calendar, Egypt, Babylon, Greece, Rome

References

Herodotus, *Historiai*

Diodorus Siculus, *Bibliotheca historica*

Macrobius, *Saturnalia*

H. E. Winlock, (1940) "The Origin of the Ancient Egyptian Calendar," *Proceedings of the American Philosophical Society*, Vol. 83. No. 3, pp. 447–64.

A. T. Grafton and N. M. Swerdlow, (1988) "Calendar Dates and Ominous Days in Ancient Historiography," *Journal of the Warburg and Courtauld Institutes*, Vol. 51, pp. 14– 42.

written by Hye Young Choi (Emeritus Professor, Chonam National University)

26

Map

I. Map

What is a Map?

A map is a storage medium that humans use to record using various symbols and characters by reducing the space they perceive. Since the map selects and reproduces only the necessary information from the myriad of spatial data, it is also an educational medium. It condenses only the geographic information that the author wants to exhibit. Traditional maps are recorded on surfaces such as paper, leather, stone, or wood. Additionally, there are other types of maps that reproduce 3-dimensional images by inscribing the altitude of objects in 3 dimensions, as well as solid objects such as globes. In the information age, maps input, store, and reproduce information in digital form and even as holograms.

Maps are generally regarded as capturing only the spatial structure of a stationary time or a specific moment; but there are cases where several eras overlap. Geography is a conceptualization of the object of space, just as history records various times, from the surroundings of humans to the birth of the universe. There is also a complex map that combines the scales of these 2 concepts and merges geography that existed in various time zones in one space. As a representative example, 'Honilgang-ri Yeokdaegukdo Jido (混一疆里歷代國都地圖),' produced by the Joseon dynasty in 1402, introduces enormous cities that once existed across history. Furthermore, maps are not necessarily objects that have existed but places created through imagination or processing.

Origin of a map

The first map was produced long before characters were created through high abstraction and synthesis because the location information of the observed natural objects, could be drawn only with intuitive interpretation. We found primitive maps carved on animal bones or painted on walls in more than 10 Palaeolithic and Neolithic sites dating back 25,000 years. They described celestial objects, which are easily observed in the surrounding terrain or the night sky. Maps at that time also had a magical meaning, conveying practical knowledge necessary for movement and resource acquisition, expressing aesthetic beauty, and representing the desired object.

More advanced maps appear along the site of the oldest civilization. 'Châatalhöyük' in south-western Anatolia, a Neolithic relic dating back to 7100 BC, was unearthed. The map excavated here possesses not only the topography structure of the excavated urban site but also natural phenomena at the time, such as volcanic activity. As such, maps in the civilized era provided geographical information necessary for preliminary administration, such as the classification of flooded areas and the current status of land management.

Emergence of the world map

If the maps of prehistoric civilizations began with realistic depictions of objects observed by the naked eye, historical civilizations launched to explain their worldview through more abstract and comprehensive regional and world maps and texts. The clay-plate world map excavated from 'Kirkuk' in Mesopotamia presents the self-centered worldview recognized by Babylonian civilization around the 7th century BC through paintings and 'Akkadian' wedge letters. Since it is broken, we cannot decode the full text. The front of this map distinguishes the central area, the round sea encompassing it, and the realms beyond the sea. The map remarks 8 cities and divides the area within the sea into swamps (Shatt al-Arab) and the Euphrates River in the area within the sea, and writes 7 or 8 area names outside the sea.

The records on the front and back contain their view of the universe, as well as the geographical knowledge observed by the Babylonians. The letters deal with a long narrative from the creation of heaven to the epic of 'Marduk', the guardian deity of Babylon. It also recorded the natural environment, characteristic animals and plants, the extent of the area, and the history of residents with different externalities for each region. Like other ancient academic fields, cartography at that time did not distinguish between the explanation of natural phenomena learned through observation and experience and the order of the universe created by God. In addition, even the scope crosses the present world, the next world, the past, and the present, and details of the world they know and the unknown world.

As such, maps that recognize the world and the universe as their centre are found in common in both the East and the West. The Persians, who followed Mesopotamian civilization, devised the concept of 'Haft-e Keshvar(the 7 areas)', which divides the world into 6 civilizations, and was later succeeded as one of the main traditions of Islamic world maps. The Greeks also produced maps centred on Omphalos, regarded as the world's navel, and it developed into a T-O world map centred on Jerusalem in later Christian civilizations. In East Asia, 'Hua(華)', a central civilized world, '4 Yi(夷)s' in the periphery, and 'Tianxiandu(天下圖)', which distinguished the barbaric world beyond, were also popular. The aforementioned 'Honilgang-ri Yeokdaegukdo Jido' also appears as the succession of a unique worldview that depicts China as the largest and 2nd most exaggeratedly under the notion that China was once the original Hua civilization.

Tradition of mathematical cartography

Humans, who used to make maps with rough observations and subjective expressions, gradually challenged scientific mapping quantified through more precise measurement and objective quantification. In particular, with the development of geometry and astronomy that calculate orientation, distance, and altitude through measurements of the daytime length and solar and lunar eclipses, scholars have secured the technology necessary for scientific maps from the size of the earth to the digitization of longitude and latitude at each point.

Among the ancient mathematical maps, the map inserted in the geographic book 'Geography' by Claudius Ptolemy, the 2nd century Greek scholar in Alexandria of Egypt, one of the astronomical centres of the world, left the greatest legacy. The book compiled the expertise and geographical knowledge of the Mediterranean Sea and Asia at the time, listed more than 8,000 regions, and gave latitude and longitude to more than 6,300 of them. In addition, the tradition set the Canary Islands (Fortune Islands in this book) in the Atlantic Ocean as a meridian in western Eurasia for over a millenia. The world map inserted in the book is not survive, but later, scholars have produced multiple versions of the map based on the latitude and longitude values written in the book.

As with other classical knowledge, Muslims are the main players who most enthusiastically studied, expanded, and developed Ptolemy's map in the Middle Ages. Unlike Greek geography, where geographical conditions forced the activity and knowledge to be limited within the Mediterranean and western Eurasia, and Persian-Indian geography, which knew the Indian Ocean well due to its geographic position, medieval Muslims were able to explore the geography across the northern hemisphere for the first time. In addition, they acquired geographical knowledge of the East and the West through a wide range of translation activities represented by the House of Wisdom and expanded and refined them with their translation and revisions. In addition, the divine obligation of Islam to pray to Mecca 5 times a day has made Muslims more dedicated than any other civilization in measuring and organizing the absolute position and relative orientation of Mecca and each point.

'Ptolemy's' map depicts the Indian Ocean as a closed sea and stops at its eastern end of the map slightly east of 'Oc-Eo', where the eastern end of the ancient Greco-Roman relics (coins of Antonius Pius) excavated. Muslims, on the other hand, extended the world map to the entire Eurasia and set its end in the Pacific and Atlantic Oceans, Silla (the ancient kingdom of Korea) and the Canary Islands. In particular, 'Caliph al-Ma'mun' (r. 813-833), an avid supporter of 'House of Wisdom', made about 70 mathematicians, geographers, and cartographers to produce a globe and a world map.

The map and globe were lost, but the contents have been preserved to this day through the geography book and map of al-Khwārazmī, who participated in the project. His geographic book, known as '*The Image of the Earth*', bears the title, *The Image of The Earth From Cities, Mountains, Seas, Islands, and Rivers extracted by Abu Jaafar Muhammad Ibn Musa Al-* Khwārazmī *from the Book Geography*. Despite its modest title, which sounds like an abbreviation of Ptolemy's book, it updated its most precise knowledge to date, including China's 4 major international ports, correcting and overcoming errors and limitations of Ptolemy's geography, such as the portrayal of the Indian Ocean as closed.

The map of 'Al-Idrīsī',' considered the peak of medieval Islamic cartography, is a representative symbol of knowledge exchange through the convergence and divergence of world-class geographic intellectuals. Roger the Second (r.-1130), the third ruler of the Norman dynasty, who overthrew the Islamic regime that had occupied Sicily for more than 2 centuries, sought to coexist with the

Fig 26–1. Al–Ma'mūn Globe, based on the Map of al–Khwārazmī, reconstructed in Sharjah Museum of Islamic Civilization, UAE, ©Jin Han, JEONG

Muslims, who were the majority in his land. When he ordered the world map project, he also reflected the convergent knowledge through the cooperation of Muslims and Christians. Idrīsī''s map (also known as Tabula Rogeriana) is not only the culmination of medieval Islamic maps but was later translated into Latin and used as a geography textbook for European universities for hundreds of years.

These maps, which were touted as scientific maps, spread unscientific myths on the one hand. The ancient Greek geography divided the earth into 7 climatic zones, named 'Klimas', according to latitude by hemisphere. In addition, they devised an environmental determinism. This thinking held that the climatic conditions per climate zone, including heat, cold, and humidity, determine the appearance and intelligence of all animals and inhabitants, the customs and the level of civilization in the society. By inheriting this idea, many Muslim geographers set up 7 or 9 climate zones (iqlīm) from the Arctic to the equator on their maps and considered that the climate zones dictate everything in each region.

For example, as you get too close to the equator, plants and animals become bizarre, and residents are depicted with ugly looks and low intelligence. On the contrary, residents adjacent to the North Pole are described as brave with robust bodies but are lewd, less intelligent, and unable to build a civilization. Instead, the inhabitants of the middle longitudinal zones are said to enjoy a beautiful appearance and developed culture. Muslims, however, praised the appearance and civilizational standards of the Chinese and Silla, even if they live in the first to third zones close to the equator.

Fig 26–2. Al–Idrīsī's globe, reconstructed and exhibited in Sharjah Museum of Islamic Civilization ©Jin Han, JEONG

The tradition of descriptive cartography

In the Middle Ages, descriptive maps with wide versatility also developed significantly different courses from such scientific maps. Since the mathematical map is described based on the absolute distance from one point to another, there is a limit to capturing the distance, route, caution, and singularities that a person needs to know when travelling the path. On the other hand, descriptive maps are much more practical for travellers and those who manage their journeys because they have been developed mainly to convey the information necessary for the actual route and process. The Persian geographic information management system, which launched the world's earliest empire, built the first highway and installed the necessary relay system, later became the standard of the western Eurasian world through the Romans.

In addition to other ancient empires developing geographic information by region and route for administration, such as taxation, information, military, and local control of the empire, Islam greatly fostered descriptive geographic methodology and map development by adding religious demands. Islam was obliged by God to make at least 1 pilgrimage to Mecca in every Muslim lifetime, and Muslim leaders were obliged to manage each route with a sacred duty to support their sacred pilgrimage, and to organize, distribute, and educate the necessary geographical knowledge. In addition to the common duty of universal Muslim pilgrimage to Mecca, Shiites and Sufis have their own pilgrimage. They have visited graves scattered throughout the world and contributed to gathering and spreading geographical information around the Islamic world.

This development of religious geography, coupled with Islamic mercantilism, distinctively contributed to Islam's advancement of comprehensive geography. Crucially, the use of compasses introduced by the Chinese developed Muslims' long-distance maritime activities and marine geography, followed by the development of the sea map. Notably, that the map produced in 1513 by Admiral 'Piri Reis' (1465-1553) of the Ottoman Empire provides the most accurate latitude map of the time using the latest map of the time, the equidistance azimuthal projection, based on his extensive navigation and naval experience in the Mediterranean and Indian Oceans. In addition, this chart is not only more sophisticated than any map from ancient time onwards in the case of describing the Americas, but it is also famous for depicting Antarctica 300 years earlier than Europe.

Exchanging Global Maps in the Age of Navigation

Through the Crusades, the Black Death, the Pax Mongolica Period and Renaissance, the completion of the Eastern Mediterranean, and the rise of the Chinese character alliance and spice demand, Europe has established a market size and system to distribute compasses, navigations systems, and Eastern specialties. Europeans, who pioneered the Cape of Good Hope bypass and transatlantic route through Portugal and Spain, soon pioneered the global circulation route and set up trade ports and colonies along the way, finally creating the first map covering the Eastern and Western Hemispheres. Closely, the Atlantic triangular trade mapped the Eastern Americas and the western coast of Euro-Africa and deepened map information on the entire Pacific and

Indian Oceans by trading silver and spices to Japan and the Philippines in the distance.

Since then, Europe has gradually begun to lead the theory and practice of mapping. European devised most of the various projections that have been used to this day and finally developed a global map and globe that provides accurate geographic information around the world while measuring the New World, which was unknown to the Old World.

As the centre of goods and human exchanges shifted from the Old Seas (Indian Ocean, Mediterranean Sea, South China Sea, and several inland seas) and Eurasia to the 3 major oceans (Atlantic Ocean, Pacific Ocean, and Indian Ocean), the hegemony of the world order also fell to Europeans. Europeans, who first sailed with the help of the 15th century Muslim 'Ahmad Ibn Majid', reintroduced geographical knowledge, maps, and globes back to the East through the maritime geography and the inland geography of Central Asia, led by Muslims, Indians, and Chinese in the past.

Since the 16th century, Western maps and globes have become top items among the most popular gifts in Asia, along with scientific machines such as telescopes and alarm clocks. Through this, power conflicts arose between progressive Asian intellectuals who wanted to expand knowledge and conservative Asian elites who were curiously examining these innovations but concerned with spreading new knowledge and worldview as the potential threat to the preserving of traditional knowledge and the existing political bodies.

For example, the intellects of the Joseon dynasty, which had a Chinese-

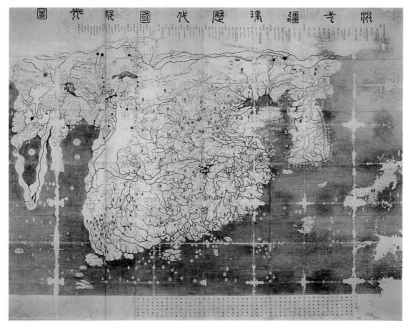
Fig 26–3. The Honil Gangni Yeokdae Gukdo Ji Do(Kangido)

centered worldview, along with Japan, Vietnam, and the old countries, were confused when they saw a map brought by small European countries stuck at the corner of their 'Honilgang-ri Yeokdaegukdo Jido.' It was neither easy to understand nor accept the reality that these so-called barbarians from small distant, countries were stirring around a much wider world with a stronger power than China.

Present and Future civilizational exchanges in mapping and cartography

A map is, after all, an integration of the information and values the author seeks to convey to potential readers. The ancient Greeks, who travelled within a relatively limited geographical confines around the Mediterranean and the Black Seas, experienced an Eastern world that remains no further east of the extreme western edge of Asia.

As they heard of India and the Scythians beyond, their concept of Asia ends around those regions during antiquity. However, their understanding of Asia gradually expanded with each discovery, such as the existence of a landmass east of India called China, and the realization that China was far larger than previously recognized.

When Muslims first became aware of the existence of a country called Silla-unknown to the Greeks-this Korean kingdom was nearing the end of its dynastic rule. However, Muslim writers, spanning from India to Iberia, continued to record Silla in their maps and various literary genres for the next 700 years, largely due to the belief that Muslim communities had resided a permanent presence there.

Before explorers ever investigated to Japan, it was prominently featured on maps as 'Zipanggu', a massive island reputed to be excessively rich in gold. This portrayal was swiftly revised after travelers visited Japan and verified that the anticipated gold reserves did not exist.

Humans continue to create maps of newly discovered areas and the frontiers they are exploring. These range from the microscopic DNA maps of the human body to the depth of ocean and the earth's interior. We even map celestial bodies floating in the vastness of the universe. Scientists produce maps ranging from the origin of the Big Bang to the edge of black holes, and they send these maps into space in anticipation of potential encounters with extra-terrestrial life. We also craft maps to navigate fictional worlds, like the map of Middle Earth from "Lord of the Rings" or Dante's depiction of hell.

The future of cartography is evolving into a new phase, characterized by the interaction between human and machine civilizations, facilitated by technological advancements. Maps are now integrated with artificial intelligence, enhancing human interaction with technologies such as robot vacuum cleaners to autonomous driving systems.

Moreover, these maps capture dynamic temporal information in real-time, rather than merely recording static spatial dart. Utilizing GPS and real-time transmission technologies people frequently access various maps- from car navigators to applications like Google Earth-to instantly navigate the most appropriate routes. This evolution is paving the way for innovative maps that support active manipulation through interactive interfaces.

Keywords

Map, Korea, Worldview, Globe, Geography

References

Jeong, Jin Han, (2020). "Creating the Medieval Islamic Geography by Using Korea," PhD diss. SOAS, University of London.

Jeong. Su-il. (2016). *The Silk Road Encyclopedia*, trans. Irvine, CA: Seoul Selection.

Morus, Iwan R., (2017) *The Oxford Illustrated History of Science*, Oxford: Oxford University Press.

Raymo, Chet. *Walking Zero*, New York: Walker & Company. 2006

Swanston, Malcolm, and Alex Swanston. (2018). *How to draw a map*. London: Harper Collins Publishers.

Image References

https://upload.wikimedia.org/wikipedia/commons/1/1d/GeneralMapOfDistancesAnd HistoricCapitals.jpg

written by Jin Han Jeong (Hankuk University of Foreign Studies)

27

Alcohol

What is an Alcohol?

Alcohol is a generic term for a compound in which a hydrogen atom in a hydrocarbon is substituted with a hydroxyl group (-OH,). In other words, it is not a single substance, but a category of substances with similar chemical structures. These range from edible ethanol to the inedible methanol, and vary from small molecules that are liquid at room temperature to larger molecules that are solid. The most common chemical formula for ethanol is $C2H5OH$, and for methanol, it is $CH3OH$.

Alcohol has been used since ancient times for a wide variety of purposes, including as medical materials, household goods, and industrial fuels.

The name 'alcohol' itself traces back to its origins and cultural exchanges. It is derived from the Arabic words 'al' (ال), and 'kuḥl' (كحل). While many scientific terms beginning with 'al-' were indeed coined by medieval Muslim scientists, the etymology of 'alcohol' referred to other materials and supplies in the older Semitic system.

The earliest use of the term 'kuḥl' was in the Akkadian 'guhālum' (𒄑𒅍𒀀𒇻), meaning shiny minerals such as stibnite and antimony. In ancient Egypt, when applying eyeliner, this shiny ore was powdered and mixed with other makeup materials to enhance adhesion and gloss. This tradition persisted in the Arab world, and in modern Arabic, kuḥl is still used as a cosmetic to darken eyelids. The term alcohol is derived from kuḥūl(كحول), an adaptation where the second vowel of the kuḥl is lengthened. The word alcohol, as we use it today, originated from adding the prefix al- to kuḥūl.

Origin of alcohol

The first time excavated use of alcohol by humans was in the form of wine, which contains alcohol naturally. Alcohol is broadly categorized into 3 types based on its production method: fermented liquor, distilled spirit, and mixed liquor. Fermented liquor results from the breakdown of carbohydrates by yeast microorganisms during the fermentation of food, a process that can also occur under natural conditions. In addition, many animals commonly encountered alcohol long before human manufactured, as the fermentation process-simple conditions like carbohydrates, moderate temperatures, wild yeast, and moisture, often occurred in nature.

Alcohol is particularly obtained in areas rich in fruits and honey, which are high in sugar and easy fermentable. Even in regions with extreme insufficient humidity and temperature, people and animals can commonly find alcohol in caves and puddles. However, naturally fermented beverages often have a low alcohol content; if the fermentation process is too rapid, the result can turn into vinegar or spoil, and too slow, alcohol may not be produced. Consequently, humans began to explore methods of crafting and preserving alcohol.

Alcohol is an efficient energy source, providing calories of 7 kcal per gram. It is rapidly metabolized and is absorbed by the body, providing instant energy. This makes it popular among both people and animals, not only for its strong fatigue reducing properties but also for its mild soothing intoxication effect, which create a pleasant sensation. Researchers such as 'Jeffrey Kahn' and 'Greg Wadley' have even suggested that the pursuit of alcohol a significant catalyst for the development agriculture and civilization. Therefore, as described later, alcohol earned the nickname 'aqua vita'.

Earliest brewage

Like the cradle of the first nomadic, agricultural, and civilized societies, and the term 'alcohol', the Middle East has the oldest brewing remains excavated today. A 13,000-year-old prehistoric burial site unearthed in a cave near Haifa in north-western Israel has yielded relics of spilled beer. This beer, made from wheat and barley, is believed to have been used in ceremonies to honour the dead.

Since high alcohol consumption causes hallucinations, it has been used in diverse types of supernatural rituals and rites, just as other hallucinogenic substances, such as cigarettes, drugs, and toxic plants, have played similar roles. Alcohol, both in the East and the West, has symbolized the strength of a warrior and a portal to the gods. Including priests of nomadic cultures and

Greek female shamanists, shamans served the god of alcohol or used alcohol in the rituals. Nomadic cultures delivered alcohol to nature, the dead, or the gods through coriander, and Christian mass and East Asian ancestral rites always included alcohol. Even in Islam, which prohibits the drinking of alcohol through the Quran, some minority sects, such as the Alevi, consider alcohol sacred and use it in essential rituals.

Neolithic traces of brewing are also most widely seen in the Middle East, but the earliest remains are in China. A pottery jar possessing the vestiges of wine made from fermented rice, honey, and fruit (hawk fruit, or grape) was discovered at the site of 'Jiahu(賈湖)' in Henan Province, China, dating back to 7,000 BC, along with early Neolithic relics. Subsequently, the ruins around Georgia in the South Caucasus region from about 5,500 years ago and the 'Hajji Firūz Tepe' site near the Zagros Mountains in north-western Iran have revealed a variety of evidence showing the Middle East's form of grape cultivation and wine brewing.

With the advent of civilization of the post-Neolithic Age, alcohol also functioned as a currency in the exchange economy and represented power, credit, and finance. Archaeological evidence and records of alcohol use began to emerge in Egypt and Mesopotamia before 3000 B.C. Inside the pyramids of ancient Egypt, records indicate that a worker was absent from work due to a hangover. Additionally, there is a text on the Urk stone plate that describes beer being provided as a wages and meals, which also recorded the wage statement. Furthermore, it managed and recorded the production and distribution of alcohol at the national level.

Ancient clay tablets from Mesopotamia depict a scene of several people sitting around a jar, drinking thick beer through reed straws stuck at the bottom. This culture of sharing the same liquid served as a sign of trust, confirming to each person that the beverage was not poisoned. While the practice of drinking from a common vessel has largely faded, the tradition of consuming thick, low-intensity alcohol grain beverages like this liquor inherits its reputation in the Middle East and neighbouring Southeast Europe until now, including 'Būẓa'(بوظة) in Egypt.

Arak, a distilled liquor blooming in the alcohol-free Islamic world

Humanity has long been aware of perils of alcohol, promoting various civilizations to attempt to enforce alcohol prohibition. However, successful instance of such regulation are rare. For example, the U.S. 'Prohibition' era provided a significant income boost for Chicago gangs, while ordinary people suffered from suffered illness or punishment from consuming bootleg liquor. Ironically, the Islamic world, which explicitly prohibits alcohol, contributed to the development of distilled liquor. Distillation improved the taste, aroma, and shelf life of alcoholic beverage compared to their fermented counterparts.

Before Islam emerged, Arabs enjoyed drinking extensively, and Muhammad, the prophet of Islam, reportedly refused to drink the pumpkin-made fermented drink 'Nabīdh(نبيذ)', which primarily signifies grape wine in modern Arabic, before receiving his revelations. However, the Quran gradually prohibited alcohol consumption clearly and strictly in 4 stages, and Muslim society also progressively banned alcohol, although not immediately, and began to implement punishment for drinking.

On the other hand, even within the Islamic world, attempts to ban alcohol often backfired due to the 'balloon effect', leading to the development of a high-end alcohol culture and the proliferation of alternative hallucinogens, such as smoking and drugs. When the caliph's faith was vigorously enforced, many Muslims were suddenly punished. However, many caliphs publicly enjoyed drinking, despite needing to set an example in their religious life, and even kept a 'Nadīm'(نديم), a drinking companion, by their side. Numerous judges who were aligned with the regime historically sought to find phrases in their faith to justify the caliph's drinking behaviour. Additionally, Muslim writers extolled alcohol by establishing wine poetry as an independent literary genre, even though references to alcohol in tribal life were only briefly mentioned pre-Islamic poetry. The sophisticated liquor culture of the Islamic world eventually spread globally through the development of a high-quality distilled liquor called Arak.

Alchemist, a leading figure in the development and spread of distilled liquor

Unlike fermented liquor, which can be produced with simple knowledge and equipment or even harvested from nature, distilled liquor requires advanced knowledge and skill, including the manufacture of distillers and mastery of distillation techniques. Therefore, the main contribution to the production of distilled liquor was not traditional brewers but scientists who consistently experimented with the most advanced chemical technology of their time.

Although very rudimentary distillation techniques are mentioned in Akkadian documents from Babylonia around 1200 BC, long before the rise of alchemy, distillation technologies had evolved significantly by the 2nd and 3rd centuries enabling the refinement of low-intensity alcohol in regions such as Greece, India, and China.

However, the chemists who achieved a high degree of pure alcohol extraction were Mediterranean alchemists and East Asian practitioners who had sought to create the mysterious substance of eternal life. The word "chemistry" is derived from the Arabic word 'al-Kīmiyyah' (الكيمياء). This morphed into 'al-Kīmī' when its gender was changed to the masculine form, and then the medieval Europeans pronounced al-Kīmī as alchemy. Essentially, chemistry was synonymous with alchemy at that time, encompassing both scientific and medical knowledge. By adding the Arabic definite article 'al' (ال) to "chemistry", it becomes '*alchemistry*,' and by removing '-stry' from it, it simplifies to alchemy. The core of this alchemy and chemistry was the 'philosopher's stone, achieved through distillation, symbolizing a high concentration of alcohol approaching the status of purity.

'Philosopher's Stone(Lapis philosophorum)' is not a material that turns lead into gold but a catalyst that converts one substance into another. From this point of view, the distillation process of producing the philosopher's stone was philosophical, methodical, and deliberate. The remarkable process by which a substance changes from solid to liquid, then to invisible vapour, and back to liquid, resulting in the formation of pure crystals, is noteworthy. This transformation is spiritual and believed to produce mystical power, enhancing vitality in the eyes of alchemists. This process of extracting the purest elements by dissolving resins and refining oils that are insoluble in water embodies the essence of medical chemistry. It refines crude substances, prevents decay, and consequently promotes health and well-being. The process of extracting alcohol was considered sacred, as the extracted alcohol either evaporated cleanly or oxidized by burning off impurities.

Muslim scientists such as 'Jābir ibn Hāayyān' (721–c. 815) and 'Abū Bakr al-Rāzi' (c. 864 or 865–925 or 935 CE) were eminent medieval physicians, pharmacists, chemists, mathematicians, and also pioneers in attempting to create the elixir(al-iksir). They could not turn lead into gold but were able to develop a method to increase relative volatility by adding salt to boiling wine. Since then, this method has helped accumulated knowledge and data on the physical and chemical principles necessary for improved distillation through various experiments, controlling more diverse materials, temperature, humidity, and mixing ratios. In addition, the experiments also led to the accidental invention of high-quality perfumes and high-purity alcohol.

The spread of pure edible alcohol developed by these Muslims under the name of 'Arak' ('Araq in Arabic) to every corner of Europe, Africa, and Asia represents a symbolic milestone in the history of alcohol exchange. The Arabic word 'Araq is derived from the word 'araqa' means sweating, named for the appearance of water forming on the surface of the distiller during the distillation process, resembling sweat. This distillation technology first flourished in Baghdad, where intellectuals gathered from around the world, translating and experimenting with knowledge, 'the Abbasid 'House of

Wisdom.' It later advanced in regions across the major cities across the Islamic world, represented by Cordoba. Iraq, the centre of the Abbasid dynasty, is 'al-i-ra-q' in Arabic. Those words share the common consonants of 'ayn(ع)'-'ra(ر)'-'qa(ق)'.

'Araq spread widely around the world along the exchange routes of global civilization. While it retained its name and distillation technology, the drink was largely localized by substituting the main and auxiliary ingredients with those available in the local environment. In Iraq, which is rich abundant with date palms, 'Araq was traditionally made from dates. Conversely, in the Mediterranean area, known for its plentiful grapes, 'Araq was mainly made from grapes.

The name Arak was simplified by the name 'Raki' as it made its way to Turkey, and upon reaching Greece, it was renamed 'Uzo'. As it spread further, the adaptation of main and auxiliary ingredients to suit each region became more pronounced.

In the Balkan Peninsula relatively close to the original source, the drink known as 'Rakiya', incorporated a mixture of local flavors including plums, grapes, apricots, pears, cherries or berries, other fruits or honey. However, in more distant regions, like France and Britain, the beverage underwent more significant modifications, resulting with a blend of a more complex and diverse array of ingredients.

Fig 27–1. Lion Rhyton, Parthian, 1st century B.C.: Wine glasses, particularly rhytons, were commonly believed to convey the power of the animal to the drinkers.[1]

The Mongols, who conquered nearly half of Asia and Europe, definitely influenced the history of distilled liquor. The Mongols, who traditionally drank a fermented drink called 'Ayran' from animal milk, began to produce and document 'Arkhi' a distilled spirit derived from livestock milk, in the 13th century upon conquering the Islamic world. They also spread 'Araq and its distillation techniques across their vast territories.

Occupied East Asia by the Mongols had limited access to dates, grapes,

---

1 Wikicommons, https://upload.wikimedia.org/wikipedia/commons/5/5d/Lion_Rhyton%2C_Parthian%2C_1st_century_B.C.jpg

horses or sheep milk, but was abundant in crops. China already had its own distilled liquor called 'Shaojiu'(燒酒), and even before the 'Yuan(元)' Period, it had adopted distillation methods from Southeast Asia and other regions. However, during the Yuan Dynasty, Chinese records launched to document the production and consumption of 'Aliqi', which was influenced by Islamic distillation techniques. In Goryeo, beyond China, distilled liquor developed around the regions of 'Kaesong', 'Andong', and 'Jeju', which were the Japanese conquest bases of the Goryeo-Mongolian alliance, and its traces are still remain intact from over 700 years ago. In Kaesong, the spirit is still known as Arakju, in Andong as Andong Soju, and in Jeju as 'Kosori.' South and Southeast

Fig 27-2. Traditional distiller of Soju(Korean Araq), Andong Soju Museum, ©Jin Han, JEONG

Asia also adopted the arak distillation technique through marine routes and consumed distilled liquor under the name of 'Arrak' or "Araq.'

Europe's Alchemy, Sources of Industrial Alcohol Production

Jabir's distillation method became the foundation for the development of European distillation technology through the works of Arabic scholars like 'Al-Kindi'(-873) and 'Al-Farabi'(-950), 'Al-Zahrawi'(936-1013) and other authors whose works were later translated into Latin and other European languages. Distillation and distilled alcohol were initially introduced in the Iberian Peninsula, Sicily, and Southeast Europe, which served as the main channels of interaction between Muslims and Europeans. By the end of the Crusades, distilled alcohol was widely recognized in Europe as 'aqua ardens'("burning water").

At that time, Europeans referred to alcohol as "aqua vita" using it to prevent diseases and developing it as a medical product. 'Taddeo Alderotti' (1223-1296), a doctor and a pharmacologist in Florence, developed a remarkable distillation method that extracted 90% of ethanol. Later in 1796, 'Johann Tobias Lowitz' obtained pure ethanol. Following these developments, scientists succeeded in developing the composition, chemical formula, and methods of synthesizing alcohol, thereby laying the groundwork for industrial alcohol production.

Today, industrial alcohol usually uses ethylene extracted from petroleum as its main ingredient. Ethanol is commonly produced by reacting with water and sulfuric acid, followed by process of liquefaction, distillation, and purification.

Ethanol, which is non-toxic upon contact with the skin and offers strong antibacterial properties at a low coast, has become a primary ingredient in medicine and beauty products applied to the skin. It is the most common disinfectant, found in wet wipes, antidote, cleaning agents, experimental reagents, and organic solvent, and is also utilized as a drug after dilution.

Ethanol is also in the spotlight as a clean energy source due to its high flammability, volatility, good thermal efficiency, stability at room temperature, and lower pollutant emission compared to methanol and other fossil fuels. Alcohol lamps serve various purposed including lighting, heating, and cooking. Additionally, ethanol is used as a colorant or decolorizer and even in thermometers.

In addition to its use as an oil substitute, ethanol serves as both a fuel and fuel additive for automobiles and as propellant for rocket projectiles. Compared to fossil fuels, this biogas is more favored over fossil fuels in the era of decarbonization because it produces cleaner exhaust gases.

Methanol is derived from wood, not petroleum. It is primarily used in industrial products and processes that do not involve living organisms due to its low flash point and emission of toxic substances. Because methanol accelerates the oxidation of metals and rubber, its use as a fuel is avoided; instead, it is specially employed for metal cleaning or paint removal.

Islam: seeking Alcohol-free world; leading Alcohol Industry

As noted earlier, one of the significant barriers to alcohol usage is Islam. Since alcohol is considered '*haram*' by Muslims, who make up nearly a quarter of the world's population, there is a significant restriction on the use of alcohol, particularly in products that come into contact with the body. The well-established 'halal' dietary laws not only restrict the consumption of alcoholic beverages, food, and sauces containing certain level of alcohol (usually 0.05-0.1%) during natural fermentation, but these laws are also progressively being applied to the production, packaging, and distribution of all products in facilities.

Recently, the inclination has been a growing preference for alcohol-free products, especially in beauty products where alcohol was previously not a concern. Additionally, alcohol-based disinfectants such as hand sanitizers are increasingly being replaced by non-alcoholic products in various ettings.

This trend became more pronounced after the COVID-19 pandemic, as the halal status of vaccines and other medicines emerged as a new topic of discussion. While the Islamic community will use ready-made products, including those containing alcohol, if there are no substitutes, they naturally prefer alternatives when available. Consequently, not only global food and consumer goods and manufactures but also medical companies have recently intensified their efforts to develop non-alcoholic products specifically for the Islamic market.

Nevertheless, the Islamic world has historically been a major contributor to and beneficiary of the development and evolution of alcohol. It is also expected to play a significant role in the use and exchange of next-generation alcohol products. Most of the ethyl alcohol is extracted from petroleum. Also, the distillation process consumes a huge amount of energy which is often supplied by inexpensive electricity generation from coal.

However, as has always been the case, the development and evolution of alcohol have been driven by exchanges among civilizations. Just as South Korea and Japan, which were used to be net oil imports, now compete for the top spot in exports of petroleum products and petrochemical goods, the production and distribution of alcohol are also sustained by global supply chains. Furthermore, the division of labour structure, where the export of raw material and the production of processed products were separate, is shifting towards collaboration. Oil-producing countries are increasingly requesting joint production or joint ventures. This remarks a new era of alcohol exchange between civilizations.

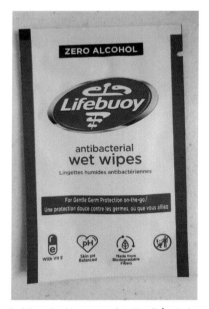

Fig 27-3. Alcohol Free Sanitizer served in Saudia's airplanes, ©Jin Han, JEONG

Keywords

alcohol, chemistry, ritual, liquor, medical science

References

Al-Hassan, Ahmad Y. (2007). "Alcohol and the distillation of wine in Arabicsources." *Artikel diakses pada* 21.

Holmyard, Eric John. (1968). *Alchemy*. Harmondsworth: Penguin Books.

Moran, Bruce T., (2005). *Distilling Knowledge: Alchemy, Chemistry, Scientific Revolution*, Cambridge, Mass.; London: Harvard University Press.

Park, Hyunhee, (2021). *Soju the Global History*, Cambridge; New York: Cambridge University Press.

Principe, Lawrence M. (2012). *The secrets of alchemy*. Chicago: University of Chicago Press.

Image References

Wikicommons: https://upload.wikimedia.org/wikipedia/commons/5/5d/Lion_Rhyton%2C_Parthian%2C_1st_century_B.C.jpg

written by Jin Han Jeong (Hankuk University of Foreign Studies)

▼

Wars

28

Crusades

General definition

The term 'Crusade' is primarily attributed to a series of military expeditions led by European kings and many important feudal lords roughly between the end of the 11th century and the late 13th century. Later, these expeditions, promoted and supported by the Latin Catholic Church of Rome, developed into religious wars and the most famous are those that took place in the Near East aimed at reconquering the Holy Land from Islamic rule, mainly in Anatolia, in the Levant (a word that can correspond to the Arabic term 'Mashriq'), in the eastern Mediterranean Sea, but also in Egypt and Tunisia.

The word 'Crusade' has been used in modern English since the early 18th century, thus long after the events had taken place. Its origin can be traced in the crossing of the term 'Croisade', attested in French around 1570, with the Spanish term 'Cruzada', also used during the 16th century and both derived from the medieval Latin 'Cruciata', past participle of the verb 'Cruciare', "sign with the cross". The noun therefore recalls the cross that those who participated in the crusades had sewn on their clothes as a symbol of their pilgrimage. At the end of 1200s, the word 'Crusade' was not attested and the same law scholars who drafted the Crusader legislation defined it as 'Iter', 'Peregrination', or 'Passagium'.

Although the term 'Crusade' has been adopted by historians to describe Christian military expeditions from 1095 onwards, the range of events to which the term has been applied is extremely broad. Historians like Thomas Asbridge, Jonathan Riley-Smith, and Giles Constable have described some different trends among scholars regarding the use of this word: "traditionalists" restrict the definition of crusade to campaigns conducted by Christians only in the Holy Land between 1095 and 1272 and then until 1291; "pluralists" speak of crusade referring to all military campaign officially promoted by a reigning Pope. The latter would more closely reflect the position of the Catholic Church (and of some authoritative medieval commentators such as Bernard of Clairvaux), according to which any military campaign officially sanctioned by a Pope would be equally valid as a 'Crusade'.

In some sources prior to the 13th century, it is possible to find the expression 'Cruce signati' regarding the crusaders, even if the Byzantine soldiers called themselves "soldiers of the cross" already in the time of the emperor Heraclius (575~641 AD).

These military campaigns were often invoked and blessed, as happened in the case of Pope Urban II who, with his heartfelt appeal to Western Christianity to help the East, contributed to the beginning of the First Crusade.

According to some historical interpretations, the crusades had an eminently religious motivation, i.e., the intention to free the land where Jesus was born, where he preached and died from Muslim occupation. Thus, in this sense, they would not have been strictly religious wars, given that the aim was never to force Muslims to change their religion. The crusaders most likely set out with their weapons and fought in the Holy Land with motivations that had very little to do with religion, rather with a desire to conquer and liberate the Holy Land itself, which inevitably involved the use of force.

Authoritative Christian sources, on the other hand, maintained the absence of guilt in killing the invading enemies of the faith. This Christian vision of a holy war that would be later the basis of the ideology of the crusade is significantly noted in 'De laude novae militiae ad Milites Templi', a treatise written between 1128 and 1136 by the Cistercian monk Bernard of Clairvaux (1090~1153).

The crusades, therefore, were not caused by abstract opposing religious visions, nor only, as certain scholars affirm, by the intention of achieving personal and material enrichment. The casus belli were the request for help, also supported by a letter from the Byzantine emperor Alexius I Comnenus, addressed by some Eastern Christian religious communities to deal with the oppression to which they were subjected by the local Muslim authorities and guarantee the safety of pilgrims who went to the Holy Land.

This does not mean that the crusades did not express significant political and economic motives that arose within the European and Byzantine medieval feudal world and, as a concrete purpose, the control of the Holy Land and the surrender of local Muslims. Crusades are also considered by some scholars as a delayed response of Christianity to the Islamic expansion of the 7th century AD, which had led to the occupation of vast territories: Spain, Syria, Palestine, Egypt, and the rest of North Africa and Mesopotamia, which had been Christian lands from the 1st to the 3rd century AD and whose reconquest was thought to be lawful.

The first crusade was called, as mentioned, by Pope Urban II during a speech given during the Council of Clermont, an assembly of Catholic clergymen and laymen which was held precisely at Clermont, then included in the Duchy of Aquitaine from 18 to 28 November 1095.

In this Council, Pope Urban II invoked military aid to the Byzantine Empire and to its emperor Alexius I Comnenus, who needed reinforcements to face the Seljuk Turks, who were conquering Anatolia after their victory over another Byzantine emperor, Romanus IV Diogenes, in the battle of Manzikiert in 1071.

The Pope's aim would have been to guarantee pilgrims free access to the Holy Land, ruled by Muslims since the 7th century AD. Scholars, however, disagree on this point. The implied intention of Urban II may have been rather that of reuniting the Eastern Christian Church with the Western one, separated following the East-West Schism, also known as the 'Great Schism', of 1054, and proposing himself as head of the reunited Christian Church.

In addition to this motivation of a religious and spiritual nature, there was another one, much more practical and, one could say, profane: the Catholic Church was at that time one of the largest feudal landowners and could have been interested in subjugating the Orthodox Church in order to extend its own political and economic jurisdiction in Eastern Europe and, at the same time, expel Muslims from the territories of the Near and Middle East and from North Africa. For these reasons, the Catholic Church assumed the role of ideological promoter of the crusades.

The success of the first crusade allowed the foundation of the first 4 Crusader States in the eastern Mediterranean Sea: The County of Edessa, the Principality of Antioch, the Kingdom of Jerusalem, and the County of Tripoli.

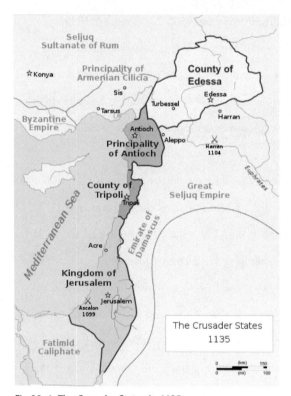

Fig 28–1. The Crusader States in 1135

Occurrence: background

The reasons for the initial success of the Crusades for the Christians are to be found above all in that great new spiritual fervor which characterized Western Europe at that time: the enthusiastic response to the preaching of Pope Urban II by all the social classes later set a precedent for subsequent military expeditions. In particular, the Pope urged the poorest social strata of the European population to seek their human and economic redemption in the East. Those who left voluntarily became crusaders by pronouncing a public vow and, in exchange, obtained the deferment of payment of their debts, the remission of sins, and plenary indulgence. In this way, huge masses of poor people took part in the Crusades to escape hunger, feudal obligations as serfs, and the miserable conditions in which they lived.

Even the most privileged and wealthy social classes, however, had their interest in participating in the Crusades: the rich feudal lords, kings, dukes, and counts were always looking for new ways to enlarge their possessions, increase their earnings, and consolidate their influence in Europe. These nobles felt threatened by the expansion of the wealth of the new bourgeois classes who had contributed to the birth of the Municipalities.

European society in the 11th century AD was in a moment of considerable economic and demographic development, following a trend that began between the 8th and the 9th century AD. However, there was a certain discomfort caused by the rules of the feudal system, according to which minor sons of noble families, who were often small landowners or knights, in the absence of the paternal inheritance, which belonged to the eldest son, had as their only choices the ecclesiastical or the military career. There were, therefore, many well-armed and equipped knights, often of French origin, who went in search of fortune and who jumped at the opportunity to leave for the Crusades to the East to obtain territories. On many occasions, they constituted the best organized and prepared departments of the Crusader armed forces.

As has been previously said, the response of the masses to Pope Urban II's invocation was enthusiastic, much more than he himself could have thought. In the First Crusade, about 40,000 people responded to his appeal, of which only a part was made up of the knights mentioned before. Eventually, most of those who took up the cross were peasants, often poor and without fighting skills. Every volunteer who became a crusader undertook to make a pilgrimage to the Church of the Holy Sepulcher in Jerusalem, and for this, he received a cross as a gift which was usually sewn onto his clothes.

The historical debate on the actual participation of the various social classes in the crusades is still ongoing. According to Thomas Asbridge and Jonathan Riley-Smith, it is misleading to argue that crusaders were motivated only by greed and the hope to find a better life, far from the hunger and poverty they lived in France. They believe that certainly greed was an important factor due to the high costs and risks involved in a journey to the Holy Land and add that many crusaders returned to their homes at the end of the pilgrimage rather than remaining in the East.

The 2 historians also argue that not all the knights who went on the crusade were minor sons of noble families or adventurers in search of fortune. Crusades were led by some of the most powerful noble lords of France who abandoned their possessions, often going so far as to sell them to afford armor, weapons, and travel for themselves and for the knights in their service. Among them, we can mention Robert Curthose, Tancred of Hauteville, Boemond I of Antioch, Godfrey of Bouillon, and Eustache III Count of Boulogne.

It is difficult to fully understand the reasons that prompted thousands of poor people, for whom there are no reliable sources, to join the crusades, just as it is complicated to understand the reasons for the most prominent

Fig 28–2. Pope Urban II preaches the First Crusade during the Council of Clermont (1095)

characters, whose stories were later put into writing by monks and clerics, but probably without due objectivity. The medieval secular world and the spiritual world of the Church were so connected that it is likely that religiosity was an important factor for many crusaders.

To try to understand what drove knights and noble lords to undertake such an expensive and dangerous mission, it is necessary to remember that they were men who had a very strong religious sentiment. In the 11th century, the culture of nobles involved a public demonstration of piety: they were known both for their military exploits and for their love for God, and it was a duty of an aristocrat to put himself at the service of the Church and the people. Crusades, therefore, constituted a further means of demonstrating their loyalty, given that by defending the Church, they defended all that was good and right in the world.

Process and development

Modern historians have expressed mixed opinions of crusaders. According to some, most crusaders were driven by a sincere love for God, but others highlighted their behaviors inconsistent with their stated goals. Crusaders and their commanders often kept the lands conquered from the Muslims for themselves instead of returning them to the Byzantines, as they had sworn to the Pope. Furthermore, crusaders were often responsible for looting, crimes, and violence of all kinds. During the First Crusade, for example, the massacres they carried out in Antioch and Jerusalem were so heinous that the Byzantines soon distanced themselves from their exploits, both because they had also plundered Christian cities and because the idea of a "holy war" with fully armed bishops, abbots, and monks was foreign to Byzantine culture.

Crusades had a profound impact on Western society: they reopened the Mediterranean routes to trade and travel, removing them from the control of the Byzantine Empire and the Muslims; they consolidated a certain collective identity of the Church of Rome led by the Pope; they provided a fruitful source of tales of heroism and chivalry which were then taken up again in chivalric literature, in philosophy and, more generally, in medieval literature.

In what is defined in Europe as the 'Near East', during the 7th century AD, there had been Arab conquests characterized by Muslim expansion: after the Arabian Peninsula, first Syria, then the cities of Antioch and Jerusalem, and all the Byzantine Mesopotamia fell under Islamic rule.

Tolerance, trade, and political relations between Arabs and Europeans went through ups and downs. Caliph al-Hakim, for example, who reigned from 1000 to 1021, had the Church of the Holy Sepulcher in Jerusalem destroyed, but his successor allowed the Byzantines to rebuild it. Although the situation was not always stable, Christian pilgrims were allowed to visit holy places, and Christian residents in Muslim lands were given the status of 'Dhimmi', with their own legal rights.

Jews and Christians, who in the Koran were called 'People of the Book' (Ahl al-Kitab in Arabic), were in fact able to remain and live in their lands, continuing to profess their faith, albeit with various limitations, but they had to pay the 'Jizya', a tax imposed on anyone who was not of Muslim faith.

In the second half of the 10th century, Byzantine Empire tried to reconquer

Syria, lost in the 7th century, and with some effective campaigns, regained possession of Cilicia and part of Syria itself. In the year 974, the Abbasid caliph of Baghdad accused the Byzantines for their "occupation of Islamic lands" and called for 'Jihad', to which fighters also responded from Central Asia. Due to contrasts between Sunnis and Shiites, however, the Muslims met defeat and in 1001, the Byzantine emperor Basil II concluded a 10-year truce with the caliph.

In 1077, Jerusalem was conquered by the Seljuk Turks and following this event, there was talk of robberies, kidnappings, and violence committed against pilgrims heading to the Holy Land. Some historians believe, however, that these episodes of violence were exaggerated or magnified to arouse an armed reaction in Latin Christians. After the disastrous Byzantine defeat at Manzikiert, in fact, the growing power of the Seljuk Turks scared the Christian world; the Byzantine Empire was going through a time of crisis, and the fear was that even Latin Christianity could be overwhelmed and conquered by the Turks themselves. Therefore, the new Byzantine emperor, precisely Alexius I Comnenus, despite the differences between the Church of Rome and that of Constantinople, decided to ask the Pope for help with Eastern Christianity. Thus, was born the First Crusade.

Crusaders, Byzantines, and Muslims from 11th to 13th century

In mid-July 1099, following the First Crusade, Jerusalem returned to Christianity, more than 4 years after the speech of Pope Urban II who had urged the West to free Christian places from Islamic rule. In 1187 however,

Jerusalem was reconquered by the Kurdish ruler and leader Salah al-Din, who took advantage of the hostility of the Byzantines towards the crusaders, often responsible for robberies and violence both in the Holy City and in the rest of the overseas military kingdoms which they had built there.

Several kings and renowned personalities of that era took part from time to time in the various crusades that took place until the late 13th century, such as Frederick Barbarossa, Richard I of England, and Philip II of France in the Second Crusade.

In 1219, Francis of Assisi arrived in the Egyptian city of Damietta along with 11 of his companions during the 5th crusade, with the aim of converting Sultan al-Kamil to Christianity and ending the fighting. The city was besieged by the Crusaders and perhaps Francis was able to cross the Muslim lines and meet the Sultan in his camps, where he seems to have stayed for a few days.

Fig 28–3. Conquest of Constantinople by the Crusaders (1204)

Welcomed with great courtesy by al-Kamil, Francis had a long conversation with him and then walked away unharmed.

According to some late sources, the Sultan appreciated Francis' words while remaining a Muslim; he also allowed Francis to visit the sacred places of the Holy Land to preach there and gave him gifts. No Arab sources, however, mention this meeting.

The 6th Crusade (1228~1229) is known as the Crusade of Frederick II Hohenstaufen. The great emperor set out for the Holy Land with a small army and arrived at Acre on 7 September 1228. Growing up in Sicily, in the multicultural Palermo of that time, Frederick II spoke 6 languages including Arabic, and in a short time, he concluded a positive negotiation with Sultan

Fig 28–4. Sixth Crusade (1228~1229): Holy Roman Emperor Frederick II Hohenstaufen (left) meets Ayyubid Sultan of Egypt al–Malik al–Kamil (right)

al-Malik, avoiding any armed confrontation thanks to the good relations he had with him. Christians would have had free access, but without weapons, to Jerusalem, Nazareth, and Bethlehem.

Frederick II discovered the Arab civilization, bringing to Europe Arab institutions, technologies, inventions, and the immense Arab libraries which conserved, among other things, many ancient Latin and Greek texts translated by Arab and Persian scholars, including Aristotle's works, which had disappeared for a 1000 year in the West.

Cultural exchanges between Europe and the Islamic world, also passing through the Byzantine Empire, were many and intense from the 11th to the 13th century, i.e., the entire period of the Crusades. Islamic contribution to medieval Europe involved various fields such as art, architecture, medicine, agriculture, music, language, science, mathematics, astronomy, and technology. The main point of diffusion of Islamic knowledge in Europe at that time were Sicily and Spain, especially the city of Toledo when it was conquered by the Castilian Christians in 1085 AD.

One of the rare sources about the crusades that don't come from the Christian West of the time is the 'Alexiad', a medieval historical and biographical text written in the form of Attic Greek around 1148 AD by the Byzantine princess Anna Komnene (1083~1153 AD), daughter of emperor Alexios I Komnenos. Anna described the political and military history of the Byzantine Empire during the reign of her father and, among other topics, in the 'Alexiad', she documents the Byzantine Empire's interaction with the crusades and highlights the conflicting perceptions of the East and West in the

Fig 28–5. The Four Commanders of the First Crusade, including Godfrey of Bouillon, in an 1883 painting by Alphonse–Marie–Adolphe de Neuville

early 12th century.

In her essay, therefore, Anna provided insight into political relations and wars between Alexios I and the West, vividly describing weaponry, tactics and battles. It has been noted that she was writing about events occurred when she was a child, so these are not eyewitness accounts; moreover, her neutrality is compromised by the fact that she praised her father and denigrated his successors. But despite her partiality, her account of the First Crusade is of great value to history because it is the only Byzantine eyewitness account available.

Anna had the opportunity to gather information from key figures in the Byzantine elite: her husband, Nikephorus Bryennios, had fought in the clash with crusade leader Godfrey of Buoillon outside of Constantinople in 1097, and her uncle, George Palaeologos, was present at Pelekanon in the same year when Alexios I discussed future strategy with the crusaders. Thus, the 'Alexiad' allows the events of the First Crusade to be seen from the Byzantine elite's perspective: it conveys the alarm felt at the scale of the Western European forces proceeding through the Empire and the dangers they might have posed to the safety of Constantinople.

Anna identified for the first time the Vlachs from Balkans with Dacians, describing their places around Haemus mountains; she also reserved a special suspicion for crusading leader Boemond of Taranto, a southern Italian Norman who, under the leadership of his father Robert Guiscard, had invaded Byzantine territory in the Balkans in 1081. Anna referred to the crusaders as "Celts", reflecting old Greek terminology for western barbarians.

In Sicily, with the Islamic conquest of the island in 965 AD and with its reconquest by the Normans in 1091 AD, an advanced Arab-Norman culture developed, represented, for example, by King Roger II of Hauteville who had Islamic poets, scientists and soldiers in his service.

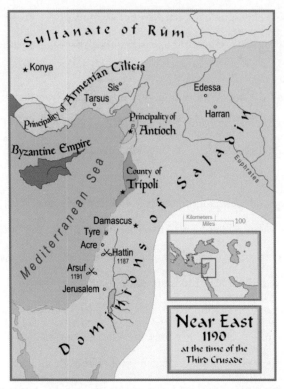

Fig 28–6. Crusaders States in 1190 at the inception of the Third Crusade

Keywords

Crusades; Pope Urban II; Byzantines; Seljuk Turks; Anna Komnene

References

Christopher Tyerman: *The World of the Crusades*. Yale University Press, 2019

Thomas Asbridge: *The Crusades: The War for the Holy Land*. Simon & Shuster, 2012

Christopher Tyerman: *The Debate on the Crusades, 1099–2010*. Manchester University Press, 2011

Giles Constable: *The Historiography of the Crusades*, 2001. In Angeliki E. Laiou and Roy P. Mottahedeh (ed.) *The Crusades from the Perspective of Byzantium and the Muslim World*. Dumbarton Oaks

Outremer; Jihad; Frank; Latin; Saracen: Oxford English Dictionary (online edition). Oxford University Press

Andrew Jotischky: *Crusading and the Crusader States*. Pearson Longman, 2004

Claude Cahen: *The Turkish Invasion: The Selchukids (1969)*, in Setton, K. A History of the Crusades: Volume I

Jacques Le Goff: *Il Basso Medioevo*, Milano, Feltrinelli, 1967

Steven Runciman: *A History of the Crusades, Volume One: The First Crusade and The Foundation of The Kingdom of Jerusalem*. Cambridge University Press, 1951

Jonathan Riley-Smith: *The Crusades: A Short History*. Second, Yale University Press, 2005

Steven Runciman: *A History of The Crusades, Volume Two: The Kingdom of Jerusalem and the Frankish East, 1100~1187*. Cambridge University Press, 1952

Image References

https://en.m.wikipedia.org/wiki/Crusader_states

https://en.m.wikipedia.org/wiki/File:CouncilofClermont.jpg

https://en.m.wikipedia.org/wiki/Sack_of_Constantinople

https://ko.wikipedia.org/wiki/%ED%8C%8C%EC%9D%BC:Friedrich_II._mit_Sultan_al-Kamil.jpg

https://mg.wikipedia.org/wiki/Kroazada_voalohany

https://en.m.wikipedia.org/wiki/File:Map_Crusader_states_1190-en.svg

written by Emiliano Pennisi (Sogang University)

29

Battle of Kadesh

Battle of Kadesh and the World's First Peace Treaty

In the 13th century BCE, the 2 strong powers, Egypt and Hittite, clashed over the hegemony of the Orient world near the current Syrian-Türkiye border. After repeating the conflicts, a peace treaty was signed between them.

The Kadesh War began during the reign of Ramesses II of Egypt and Muwatallis II of the Hittites, and a peace treaty was signed about 16 years later. For 16 years, Ramses II continued to rule Egypt as a pharaoh, while the

Hittites changed kings twice due to various circumstances. Thus, the Hittite treaty in Egypt was signed between Hattusillis III (King of the Hittites) and Ramses II (Ramses the Great), not between Muwatallis II during the Kadesh War.

The Egyptian-Hittite peace treaty is the earliest known surviving peace treaty, which was drawn up in 1,271 BCE, also called the Treaty of Kadesh, for which the versions of both sides have survived. 2 copies of the treaty were made, one in hieroglyphics and the other in the Mesopotamian language of Akkadian (or Babylonian-Assyrian).

The about forty lines of the Egyptian Kadesh Treaty version were engraved in hieroglyphics on the walls of 2 temples, the Rameseum for the funeral of Ramses II and the Precinct of Amun-Re at the temple of Karnak. Its Hittite version remains on clay tablets excavated from the ruins of Hattusa, now in Türkiye.

Regional Circumstances

Ancient Egypt had built around fertile land along the Nile River, and sought to expand its territory to Sudan to the south and to Asian continent through the Sinai Peninsula to the northeast for thousands of years. During the 'New Kingdom' period from the 15th to the 11th centuries BCE, Asian land was particularly active, and Palestine and Lebanon were largely Egyptian territory, as well as Kadesh, a key point that could be seen as far as Anatolia by the Seti I of the 18th Dynasty.

However, a series of powerful races and countries emerged in Asia. Among them there was Hittite, who had once emerged as the loser of the East area, with iron weapons and excellent cavalry-tank troops. Hittite regarded Egypt's entry into Asia as a significant threat. Thus, Hittite's Muwatallis II moved the capital from Hattusa to Tarhuntasa in the south and converted Kadesh back into the land of Hittite. It stimulated Ramses II, the son of Seti I and the ambition of a conqueror, so that a fight of the century was inevitable.

Battle of Kadesh: the Confrontation of the Century

During the reign of Ramses II in the 13th century BCE, Egypt competed with the Hittites over Palestine. In 1274 BCE, Ramses II headed to Kadesh with about 20,000 soldiers from four legions, and King Muwatallis II of Hittite confronted with about 50,000 troops. It was the first world war of humankind in which Egyptian and Asian civilizations collided.

Egypt struggled so hard but Ramses whom false information leaked by Muwatallis deceived, made the mistake of dividing the troops in half while crossing the Orontes River. At this opportunity, Hittites launched a surprise attack, and Ramses was on the verge of being killed or captured. However, while Muwatalliss was not putting all his forces in at once with excessive caution, the Egyptian army's successor joined the battlefield, and the Hittites could no longer maintain their overwhelming advantage in the early stages of the battle. In the end, Ramses crossed the river safely and retreated, and the two military camps confronted each other for some time on either side of the Orontes River, and each turned their steps and returned home.

The War and Its Aftermath

As such, the showdown of the century ended in terms of battle, and strategically, it could be concluded that Egypt failed to recapture its goal, Kadesh. However, Ramses glorified it as his heroic victory and fabricated it to promote it. This is because he was a man who could not lose, 'Shining forever like the sun.' Fortunately, the media was not as developed as it is now. Therefore, it was not difficult for the people to know what happened far outside the country. Ramses considered himself a hero by sending troops to Asia to make the hero story true. Hittite shook off the challenge every time, but in the meantime, things were changing.

Muwatallis died 2 years after the battle of Kadesh, and the throne was succeeded by his son, Mursilis III. Since Mursilis III was still young, he appointed his uncle Hattusillis, who had strong political influence since his father's time, as governor of the northern region and tried to keep him away from the royal palace. However, Hattusillis staged a coup around 1267 BCE, overthrowing his nephew from the throne and becoming Hattusillis III. However, because there were still lots of supportive forces for Mursilis, Hattusillis appointed Mursilis as governor of the southern region, just as his nephew did, and even planned to assassinate him secretly. Accordingly, Mursilis defected to Egypt and sought to regain the throne by relying on Ramses II. Egypt did not recognize Hattusillis as the king of Hittite, and it was about to start a new war again. It was about to put forward Mursilis as the justification for 'punishing the haters of Hittite.'

Hattusillis, who had become so complicated, had to think about the pressure of Assyria to make matters worse. The emerging power, Assyria, had engulfed Babylon and invaded Syria, posing the strongest threat to Hittite, which was slowly entering a period of decline. Hattusillis finally had to make a big decision because of being surrounded by enemies.

In about 1,259 BCE, Hattusillis' envoy, who came to Phiramses, Egypt, presented Ramses with a silver plate with inscriptions. It was the first draft of the Hittite-Egypt Treaty (the Kadesh Agreement). Hattusillis made a reasonable judgment of reconciliation with one of the enemies before and after, and of making a joint confrontation against the other.

Ramses didn't mind this either because if Hittite falls to Assyria, Egypt may be trampled on the horse's hooves, and there was a limit to misleading the people with exaggerated propaganda. For Ramses, if conquering Asia was practically difficult, he could have ended the myth by creating an image of 'generously accepting the peace that Hittite begged for'. Therefore, Ramses did not put this treaty in the archives of the royal palace. Instead, he carved it on the wall of the temple as a means of showing off.

The Contents of the Treaty and Its Historical Significance

* Treaty between the Hittites and Egypt

No.	Provisions	Keywords
I	Preamble	Hatti: **Hattusilis**, Mursilis, Suppiluliurmas Egypt: **User-maat-Re** (**Ramses II**), Men-maat-Re (Seti I), Men-pehti-Re (Ramses I)

No.	Provisions	Keywords
II	Former Relations	From this day, maintaining the present border line in order not to permit hostility to occur between them forever
III	The Present Treaty	Keeping the good peace and the brotherhood between us (for generation) forever
IV	Mutual Renunciation of Invasion	Modern type of a non-aggression pact
V	Reaffirmation of Former Treaties	Reaffirming the former treaties
VI	A Defensive Alliance for Egypt	Modern type of a mutual defense treaty (MDT)
VII	A Defensive Alliance for Hatti	
VIII	The Contingency of Death?	Continuity of the treaty
IX	Extradition of Refugees to Egypt	Modern type of an extradition treaty
X	Extradition of Refugees to Hatti	
XI	The Divine Witnesses to the Treaty	Witnesses (Divine): a thousand gods
XII	Curses and Blessings for the Treaty	In compliance with the treaty
XIII	Extradition of Egyptians from Hatti	Modern type of extradition treaty
XIV	Extradition of Hittites from Egypt	
XV	Description of the Tablet	

* **Reference:** *Treaty, Law and Covenant in the Ancient Near East.*

The treaty was signed because both sides insisted on a great victory.

However, both sides needed both sides needed it, and the treaty, which has both parties' records, is a rare and historically valuable diplomatic document in ancient history. Also, although the treaty was signed in ancient times, its contents were surprisingly modern. The 2 sides agreed to establish peace permanently without invading the other country's territory and agreed to cooperate in the event of foreign invasion or domestic disturbance.

In addition, political asylum seekers are arrested and sent back by both sides, but no matter what status the political prisoner holds, he or she shall not be punished for his or her crimes, including direct or wife-in-law. It even stipulates that no harm should be inflicted on one's body.

As shown in the above table, the treaty consisted of 15 provisions, including the preamble. Surprisingly, the contents of the treaty proclaim the establishment of a peace in the modern sense. It stipulated the mutual inviolability of the modern international societies between countries, and more surprisingly, it stipulated a mutual defense treaty (MDT) and contained information about a modern type of extradition treaty.

The preamble, which is not in Hittites' one, was added with praise for Ramses, and the expression of the text was slightly modified to express both Ramses and Hattusillis as 'King' in Hittites' one, while Ramses and Hattusillis were differentially expressed as 'Prince' in Egypt. However, the essential content of the treaty remained the same. After confirming the principle of mutual non-aggression and recognizing the existing bilateral border (which eventually cemented Kadesh as the territory of Hittite), the principle of bilateral defense alliance was specified.

Subsequently, there is a provision that if an important figure or city of the two countries betrays, defects, or surrenders to the other country, the two countries should not accept it and return the person who has fled immediately. And then there is the oath to the thousands of gods that exist in Egypt and the Hittites, and somehow, the content after that is severely damaged. So if one looks at Hittites' one, it is imperative from Hattusillis's point of view.

The content, which is awkward for an international treaty clause, reveals that Hattusillis's decision to sign a peace treaty with Ramses was to ensure personal safety and national security. Since he took his nephew's throne in a coup, he was not always free from legitimacy disputes, and he was always worried that someone might take his or her successor's throne by coup or assassination. Therefore, the provision of repatriation of asylum seekers was made to regain Mursilis, who had fled to Egypt, and to borrow Egypt's power to relieve him in the future.

Therefore, this treaty becomes a more regrettable treaty for Hittites and the fact that Hattusillis sent his eldest daughter to Ramses' wife with a considerable amount of dowry after the treaty was signed supports this point. As a result, Ramses, who could better use the treaty to idolize it, refused to repatriate Mursilis until the end (and thus partially violated the treaty) but supported Hattusillis to succeed to power safely. As stated in the treaty, Egypt and Hittite never went to war again, and the Orient enjoyed relatively long peace until 1,180 BCE when Hittite was attacked and virtually defeated by 'the peoples of the sea' (though considered the ancestors of the Greeks and Italians) on the Mediterranean side. In other words, the peace treaty and the Egyptian-Hittite alliance had a apparent deterrent effect on Assyria.

However, the reform of the Egyptian army was delayed due to the war. It rapidly weakened from the next dynasty, the 20th Dynasty of Egypt, and from the 21st Dynasty of Egypt, it was an opportunity to collapse as a conquered.

Hittites also collapsed around 1,200 BCE due to the rapid weakening of power after consuming national power in the war. Since then, small countries have been scattered in Anatolia for about 1,000 years.

Epilogue

Unlike today's treaties, where only one edition existed, the Hittite-Egypt Treaty was carefully agreed upon and selected not only for the preamble but also for each word of the agreement. It also shared the nature of an agreement between states and personal promises between monarchs, and some contents were not kept in the end (unconditional repatriation of asylum seekers from other countries). However, most of them were observed for an incredibly long time in the ancient world, where the only power was justice. Such appearances are not uncommon in modern times.

While the 'treaties' until then were generally subordinate treaties in which winners forced losers to fulfill particular demands, this treaty was an equality treaty in which equal subjects reasonably agreed on principles such as mutual recognition, mutual inviolability, and equality. Civilized conflict resolution methods such as 'talk rather than fist' and 'think from each other's point of view and make concessions' existed far back in the Near East, and the promises and reconciliations made accordingly were guaranteed forever by 'thousands of gods present on each other's land.'

It contains principles that should also be respected in today's international politics, and thus, a replica of the treaty text is placed at the UN headquarters. The replica of the Kadesh Peace Treaty is a gift from the Government and people of Türkiye to the United Nations. It is the replica of the original treaty signed by Hattusillis III, King of the Hittites, and Ramses II, King of the Egyptians. The clay tablet, which records the text in cuneiform script, was found in 1906 in central Anatolia on the site of the old Hittite capital, Hattusas (the present Bogazkoy). The replica was made by Sadi Calik, a sculptor and lecturer at the Istanbul College of Fine Arts.

References

Healy, Mark. 1993. *Qadesh 1300 BC: Clash of the Warrior Kings*. Oxford: Osprey Publishing Ltd.

Kitchen, Kenneth A., and Paul J. N. Lawrence. 2012. *Treaty, Law, and Covenant in the Ancient Near East*. Wiesbaden: Harrassowitz Verlag.

Image References

UN7755654_2d4_. United Nations.

written by Byoung Joo Hah (Busan University of Foreign Studies)

▼

Ethnicities and Migrations

30

Muslim Diaspora in North Africa

Who are the North African Muslims?

The ancient Greeks used the name Lybian to refer to the indigenous inhabitants of Maghreb as a blanket term, distinct from the colonizing Phoenicians and Greeks. The Romans used the name 'Moor', meaning "black-skinned," to refer to the inhabitants of the Berber countries of North Africa, and the Arabs called them

'Barbari' in Arabic, a transliteration of "Berber," meaning "unpeopled. In this article, "North African Muslims" refers to the "Muslim Moors" who, through the conquest of the Iberian Peninsula, became the ruling power of Spain during the Middle Ages(711-1492), and their descendants, the "Moriscos," who were expelled from Spanish society after the Reconquista victory over the Spanish kingdoms.

Etymologically, the word "Morisco" is derived from "Moorish". While "Moor" refers to the Muslim inhabitants of North Africa and the Iberian Peninsula, "Moriscos" refer to Muslims who were forcibly converted to

Christianity in medieval Spain.

The Moors were initially Islamized Berbers from North Africa, and the Arab conquest led to their Islamization, with the majority speaking Arabic. They lived mainly in the Maghrib (Mauritania, Morocco, Algeria, Tunisia, Libya, etc.), a region west of the Nile River in Egypt. In general, the term "Moors" refers to the nomadic, intermarried, Arabized Berbers of the Maghreb in North Africa. They have a common Arabic dialect and lifestyle (desert civilization).

Depending on the historical time and space, the definition of "Moors" varies and is often ambiguous: "the old name of a North African people", "the inhabitants of Western Sahara (mainly Mauritania)", "people who lived in Africa, Turkey", "Islamized Berbers from the Middle Ages", "Berbers who conquered Spain in the Middle Ages", "Saracens who lived in Spain from the Muslim conquest until their expulsion by order of Felipe III", etc.

This helps us understand the complexity of race and ethnicity in North Africa. Early on, the peoples of North Africa experienced a transnational diaspora of migration and settlement, as evidenced by the mixed-race Arab Berbers. Moreover, the specificity of the North African Muslim diaspora seems to lie in its spatial circularity (from North Africa to the Iberian Peninsula and back to North Africa) and temporal connectivity (the settlement of the ancestral Moors and the expulsion of the descendant Moriscos).

The formation of an incomplete Morisco society

Beginning in 718, the Spanish Christian kingdoms of the Iberian Peninsula began a war of reconquest that culminated in the conquest of the last remaining Muslim kingdom, Granada, in 1492. Immediately after the conquest, Spain expelled the Jews and converted the remaining Jews to Christianity. On February 14, 1502, by edict of Felipe II, the Moriscos of Spain were also forced to convert to Christianity. All Muslims in the Kingdom of Castile were forced to choose between expulsion and conversion. Muslims, many of whom worked in agriculture or menial jobs, were unable to leave their ancestral lands where they had lived for hundreds of years. Thus, Morisco society was formed around the forced conversion of Muslims to Christianity.

Fig 30–1. The Moriscos of Spain
as depicted by Christoph Weiditz in the 1530s (Public domain)

The Moriscos' problem was most acute in the Kingdom of Aragon. The Kingdom of Valencia had 130,000-140,000 Moriscos, a third of its population. Spanish society's view of them was divided. Aragonese nobles and farmers who relied on Moriscos' labor, as well as the financiers and wealthy citizens who paid them, were friendly, while lower-class Christians who were jealous of those who had become wealthy thanks to Moriscos' labor were hostile. The Moriscos in the Kingdom of Castile were even more problematic than in Aragon. They were employed mainly as porters and handymen; they worked harder than Christians but were paid less. Naturally, employers favored Moriscos. In 1598 when Felipe III (1598-1621) ascended the throne, Spain was in total trouble. The Kingdom of Castile suffered from bad years, famine, and plague, which caused the population to plummet, which in turn caused labor shortages and higher wages.

Forced Conversions and Pure bloodism

Religious and racial tolerance disappeared in the wake of the Inquisition. Internationally, the defeat of the Invincible Armada in the war with England and the fruitless war with the Dutch led to the disappearance of optimism in Spanish society and a sense of cynicism and defeat. If he resumed the war with the Dutch (1567-1648) and lost, despite the royal deficit, he would be responsible for both bankruptcy and defeat. He decided to sign a twelve-year armistice with the Dutch. The Duke of Lerma used the Moriscos as a scapegoat to divert public attention. He had already expelled the Jews shortly after his conquest of the Kingdom of Granada in 1492 and did the same for the Muslims in 1502. Unlike the Jews, most Muslims chose to convert.

Demagogues blamed Moriscos for Spain's recent economic crisis and lack of jobs, as well as Spain's defeat in the wars against the heretical English and Dutch. Public sentiment was stirred, and hostility toward Moriscos was high.

The Lerma regime decided to exile the Moriscos, and on April 9, 1609, King Felipe III signed the decree of exile.

Spain's Convivencia experiment

A century later, the converted Moriscos had intermarried and changed their appearance to the point where they were indistinguishable from "longtime Christians." They also became Castilian-speaking, losing their Arabic usage, and similarly, despite their lack of knowledge of Islamic rituals, many Moriscos practiced them in secret, i.e., they were nominally Christian. In this way, they maintained a segregated religious life at some distance from Spanish society and sought to retain their ethnic and cultural identity, including the clothing, music, and cuisine of their ancestors, the Moors.

They resisted complete assimilation, especially when Charles V, King of

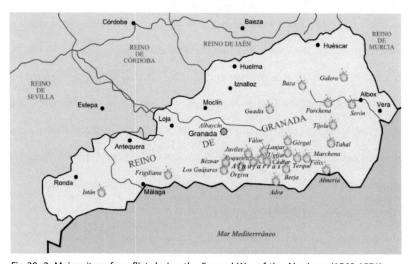

Fig 30–2. Major sites of conflict during the Second War of the Alpujarras(1568-1571)

Spain and Emperor of the Holy Roman Empire, forced the Moriscos to convert between 1525 and 1526.

A key event was the Revolt of the 'Alpujarras' (1568-1571), led by the Moriscos of Granada.

From then on, until 1608, the policy toward the Moriscos was conversion, and it was only in 1608 that deportation began to be seriously considered. The distribution of the Moriscos within Spain varied considerably: While the Moriscos' population was negligible in Castile and throughout the north and northwest, as it was in Aragon and Catalonia, they were most densely populated in the Kingdom of Valencia, where they constituted one-third of the population, and in the Kingdom of Granada, where they constituted more than 55%. Based on these calculations, the number of Moriscos subject to

Fig 30–3. Expulsion_moriscos_Valencia.jpg encia

expulsion was estimated to be a minimum of about 325,000 and a maximum of 1,000,000 out of a total population of 8.5 million in Spain. It was decided that the deportations would begin with the most populous province, the Kingdom of Valencia.

Expulsion of the Moriscos of Valencia

At the time, opinions were divided in Spain regarding the expulsion of the Moriscos. The aristocracy of the kingdoms of Aragon and Valencia were opposed to the expulsion of the Moriscos because they relied on them for labor to manage their farmlands. The peasants of the region, on the other hand, viewed the Moriscos as competitors. Moreover, the fact that the Moriscos' population growth rate was significantly higher than that of the Christians made them fearful and victimized.

The forced conversion of the Moriscos began first in the Kingdom of Castile in 1502 and much later in the Kingdom of Aragon in 1526. This was due to pressure from the nobility of the Kingdom of Aragon to delay the forced conversion of the Moriscos, arguing that they needed to be prepared to build new churches for the new Christians to practice their religion.

Spanish Christian society linked race and religion to 'Otherize' the Moriscos. In 1478, King Fernando and Queen Isabella established the Inquisition and adopted the concept of "purity of blood" (*Liempieza de Sangre*), which legalized discrimination against Muslims, Jews, or those with "heretical" ancestry. Spaniards also suspected the Moriscos of having ties to Turks, Barbary pirates, and even the French, who plundered the Spanish coast. Spaniards saw this as a threat to Christianity, especially the lower classes, who blamed the Moriscos for their poor lives, and the Spanish crown and church justified the mass expulsion of the Moriscos in the name of "religious unity".

The expulsion of the Moriscos and its current implications

On September 22, 1609, King Felipe III decided to expel the Moriscos from Spain, issuing a decree that "All Moriscos shall be expelled from this kingdom and banished to Barbary (North Africa)".

Beginning on September 30th, 1609, some 280,000 Moriscos were delivered to various port cities in southern Spain, where they were required to pay for their journey. The first batch of Moriscos were taken to the ports of Oran,

Fig 30–4. 1609: What did Denia look like, from which 42,000 Moors were expelled? Embarkation of the Moors at the port of Denia. Vincent Mestre, 1613.

where they were treated poorly and even attacked by the locals. These rumors caused great fear among the Moriscos who had not yet been deported, and on October 20, protests against the deportations took place. The deportation of the Aragonese Moriscos was followed by the deportation of the Catalan Moriscos.

The Moriscos of the kingdoms of Aragon and Castile were the most likely to attempt to cross the Pyrenees; some took the route through Catalonia to the French Languedoc cities, while others went up the Atlantic coast and settled as far as Bayonne, St. Jean de Luz, and beyond Bordeaux. On the other hand, most Moriscos settled in Morocco, Algeria, Tunisia, or other parts of the Ottoman Empire.

LAS EMIGRACIONES MORISCAS DEL SIGLO XVII

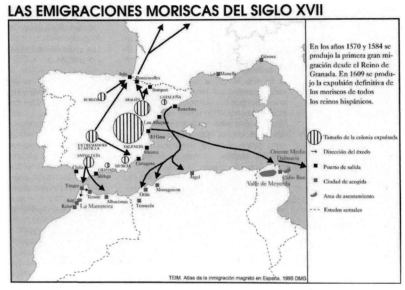

Fig 30—5. Moriscos emigrations in the 17th century(English title)

Today, most of the Moriscos' diaspora is scattered throughout North African countries. In Morocco, the descendants of the Moriscos live mainly in Rabat, Salé, and the northern cities of Chefchaouen, Tetouan, and Tangier. When they left Spain, the Moriscos left behind everything but their culture and traditions. Their influence is still evident in costumes, music, food, and architecture, etc.

Although the Moriscos were eventually expelled from their Iberian homeland, their legacy remains. The city of Chefchaouen, founded in 1471 by 'Ali Ben Rachid', the last ruler of the Kingdom of Granada, is architecturally similar to Granada, with its alleyways, minarets, mosaics, blue wall coloring, and houses, etc.

Moriscos traveled by various routes and ships to Africa, France, Turkey, colonial Latin America, and beyond, or sought refuge over the Pyrenees to cities in France or on the Atlantic.

Henri Lapeyre estimates the number of deported Moriscos at around 300,000. At the time, few Moriscos refused to be expelled, but few wanted to leave the land. In other words, for them, the Iberian Peninsula and North Africa were as much their land as their ancestors. Nevertheless, even after the expulsion, they quickly adapted to their new environment and did not resort to piracy to seek revenge for their expulsion.

As Enrique Dussel has argued, the Reconquista was part of Spain's formation of the modern subject of the self. As a center against a periphery, Spain, through the reconquest of Granada, drew a sharp distinction between the Christian conquerors as "subjects" and the Muslim subjects as "others."

In this sense, We can say that Spain's religious convivencia was absent, an experiment in coexistence.

Today, the Moriscos' diaspora has expanded beyond the Maghreb, settling in France, Turkey, Latin America, and elsewhere. The brutality and injustice of the expulsion must be reassessed from a modern perspective. An apology and reconciliation process is needed for the victims of the expulsion. In fact, in October 2015, the Spanish government enacted a law granting citizenship to Spanish Jews. However, there is no apology or citizenship for the descendants of the expelled Moriscos.

Today's Spain still seems to have a double standard when it comes to genuine apologies and reconciliation with religious minorities in its history. I wonder if Spain today is still experimenting with convivencia as it did in medieval Spanish society. As a member of the European Union, Spain's political concerns are also a big factor in finding a solution. Spain's claim to cultural pluralism or coexistence is incomplete, as political and diplomatic considerations do not give their descendants the right to return.

North African Muslim Diaspora

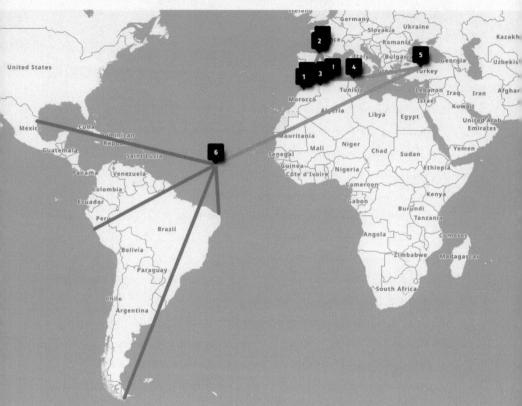

① Morocco
(Rabat, Sale, Chefchaouen, Tetouan, Tangier)

② France
(Bayonne, Saint–Jean–de–Luz, Bordeaux)

③ Algeria (Algiers, Tlemcen, Mostaganem)

④ Tunisia*

⑤ Turkiye*

⑥ Colonial Latin America

* Difficult to identify the specific city

Scan the QR code
to view the map.

Keywords

Spain, Expulsion, Morisco, Diaspora

References

Vincent Monteil, *Les Arabes*, N.722, Que sais-je?, PUF. 1959

Henri V. Vallois, *Les Races humaines*, N.146, Que sais-je?, PUF, 1967

Donghun Song, *The birth of the Age of Navigation*, Sigongsa, 2019

Marc Terrisse *La diaspora morisque: une histoire globale méconnue*, pp. 124-129.
1315, 2016
https://doi.org/10.4000/hommesmigrations.3737

Marc Terrisse, *La présence arabo-musulmane en Languedoc et en Provence à l'époque médiévale*, pp. 126-128, 1306, 2014
https://doi.org/10.4000/hommesmigrations.2837

Louis Cardaillac, Vision des morisques et de leur expulsion, quatre cents ans après, pp. 407-418. https://doi.org/10.4000/cdlm.4945

Youssef El Kidi, *The Expulsion of Moriscos from Renaissance Spain*, 2018 https://insidearabia.com/egypts-waning-geopolitical-position-mena-region

M. Bernard Vincent, L'expulsion des Morisques du Royaume de Grenade et leur répartition en Castille(1570-1571), Mélanges de la Casa Velazquez, pp.211-246. tome 6, 1970
https://persee.fr/doc/casa_0076-230x_1970_num_6_1_1019

Castillo Alvaro, Henri Lapeyre, *Géographie de l'Espagne morisque*, In: Annales. Economies, sociétés, civilisations, 18e année, N.4, pp. 800-802, 1963
https://www.persee.fr/doc/ahess_0395_649_1963_num_18_4_421056_t1_0800_0000_2

Grand Larousse de la Langue Française, 1971-1978, Paris : Larousse.

Trésor de la Langue Française, 1978, Tome 1-16, Paris : CNRS

Image References

https://commons.wikimedia.org/wiki/File:Weiditz_Trachtenbuch_105-106.jpg
https://en.wikipedia.org/wiki/Rebellion_of_the_Alpujarras_(1568%E2%80%931571)
https://en.wikipedia.org/wiki/Expulsion_of_the_Moriscos

written by Eunsoon Choi (Korea Maritime & Ocen University)

31

Norman Sicily

Norman Conquest of Sicily

In the 10th and 11th centuries, it was considered fashionable to go on a pilgrimage to the Holy Land with a unique religious fervor in Norman society. Around 1015, about 40 adventurous young Normans from Normandy made a pilgrimage to the province of Apulia in southern Italy, and found the cave shrine of the Archangel Michael at Monte Gargano in the north of the province. The pilgrims saw this sparsely populated and desolate region as a challenging opportunity and were hired as mercenaries by the local Lombard leaders.

When the news reached Normandy, young people flocked to southern Italy one by one in search of an adventure of riches. The Normans who moved so southern Italy at the time worked as mercenaries and soon after their employment, they demanded their wages for land on which they could settle. Accordingly, Sergius, Duke of Naples, ceded the region of Aversa in 1030, when the Norman advance went swift. In 1053, they easily defeated a large army raised and led by Pope Leo IX himself at Civitate in Apulia.

At that time, the most powerful of the Norman chieftains came from the family of Tancred of Hauteville, a humble knight under the command of the Duke of Normandy. 8 of Tancred's 12 sons came to Italy, 5 of whom became first-class leaders. Robert Guiscard (c. 1015-1085), the eldest of the 8 immigrants, was particularly gifted. Giscard was count of Apulia and Calabria from 1057 to 1059, after his victory at the Battle of Civitate.

At that time, the papacy was in conflict with the antipope Benedict X and Nicholas II ahead of the election of the pope in 1058. Nicholas II, a native of Burgundy, convened a synod on his way to Rome, declared Benedict X antipope, and excommunicated him at the same time. He then arrived in Rome, where, with the support of the Normans, he engaged in battle against the antipope Benedict X and his supporters. The first battle occurred at Campania in early 1059, in which Nicholas II was unable to achieve a complete victory. However, in the second half of the same year, Nicholas II's armies conquered Praeneste, Tusculum, and Numentanum. He then proceeded to capture Galeria, forcing Benedict X to surrender and withdraw his claims to the papal throne.

Also, Nicholas II needed amicable relationship with the Normans to secure his position. For the Nicholas II, who hoped to recapture Sicily which had been conquered by the Muslims, the Normans appeared to be the right force to do. In 1059, a new alliance was concluded at Melfi between the Roman Curia and the Normans. Nicholas II presided over a solemn ceremony in which Apulia, Calabria, and Sicily were designated as new duchies, conferring titles on Guiscard. He also installed Richard of Aversa, a native of eastern

Normandy, as duke of Capua. Through the process, Nicholas II obtained an oath from the Norman leaders of future allegiance as well as protection of the church. This freed the pope from being subject to the power of the Roman aristocrats.

At that time, most of Apulia and Calabria belonged to the Byzantine Empire. Also, Sicily was still in the hands of the Arab Muslims. However, Giscard legally strengthened his position supported by the conferred title by the pope, and obtained a 'license of conquest' to conquer Apulia, Calabria, and Sicily. He took Apulia and Calabria from the Byzantine Empire by 1060, and in 1061, along with his youngest brother, Roger, plotted to invade and take Sicily.

At the time of its conquest by the Normans, Sicily was inhabited by a mixture of Christians, Arab Muslims, and Muslim converts. Arab Sicily was originally under the control of the Aghlabids and the Fatimid Caliphate, but in 948, the Kalbids took control of the island and held it until 1053. A succession crisis occurred between the 1010s and 1020s, which makes the island came under the intervention of the Zirids of Ifriqiya.

In 1060, Sicily was in total chaos. After the abdication of Emir of the Kalbids in 1053, the country was divided by civil war in the following years. Moreover, the rulers of Tunisia's powerful Zirids, who were once patrons and protectors of Sicilian Muslims, have been severely weakened by wars with Cairo, invasions of new Arab tribes in Yemen, and domestic civil wars. As a result, central rule in Sicily collapsed, split between 4 feuding qaids (leaders).

Amid widespread chaos, rebellion, and near-anarchy, the island's indigenous

Christian communities, primarily in the Valdemon region around Mount Etna in the northeast, sought ways to gain greater autonomy and external Christian protectors. This community came to watch with some interest the Norman advance into Calabria. Some accounts say that, during the summer of 1060 they sent envoys to Roger at Mileto to ask for help, but the immediate intervention of the Normans did not go their way, and the intervention was decided by the Normans. Since then, they had a far more persuasive and powerful negotiator, one of the 4 feuding qaids. It was Ibn al-Timnah, a qaid of Syracuse, who offered to lead the Normans into Sicily. A despicable villain even by the standards of the time, Ibn al-Timnah defeated and killed his predecessor, Ibn al-Maklati, not only usurping his position but also gaining control over most of the southeastern part of the island. His expansionist policies quickly brought Ibn al-Timnah into conflict with his neighbor, Ibn al-Hawas, who ruled Agrigento and the island's central region. Ibn al-Timnah was defeated in several battles, and Ibn al-Hawas pursued him. In desperation, Ibn al-Timnah crossed the strait to Mileto and offered Roger a deal he could not refuse. What he offered was a rebellion against his fellow Muslims, an alliance to seize power in eastern Sicily, and the remaining cooperation of his troops. And it appears that Roger's acceptance of the deal was more implusive than his brother.

In May 1061, Robert Guiscard and Roger first invaded Sicily to gain control of the strategically important Strait of Messina. Roger first crossed the Strait of Messina and landed at night, surprising the Arab forces in the morning. Arriving later that day, Robert Guiscard's troops found Messina abandoned without resistance. Robert Guiscard immediately fortified the city and allied himself with Ibn al-Timnah against his rival Ibn al-Hawas. Then Robert Giscard, Roger, and Ibn al-Timnah proceeded to the center of the island. They were attacked by resistance from Centuripe, but passed through Frazzanò and Pianura di Maniace and captured Paternò. He took his army as far as Castrogiovanni (modern Enna), the strongest fortress in Sicily. Although the garrison was defeated, the fortress was not taken, and as winter approached Robert Guiscard returned to Apulia. Before leaving Sicily, he built a fort at San Marco d'Alunzio, the first fort built by the Normans in Sicily. Robert Guiscard returned to Sicily at the end of the 1061 and captured Troina. Following his return, in June 1063 at the Battle of Cerami, Robert Guiscard defeated a Muslim army and secured a stronghold for the Normans on the island of Sicily.

In 1064, Robert Guiscard went back to Sicily and attempted to go to Palermo bypassing Castrogiovanni, but this expedition was ultimately canceled. Meanwhile, Robert Guiscard nominated Roger Count of Sicily and placed his county under the Duchy of Apulia. In dividing the island with his brother, Robert Guiscard retained half of Messina and the Christian enclave of Val Demone, leaving the rest to his brother Roger, including lands not yet conquered. When Robert Guiscard invaded Palermo again in 1071, only the castle fell, and the citadel did not fall until January 1072.

With the fall of Bari in 1071, the last Byzantine stronghold in Italy was lost. The Norman conquest of the Byzantine territories in Italy was thus completed. With the fall of Palermo to the Normans in early 1072, the remaining Arab strongholds in Sicily disappeared. Also in 1075, Salerno, the last independent Lombard principality, was conquered by the Normans. This brought all of Italy south of the Garigliano River under the rule of the Normans, led by Roberto Guiscard.

For centuries Sicily had been called Magna Graecia, and by 1070 it had a stronger Greek element than Italy. The majority of the inhabitants spoke Greek. Also, most of the ceremonies were performed in the Greek style in churches and monasteries. Apulia and Calabria were still called 'themes' as they were under the Byzantine Empire, and officials leading important organizations retained their Byzantine titles such as military governor, viceroy, or eparch as before. Therefore, it was not surprising that Guiscard claimed to be successor of the Roman emperor as far as the Italian territories he ruled were concerned, and even dreamed of the Byzantine throne. However, the dream was also unknowingly inspired by Byzantium. In 1073, he received 2 letters from Michael VII Dukas. In exchange for a military alliance, it was a proposal to marry the emperor's brother born in the imperial family to the most beautiful of Guiscard's daughters. When there was no reply, Michael VII sent another letter appointing his newborn son Constantine as his future bridegroom and offering him 44 Byzantine medals and 200 pounds of gold annually. Guiscard did not hesitate any longer. Soon after his acceptance to the offer, the bride left for Constantinople.

In 1077, Roger laid siege to Trapani, one of the 2 remaining Arab strongholds on the west side of Sicily. With food supplies cut off, Trapani soon surrendered. In 1079 Taormina was besieged, and in 1081 Catania, held by the Syracuse emir, was conquered. Roger left Sicily in the summer of 1083 to assist his brother on the Italian mainland. However, when his son Jordan rebelled in Sicily, he returned and subjugated his son. In 1085, he was finally able to mount an organized expedition. On May 22nd, Roger and his army approached Syracuse by sea, and on May 25th, Roger's army and the Emir's navy engaged in a harbor, while Jordan's army besieged the city. When the city surrendered in March 1086, only Noto was still under Muslim control. In February 1091, Noto surrendered, and the conquest of Sicily was completed.

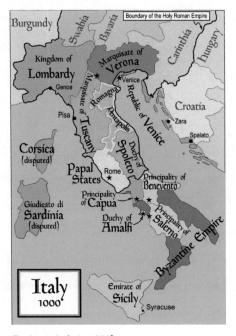

Fig 31–1. Italy in 1000[1]

---

1 https://en.wikipedia.org/wiki/Norman_conquest_of_southern_Italy

In 1091, Roger invaded Malta and subdued the walled city of Mdina. He taxed the island, but allowed the Arab rulers to continue their rule. In 1127, Roger II abolished the Muslim government , replacing it with Norman officials. And under Norman rule, Arabic, spoken by Greek Christian islanders for centuries during Muslim rule, became Maltese.

Fig 31–2. Italy in 1084[2]

Fig 31–3. Kingdom of Sicily in 1154[3]

2 https://en.wikipedia.org/wiki/Norman_conquest_of_southern_Italy

3 https://en.wikipedia.org/wiki/Norman_conquest_of_southern_Italy

Fig 31–4. Cappella Palatina in Palermo, Sicily[4]

Keywords

Normans, Sicily, Roger, conquest, Arab Muslims

References

Brown, R. Allen (1984). *The Normans*. Woodsbridge, Suffolk: Boydell & Brewer.
    Joranson, Einar (1948). "The Inception of the Career of the Normans in Italy:
    Legend and History." *Speculum*. 23(3): 353-396 .

Rogers, Randall (1997). *Latin Siege Warfare in the Twelfth Century*. Oxford: Oxford
    University Press.

---

4 https://en.wikipedia.org/wiki/Cappella_Palatina

Rogers, Clifford J. (2010). *The Oxford Encyclopedia of Medieval Warfare and Military Technology*: Vol. 1. Oxford: Oxford University Press.

Curtis, Edmund (1912). *Roger of Sicily and the Normans in lower Italy, 1016-1154*. New York and London: The Knickerbocker Press.

Malaterra, Galfredus and Wolf, Kenneth Baxter (2005). *The deeds of Count Roger of Calabria and Sicily and of his brother Duke Robert Guiscard*. University of Michigan Press.

Britt, Karen C. (2007). "Roger II of Sicily: Rex, Basileus, and Khalif? Identity, Politics, and Propaganda in the Cappella Palatina." *Mediterranean Studies*, Penn State University Press. 16(1): 21-45.

Cilento, Adele and Vanoli, Alessandro. *Arabs and Normans in Sicily and the South of Italy*. Riverside Book Company, INC, 2007.

Loud, G. A. (2000). *The Age of Robert Guiscard: Souther Italy and the Norman Conquest*. London: Routledge.

Weber, Nicholas (1911). "Pope Nicholas II." *The Catholic Encyclopedia* Vol. 11. New York: Robert Appleton Company.

Chisholm, Hugh (1911). "Nicholas (popes)." *Encyclopædia Britannica*. 19 (11th ed.). Cambridge University Press. 649-651.

written by Chagyu Kim (Myongji University)

32

Muslim Sicily

The Muslim conquest of Sicily began in 827 and lasted for a long period of 75 years, until 902, when the last remaining Byzantine stronghold, 'Taormina', fell. At that time, Sicily was an island located in the middle of the

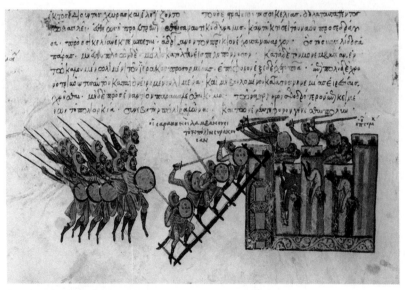

Fig 32–1. Muslim conquest of Sicily

Mediterranean Sea and was the most important commercially and politically. For ambitious African rulers, it was a stepping stone to the gateway of Italy and the Adriatic Sea. For this reason, Sicily became an early target for attacks by Muslims.

Abd al-Rahman al-Fihri, ruler of Ifriqiya, concluded the consolidation of power in North Africa and Spain, before launching an attack to capture Sicily and Sardinia in 752-753. However, his attacks were thwarted by a Berber rebellion.

Later, the Arab conquest of Sicily was postponed to a later date by the establishment of the Aghlabid dynasty in North Africa. The reason is that from that time until the 820s, the Aghlabids were preoccupied with their rivals, the Idrisids, located in western North Africa. That is why Ibrahim decided in 805 to conclude a ten-year truce with the Byzantine ruler of Sicily. This truce was renewed in 813 by Ibrahim's son and successor Abu'l-Abbas. During that time, the Aghlabids traded with Sicily.

However, peace between the Aghlabid dynasty and the Byzantine Empire could not last forever. Because in 827 Euphemius commander of the Sicilian fleet, rebelled. The rulers of the Aghlabid dynasty of North Africa used the rebellion as an opportunity to attack Sicily. The Arabs attacked the West first to conquer Sicily. This can be attributed to four reasons. First, the western part of Sicily is closer to North Africa than the eastern part. This is advantageous for military transportation or material transportation. Second, the eastern part of Sicily is more mountainous than the western part, so it is not easy to procure supplies or food during military operations, and it is not easy to wage war in relation to the ambush of the enemy even during military operations. Third, the western region of Sicily was more distant from southern Italy and the Balkans, where the Byzantines lived, than the eastern region. Fourth, the power and wealth of Sicily were concentrated in the eastern region, and the residents of the western region were dissatisfied.

On June 17, 827, Asad set out from Sousse with over 100 ships carrying 10,000 infantries and 700 cavalries and arrived at Mazara in western Sicily. At that time, there were about 2,000 Byzantine troops guarding all of Sicily. Asad's army carried out regional plunder, traversing the island along ancient Roman roads to lay siege to Syracuse, the capital of Sicily, located in the southeastern Val di Noto. His siege failed because the Byzantine fleet, supported by Venice, arrived at the right time to aid Syracuse. Asad found Sicily more challenging to conquer than he thought. So he decided to slowly advance the war and conquer Sicily by dismantling the opponents one by one. Thus, the conquest of Sicily was gradual, and, with considerable resistance and internal struggle, it took some 75 years for Byzantine Sicily to be entirely conquered.

In September 831, the Muslim army obtained the surrender of Palermo after a siege of nearly a year. After that, the Muslims seem to have temporarily put off an attack on eastern Sicily due to an attack on Calabria in southern Italy. The commanders of the Aghlabid Dynasty targeted the Calabrian region for the idea of quickly attacking it to gain loot or reduce the animosity created between their classes because it was a region without systematic attempts to defend itself or build defenses against aggression. Muslim attacks on the

Italian peninsula have been intermittent, but records of events in the 800's are sparse. Nevertheless, there are three incidents related to the development of Muslim-Christian relations in southern Italy. First, Muslims played a role in the division of Benevento. Second, Muslim raids, including naval attacks on Rome, were economically, politically, and propaganda effective. Third, the Muslim Emirates were established in Bari and Taranto.

The success of the Aghlabids outside Val di Mazara at the beginning of the conquest was not only disjointed but sporadic. The Muslims captured Messina in late 842 or 843 with Naples support. However, Muslims could hardly penetrate the mountainous northeastern region of Val Demone. On the other hand, although many important fortified areas to the east, such as Taormina, Catania and Syracuse in the southeastern part of the island, Val di Noto, which occupies one-third of the island, remained in Byzantine hands, Modica was captured in 845 by a Muslim raid.

Meanwhile, since Byzantium had a peace treaty with the Abbasids, the Byzantines in Sicily received reinforcements from the theme of Charsianon in eastern Asia Minor. However, the Byzantine army, which encountered the Muslims, suffered a disastrous defeat, losing 10,000 soldiers. This defeat quickly worsened the Byzantine camp. In 846, Leontini fell, followed by 'Ragusa' in 848. Thus, the Byzantine Sicily gradually fell into the hands of the Muslims. However, the complete Arab conquest of Sicily was delayed by the failure of the initial Muslim assaults on Cefalù and several occasions against Castrogiovanni in 838.

In the case of Cefalù, a port city located in the center of the northern coast of Sicily, it was helped by the Byzantine fleet, which appeared occasionally. Because of this help, Cefalù was able to hold out for another 20 years without being quickly captured by the Muslims. However, Cefalù's surrender precipitated another attack on the hitherto impregnable fortress of Castrogiovanni in central Sicily. After the fall of Palermo, the Byzantines emphasized the strategic and political importance of Castrogiovanni, along with the importance of Syracuse. During the 830-840's, the Muslims attacked Castrogiovanni five times. Although its external defenses were sometimes broken and loot was taken, Muslim forces were unable to take the stronghold. However, Castrogiovanni fell on 24 January 859 and was thoroughly plundered.

After the fall of Castrogiovanni in 859, the Aghlabids ruled central Sicily. After the loss of Castrogiovanni, the Byzantines sent troops into Sicily to defend what remained of eastern Sicily. Their appearance coincided with the rebellion of cities in the southwest, including Agrigento, Caltabellota, and Platani. However, the Eastern Byzantines did not seem to have taken advantage of these revolts. In any case, Muslims conducted annual expeditions against Christians living in cities in southeastern Sicily.

In 869, while retreating from a summer attack against Syracuse, Khafāja (862-9 AD, the governor-general of Sicily of the Aghlabid Dynasty) was killed by a soldier. Soon after, his son 'Muhammad' was declared the successor and received approval from Ifriqiya. In August 870, during Muhammad's reign, Malta was completely destroyed by an expedition from Sicily. The efforts of Byzantium to save were futile; the Byzantine governor of the island was murdered, and the bishop was taken to Palermo. However, Muhammad, like his father, was killed in unclear circumstances by his eunuch slaves in the following year, 871. The failure of the expedition to southeastern Sicily, the death of Khafāja and his son Muhammad, and the appearance of six governors over three years revealed the temporary instability of the Sicilian Muslim government.

Meanwhile, in the Italian peninsula, the Muslims also lost their foothold after the failed siege of Salerno and the loss of Bari in 871. By contrast, the

Fig 32–2. Battles around the Medieval Sicily

Byzantine Empire permanently regained Bari and subsequently reestablished its power in Apulia. However, in 877, Syracuse was blocked by land and sea for a long time and could not be rescued by the Byzantine fleet. The war involved sophisticated siege techniques, including the groundbreaking weapon of the catapult, which was probably first used at the siege of Salerno. The defenses of Syracuse fell in May 878. Christians and Jews there were not massacred, but many broke out in Palermo.

In March 890, a rebellion broke out in Palermo. This rebellion was initiated by Sicilian Arabs against the Ifriqians of Sawada. This rebellion, linked to a major rebellion in Ifriqiya itself in 894-895, not only ended Muslim attacks against the Byzantines, but also resulted in a truce with the Byzantines in 895-896. In 898, a large-scale civil war broke out between the "Arabs" and the "Berbers." In response, 'Ibrahim II' dispatched his son Abu'l-Abbas Abdallah, who had suppressed the rebellion in Ifriqiya, to Sicily. Negotiations between

Fig 32–3. Aghlabid quarter–dinar, minted in Sicily, 879

the Ifricians and their rival Sicilian faction broke down. Abu'l-Abbas Abdallah marched on Palermo and captured it on September 18, 900. Several rebels fled to the Byzantines in Taormina, some even to Constantinople. Abu'l-Abbas Abdallah suppressed the rebellion without delay. He then marched to attack the Byzantines, devastated the area around Taormina, and laid siege to Catania before returning to Palermo in winter, but failed to capture it. Taormina, on the eastern coast, was the last important Byzantine fortress to withstand a two-year siege, but eventually fell on August 1, 902, followed by a massacre. This completed the conquest of Sicily by the Arabs.

Then, until 1091, Palermo was the capital of the Emirate of Sicily and became a major cultural and political center of the Islamic world. The new Arab rulers initiated land reforms and further improved the irrigation system through qanats. Palermo also flourished in trade and agriculture and became one of the largest and wealthiest cities in Europe. Sicily was multi-denominational and multilingual, developing a unique Arab-Byzantine culture that combined aspects of Muslim Arab and Berber migrants with elements of the local Greco-Byzantine and Jewish communities. However, those who formed the majority of the Muslim community in Sicily were Sunnis. The majority of Palermo's people were Sunnis and showed hostility towards the Shia Kalbids. After suppressing a sectarian rebellion, the Fatimid caliph Ismail al-Mansur appointed al-Hassan al-Kalbi (948–964) as Emir of Sicily. He successfully controlled the constantly revolting Byzantines and established the Kalbid dynasty. However, with Emir Yusuf al-Kalbi (986–998) a period of steady decline began. Then, under al-Akhal (1017–1037), dynastic conflicts intensified, leading to internal fragmentation and eventually being conquered by the Normans.

Keywords

Muslim Sicily, Byzantine Sicily, Aghlabid dynasty, Ifriqiya, Emirate of Sicily

References

Ahmad, Aziz (1975). *A History of Islamic Sicily*. Edinburgh: Edinburgh University Press.

Amari, Michele (1933). *Storia dei musulmani di Sicilia*. vol. I (ed. and rev. by C. Nallino), Catania.

Brown, T. S. (1995). 'Byzantine Italy c. 680-c. 876', in *New Cambridge Medieval History II, c.700-c.900*. Rosamund McKitterick, ed. Cambridge.

Cilento, Adele and Vanoli, Alessandro (2007). *Arabs and Normans in Sicily and the South of Italy*. Riverside Book Company, INC.

Crawford, F. M. (1900). *The Rulers of the South: Sicily, Calabria, Malta*. 2 vols. London: Macmillan.

Finley, M.I., Smith, D. M. and Duggan, Christopher (1986). *A History of Sicily*. Chatto & Windus.

Ibn al-Athīr (1987-8), BAS2 Ar. Biblioteca arabo-sicula, ossia raccolta di testi arabici che toccano la geografia, la storia, le biografie e la bibliografie della Sicilia. 2nd rev. edn, M. Amari and U. Rizzitano, 2 vols, Palermo.

Kreuts, Barbara (1991). *Before the Normans: Southern Italy in the Ninth and Tenth Centuries*. Philadelphia.

Metcalfe, Alex (2009). *The Muslims of medieval Italy*. Edinburgh: Edinburgh University Press, 2009.

Skylites, John (2010). A Synopsis of Byzantine History, 811-1057. introduction, text and notes translated by John Wortley. Cambridge: Cambridge University Press, 2010.

Treadgold, Warren (1997). *A History of the Byzantine State and Society*. Stanford, CA: Stanford University Press.

Kim, Chagyu (Sept. 2014). The Arab Conquest of Sicily and the Byzantine Response. *Journal of Middle Eastern Affairs*, 13 (4): 31-61

Image References

https://en.wikipedia.org/wiki/Muslim_conquest_of_Sicily

https://www.quora.com/Muslims-ruled-the-island-of-Sicily-for-almost-a-century-and-a-half-Moreover-Arabs-had-influence-in-places-of-Sicilian-rulers-along-with-the-Greeks-So-why-is-there-not-any-Muslim-Arab-culture-or-descendants-in-there

https://en.wikipedia.org/wiki/Muslim_conquest_of_Sicily

written by Chagyu Kim (Myongji University)

33

Sicily under Frederick II

Frederick II's reign in his kingdom in Sicily

Fig 33–1. Emperor Frederick II

Frederick II (1194-1250) was the last Holy Roman Emperor of the Hohenstaufen dynasty. He was King of Sicily from 1198 (1197-1250), King of Germany from 1212, King of Italy and Holy Roman Emperor from 1220, and also King of Jerusalem from 1225. When Heinrich VI (1190-1197) died in 1197, he left a son named Frederick, who was brought up at the worldwide court of his mother, Constance, in Sicily. However, when his mother Constance died the following year, he inherited the rule of Sicily. History may remember him as Emperor of the West, but he never forgot that he was also King of Sicily, the grandson not only of Barbarossa but of Roger II as well.

Meanwhile, Pope Innocent III(1198-1216) was very opposed to the revival of the private union between Germany and the Norman kingdom of Sicily, and he induced the German princes not to elect Frederick as their king. Instead, he advocated the election of Otto IV, the son of Henry the Lion. Once on the throne, however, Otto asserted his emperorship as thoroughly as the Hohenstaufen rulers did. Otto promised to return all the papal territories that had been taken by the emperor, but he took no action to fulfill the promise. Moreover, he gathered an army and intended to invade Sicily. In relations with Germany, Italy, and the Church, although he proved to have no preeminent governing power, the Pope and the princes were all forced to follow the young Frederick. In response, Pope Innocent III received a promise to give up Sicily if he became emperor and appointed the young Frederick as his candidate for emperor. The Pope's insistence on Frederick II's renunciation of the Kingdom

Fig 33–2. Emperor Frederick II, the Wonder of the World and the Art of Falconry

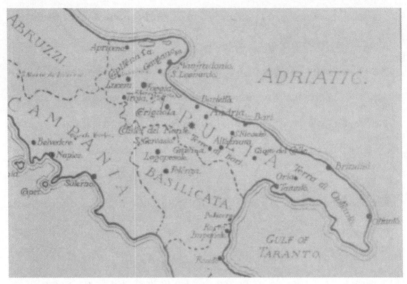

Fig 33–3. Some of Frederick's castles and hunting lodges

of Sicily was, at least in theory, to emphasize independence from the Empire. In 1211, Frederick was elected king of Germany, and a few years later, in 1220, he was crowned emperor. The background of Frederick's being able to become the ruler of Germany was the Battle of Bouvines in 1214. In this war, King Philip Augustus of France defeated Otto's army.

After ascending the throne, Frederick II's political objective was to rule over a vast territory stretching from Sicily, Italy, and Germany. He also displayed an insatiable artistic and intellectual curiosity, which earned him the nickname 'Stupor Mundi' (Wonder of the World). Frederick II's political breakthrough began in 1212 when he claimed the title of King of the Romans. From 1215, no one opposed his claim. The Papacy thus met its enemy, Frederick II of

Hohenstaufen, the most powerful man in its long history.

Honorius III (1216-1227), who succeeded Innocent III, was a gentle pope. Frederick II ingratiated himself with the new pope by taking part in a crusade and promising to return some of the papal territories that had been in the hands of the emperor since the reign of Frederick Barbarossa. Fascinated by this promise of Frederick, who had never intended to fulfill it, Honorius made the great mistake of crowning Frederick II without ceding Sicily. Frederick II thus devoted all his energies to securing his power in the Kingdom of Sicily and Central Italy. In Central Italy, he replaced the German officials seated by his grandfather and father with Sicilians of much lesser repute. Even the gentle Honorius III became intolerant of Frederick II towards the end of his reign.

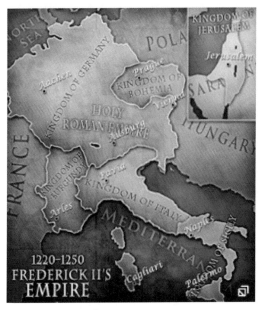

Fig 33–4. FrederickII's Empire1220–1250

Fig 33–5. Frederick II (left) meets Al–Kamil (right). Nuova Cronica, c.1348

Frederick II was Emperor of Rome from his papal coronation in 1220 until his death. That is why the pope recognized him as the most threatening person. In the war with the papacy, which was surrounded between Frederick II's lands in northern Italy and his Kingdom of Sicily in the south, Frederick II was excommunicated three times. It was because of his stubborn and radical nature that he was at odds with the Popes, and he pursued his ambition to unite Italy and Sicily. That is why Frederick II was often maligned in the papal annals of his time and later.

Pope Gregory IX (1227-1241) was a fiery character and would not tolerate any infringement of papal rights. As soon as he became pope, he excommunicated Frederick II for breaking his oath to join the Crusades, even calling him the Antichrist.

Fig 33–6. The Battle of Cortenuova against the 2nd Lombard League (1237), Nuova Cronica c. 1348

Frederick II was half Sicilian by blood and even more so by his taste. Frederick II attempted to consolidate his dominion in Germany in his early years. But he couldn't realize his intention. He ceded extensive rights and judicial authority to the princes of various provinces in order to be crowned emperor. Accordingly, he handed over the administration of the empire to the German princes. As a result, he stayed in Germany until 1220, but it was only to reorganize Germany so that he could care about it less than possible, and after leaving Germany, he stopped by only for a short time. Thus, to establish his son Henry as German king in Germany, where he did not have confidence, and to leave Germany as a province, he made an agreement with the German clergy and secular princes and the holy princes and an agreement for the benefit of the princes. Still, these agreements eventually ruined his plans and led to the rebellion of his son Henry.

At that time, the great princes generally did not feel a sense of responsibility towards Germany. No effective system was established to deal with public issues. The princes arbitrarily taxed the masses. They also asserted their individual and territorial rights. They obstructed all attempts to establish the emperor's centralized sovereignty, and as they envied and shunned the emperor's prerogatives, they devoted themselves to undermining the emperor's authority. They even led several revolts in collusion with the son of Frederick II.

Meanwhile, Frederick II established an efficient bureaucracy in Sicily and southern Italy, similar to that of modern centralized kingdoms. In Italy, public administration was conducted by Frederick II with extreme caution, unlike in Germany. He perfected his bureaucracy on the basis of that of his Germanic

Fig 33–7. Frederick II's troops paid with leather coins during the Siege ofFaenza(1240-41), Nuova Cronica c. 1348

Fig 33–8. The Battle of Giglio against Gregory IX in 1241, Chronica Maiora (1259)

predecessors and further developed it. Competent officials were chosen regardless of their religion or social status, laws were made uniform in many places, trials were strictly administered, and churches, lords, and city officials were obliged to obey the king's decrees.

The trial of the prosecution and the collection of taxes were the responsibility of central officials. Trade was facilitated by gold coins, whose value and circulation were stable. Moreover, obstacles such as inland taxes and tolls did not exist. The 'Constitution of Melfi' in 1231 concretely expressed the principles of Frederick's Government plan. Frederick founded the University of Naples and protected and developed the sciences and arts. He also tried unsuccessfully to extend his rule into northern Italy, where economically prosperous cities first seized the initiative and established a vibrant republic away from feudal traditions. With Milan at the head, all these cities betrayed the emperor and maintained their independence.

In foreign affairs, Frederick II turned his principal attention to the eastern part of the Mediterranean instead of the Byzantine Empire, which Henry

VI was determined to conquer which at that time had already fallen into the hands of Venice and the French. After the Fifth Crusade failed to advance at Damietta in Egypt and failed in 1217, Innocent III's successor, Honorius III, ordered Frederick II to flee abroad. Not indifferent to the opportunity to control his power by launching him into his venture, he urged the emperor to try again.

Frederick II promised to undertake the task, and he decided to ascend to the throne as king of the defunct kingdom of Jerusalem by marrying the heiress of Jerusalem. However, he failed to carry out his plan, and after several years of delay, Honorius' successor, Gregorius IX, excommunicated him. But just then, the infighting among the Muslims gave the emperor an advantage,

Fig 33–9. The wooden city of Vittoria is charged at the siege of Parma 1248

baroiu. Et quelli dretentano parte Guelfa ntelachrefa comtaagrone spue

citate. Et olive aeno quelli telaciou te 61 tulurn ntum glaltn nobolugh

Fig 33–10. The capture of King Enzio a son of Frederick at the Battle of Fossalta 1249

and he decided to attempt an expedition. He set out for Egypt and in 1229, secured Jerusalem, Bethlehem, and Nazareth through a treaty with the Turkic ruler Al Kamil, where he recognized the pagans the right to keep their faith. Although under pressure of excommunication, he ascended the throne as king of Jerusalem. The Pope, enraged by this, issued a ban on the Holy Land, but it was ineffective.

Frederick retained the territories he had acquired and exercised his dominion for 15 years. Eventually, however, feuds between the various commercial and religious groups in the region and struggles between the lords and officials of the empire led to infighting, leading to the reoccupation of the region by the Turks. The fate of Jerusalem highlighted the problems that always accompany relations between emperors and popes. The popes unconditionally supported the enemies of the emperor at home and abroad. Popes repeatedly used the weapon of excommunication against the emperor. The pope's opposition made the lasting success of the emperor's business impossible, and after fighting against this undue discrimination, Frederick died in 1250; there was no guarantee that he would have been able to continue his work even if he had lived.

Within a generation, the House of Hohenstaufen was completely cut off. Frederick's successors, Konrad IV (died 1254), Manfred (died 1266), and the young Conradin, beheaded in 1268 by order of the invader Charles of Anjou, etc. was found to be incapable of carrying on his business. Having conquered Sicily and Naples, Charles imposed a strict rule on himself and used the administrative system established by the Norman rulers and the Hohenstaufen government to extract the maximum from the unfortunate country. When he finally forced the cost of war on Sicily to attack the resurgent Byzantium, the people, outraged by the misdeeds of his troops, rose against the French and ousted the French through the so-called 'Sicilian Vespers' in 1282.

In Germany, meanwhile, Frederick's death soon ushered in an era of turmoil. For nearly twenty years, during the so-called 'Interregnum' (1256-1273) period, no new king or emperor could take charge of the empire.

Keywords

Fredrick II, Sicily, Holy Roman Emperor, Hohenstaufen dynasty, Pope Innocent III, Stupor Mundi

References

Abulafia, David (1992). Frederick II: A Medieval Emperor. Oxford University Press.

Allshorn, Lionel (1912). Stupor Mundi: The Life & Times of Frederick II Emperor of the Romans King of Sicily and Jerusalem 1194-1250. University of Michigan Library.

Detwiler, Donald S. (1999). *Germany: A Short History*. Southern Illinois University Press.

Kantorowicz, Ernst (1957). Frederick the Second, 1194-1250. Frederick Ungar Publishing Company.

Kington, T. L. (1862). History of Frederick the Second. Kessinger Publishing.

Luchaire, A. (1905-1908). Innocent III, 6 vols..

Norwich, John Julius (2015). Sicily: An Island at the Crossroads of History. Random House.

Weiss, Roberto (1973). The Renaissance Discovery of Classical Antiquity. Hunanities Press.

Image References

http://www.bestofsicily.com/mag/art57.htm

https://beyondforeignness.org/8966

https://beyondforeignness.org/8966

https://en.wikipedia.org/wiki/Frederick_II,_Holy_Roman_Emperor#/media/File:Friedrich_II._mit_Sultan_al-Kamil.jpg

https://en.wikipedia.org/wiki/Frederick_II,_Holy_Roman_Emperor

https://en.wikipedia.org/wiki/Frederick_II,_Holy_Roman_Emperor

https://en.wikipedia.org/wiki/Frederick_II,_Holy_Roman_Emperor

https://en.wikipedia.org/wiki/Frederick_II,_Holy_Roman_Emperor

https://en.wikipedia.org/wiki/Frederick_II,_Holy_Roman_Emperor

written by Chagyu Kim (Myongji University)

34

Muslim Iberia (Iberian Peninsula)

Iberian Peninsula

Geographical Location

The Iberian Peninsula is located in southwestern Europe. It borders the Atlantic Ocean to the west and the Mediterranean Sea to the south and east. The Pyrenees Mountains form the natural boundary between the Iberian Peninsula and the rest of Europe, separating it from France to the north. As seen in the following map, the Iberian Peninsula is geographically distinguished by its surroundings. In the south, it is separated from North Africa by the narrow Strait of Gibraltar. Its northern, western, and southwestern coasts borders the Atlantic Ocean, while the southern and eastern shores are embraced by the Mediterranean Sea. Cape Roca, located in Portugal, marks the furthest western point of continental Europe.

Currently encompassing an area of approximately 230,000 square miles, Spain occupies the northwest, east, and central parts of the peninsula, representing approximately 84.5% of its total area, which is equivalent to 492,175 square kilometers. Spain shares borders with Portugal to the

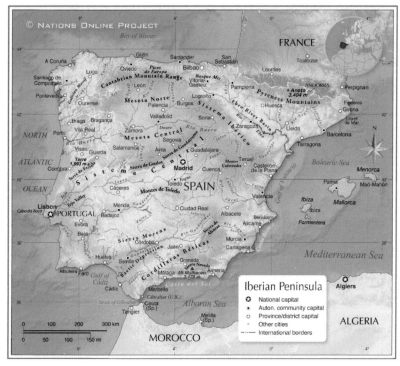

Fig 34–1. Map of the Iberian Peninsula at present

northwest and west, Andorra and Southern France to the north, and Gibraltar
to the south. Portugal, on the other hand, is the largest country on the
peninsula, covering around 15.3% of its total area, which is approximately
89,015 square kilometers. Portugal shares its eastern and northern borders
with Spain.

Besides Spain and Portugal, the Iberian Peninsula also encompasses the
countries of Andorra and the British Overseas Territory of Gibraltar. Andorra,
a small country entirely located on the Iberian Peninsula, covers an area of 468

413

square kilometers. The presence of France on the peninsula is represented by the 'Pyrénées-Orientales' region, which constitutes around 0.1% of the total area, equivalent to approximately 539 square kilometers. Lastly, Gibraltar, situated at the southern tip, occupies a mere 7 square kilometers of the peninsula.

Historical Background:

The term "Iberian" commonly refers to Portugal and Spain, comprising the Iberian Peninsula. It originates from the Ebro River, known as 'Hiberus' in Latin and 'Iberos' in ancient Greek, which flows through the northern and northeastern regions of the peninsula, primarily in Spain, before reaching the Mediterranean Sea. The Greeks called Spain Hiberia due to the presence of the Ebro River, and its inhabitants along the riverbanks were known as Iberians. The exact meaning of 'Hiber' or 'Iber' remains uncertain. Basque speakers suggest that 'ibar' denotes a "watered meadow" or "valley," while 'ibai' means "river." However, no conclusive evidence links these Basque words to the Ebro River. The term 'Iberian Peninsula' was coined by 'Jean-Baptiste Bory de Saint-Vincent' in 1823.

The history of the Iberian Peninsula stretches back thousands of years. The region has been inhabited since prehistoric times, with evidence of human presence dating back to the Paleolithic era. Various ancient civilizations, such as the Celts, Phoenicians, Greeks, and Carthaginians, established settlements on the peninsula.

One of the most influential civilizations in the Iberian Peninsula's history was the Roman Empire, which conquered the region in the 2nd century BCE. Roman rule lasted for several centuries leaving a significant imprint on the peninsula's culture, infrastructure, and language. The fall of the Western Roman Empire in the 5th century CE led to a period of political fragmentation and the arrival of various Germanic tribes, such as the Visigoths and Vandals.

In the 8th century, during medieval times, the Muslim Moors from North Africa conquered the Iberian Peninsula, introducing Islam and establishing the Umayyad Caliphate. During their rule, the Moors controlled a significant portion of the peninsula for several centuries. The following map shows the lands ruled by Muslims the "Caliphate of Cordoba", and the Christian kingdoms ruling other territories in the north of the peninsula. The Muslim influence of that era left a profound and enduring mark on various aspects, including architecture, agriculture, science, and culture. This era of Muslim rule is commonly known as the "Golden Age" of Al-Andalus. It was characterized by a notable atmosphere of peaceful coexistence, referred to as "convivencia," in which Jews and Christians lived alongside Muslims under Muslim rule. This period fostered cultural exchange, intellectual development, and artistic achievements that shaped the diverse heritage of the Iberian Peninsula.

The Christian kingdoms in the north gradually reconquered the peninsula from the Moors in a process known as the 'Reconquista'. This prolonged process eventually led to the establishment of the Kingdom of Spain and the Kingdom of Portugal in the 15th century. However, this transition resulted in the expulsion or forced conversion of numerous Muslim and Jewish

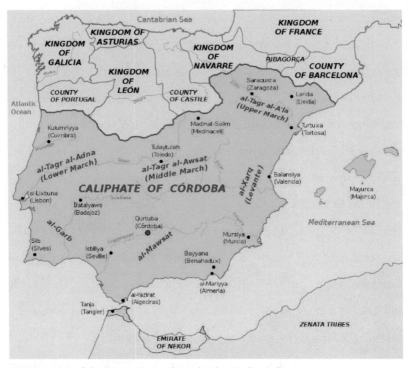

Fig 34–2. Map of the Iberian Peninsula under the Muslim Rule

individuals from the Iberian Peninsula. This had profound demographic and cultural implications, as it shaped the religious and ethnic makeup of the region during that era.

Simultaneously, this era of establishing Christian kingdoms coincided with the commencement of the Age of Exploration. Both Spain and Portugal embarked on global expansion, significantly impacting world history. Spain emerged as a major colonial power in the Americas, while Portugal established crucial trade routes to Africa, Asia, and Brazil. These developments marked a period of extensive exploration, territorial acquisition, and influence for both nations, leaving an indelible mark on the history of the Iberian Peninsula and the wider world.

Throughout its history, the Iberian Peninsula has seen significant cultural exchange, conflicts, and a blend of different traditions and influences. It is known for its vibrant art, literature, music, and culinary traditions. Today, Spain and Portugal are independent nations but continue to share a common cultural heritage and close ties, making the Iberian Peninsula a fascinating and diverse region.

Cultural Crossroads on the Iberian Peninsula:

Throughout history, the Iberian Peninsula has been a melting pot where diverse cultures converged and intermingled. It served as a meeting point for various civilizations, including Celts, Phoenicians, Greeks, Carthaginians, Germans, Romans, Jews, and Moors. These peoples, with their rich cultural backgrounds, inhabited and coexisted on the peninsula, leaving lasting imprints on its heritage.

Since ancient times, the Romans, renowned for their vast empire, have conquered and established their presence in Iberia, shaping its governance, infrastructure, and cultural landscape. As a result of Roman rule, the beliefs of the peninsula transitioned from paganism to Christianity. Initially, Christians faced persecution until the Roman emperor Constantine I, in the 4th century, adopted Christianity to emerge as the official religion of the entire empire, including the Iberian Peninsula.

417

Judaism also found a significant presence on the Iberian Peninsula as a result of Jewish migration during their diaspora, seeking refuge and settlement. The Jewish community made valuable contributions to the intellectual and artistic advancements of the region, particularly during the period of Muslim rule. The Jews, who had faced persecution under the prolonged Christian dominion, were welcomed by the Muslim conquest and found support under Muslim rule.

Their participation in various fields, including science, philosophy, literature, and commerce, enriched the cultural and intellectual landscape of the peninsula. The Jewish community's collaboration with Muslims fostered an atmosphere of exchange and cooperation, leading to advancements in various disciplines. The interplay between Jewish and Muslim scholars resulted in significant contributions to fields such as medicine, mathematics, astronomy, and philosophy.

With the Muslim conquest during medieval times, Islam was introduced to the Iberian Peninsula, gradually leading to an Islamization process that reshaped the demographic structure, establishing a Muslim majority for centuries. The Muslim rule brought significant contributions to architecture, agriculture, science, and culture, fostering a vibrant period of coexistence within the diverse religious landscape of the peninsula. During the reign of the Umayyads in Al-Andalus, a mixed society emerged where Christians were not compelled to convert to Islam. They were allowed to freely practice their religion, resulting in the emergence of a distinct group known as the 'Mozarabs'. The Mozarabs were influenced by Arab culture, which is seen in various aspects of their lives, including traditions, food, clothing, architecture, and language, particularly the Arabic language.

This cultural blending and coexistence between Muslims and Christians can also be observed in intermarriages among the ruling elites of Al-Andalus. 'Abd AI-Rahman III', the first Umayyad Caliph of Al-Andalus, had a Christian Basque princess as his grandmother, and his successor, 'Al-Kaham II', married a Basque girl. Similar examples can be found in earlier generations, such as the marriage of 'Abdel Aziz', the son of 'Musa ibn Nusayr', the Arab ruler who initiated the Muslim conquest, to the wife of the last Visigothic ruler of the Iberian Peninsula, Rodrigo.

While peaceful coexistence between Muslims and Christians under Umayyad rule in Al-Andalus is evident, it is essential to acknowledge that there were non-peaceful practices as well. An example of this is seen in the intolerant attitude of the Umayyads towards fanatical Christian martyrdom movements in Cordoba during the ninth century. Christians publicly insulted Islam's prophet, despite warnings of execution. In response, the Muslim government imposed oppressive measures such as increased taxes, closure of monasteries, and dismissals from government positions. However, this movement was short-lived and not representative of the overall atmosphere of Convivencia.

The impact of this peaceful environment can be seen in the advanced civilization that flourished in Al-Andalus. Many Andalusian scientists and scholars made significant contributions in various fields, benefiting not only Al-Andalus but also Christian Europe. Al-Andalus became a center of enlightenment during the medieval period when Christian Europe was considered intellectually backward. Muslim efforts in fields such as medicine, mathematics, astrology, physics, and other areas of knowledge influenced the Christian world for centuries.

Furthermore, Muslim rulers showed a great interest in spreading knowledge and literacy, particularly the Arabic language, which played a significant role in the cultural exchange between Muslims and Christians. The use of Arabic among Mozarabs continued until the thirteenth century, and young Christians in Cordoba showed fluency in Arabic surpassing their knowledge of Latin. The influence of Arabic can still be seen today in Spanish language, which includes numerous words of Arabic origin.

Christianization once again became a dominant force in the Iberian Peninsula after the Christian kingdoms successfully completed the Reconquista of the whole Iberian Peninsula by 1492, reclaiming the territories that had been under Muslim rule for more than seven centuries and thus bringing an end to Muslim rule in the region. In this Christianization process, the Catholic Church played a central role in actively promoting the conversion of the population to Christianity.

The Christianization of the Iberian Peninsula involved various policies and approaches. One approach was through the establishment of new Christian institutions, such as churches, monasteries, and cathedrals, which became centers for religious instruction and worship. These institutions not only served as places of faith but also played important roles in shaping the social, cultural, and political life of the communities. Christianization policies also included legislation and laws that aimed to suppress or eradicate other religious practices. The authorities enacted measures that prohibited the open practice of non-Christian religions and imposed penalties on those who deviated from the prescribed Christian doctrines. As a result of these policies, the religious landscape of the Iberian Peninsula underwent significant changes. The once-diverse religious practices that had thrived under Muslim rule, such as Islam and Judaism, faced increasing restrictions and persecution.

On the other hand, the imposition of Christianity as the dominant religion in the Iberian Peninsula had profound effects on the social, cultural, and religious life of the region. It shaped the values, customs, and beliefs of the population, establishing a predominantly Christian identity that persisted for centuries. Overall, the Christianization of the Iberian Peninsula following the Reconquista significantly contributed to the formation of its present demographic, religious, and cultural landscape while it had complex and lasting consequences for the diverse religious communities that once flourished on the peninsula.

As a result of this long history of cultural exchange, we can note that the Iberian Peninsula stands as a cultural crossroads, where numerous civilizations and peoples have converged throughout history. It has witnessed the mingling of various peoples of cultural diversity, leaving indelible marks on its heritage. This fusion of cultures has created a unique and intricate cultural fabric that continues to shape the region's identity and inspire its inhabitants. The Iberian Peninsula remains a testament to the power of cultural exchange and the richness that emerges when diverse influences come together. This blending of cultures and peoples on the Iberian Peninsula resulted in a rich tapestry of

Fig 34–3. Mosque–Cathedral of Córdoba

diversity, where traditions, languages, and artistic expressions merged, giving rise to a unique and intricate cultural fabric that continues to influence the region to this day.

The remaining architectural structures today provide substantial evidence of cultural blending. One notable example is the Mosque-Cathedral of Córdoba, whose very name reflects the fusion of Islam and Christianity. The mosque, originally built by the Umayyad ruler ' 'Abd ar-Raḥmān I' between 784 and 786, underwent significant expansions during the 9th and 10th centuries, effectively doubling its size and establishing it as one of the largest religious structures in the Islamic world. However, following the year 1236, the former mosque was repurposed as a Christian cathedral, leading to alterations in its

Moorish architectural features during the 16th century. These modifications included the installation of a central high altar, a cruciform choir, numerous chapels, and a 90-meter-high belfry in place of its original Islamic minaret. Despite its current function as a church, the monument's structure evolved over centuries, blending diverse architectural styles. Islamic influences can still be readily observed in its architecture.

Iberian Peninsula's Impact on European Civilization:

The Iberian Peninsula contributed to the development of European civilization and renaissance through many aspects. Its geographical location at the southwestern corner of Europe made it a crucial crossroads for various civilizations and trade routes throughout history. Its proximity to Africa and the Mediterranean Sea facilitated cultural exchanges and influenced the development of European civilization. The peninsula's strategic position also made it a coveted territory for ancient empires, leading to conflicts, conquests, and the establishment of diverse cultures and influences.

Throughout history from ancient times to the present day, the Iberian Peninsula has witnessed the settlement of diverse racial groups, blending together to create a distinctive cultural fusion. The Celts, Phoenicians, Greeks, Carthaginians, Romans, Visigoths, Jews, and Muslims all left their mark on the region, contributing to a rich tapestry of traditions, languages, and artistic expressions. These cultural exchanges resulted in the fusion of diverse elements, such as architecture, language, cuisine, and music. The legacy of this cultural fusion can still be seen today in the vibrant traditions and heritage of

Spain and Portugal.

One of the most significant impacts on European civilization came from the Muslim rule of the Iberian Peninsula, known as Al-Andalus. For centuries, Muslim rulers fostered a flourishing civilization characterized by advancements in science, arts, philosophy, and architecture. The Islamic influence in Al-Andalus introduced new knowledge and technologies to Europe, preserving and translating ancient Greek and Roman texts and contributing to the European Renaissance. The legacy of Al-Andalus can be seen in the architectural marvels, such as the Alhambra in Granada and the Great Mosque of Córdoba.

The Iberian Peninsula played a pivotal role in the Age of Exploration and European maritime expansion. Spanish and Portuguese explorers like Christopher Columbus, Vasco da Gama, and Ferdinand Magellan embarked on daring voyages from the peninsula, opening up new trade routes and making groundbreaking discoveries. The exploration of the New World, including the Americas, transformed European history, economy, and culture. The wealth and resources brought back from the colonies fueled the growth of powerful empires, such as the Spanish Empire, and had a profound impact on Europe's global influence.

Overall, the Iberian Peninsula's impact on European civilization can be seen in its strategic location, cultural fusion, Islamic influence, and contribution to exploration and discoveries. These factors have shaped the history, heritage, and interconnectedness of Europe, leaving a lasting imprint on the continent's cultural, intellectual, and artistic development.

Keywords

Iberian Peninsula, Spain, Portugal, Muslims, Christians

References

Ahmed, Mona F. M., (2021) "A Comparative Study of Convivencia in Medieval Sicily and Al-Andalus", Mediterranean Review, Vol. 14, No. 1, pp. 31-60.

Ahmed, Mona F. M., (2019) "Presence of Islam in Spain Since the Reconquista", Annals of Korean Association of Islamic Studies (KAIS) (한국이슬람학회논총), Vol. 29, No. 3, 31, pp. 79-114.

Ahmed, Mona F. M., (2019) "Muslim and Jewish Minorities in the Medieval Iberian Peninsula After the Reconquista", Journal of Middle Eastern Affairs (JMEA) (중동문제연구), Vol. 18, No. 3, 30, pp. 25-58.

Britannica, T. Editors of Encyclopaedia (2022, September 9). *Iberian Peninsula*. *Encyclopedia Britannica*. https://www.britannica.com/place/Iberian-Peninsula

Carr, R. (2003). "Spain: A History." Oxford University Press.

"Iberian Peninsula", World Atlas, https://www.worldatlas.com/peninsulas/iberian-peninsula.html

"The Iberian Peninsula". Encyclopedia of European Social History. Encyclopedia.com. (May 4, 2023). https://www.encyclopedia.com/international/encyclopedias-almanacs-transcripts-and-maps/iberian-peninsula

"Topographic Map of the Iberian Peninsula", Nations Online Project. https://www.nationsonline.org/oneworld/map/Iberian-Peninsula-topographic-map.htm

Weaver, Stewart A., (2015) 'The age of exploration', Exploration: A Very Short Introduction, Very Short Introductions (New York, 2015; online edn, Oxford Academic, 22), https://doi.org/10.1093/actrade/9780199946952.003.0004, accessed 21 May 2023.

Image References

Nations Online Project (https://www.nationsonline.org/oneworld/map/Iberian-Peninsula-topographic-map.htm)

Tyk, Wikimedia commons, Caliphate of Córdoba, circa 1000, 26 Aug. 2017. https://commons.wikimedia.org/wiki/File:Califato_de_C%C3%B3rdoba_-_1000-en.svg

José Puy, "Historic Centre of Cordoba", Institute of Cultural Heritage of Spain. Ministry of Education, Culture and Sport. https://whc.unesco.org/en/list/313/gallery/

written by Mona Farouk M. Ahmed (Busan University of Foreign Studies)

35

The Germanic Migration

1. Introduction

The 'Germanic migration', also known as the 'Völkerwanderung', was a pivotal event in European history. Over several centuries, Germanic tribes left their homes in northern Europe and migrated south, challenging existing empires and establishing new states.

This turbulent period had a profound effect on the culture, language, and society of Europe and laid the foundation for the emergence of modern European nations.

The Germanic migration in Europe was a complex process that spanned two centuries (375-568 AD) and resulted in a profound reorganization of the Germanic and Romance populations. This reorganization shaped the political, social, and cultural-religious structure of Europe until the Middle Ages.

2. Background and Initiators of the Germanic Migration

2.1 Definitions

The Germans

Among the English, the Germans are called 'Germans', among the French

'Allemands'. In Germany, there are Swabians, Franks, Saxons, and Thuringians. Whether Alemanni, Swebs, Franks, Saxons, Thuringians, or Goths, whether Vandals, Alans, Burgundians, and Lombards or Angles, Saxons, and Jutes, all these tribes are former Germanic tribes. Germanic is a collective term for various groups of peoples in northern, eastern, and central Europe in the centuries around the turn of the millennium; the groups themselves did not know a name for their entirety.

The Germanic Migration or die Völkerwanderung
(in German: migration of the Folks)

In German, the migration of the Germanic tribes is often called the 'Völkerwanderung' (Migration of the folks).

But the term Völkerwanderung is considered problematic as it refers to the events of late antiquity related to the migratory movements of Germanic tribes and their confrontation with the Roman Empire as well as the emergence of the successor states.

Widely accepted is the chronological classification between 375 (the first mention of the Huns) and 568 AD (the immigration of the 'Lombards' into Italy).

In a narrower sense, a "folk" is a group of people who share a similar biological and/or cultural "ancestry" (language, customs, etc.).

However, this was not the case with the groups of people who were on the move at the time of the migration of people. They were not folk, but individual Germanic tribes with different languages/dialects and customs or heterogeneous tribal associations (mergers of different tribes). Such tribal associations were not formed on the basis of equal biological or cultural descent, but for political reasons, for instance: Tribes formed communities of purpose in order to better assert common interests. Therefore, in the context of the Völkerwanderung, it is better to speak of "tribal associations" than of "a folk".

In today's Spanish, Italian, or French, one speaks of 'barbarian invasions' (invasiones bárbaras, invasioni barbariche/grandes invasions - invasions barbares), which has a decidedly negative connotation. Several terms are used in English: Migration period as well as Barbarian invasions or more recently Barbarian migrations.

These migratory movements were seen as the main reason for many social and power-political conversions that took place at the time - due to this, the term "Völkerwanderung" (migration of the folks) also established itself as an epochal designation for the period just named.

Since the era of the Germanic migration led to great social and political changes in Europe, it is also seen as a transition from the ancient to the medieval world.

And the so-called 'Wanderung' of tribal associations should also be looked at a little more closely. It was not a matter of tribal associations wandering through areas in order to arrive back at their starting position at the end. In the Germanic migration, they left their homeland for good and set off in search of new living space. "Migration" is the movement of people from their homeland to another country/territory with the aim of finding a new place to live.

2.2 Causes and triggers of the Germanic Migration

The history of the Germanic migration is complex and multi-layered and can be traced back to various factors.

Causes for the Germanic migration from the 3rd to the 6th century include climate deterioration, flooding (e.g. at the North Sea), overpopulation, land shortage and food problems, violent displacement by warlike neighbouring peoples, and news of favourable living conditions in the Roman Empire.

In the Germanic areas, the climate became increasingly cold it became colder and colder, resulting in poor harvests and consequently famine. The agricultural yield was no longer sufficient as a basis for nutrition. The famines were additionally aggravated by the population growth within the Germanic tribes.

(In the 2nd and 3rd centuries, Germanic tribes repeatedly crossed the borders of the Roman Empire (e.g. Cimbri, Teutons, Swebs, Marcomanni, Alemanni or Franks). However, the advance of the individual tribes had no lasting effects, and there were no formative shifts of people. Apart from the short-term incursions, relations with the Germanic tribes on the Roman borderline had so far been largely peaceful: Germanic peoples had been active as allies in the Roman army and the administration, sometimes in high-ranking positions; furthermore, there had been barter trade between Romans and Germanic peoples.)

The actual trigger of the Germanic migration was also the so-called "Hun storm" in 375 A.D. The Huns were a Eurasian nomadic tribe from the steppes of Mongolia who had been driven out by the Chinese after centuries of fighting. With their advance to the west they in turn, released an increasing spread of various displaced Germanic tribes: The Germanic migration.

3. Process and Development of the Germanic Migration

The Hunnic nomads pushing westwards from the Central Asian steppes triggered a domino effect. In their advance, they drove whole peoples who did not want to submit before them. Within a few decades, the map of Europe was completely changed. The 'Mongol horsemen' set in motion the ethnic groups that had settled before their invasion. Celts, Germanic tribes, and Slavs went in search of new settlement areas. They passed on the pressure of the migratory movement and annexed tracts of land, which in turn were abandoned by the inhabitants to seek safety. The migrating tribes usually moved in large groups and often fought against local tribes and rulers to acquire land and resources.

Huns, Goths and Germanic tribes

The Mongol horsemen of the Huns first encountered the 'Ostrogoths' and the 'Visigoths' (Goths) on their migration to Western Europe around 375. While the Ostrogoths, who had settled north of the Black Sea, were crushed, the Roman Emperor 'Theodosius I' (*347, †395, Emperor since 379) allied himself with the 'Visigoths'.

The Visigothic tribes left their settlement areas at the mouth of the Danube. They initially received permission from the Roman Emperor 'Valens' to settle on Roman imperial territory and thus find safety. Soon however, the migratory pressure of the advancing Visigoths led to an open confrontation with Rome.

From 375 AD onwards, Germanic tribes invaded the Roman Empire on a massive scale. When the Romans held off the invading Germanic tribes for two years and refused them settlement areas, the 'battle of Adrianople' (today the Turkish city of Edirne) took place in 378 AD, in which the Romans suffered a crushing defeat at the hands of the Visigoths. As a result, the Visigoths settled firmly in what is now Bulgaria, and the following Roman emperor had no choice but to tolerate the Visigoths' new domain on his territory.

The Visigoths were thus the first Germanic tribal association to officially settle in the Roman Empire during the migration of peoples, with the emperor's permission.

The Visigoths under 'Alaric' conquered and plundered Rome in 410 AD. They then moved to Spain, where they settled from the Loire to the Strait of Gibraltar. At the battle of the 'Catalaunian Fields' in Champagne in 451 AD, the Romans and Visigoths together repelled a further advance by the Huns under their king 'Attila' (†453).

The "Wandering League" of the Vandals, Alans and Swebs

Other Germanic tribes that fled from the approaching Huns were the Vandals, Alans and Swebs. The Vandals came from eastern Central Europe; the Alans were originally a tribe of Iranian origin north of the Caucasus. The Swebs were Elbe Germanic tribes, but partly settled in south-west Germany and formed the ethnic basis of the 'Alemanni' (today Swabia). Another part of the Swebs, who had their settlement area east of the Danube, joined forces with the Vandals and the Alans to form a so-called 'Wanderbund'. Together, they travelled through what is now southern Germany, crossed the weakened Rhine border near Mainz in 406 AD and went marauding through Gaul.

While some of the Alans and the Swebs were able to prevail against the Visigoths and remained in Gaul, the other tribes marched on to Spain. There the Swebs were pushed away by the Visigoths to northwestern Spain, where they established an independent empire that held out until 585 AD.

What the Visigoths had not succeeded in doing, the Vandals now reached North Africa, which was under Roman rule, in 429 AD under their leader 'Geiserich' (* around 389, †477). There, they conquered Carthage, the granary of Rome, and thus controlled the grain supply to Italy. The Vandals dominated the western Mediterranean and conquered and sacked Rome from North Africa in 455 AD. 'Pope Leo I the Great' (†461, Pope since 440 AD) kept the conquerors from severe destruction. In 476 AD, the last Western Roman emperor, 'Romulus Augustulus', was deposed by the Germanic troop leader 'Odoacer' (b. c. 433; †493). Odoacer became king of Italy.

Burgundians

The Burgundians also crossed the Rhine in 406/07 and settled around Worms and Speyer in 413 by an alliance treaty with Rome. In 436, on behalf of the Western Roman commander 'Aetius', there were fierce conflicts with the Huns. They led to a severe defeat of the Burgundian Empire and its king 'Gundahar' (Gunther) - and formed the background of the Nibelungen saga. The Burgundians then settled in the area of the rivers Rhône and Saône and founded their empire there (443-534). Even today, the French region of Burgundy bears witness to the settlement of that time, although it was further east.

The Franks

The Franks were a tribal confederation of several small Germanic tribes of the eastern Middle and Lower Rhine.

The Frankish Empire was the only permanent foundation of an empire on Roman soil. Of all the Germanic empires, it was the most important great power until the beginning of the Middle Ages, and it determined the political order of Western and Central Europe. The fact that both tribes of the Franks - the Salians and the Rhine Franks - had gradually migrated into Gaul and asserted themselves as Roman allies in Toxandria (North Brabant) in the 4th century had a favourable effect.

'Chlodwig''s conversion to Christianity in 497/98 - and thus also that of the Franks - was of great importance for the formation of the empire. With this religious and, at the same time, political step, he created a close link between the kingdom and the papacy and won over the Christian ruling class of the country, the bishops and abbots. Secondly, the Catholic confession supported the hostility towards the Arian Visigoths. And thirdly, the Frankish-Germanic and the Gallo-Roman populations could now intermingle. Their merging was one of the most important domestic factors for the permanence of the empire.

The Franks subjugated or expelled other Germanic tribes: they defeated the Alemanni in 496 and expelled the Visigoths from their 'Tolosan Empire' in 507 - despite the Germanic alliance by the Ostrogoth 'king Theoderich'. After the death of 'Chlodwig' in 511, his successors also brought the kingdoms of the 'Thuringians' (531) and the 'Burgundians' (534) under their rule. The Frankish Empire now stretched from the Atlantic to the Main and from the Pyrenees to Friesland.

The Jutes, Angles and Saxons

The Roman province of Britain had already been abandoned by the Romans in 410; the Roman protection troops that had long besieged Britain had left. The now-ruling local princes recruited Germanic mercenaries, who were probably the first to launch the invasion of Germanic tribes into Britain.

The Jutes (from Jutland), the Angles (from southern Schleswig), and the Saxons (from the area between the Weser and the Elbe) invaded Britain in 449. Around 500, the advance of the Germanic tribes was temporarily halted (the legend of King Arthur is about this victory over the Germanic tribes). But the far-reaching conquests of the Jutes, Angles, and Saxons could not be stopped. They drove out the Celtic natives (also into Gallic Brittany, which still bears the name of the Britons) and founded Anglo-Saxon kingdoms - the name England goes back to the Angles. At the end of the 8th century, the Normans ("Vikings") began their depredations and later took over the rule of the Anglo-Saxon kingdoms.

The Lombards

The Lombards, originally from Scandinavia, had settled on the Elbe, had penetrated Pannonia since the 2nd century, and had founded a Lombard empire there. After they invaded northern Italy in 568, a second empire arose under 'King Alboin'. The conquests of central Italian territories also came to an end around 650 and resulted in Italy splitting into a Lombard (later imperial) and a Byzantine (later papal) part. In 774, the Lombard Empire was taken possession of by 'Karl the Great' took possession of the Lombard Empire.

The invasion of Italy by the Lombards in 568 marked the end of the Germanic migration. It was not until the Viking raids in the 8th-10th centuries that it finally came to an end.

The Byzantine Emperor JUSTINIAN I.

'Justinian I' became the Eastern Roman Emperor in 527 and played a decisive role in the further development of the Roman Empire during the four decades of his reign. He saw himself as the successor to the great Roman emperors; accordingly, his main foreign policy goal was to restore the old borders of the Roman empire.

With the help of his two commanders, 'Belisar' and 'Narses', he conquered and destroyed the Vandal Empire in 534/35 and, after a 20-year war, the 'Ostrogoths' in 553; shortly before, he had wrested the southern tip of Spain from the Visigoths. When he died in 565, he had at least reincorporated the Mediterranean area (North Africa, Italy, southern Spain, and the Mediterranean islands) into the Byzantine Empire. Most of the reconquests were soon lost again under his successors.

The end of the Western Roman Empire

In the following decades, sub-groups of the Visigoths spread across Greece and Italy to the areas of present-day Spain. However, the Goths were not the only Germanic tribal group that pushed into the Roman empire. The Franks, for example, migrated across the Rhine and settled in what is now northern France.

Although the tribes were on foreign territory, they took advantage of the growing power-political instability of Rome to increasingly break away from the central power of the Empire and become sovereign. Thus, over time, more and more autonomous Germanic territories emerged, which the 'Imperium Romanum' soon could not keep under control and, therefore, had to abandon.

The Vandals also went on a "migration" and covered many further distances than some other tribes - they even went through France and Spain to the north coast of Africa and back to Italy.

Thus, in 455 AD, the Vandals attacked Rome, led by 'Geiseric', the warlord and king of the Vandals. The city was completely sacked - another crushing defeat for the Western Roman Empire in the course of the Germanic migration.

The Western Roman Empire increasingly lost power and ground under the influence of the Germanic tribal associations and their established dominions. In addition, the power-political and organizational structures of the Roman Empire were disintegrating more and more - the Empire was on the verge of disintegration.

Odoacer and the last Roman Emperor

Finally, in 476 AD, the last great internal political conflict occurred that would finally seal the downfall of Western Rome.

The Roman military still had some Germanic auxiliaries, but they, too, used the growing unrest in the Empire to their advantage. The auxiliaries demanded settlement areas in Italy and fair payment for their continued military services. However, the Roman Emperor Romulus Augustulus (then still a minor), or rather his government representative, refused to meet the Germanic demands.

This led to a mutiny of the Germanic troops under the commander 'Odoacer' in 476 AD. The 'Teutons' emerged successfully from this battle; Odoacer deposed 'Augustulus' and founded his own kingdom in Italy. With this, Odoacer not only finally ended Roman imperial rule, but also the existence of the Western Roman Empire.

After the end of the Western Roman Empire in 476 AD, however, the migration of peoples was not yet over. The migration movements continued, and numerous smaller and larger Germanic dominions were established.

But soon, there were concentration processes, i.e. mergers of tribes. Smaller tribes/tribal associations were taken over by a few large and powerful Germanic dominions.

The 'Visigoths', for example, incorporated many tribes that settled in Spanish territory and became the dominant Germanic power there.

In Central Europe, in what is now France, a similar process took place. There, the tribe of the Franks established itself and took over the Germanic leadership role by integrating other tribes.

End of the Germanic Migration

From 493 AD, Italy was under the rule of the Ostrogoths. The Ostrogoth king Theoderic succeeded in defeating Odoacer and taking over his empire;thus, the Ostrogothic Empire came into being. However, as early as 562 AD, the Ostrogothic Empire was crushed, namely by an attack from the Eastern Roman Empire. Large parts of Italy, however, were to remain in Eastern Roman hands for only about six years. In 568 AD, the Ostrogoths advanced from Pannonia (in the area of present-day Hungary) in Italy as far as Rome.

The last major migration movement in the course of the Germanic migration was undertaken by the Lombard tribes. In 568 AD, they moved from the territories of present-day western Hungary across the Alps and invaded Italy, which was dominated by Eastern Rome. The Lombards succeeded in occupying northern Italy and founded the Lombard Empire there.

The Lombard Empire was the last new dominion, the last new empire created by the Germanic tribes - this is why many historians see the year 568 AD as the end of the Germanic migration.

It was not until 200 years later (774 AD) that 'Karl the Great', King of the Franks, defeated the Lombards. But it was not only the Lombards that he subjugated, but also all sorts of other tribes and peoples. Of the tribes that had once become independent through the migrations, only the Frankish Empire but the migrations were not without consequences.

4. The impacts of Germanic Migration on Europe

The Germanic migration in Europe lasted about 200 years (from 375 to 568) and led to a fusion of ancient Roman culture, the way of life of the Germanic peoples, and Christianity.

As a result of the Migration of Germanic tribes, the Western Roman empire came to an end and new Germanic empires arose in the East.

Internal problems and the military protection of the 15,000 km long borders of the empire, which stretched over three continents, made the domination of the Roman Empire more difficult. With the invasion of the Parthians or Persians in the East and the Germanic tribes in the north around 250, the Roman Empire began to disintegrate. The former great empire was replaced by individual Germanic dominions and kingdoms (e.g. the Frankish Empire), which henceforth determined the power-political fate of Europe.

Notable empires were the Vandals in Africa, Sardinia, and Corsica, the Visigoths in Spain, and the Ostrogoths under Theodoric the Great in Italy, with their capital at Ravenna (Goths).

The Germanic migration had a profound impact on Europe and the world in various areas such as culture, society, politics, and economy. Some of the most important impacts are listed below:

Linguistic and cultural changes: The migrations of the Germanic peoples spread new languages and cultural traditions in Europe. For example, the Germanic language became dominant in many parts of Europe and influenced the development of other languages. The migrations of the Germanic peoples also led to an exchange of cultural elements and ideas between the Germanic peoples and other cultures. For example, the art and music of the Germanic peoples incorporated elements from other cultures and developed them further.

Political changes: The Germanic migration led to the collapse of the Roman Empire and the emergence of numerous Germanic empires. This led to a reorganization of the political balance of power in Europe and laid the foundation for the emergence of modern states and nations.

Social changes: The Germanic migration led to profound social changes in Europe. The founding of new settlements and the takeover of territories led to a mixing of cultures and peoples. The emergence of new social forms, such as nobility and serfdom, also shaped European society for a long time.

Economic impact: The Germanic migration also influenced Europe's economy. New trade routes were opened, towns and markets were established, and the development of trade and crafts was advanced. The exploitation of resources and raw materials in the conquered areas also had an impact on the economy of Europe. Larger trading centers emerged, and the economy became more trade-oriented. Trade contacts were also established over greater distances and there was a lively exchange of goods and ideas.

But the social consequences of the Germanic migration were also undeniable - the migration processes led to a cultural exchange between the Germanic tribes and the former inhabitants of the Imperium Romanum. The resulting cultural landscape shaped European society for many centuries.

In summary, it can be said that the Germanic migration Period was a time of upheaval for the Germanic peoples. Changes occurred in the political structure, economy, and culture. New states and kingdoms emerged, and there was increased integration and acculturation with other cultures.

All in all, the Germanic migration has had a profound impact on Europe and the world that is still evident today. Due to the serious territorial and social reorganization that the epoch of the German migration brought with it, it is also referred to as the transition from antiquity to the Middle Ages.

5. Conclusion

The Germanic tribes were a group of tribes that lived in Europe and made an important contribution to the history of the continent. Their migrations, also known as the Germanic migration or "Völkerwanderung", took place from about 375 to 568 AD.

During this time, many Germanic tribes migrated from their original settlement areas and moved to different regions of Europe, including the Roman provinces. It is assumed that the causes for the migrations of the Germanic tribes were manifold, including environmental factors, population growth, and political conflicts.

The Germanic migration had profound effects on culture, society and politics in Europe. The most well-known events of the Germanic migration include the fall of the Western Roman Empire, the founding of new kingdoms such as the Frankish Empire, and the spread of Christianity.

The Germanic migration is summarised in 8 key points:

375 AD: The Huns arrived in Europe and conquered the 'Ostrogoths'. The Visigoths were able to flee to Roman territories.

378 AD: a dispute between the Romans and the Visigoths over settlement areas led to the 'Battle of Adrianople', which the Visigoths won.

410 AD: The Visigoths besiege and sack Rome.

443 AD: The Roman Emperor 'Aetius' made common cause with the Hun King 'Attila' to repel hostile Germanic tribes.

451 AD: The Huns were betrayed by the Romans. The Romans defeated the Huns with the help of Germanic tribes. The Huns were forced to retreat.

476 AD: Odoacer deposed the last Roman emperor. He only lasted 17 years before being defeated by Theodoric.

553 AD: Justinian defeats the 'Ostrogoths' and most of the other Germanic tribes. His successor, however, failed against the 'Lombards'.

774 AD: 'Karl the Great' managed to defeat the 'Lombards' and was crowned Emperor by the Pope in 800.

Overview of the Germanic kingdoms

419-507 'Tolosan' kingdom of the Visigoths in Aquitaine

507-711 Second 'Visigothic' kingdom in Spain

493-553 'Ostrogothic' kingdom in Italy

429-534 Vandal Empire in North Africa

443-534 Empire of the Burgundians

From 486 Merovingian Frankish Empire

449-8th/9th century Anglo-Saxon kingdoms

568-774 Lombard kingdoms

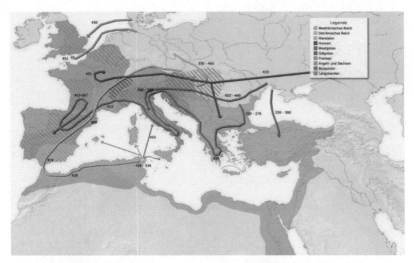

Fig 34–1. Germanic tribes and the routes of their migration (375-568 AD)

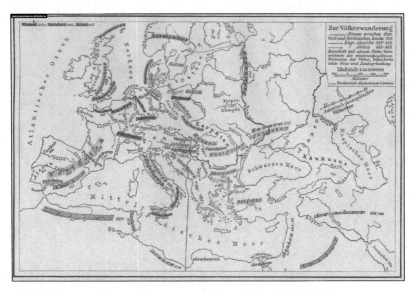

Fig 34–2. Germanic tribes and the routes of their migration (375-568 AD)

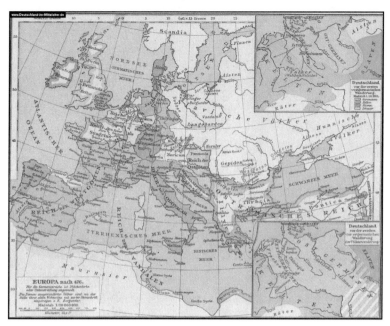

Fig 34–3. The waves of the Germanic Migration until 476

Fig 34–4. Europe in 526 AD: Of the many Germanic empires that emerged with the fall of Western Rome (476), only the Frankish Empire ultimately survived. Under Karl the Great, it became the foundation of medieval Europe in the 8th century.

Keywords

Germanic Migration, die Völkerwanderung, Germanic tribes, Battle of Adrianople,
Roman Empire, (Huns, Goths etc.)

References

Demandt, A. (2016). Untergang des Römischen Reichs. Das Ende der alten Ordnung.
    In: FAZ 22.01.2016.

Engels, Ch. (2005). Die Völkerwanderung. Europa zwischen Antike und Mittelalter.
    In: Knaut, M./Quast, D. (Hrsg.). Archäologische Informationen 28/1&2, 2005,
    Sonderheft 2005 der Zeitschrift Archölogie in Deutschland. Stuttgart S. 187–190

Ewig, E. (1991). Die Namensgebung bei den ältesten Frankenkönigen und im
    merowingischen Königshaus. In: Francia 18,1. Sigmaringen. Jan Thorbecke. S.
    21–69.

Halsall, G. (2013). The Barbarian Migrations and the Roman West, S. 376–568.
    Cambridge University Press.

Heather, P. (2014). Empires and Barbarians: The Fall of Rome and the Birth of
    Europe. Oxford University Press.

Heinen, H. (2000). Reichstreue Nobilität im zerstörten Trier. In: Zeitschrift für
    Papyrologie und Epigraphik 131. Bonn. Dr. Rudolf Habelt GmbH. S. 271–278.

Kulikowski, M. (2018). Imperial Tragedy: From Constantine's Empire to the
    Destruction of Roman Italy AD 363–568. Profile Books.

Marti, R. (2000). Zwischen Römerzeit und Mittelalter. Forschungen zur
    frühmittelalterichen Siedlungsgeschichte der Nordwestschweiz (4–10
    Jahrhundert). Archäologie und Museum 41, Liestal. 2 Bde.

Meier, M. (2017). Die „Völkerwanderung". In: Geschichte für heute Heft 2. Frankfurt
    a. M. Wochenschau. S. 5–31

Meier, M. (2018). Der letzte Römer? Zur imperialen Politik des Aetius. In:
    Heidelberger OJS-Journal. Universität Heidelberg online. S. 209–224
    [https://journals.ub.uni-heidelberg.de/index.php/bjb/article/download/70706

/64063].

136 PL-Information 1/2022

Pädagogisches Landesinstitut (2022). Der Untergang des römischen Rieches-Kritisch betrachtet und spielend gelernt, Rheinland-Pfalz Speyer.

Pohl, W (2002). Die Völkerwanderung. Eroberung und Intergration, German Historical Institute Paris.

Pohl, W. (2018). The Avars: A Steppe Empire in Central Europe, 567-822. Cornell University Press.

Selvaggi, R. (2019). Erfolgreiche Vertragskonzepte oder foedera incerta? - Die weströmische Außenpolitik des 5. Jahrhunderts im Spiegel der römisch-germanischen Vereinbarungen. Diss. Hamburg.

Hamburg University Press E-book

[https://hup.sub.uni-hamburg.de/oa-pub/catalog/book/131].

Steinacher, R. (2017). Wanderung der Barbaren? Zur Entstehung und Bedeutung des Epochenbegriffs „Völkerwanderung" bis ins 19. Jahrhundert. In: Vom Wandern der Völker. Zur Verknüpfung von Raum und Identität in Migrationserzählungen. Hrsg. Gehrke, H.-J.; Hoffmann, K.P.; Wiedemann, F. (Berlin Studies of the Ancient World 41). Berlin. S. 65-93.

E.book

[https://refubium.fu-berlin.de/bitstream/handle/fub188/22304/ bsa_041_03.pdf;jsessionid=A888C8C4F56A61F2353EAF7B63EA68EC?sequen ce=1 oder

https://www.topoi.org/publication/42120/]

Tschernjak, A. (2003). Sidonius Apollinaris und die Burgunden. In: Hyperboreus 9 Fasc.1. St. Petersburg (Bibliotheca classica Petropolitana).

[http://www.bibliotheca-classica.org/sites/default/files/Tscher@5-Prn.pdf].

Waldman, C. (2006). Encyclopedia of European Peoples. Infobase Publishing.

The Cambridge Ancient History 14, 2000.

Wiedemann, Felix/ Hofmann, Felix/ Gehrke, Hans-Joachim (eds.) | Vom Wandern der Völker. E-book https://edoc.hu-berlin.de/bitstream/handle/18452/18828/bsa_041_00.pdf?seq uence=1

Image References

epoc / EMDE-Grafik

written by Chin-Sung Dury, Chung (Korea Maritime & Ocean University)

▼

Intellectual Traditions

House of Wisdom

The Abbasid era (750-1258) is considered as a golden age in the history of Arab Islamic civilization because the base of Arab Islamic culture was settled and developed owing to the rulers' policies for encouraging sciences by accepting and accommodating various foreign cultures. The highly developed sciences of this period greatly influenced Europe beyond the Arab Islamic world. The driving force of cultural and academic development in the Abbasid era was due to the role of the House of Wisdom. As for the House of Wisdom, it was a royal academic institution that served as a library, translation center, academic writing center, astronomical observatory, and university.

Establishment and Name

There are various theories about the background and time of the establishment of the House of Wisdom. In general, this institution started with the purpose of storing various foreign books obtained in the early Abbasid era, and it prepared the base of translation owing to the translation policy of 'Khalifah al Manṣūr'(r. 754-775) and the fields of academic activities were expanded during 'Khalifah Hārūn al Rashīd' (r. 786-809) and it was settled as an organized academic institution in the 833 during period of 'Khalifah al Ma'mūn' (r. 813-833). After that, it was known that it played an active role until the era of 'Khalifah al Mu'tasim' (r. 833-842) and gradually decreased from the era of 'Khalifah al Mutawakkil' (r. 847-861) and maintained only the library function until the perish of the Abbasid dynasty in 1258. After the 'Khalifah al Mutawakkil' period, the function was maintained around the library, and academic institutions named the House of Wisdom appeared in each small country within the Abbasid Empire.

The exact location of the House of Wisdom is unknown. It is guessed that it was inside the palace or in an independent building near the palace, and it is possible to speculate that it was in a special building inside the palace. Names of Houses of Wisdom were various, like 'Bayt al Ḥikmah', 'Ḍār al Ḥikmah', and 'Khijānat al Hikmah'. 'Ḥikmah', which was interpreted as 'wisdom', meant knowledge, reason, and philosophy. Here, philosophy was a synonym for Greek philosophy, and the term philosophy at that time was a concept encompassing various sciences.

Function of Library

The function of the House of Wisdom as a library was very systematic. The space was divided for each task, so separate rooms were prepared for translation, supervision, copying, research, reading, and discussion. desks, chairs, and writing instruments such as paper and pens were provided in reading rooms and stack rooms. There were board facilities for scholars and welfare facilities such as music rooms and rest halls were also provided. A collection of books was provided through various methods and channels. In the early days, books were collected by obtaining books as booties in the process of Islam's conquer or by dispatching purchasing delegations as the policy. For example, Khalfah al-Manṣūr brought books on 100 camels due to a peace treaty with the Roman king, and Khalifah Hārūn al-Rashīd obtained books from Ankara, Rome, and Umuriya (Amorium), and Khalifah al-Ma'mūn sent a personal letter to the Roman king to obtain books or he sent scholars fluent in Greek and Syrian to Rome to bring books from the library of Constantinople, built in 336.

Books were classified by subjects, and the titles of the books were marked with serial numbers and kept in the stack rooms. It is presumed that the book classification method, which is close to today's book list system, was already applied at that time. As for the lost books which were included in the book list but were not actually provided or the books which were not prepared among the entire collection were posted through a separate manual.

Borrowing books was also available. Borrowing books inside the library was available without any additional conditions, while taking books outside the library was possible within up to two months with a certain amount of deposit only for those with credit.

The works of scribes and translators were very important in managing the House of Wisdom. The fact that most books were prepared by transcription and translation at that time shows that the duties of scribes and translators were so important. Hundreds of scribes resided in the House of Wisdom and transcribed many books. At that time, there were two methods of transcription: the first was a method in which a scribe transcribed a book and then several scribes reviewed the contents, and the second was a method in which several scribes shared the transcription of the book and then reviewed it together. At that time, sincerity and responsibility were essential to scribes, and they were respected by the people.

All the rulers, including Khalifah Hārūn al-Rashīd and Khalifah al-Ma'mūn, put huge budgets into library finance. A large budget was spent on labor costs for scholars, scribes, translators, bookbinders, and general managers, and a large amount was spent on materials such as paper, ink, and pens, as well as repair and maintenance costs for books and facilities.

Fig 36-1. Scholars in the House of Wisdom

The management system was divided into two levels: one is the general manager or the head of the library, referred to as 'al khāzin' or 'al 'Amīn', and another is the person in charge, referred to as 'al mushrif' or 'al munāwil'. As for al khāzin or al 'Amīn, he was responsible for academic or administrative supervision, such as purchasing books, checking book lists, and managing translators and scribes. Therefore, he was often appointed among scholars and writers. As for al mushrif or al munāwil, he was the manager of the bookshelf and reading room, and was responsible for guiding library users to the bookshelf or helping them to find books.

Influence on Exchange of Mediterranean Civilization

The House of Wisdom, that was the origin of the libraries in the Arab Islamic world, has become a catalyst for the creation of numerous libraries and the development of sciences not only in the eastern Arab region but also throughout the entire Islamic world. As a result, the Fatimid dynasty in the Maghrib and the Umayya dynasty in Andalus immitated the House of Wisdom and built many libraries and started to compete with the Abbasid dynasty in the eastern Arab region. The governor of Cairo, 'Amru Allah', established a library called 'Dār al-Ḥikmah', and 'Khalifah al Hukum bin al Nāṣir' of the Umayyad dynasty in Andalus established a library in Cordoba, obtaining books from all over the world. The establishment of libraries by each local ruler had a broad derivative effect, creating numerous libraries in the regions, for example, 'al 'Azīz' library in Cairo and 'al-Zahra' library in Cordoba. These two libraries, together with the House of Wisdom in

Baghdad, formed the troika of the libraries, and led the academic development and revival.

The function of Translation Center

The House of Wisdom was a center for the acceptance of foreign studies and academic development, and translation activities were its most important engine of it. Various studies in Greece, Persia, and India were translated into Arabic promoted deep research and writing and created unique studies of Arabs. The translation policy lasted for about two centuries since it was started in the Khalifah al-Manṣūr era, and it peaked during the Khalifah al-Ma'mūn era. The translation policy of the Khalifah al-Manṣūr emphasized the translation of Persian astrological books to pursue stability by making sure of the support of the Persian Zoroastrians who sympathized with the Abbasid Revolution. In contrast, translation policy of the Khalifah al-Ma'mūn emphasized the translation of logic books needed to win the religious doctrinal debate. However, translation activities became decentralized and localized after Khalifah al Muʿtaṣim era because the centralized rule of the Abbasid Empire was weakened after him. Since then, the translation activities have been supported by the Amir or Sultan of each small country.

The lineages and religions of the translators of the House of Wisdom varied, especially the Persian mawālī and Syrian Christians who worked actively. Translations were done in all ways to pursue accuracy and expertise, such as using mediating languages, tuning literal translations and free translations, progressing primary translation and professional supervision, and re-translation and revision of previous translations. An original text in each field of study was translated by several translators at the same time or re-translated in later generations. In addition, explanations and annotations of the original text appeared, and the books which supplemented or criticized the original text appeared, and these books were compiled as educational textbooks. In that sense, the translator was a scholar and, a writer and an educator.

The translation activities of House of Wisdom were done very systematically. The translation manager was in charge of all processes, which were divided by kinds of studies, languages, and functions. The person in charge and the assistant worked together for each division to improve the accuracy and efficiency of translation. In addition, there were departments and professional

Fig 36–2. al Khwarizmi's *Kitab al Jabr*   Fig 36–3. 13th century Arabic translation of *DE Materia Media*

translators dedicated to each language such as Greek, Pahlavi, and Syrian. Financial support for translation activities began in Khalifah and spread to ministers, soldiers, wealthy merchants, and landlords. For example, Khalifah al-Ma'mūn gave gold as much as the weight of the translated book to someone who translated Greek books into Arabic and paid high salaries to other major translators. Not only Khalifah but also social high-class people and scholars spared no investment to get the translations they wanted. Such stable financial support motivated better translators and scholars to gather at the House of Wisdom.

Function of Astronomical Observatory

Khalifah al Ma'mūn was well acquainted with all kinds of sciences throughout his life, especially in astrology. He built two astronomical observatories, one in 'al Shammāsiyah' district of Baghdad and another in Mountain Qasion in Damascus in 830. He built the observatories by taking the advice of 'Sind bin Ali', a Jewish convert to Muslim, and appointed him as the construction supervisor of the Baghdad Observatory. Based on the Baghdad Observatory, seven branches of 'Bayt al Ḥikmah' were constructed in Baghdad, and each was named after seven stars. The construction of seven branches aimed to more accurately observe the movement of stars and celestial bodies in various places. This point proves that the spread of the House of Wisdom was intended to strengthen the function of the observatory. Many historians say that the rulers' demand for astrology is a key reason for the development of observatories.

This is because many rulers asked astronomers for astrological secret information. In other words, it turns out that the observatories were installed because of the rulers' interest in astrology above all else. Some observatories were built within or near the royal court, and astrologers and astronomers gave astrological advice to the rulers. After all, the establishment of the observatories was for accurate astrological predictions, which ultimately were for maintaining royal authority and expanding the empire.

Khalifa al-Ma'mūn held regular discussions with astronomers or astrologers at the observatory and ordered them to observe the movements of stars by using of observation instruments. He ordered 'Sind bin Ali' to measure the circumference of the Earth, so 'Sind bin Ali' went to the 'Sinjar' Desert in Iraq, where, after two years of hard work, he figured out the circumference of the Earth and produced an astronomical table.

Fig 36–4. Astrolabe

Catalyst for the construction of the Mediterranean Observatories

The House of Wisdom in Baghdad made the tradition of establishing and managing observatories by many khalifas, local governors, scholars and wealthy people. They were highly interested in the operation of observatories and astronomical instruments, and they maintained personal ties with famous astronomers. The second largest observatory after the Observatory in Baghdad was established in Cairo during the Fatimid dynasty. Khalifah 'al 'Azīz' (r. 975-996) established an observatory on Mt. Muqaddam in 977, two years after accession to Khalifah, and appointed the astronomer and astrologer 'Abdul Rahman bin Yunus' as a supervisor and he began astronomical observation.

Many observatories attracted excellent astrologers, astronomers, mathematicians, physicists, and geographers and they began to discuss, translate, and write, and the observatories became teaching places for students. Like the functions of prominent universities these days, the medieval Islamic Observatories and the royal courts invited excellent scholars and professors. And they acted like magnets, attracting not only students but also other scholars from all over the Islamic world. The Observatories played important roles in the academic development of the Abbasid Empire.

However, the observatories did not last long. The reason was that the observatory did not benefit from the Islamic Religious Fund, so it disappeared at the end of its founder's life. The longest durability of the observatory was 30 years. The relatively short lifespan of the observatories suggests that they were important to Islamic religions but were not essential to the practice of faith. In addition, it cannot be overlooked that the observatories were continuously attacked by Islamic theologians as they were used as tools for astrology.

Spread of House of Wisdom

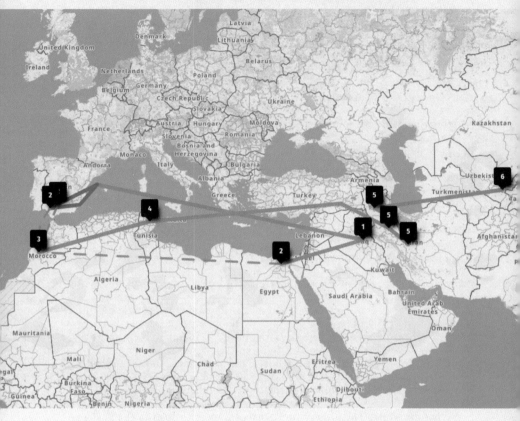

① Iraq (Baghdad)

② Egypt (Cairo) (Around 1010)*
   Spain (Cordoba) (Around 900~1000)*
   Spain (Seville) (Around 1200)*

③ Morocco (Marrakesh) (Around 1200)**

④ Tunisia (Kairouan) (1386)

⑤ Iran (Hamedan) (1023)
   Iran (Isfahan) (1070)
   Iran (Maragheh) (1259)

⑥ Uzbekistan (Samarkand) (1400)

* Assumed to have been disseminated simultaneously from Iraq.

** It is impossible to confirm whether the point of origin for the spread is Egypt or Spain.

Scan the QR code
to view the map.

Keywords

House of Wisdom, Khalifah Hārūn al Rashīd, Khalifah al Ma'mūn, Library, Translation Center, Astronomical Observatory

References

Lee Dong-eun. 2014. "A Study on the Effect of Bait al-Hikmah on Development of the Knowledge in Arab Islam World - A Focus on Library -" *Journal of Middle Eastern Affairs*,13-1. Institute of Middle Eastern Affairs.

Lee Dong-eun. 2014. "A Study on the Effect of Bait al-Ḥikmah on the Development of the Knowledge in Arab Islam world - A Center for Translation -" *Arabic and Arabic Literature*.18-1. Korean Association of Arabic Language & Literature.

'Aṭṭā' 'Allah, Khuḍar Aḥmad.1989. *Bayt al-Ḥikmah fī 'Aṣr al-'Abbāsī*. Cairo: Dār al-Fikr al-'Arabī.

Gutas, Dimitri. 1998. *Greek thought, Arabic culture*. New York: Routledge.

Hamādah, Muḥammad Māhir. 1996. *al-Maktabāt fī al-Islām*. Beirut: Mu'asassāt al-Risālah.

Hasan, Said Ahmad. 1984. *'Anwa' al Maktabat fī al 'Alamaini al 'Arbī wa al Islamī*. Amman: Dar al Farqani al Nashr.

Muaḥmmad, Yūsuf. 1996. *al-Injāzāt al-'Ilmiyah fī al-Ḥadārat al-Islāmiyah*. Amman: Dār al-Bashīr.

Image References

Picture1: Scholars in Library

    https://narsid.com/The-House-of-Wisdom

Picture2: al Khwarizmi's *Kitab al Jabr*

    https://en.wikipedia.org/wiki/House_of_Wisdom

Picture3: 13th century Arabic translation of *DE Materia Media*

    https://en.wikipedia.org/wiki/House_of_Wisdom

Picture3: Astrolabe

https://100.daum.net/encyclopedia/view/b14a1867a

written by DongEun Lee (Dongguk University)

37

Mathematics

Islamic Mathematics: The Characteristics of Early
Abbasid Mathematics and Its Contemporary Significance

al-Khwarizmi, the Mathematician of the House of Wisdom

The mathematicians who made the greatest achievements in mathematical discovery and transmission in the 9th century were 'al-Khwarizmi' in the first half and 'Thabit ibn Qurra' (826–901) in the second half.

Thabit was a physicist, philosopher, linguist, and mathematician. He produced the first satisfactory revised translation of Euclid's *Elements*. He translated the writings of 'Apollonius', 'Archimedes', 'Ptolemy', and 'Theodosius' and developed the *Almagest,* translated by 'Ishaq ibn Hunain' (809–873). He also left his writings on astronomy, conics, elementary algebra, magic squares, and amicable pairs. Thabit is a mathematician who invented the first algebraic method to generate some amicable numbers, and 'L. Euler' (1707–1783) calculated fifty-nine amicable numbers based on Thabit's method.

'G. Sarton', in his book *Introduction to the history of science,* says of al-Khwarizmi that he was "one of the greatest scientists of his race and the greatest of his time." The first half of the 9th century is characterized by

Sarton as "the time of al-Khwarizmi." Al-Khwarizmi flourished at Bagdad under caliph 'al-Mamun' (813-833). al-Mamun encouraged al-Khwarizmi to write in the House of Wisdom. He was active around 825. al-Khwarizmi also absorbed Greek and Byzantine knowledge and encountered and translated precious books in Sanskrit from India in the first half of the ninth century. In 772, a great astronomer brought Sanskrit astronomical texts called *Siddhanta* to the palace of 'al-Mansur' (reigned 754-775) in Baghdad. The author was 'Brahmagupta', a mathematician and astronomer. 'al-Fazari' translated them into Arabic by the order of al-Mansur and published them as *Sindhind* around 775. Currently, only fragments remain. H. Eves claimed that the visit of an Indian astronomer indicated the introduction of the Hindu number system into Arabic mathematics. al-Khwarizmi wrote an astronomical table around 825 based on *Sindhind*. 'D. Smith' introduced six astronomy-related scholars active in Baghdad during the reign of al-Mamun: 'al-Tabari', 'al-Nehavendi', 'al-Mervariiudi', 'al-Astorlabi', 'Messahala', and 'Alfraganus'. The development of mathematics and astronomy continued for 150 years after al- Mamun's death.

al-Khwarizmi learned the Hindu arithmetic system through Hindu astronomy in Baghdad. One of the surprising shocks he received was the role of the number zero introduced by Brahmagupta to arithmetic. al-Khwarizmi authored an untitled book on arithmetic on how to count with the Hindu number system, which played a crucial role in spreading the Hindu-Arab number system widely throughout the Arab world and Europe. Because of this book, which began as "Dixit Algorizmi" (al-Khwarizmi has said), the word

Fig 37–1. al–Khwarizmi, Khiva (Photo: Author)

'algorithm' came to mean the calculation rules in the Hindu–Arabic numeral system.

al-Khwarizmi continued to author books on algebra, astronomy, and arithmetic until his death around 850. These were translated into Latin by 'Robert of Chester', 'Gerard', and 'Adelard' in the 12th century and profoundly influenced Europe. 'Fourani' argued that this fusion of academic elements is significant. Moreover, the traditions of Greece, Iran, and India could be fused into one, just as the Abbasid dynasty united the Indian Ocean and Mediterranean world into a single trading bloc. A. Fourani cited the expression that, for the first time in history, the internationalization of learning has taken place on a grand scale.

Characteristics of Early Abbasid Mathematics

The Abbasids inherited the unit fraction system and the *regular falsi method* of the ancient Egyptians. This is a method of evaluating an equation by putting strategic values in a given equation and finding a final solution that satisfies the given equation based on them. 'Ahmes' (17ᵗʰ Century BCE),[1] in October of the year 33 of 'Apophis', 'Hyksos Dynasty', used the system of unit fractions including two-thirds. In addition, he used a test solution in solving the equation in Problem 24. 'Fibonacci', who was influenced by medieval Islamic mathematics in the Mediterranean region, dealt with unit fraction decomposition of fractions and the regular falsi method in his book *Liber Abaci* in further developed these methods in his book Liber Abaci in 1202. His work not only advanced the unit fraction decomposition of fractions and the regular falsi method, but also highlighted the cross-cultural influences in the development of mathematics. 1202. Unsurprisingly, these methods were used during the Abbasid era.

In his *Algebra*, al-Khwarizmi dealt with the geometric solution to the irrational number that Plato dealt with in ancient Greece. al-Khwarizmi treated the diagonal property[2] in isosceles right-angled triangles using figures

---

1 A text written by Ahmes in the 33rd year of the Apophis' reign shows how to solve 87 various problems in arithmetic and geometry. In his preface, Ahmes mentions that he is acting as a scribe, copying a document written in the twelfth dynasty (c. 1990 – 1780 BCE). A note on the back of the book refers to "Birth of Set and ISIS" in the eleventh year of an unknown pharaoh's reign, which M. Bernal has argued as equating to 1628 BCE as the eleventh year of Apophis, based on the Thera eruption. According to this claim, I propose that Ahmes wrote the book in approximately 1606 BCE. This document used to be called the Rhind Mathematical Papyrus. Nowadays, it is believed more proper to name the papyrus after the author rather than the man who bought it.

2 He mentioned the properties of a right triangle:

and descriptions remarkably identical to those used by Plato in his dialogue *Meno*. Of course, this is a coincidence because there is no record that Plato's writings were translated during the time of al-Khwarizmi.

There are two possibilities. al-Khwarizmi judged that Euclid's *Elements* (Book I, Proposition 47), which dealt with general right triangles, was complicated and simplified the conditions for isosceles right-angled triangles. The other is that because Indian scholars visited Baghdad, al-Khwarizmi recognized the geometric proof of the diagonal property in the isosceles right-angled triangle by Indians and reflected this figure and proof method in his book.

al-Khwarizmi's treatments of 'Pi' can be influenced by Ancient Greece, India, and Old Babylonia (2000–1600 BCE). In his *Algebra* (Chapter 8. Measurement[3]), he had three circumferences, Archimedes' 3 1/7, 'Brahmagupta' (c.598–c.668)'s , and 62832/20000 of 'Aryabhata' (476–c.550) were used. The circumference of a circle with a diameter of 7 was used as 22 without explanation. On the other hand, the method of presenting the diameter and circumference at the same time was the method used in Mesopotamia. The Old Babylonians expressed the circle in a way, such as '60 for the circumference and 20 for the diameter', as described by al-Khwarizmi. A similar description is given in 1 Kings 7:23 (And he made a molten sea, ten cubits from the one brim to the other: it was round all about, and his height was five cubits: and a line of thirty cubits did compass it roundabout.) Here 'he' is Solomon.

Observe, that in every rectangular triangle the two short sides, each multiplied by itself and the products added together, equal the product of the long side multiplied by itself.

3 Ganz (1929) also sees this chapter as being influenced by Hebrew geometry written around 150.

The equations show that the tradition of mathematics from the Old Babylonian period continued through ancient Greece to the al-Mamun period. al-Khwarizmi's *Algebra* was written half a century after Euclid's *Elements* was translated and provided the motivation for translating *Arithmetica* by 'Diophantus' of Alexandria (third century). Thus, al-Khwarizmi does not appear to have been influenced directly by Diophanthus. On the other hand, al-Khwarizmi was influenced by Euclid's Elements, considering that he used a geometric method in solving quadratic equations. On the other hand, the Babylonians already dealt with important equations from 2250 BCE, including those in Euclid's *Elements* and Diophantus's *Arithmetica*. For example, Euclid treated the quadratic equation $x^2+x=1$ geometrically in Book II (Proposition 11) of the *Elements*, and al-Khwarizmi provided a geometric proof of $x^2+10x=39$. These equations are of the same form as the Old Babylonian equations. The Babylonian method of solving equations influenced ancient Greek and Arab algebra and is believed to have determined the nature of al-Khwarizmi's algebra.

Modern Significance of Early Abbasid Mathematics

al-Khwarizmi's Algebra solved quadratic equations, measured the area and volume, and made complex calculations involved in inheritances, legacies, partition, law-suite, and trade. The words, al-jabr and al-muqabala, appearing in the title of Algebra, can be translated as restoration and reduction. The etymology of the Arabic word 'al-jabr' is Babylonian and means equation. The word algebra comes from the Arabic word 'al-jabr'. al-Khwarizmi used restoration and reduction without explanation. "Restoration" meant the transposing of negative terms to the other side of the equation; by "reduction," the uniting of similar terms. For example, $x^2-4x = 2x+5$ passes by al-jabr into $x^2=4x+2x+5$, and this, by al-muqabala, into $x^2=6x+5$. Al-Khwarizmi's Algebra is translated as 'A short book on the calculus al-jabr and al-muqabalah' or 'The condensed book of completion and restoration'.

al-Khwarizmi did not use letter symbols, whereas Diophantus used unknowns through the contraction of words. The equation, $x^2+10x=39$, appears in al-Khwarizmi's book as "a Square and ten Roots are equal to thirty-nine Dirhems." From this point of view, al-Khwarizmi's work on quadratic equations is not similar to that of Diophantus or the Old Babylonians. As 'G. Toomer' noted, "al-Khwarizmi's scientific achievements were at best mediocre, but they were uncommonly influential." In response to this controversy, however, 'J. Derbyshire' pointed out how difficult it was to develop symbolic algebra and cited Johnson's argument: "The wonder is not that it took us so long to learn how to do this stuff; the wonder is that we can do it at all." 'Hughes' asserted, "Even if he was influenced by Diophantus or Euclid, no one can deny that he created a completely new method of solving problems by formalizing the form of equations."

al-Khwarizmi's algebraic achievement was to set forth the concepts of equations as objects, classify them into linear and quadratic forms for an unknown, and propose solutions for each. His classification was into six fundamental types of equations, which we would write in modern notation as

(1) $ax^2 = bx$ (2) $ax^2 = c$

(3) $bx = c$ (4) $ax^2 + bx = c$

(5) $ax^2 + c = bx$ (6) $bx + c = ax^2$

One reason for these six type classifications is that Islamic mathematicians did not deal with negative numbers at all. By the way, 'Omar Khayyam' was the first to consider all types of cubic equations that possess a positive root. He classified cubic equations of integer polynomials and claimed that the solution of cubic equations can be obtained by means of intersections of conic sections. He only found positive solutions using geometric methods, but it was not until the 17th century that 'Descartes' established a relation between geometry and algebra. Descartes' methods are similar to those of Omar Khayyam, but Descartes realized that certain intersection points represented negative roots and imaginary roots.

al-Khwarizmi's place in the history of mathematics is characterized by his introduction of modern forms and methods without using the older methods of Old Babylonia or Ancient Greece. His achievements can be summarized as "creating new mathematical ideas", which he referred to as the founding purpose of al-Mamun's House of Wisdom.

Based on the preface of al-Khwarizmi's *Algebra*, considered a primary source, and the information recorded in *Fihrist* to some extent, al-Khwarizmi was the foremost mathematician of the early Abbasid Caliphate, representing the pinnacle of wisdom as an academy. In the preface of *Algebra*, al-Khwarizmi mentioned the problem of inheritance as the primary purpose of his work, dedicating half of the book to providing solutions for 34 various inheritance problems. Owing to the difficulty in calculating inheritance based on the Quran and Hadiths during the early Abbasid dynasty, there was a need to establish inheritance calculation methods through numerous examples and educate the scribes and bureaucrats on inheritance calculations. Consequently, Caliph 'al-Mamun' encouraged al-Khwarizmi to write the book. He attributed the great value of algebra to solving inheritance problems.

The thirty-four problems of inheritance distribution calculations can be used to estimate the mathematical level during the early Abbasid dynasty. The Egyptian unit fraction system with the greedy algorithm and *the regular falsi method* was still used. The influence of ancient Egypt, Mesopotamia, ancient Greece, the Hellenistic era, and India's arithmetic and geometry can also be observed. As observed in the characteristics of Islamic scholarship, the Abbasid dynasty inherited and developed elements of the previous mathematical traditions existing in this region and beyond, which were then spread to Europe through the area of Spain, as currently known today. As argued by 'Katz', even after the House of Wisdom closed its doors over two hundred years later, the rulers of Islamic dynasties continued to support and encourage the pursuit of knowledge by scientists, recognizing its practical and applied value.

Keywords

Islamic Mathematics, Algebra, The House of Wisdom, al-Khwarizmi

References

Bashmakova, I., and Smirnova (2000) (), G. *The Beginning and Evolution of Algebra*. Washington: MAA.

Berggren, L(2003). *Episodes in the Mathematics of Medieval Islam*. New York: Springer.

Bürk, A. (1901) "Das Āpastamba-Śulba-Sūtra, Herausgegeben, Übersetzt und Mit Einer Einleitung Versehen." *Zeitschrift der Deutschen Morgenländischen Gesellschaft* (in German) 55: 543-591.

Burton, D. (2007).*The History of Mathematics: An Introduction*. New York: McGraw-Hill.

Chace, A. (1979) *The Rhind Mathematical Papyrus*. Virginia: NCTM.

Derbyshire, J. (2006) *Unknown Quantity*. New York: Joseph Henry Press.

Eves, H. (1990). *An Introduction to the History of Mathematics*. New York: SCP.

Fibonacci. (2003). *Liber Abaci*. Translated from Latin by L. Sigler. New York: Springer-Verlag.

Friberg, J. (2007). *A Remarkable Collection of Babylonian Mathematical Texts*. New York: Springer-Verlag.

Fourani, A. (1991). *A History of Arab Peoples*. New York: Warner Books.

Ganz, S. (1929) "The Mishnat Ha-Middot or the First Hebrew Geometry written About 150 C.E." *Hebrew Union College Annual* 6: 263-276.

Gandz, S. (1937). "The Origin and Development of the Quadratic Equations in Babylonian, Greek, and Early Arabic Algebra." *Osiris* 5: 405-557.

Guttas, D. (1998). *Greek Thought, Arabic Culture*. New York: Routledge.

Hughes, B (1986). "Gerard of Cremona's Translation of al-Khwārizmī's al-Jabr. A Critical Edition." *Medieval Studies* 48: 211-263.

Jaouiche, K.(2011). "India's Contribution to Arab Mathematics." *Indian Journal of History of Science* 46(2): 1-16.

Karpiniski, L. (1915). *Robert of Chester's Latin Translation of the Algebra of al-Khowarizmi*. New York: The Macmillan Company.

Katz, V. (1995). "Ideas of Calculus in Islam and India." *Mathematics Magazine* 68: 163-174.

Lorch, R (2001). "Greek-Arabic-Latin: The transmission of Mathematical Texts in the Middle Ages." *Science in Context* 14(1/2): 313-331.

Rosen, F. (1986). *The Algebra of Mohammed Ben Musa.* New York: Georg Olms Verlag.

Smith, D. (1958). *History of Mathematics.* Vol. 1. New York: Dover.

Suzuki, J. (2002). *A History of Mathematics.* New Jersey: Prentice Hall.

Yan, S. (1996). *Perfect, Amicable and Sociable Numbers.* New Jersey: World Scientific.

written by Jenam Park (Inha University)

38

Renaissance

General definition

The Renaissance is a period in European history that developed between the 15th and the 16th century, marking the transition from the Middle Ages to the Modern Era. It occurred after the Crisis of the Late Middle Ages and was associated with deep social changes. Its chronological limits know wide differences according to the various disciplines and geographical areas and could be fixed between the middle of 14th and the late 16th century.

Experienced by most of its protagonists as an era of change, as it was previously said, and a cultural movement, the Renaissance proposed a new way of conceiving human life and the world, thus developing the ideas of Humanism born in the literary field in the 14th century thanks to the revived interest for classical studies regarding Latin and vernacular languages, especially by the Italian scholar and poet 'Francesco Petrarca' (1304~1374), commonly anglicized as Petrarch and also influencing the figurative arts and philosophy for the first time.

This new frame of thinking became manifest in art, architecture, politics, science, literature, music, philosophy, technology, religion, and other aspects of intellectual inquiry: an early example was the development of linear perspective and other techniques of rendering a more natural reality in painting. Many scholars argue that the first traces of the ideas of the Renaissance had their origin in Florence at the turn of the 13th and the 14th century, during the period that some historians refer to as the "Italian Proto-Renaissance literature", with the Divine Comedy of 'Dante Alighieri', the Canzoniere of 'Petrarch', the Decameron of 'Giovanni Boccaccio' and with the paintings of 'Giotto di Bondone'.

In modern art history textbooks, Giotto is considered one of the forerunners of the Renaissance, thanks to his innovative artistic technique, which will then be taken up and enhanced by another great painter: Masaccio.

Although, therefore, the Renaissance saw revolutions in many intellectual and social pursuits, such as the introduction of modern banking and accounting, it is perhaps best known for its artistic developments and the contributions of such polymaths as 'Leonardo da Vinci' and 'Michelangelo', who inspired the term Renaissance man. In his essay Lives of the Most Excellent Painters, Sculptors and Architects, first published in 1550 and then in a second enlarged and updated edition in 1568, the Italian historian, painter and architect 'Giorgio Vasari' (1511~1574) first used the term 'Rinascita', "rebirth" in English, even if this renewed awareness of descent and connection with the ancient world, through the revival of the ways of the classical Greek and Roman age was not only a characteristic of Vasari's epoch.

During the Middle Ages there had been various rebirths or revivals: the Langobard rebirth; the Carolingian one; the Ottonian one; the Rebirth of the Year 1000 and the Renaissance of the 12th century.

The Renaissance began in Florence, then the capital of the Florentine Republic, one of the many states into which Italy was divided. Various theories have been proposed to explain its origin and characteristics, and it has long been a subject of debate why this cultural movement developed in this very city and not somewhere else in Italy. Scholars highlight the social and political peculiarities of Florence, emphasizing the role played by the Medici, a banking family and later ducal ruling house in patronizing the arts, and the migratory waves of Byzantine Greek scholars who arrived in Italy in the aftermath of the fall of Constantinople to the Ottoman Turks (June 29, 1453) which led to the end of the Byzantine Empire. The knowledge of the precious texts of these scholars allowed the Italian humanists to renew their contacts lost for centuries with the remains of ancient Greek culture.

The new figurative language of the Renaissance, linked to a different way of thinking about humanity and the world, therefore, takes its cue from the Florentine culture and from Humanism, which had already previously counted important personalities among its ranks, such as 'Petrarch' and 'Coluccio Salutati' (1332~1406). The artistic innovations proposed in the early 15th century by authoritative artists such as 'Filippo Brunelleschi', 'Donatello', and 'Masaccio', respectively, in architecture, sculpture and painting, were not initially welcomed by their clients and indeed remained for about 20 years a largely misunderstood artistic change before the then dominant International

Gothic. Subsequently, however, the Renaissance became the most appreciated figurative language and its culture gradually spread to other Italian states, such as the Republic of Venice, the heart of a Mediterranean empire that controlled the trade routes with the East since its participation in the Crusades; in the Papal States, where Rome was largely rebuilt by the Renaissance 'Popes Julius II' (born Giuliano Della Rovere) and 'Leo X' (born Giovanni di Lorenzo de' Medici), and progressively, from the late 15th century, in many areas of Europe.

Fig 38–1. The main States in the Italian Peninsula at the end of the 15th century

The Renaissance style, after its beginnings in the first 20 years of the 15th century, spread with enthusiasm until the middle of the century, with experiments based on a technical and practical approach. A second phase occurred at the time of 'Lorenzo de' Medici' (1449~1492), who committed himself to a more intellectualist accommodation of the new currents of thoughts and who was an extraordinary artistic patron, encouraging his countrymen to commission works from the major Florentine artists, including 'Leonardo da Vinci', 'Sandro Botticelli', 'Michelangelo Buonarroti', 'Neri di Bicci' and 'Filippino Lippi'.

Just Leonardo da Vinci and Michelangelo Buonarroti, together with 'Raffaello Sanzio', are the protagonists of the last phase of the Renaissance, datable between 1490 and 1520, which is defined as "mature" and with their art, these 3 masters influenced the following generations of artists.

Overview and Background

There are at least 2 aspects that unequivocally characterize the Renaissance with respect to the previous experiences: its great diffusion in Europe and its spontaneous continuity; the awareness of the fracture between the modern world and antiquity, which did not mean, however, the rejection of the past, but a different interpretation of it. The past that Renaissance scholars loved to recall was not something courtly and mythological, but through modern tools such as philology, history and inductive reasoning, they sought a representation of the ancient world as close to reality as possible. In the artistic field this led to greater attention to man as an individual, both in physiognomy and anatomy.

There is much debate about whether to consider the Renaissance as a moment of rupture or, vice versa, as a phase of continuation of the Middle Ages. Changes obviously did not happen suddenly, and in general, the medieval legacy was preserved.

One of the great scholars of the Renaissance, the Swiss historian 'Jacob Burckhardt' (1818~1897), supported the thesis of discontinuity concerning the Middle Ages, stating that medieval man had, in his opinion, value only as a part of a community, while only with the Renaissance, first in Italy, a freer and more individualistic attitude of people towards life in its various aspects would have started. Jacob Burckhardt defines the Middle Ages as transcendent, theocentric, universalist, and the Renaissance as immanentist, anthropocentric and particularist. He argues that the new perception of man and the world around him would have been very different from that of previous centuries and that the individual would have been seen as a unique subject capable of self-determination and of cultivating his abilities with which he can win the Fortune (understood in the Latin meaning of "fate", "destiny"), dominating nature by modifying it at will.

The famous Latin statement 'homo faber ipsius fortunae', "every man is the architect of his own fortune", which was also quoted in the oration 'De hominis dignitate' by 'Pico della Mirandola', is a sort of manifesto of the Renaissance thought, where man is seen as "free and sovereign architect of himself", with the presence of God relegated in the background. The enhancement of all human capabilities is at the basis of the dignity of the individual person, with the refusal of the separation between spirit and body: the pursuit of pleasure and worldly happiness would no longer be seen as guilty and dishonest, but rather praised in all its forms, as the learned humanist 'Lorenzo Valla' (1407~1457) wrote in his work De Voluptate.

A new value is given to dialectics, the exchange of opinions, and to comparison. It is no coincidence that a large part of humanistic literature is in the form of dialogue, such as in the Secretum, a work in Latin prose conceived and composed by Petrarch between 1342 and 1358. This new conception spread with enthusiasm but was based on individuals and was not without dark and distressing sides, unknown in the reassuring medieval conceptual systems. The uncertainties of the unknown replaced the Ptolemaic certainties, faith in Providence was approached by the fickler Fortune and the responsibility of self-determination entailed the anxiety of doubt, error and failure. This reverse

Fig 38-2. La Città Ideale (The Ideal City), 1470~1490, a tempera painting which represents the Renaissance theoretical concept of a modern city. By an unknown author, it is attributed to various artists such as Piero della Francesca, Giuliano da Sangallo and Fra'Carnevale.

of the coin reappeared every time the fragile social, economic, and political balance was broken, removing support for ideals.

At the beginning of the 20th century, however, the ideas of 'Jacob Burckhardt' were questioned and, above all, by the German historian 'Konrad Burdach' (1859~1936), one of the major supporters of the thesis of continuity between the Middle Ages and Renaissance. According to Burdach, there would be no break between the 2 periods constituting a single era, and to find a "rebirth", one would have to go back even to the 11th century. He notes that the themes of the 'Lutheran Reform' were already discussed in medieval heresies, that the Middle Ages and the Renaissance have classical world as a common source, and that the concepts of rebirth and self-renewal were found in the Middle Ages, for example in the thought of 'Joachim of Fiore' and 'Francis of Assisi', who aimed to rediscover the inner dimension of individuals.

'Petrarch' and 'Marsilio Ficino' revived the Neoplatonic spirit that had already emerged in the 13th century with 'Bonaventure'. There would, therefore, be no rejection of God but rather a ferment of strong religious renewal. The Christian faith, moreover, had never led to a debasement of human prerogatives, not even in the Middle Ages. According to 'Burdach', in the Renaissance there was only a greater desire to rediscover oneself, and medieval asceticism was also present in the Renaissance itself, for example, in characters such as 'Girolamo Savonarola' and 'Martin Luther'.

Italian philosopher 'Eugenio Garin' (1909~2004), an authoritative scholar of Humanism and the Renaissance, believes that the humanistic experience has as its fundamental characteristic the spiritual, moral and civil formation of man,

Fig 38–3. The Creation of Adam (circa 1508~1512). A fresco painting by Michelangelo, which forms part of the Sistine Chapel's ceiling

obtained with the study of Latin and Greek classics. Humanistic philology leads to the formation of a critical spirit to give a sense of the historical dimension for which humanists were aware of their detachment from the ancient world. It also renews aesthetic taste and establishes in people the sense of life as a civil dimension and as an awareness of the possession of all the abilities placed in them by nature.

Process and development

The 15th century was a time of great economic, political, religious, and social changes, including the expansion of the Ottoman Empire following the conquest of Constantinople, the birth of modern European states such as the monarchies of France, England, and Spain, the Empire of Charles V, the discoveries of America, and the Protestant Reformation.

After the economic and social instability of the mid-14th century, caused by bank failures, famine, and the Black Death, Florence was on its way to recovery. The population began to grow and with the domination of the upper middle class, public construction sites were reopened in the city. However, the Milan Visconti family's threat loomed over the recovery.

By the late 14th century, Milan had become a centralized monarchy under the rule of the Visconti family. 'Gian Galeazzo Visconti', who ruled the city from 1378 to 1402, was renowned both for his cruelty and his abilities. He planned to conquer Florence and include it in an Italian nation-state ruled by Milan, and for that purpose, he launched a series of wars, defeating the coalitions led by Florence. This culminated in the 1402 siege of Florence when it looked as though the city was doomed to fall, but then suddenly Gian Galeazzo died, and his empire collapsed.

The German American historian Hans Baron argues that one of the first causes of the early Renaissance was precisely this long series of wars between Florence and Milan during which the leading figures of Florence, such as 'Leonardo Bruni', rallied the people by presenting these wars as ones between the free republic and a despotic monarchy, between the ideals of the Greek and Roman Republics and those of the Roman Empire and Medieval Kingdoms. This time of crisis in Florence was when the most influential figures of the early Renaissance were coming of age, such as 'Lorenzo Ghiberti', 'Donatello', 'Masolino da Panicale' and 'Filippo Brunelleschi'. Imbued with this republican ideology, they later went on to advocate republican ideas that were to have an enormous impact on the Renaissance.

Fig 38–4. Sandro Botticelli, The Birth of Venus (circa 1484~1486). Uffizi Gallery, Florence, Italy

Until the late 14th century, prior to the 'Medici', Florence was led by the 'House of Albizzi', whose main challengers were the Medici themselves, first under 'Giovanni de' Medici' and later under his son 'Cosimo de' Medici' who realized that to protect the interests of his family, he had to take over the government of Florence to have greater control over city politics. Having therefore entered conflict with the 'Albizzi' and with the 'Strozzi', another powerful Florentine family, 'Cosimo' was first sent into exile. However, the following year, he returned triumphantly in Florence acclaimed by the citizens who named him 'Pater Patriae' and drove away his enemies.

This was the first major success of the Medici, who would henceforth rule Florence for about three centuries. In 1439, 'Cosimo de' Medici' fulfilled his dream of a new Rome in Florence by hosting the Byzantine emperor 'John

VIII Palaeologus' and his entourage of scholars during a Council convened by 'Pope Martin V'. Their presence greatly influenced Florentine cultural life: ancient Greece began to be studied with renewed interest and especially the Neoplatonic school of thought.

Cosimo was briefly succeeded by his son 'Piero de' Medici', and then, in 1469, his 21-year-old grandson Lorenzo rose to power. Notoriously famous as "the Magnificent", 'Lorenzo de' Medici', after a critical beginning due to the Pazzi Conspiracy in 1478, led Florence into an era of peace, prosperity and notable cultural achievements until he died in 1492. Florence was one of the most important cities in Europe and the driving force of the political and artistic ideas of the Renaissance. Significant was the first decoration of the Sistine Chapel in the Vatican, carried out by a team of artists including 'Sandro Botticelli', 'Domenico Ghirlandaio', 'Pinturicchio' and 'Pietro Perugino'.

'Lorenzo' was the first of the Medici family to be educated from an early age in the humanist tradition, and with his death a period of crisis and rethinking began.

Pinpointing the end of the Italian Renaissance is a complex and debated issue. For many, the rise to power in Florence of the austere monk 'Girolamo Savonarola' between 1494 and 1498 marks the end of the city's flourishing. He came to power and created a theocratic republic by taking advantage of the political and social crisis that was affecting the Italian peninsula to oppose the secularism of the Renaissance. His clash with Pope Alexander VI Borgia decreed his end: the monk was condemned as a heretic and burned in Piazza della Signoria in Florence.

Other scholars account traces of the end of the Renaissance to the foreign invasions of Italy known as 'Italian wars', which began in 1494 and continued for decades throughout the 16th century in the context of a conflict between France and Spain for control of Italian territories. British philosopher and mathematician 'Bertrand Russell' dates the end of the Renaissance to May 6, 1527, when Spanish and German troops sacked Rome. This event partly marked the end of the role of the Papacy as the patron of Renaissance art and architecture.

With the political and economic decline in the Italian peninsula, the Renaissance entered its descending phase, as those creative forces that had

Fig 38–5. Piero della Francesca, The Flagellation of Christ (circa 1468~1470). Galleria Nazionale delle Marche. Urbino, Italy

given it vigor were extinguished. The unfortunate Italian political events made faith in the individual's abilities typical of the Renaissance waver, making superstition, hope in miracles, and a sense of precariousness resurface.

Many historians place the transition from the Renaissance to Mannerism in Italy, as regards art and literature, between the 1520s and the middle of the same XVI century. During this period, a certain number of Italy's greatest artists chose to emigrate, and it suffices to recall the example of Leonardo da Vinci, who left for France in 1516.

Greco-Byzantine and Islamic influence in the Renaissance

Many modern historians consider the migration waves of Byzantine Greek scholars in Italy following the end of the Byzantine Empire in 1453 a crucial event for the revival of Greek and Roman studies, art, and sciences in the West and, therefore, for the formation of the typical characteristics of Humanism and the Renaissance.

These scholars brought to Western Europe the relatively well-preserved remnants and knowledge of their Greek civilization, which mainly had not survived the Early Middle Ages in the West. According to the Encyclopedia Britannica, "many modern scholars agree that the exodus of Greeks to Italy marked the end of the Middle Ages and the beginning of the Renaissance, although few scholars date the start of the Italian Renaissance this late".

The main role of Byzantine scholars within Renaissance humanism was teaching the Greek language to their Western counterparts in universities or privately and spreading ancient texts. Their forerunners were 'Barlaam of

Calabria' and 'Leonzio Pilato', 2 translator both born in Calabria, southern Italy, and whose impact on the humanists was indisputable.

Although ideas from ancient Rome already enjoyed popularity with the scholars of the 14th century, the lessons of Greek learning brought by the Byzantine intellectuals changed the course of the Renaissance: history and philosophy were affected by the texts from Byzantium. The thoughts of Aristotle and Plato were fundamental to the Renaissance, as they caused debates over man's place in the universe, the immortality of the soul, and the ability of man to improve himself through virtue. Among the various Greek texts translated into Latin by Byzantine and Italian scholars are those of Homer, Plato, Strabo, Plutarch, Xenophon, Thucydides and Herodotus.

In many Italian Renaissance paintings, a decorative motif known as pseudo-Kufic recalls the Kufic script, an ancient calligraphic style of the Arabic language. The reason for the incorporation of pseudo-Kufic in Renaissance works is still being determined. It seems that Westerners mistakenly associated 13~14th century Middle Eastern scripts as identical to the scripts current during Jesus's time, and thus found it natural to represent early Christians in association with them.

Scholars claim that "In Renaissance art, pseudo-Kufic script was used to decorate the costumes of Old Testament characters like David".

Carpets of Middle Eastern origin with geometric designs from Anatolia, Persia, Armenia, Azerbaijan, the Levant, the Mamluk state of Egypt, or Northern Africa were used as decorative features in Western European paintings from the 13~14th century onward, especially in religious paintings both in the Middle Ages and in the Renaissance.

They are known to have been produced about a century earlier, in the 13th century, among the Seljuks Turks of Rum in eastern Anatolia, with whom Venice had had commercial relations since 1220. One of the first uses of an Oriental carpet in a European painting is Simone Martini's Saint Louis of Toulouse Crowning Robert of Anjou, King of Naples, painted in 1316-1319, while a typical example of Turkish carpet is the one at the feet of Virgin Mary in the 1456-1459 San Zeno Altarpiece by 'Andrea Mantegna'.

Such carpets were often integrated into Christian imagery as symbols of luxury status of Middle Eastern origin, and together with pseudo-Kufic scripts, offer an interesting example of the integration of Eastern elements into European painting.

Fig 38–6. Leonardo da Vinci, Monna Lisa (circa 1503~1506). Louvre Museum, Paris, France

Keywords

Florence; Renaissance; Medici family; Leonardo da Vinci; Michelangelo Buonarroti

References

Giorgio Vasari, Le vite de' più eccellenti pittori, scultori, architettori; The Lives of the Artists , from the original 1568 edition. English translation by George Bull, Penguin, 1965

Jacob Burckhardt, (The Civilization of the Renaissance in Italy. Basel 1860 and 1878

Vincent Cronin, , The Flowering of the Renaissance. 1969

Vincent Cronin, ,The Renaissance. 1992

Denys Hay,). The Italian Renaissance in Its Historical Background. Cambridge University Press. 1977

Eugenio Garin,). Medioevo e Rinascimento. Studi e Ricerche. Laterza 2005

Hans Baron, The Crisis of the Early Italian Renaissance: Civic Humanism and Republican Liberty in an Age of Classicism and Tyranny. Princeton University Press. 1966

Bernard Berenson, The Italian Painters of The Renaissance. London. 1962

Image References

https://en.wikipedia.org/wiki/List_of_historical_states_of_Italy

https://it.wikipedia.org/wiki/Citt%C3%A0_ideale_(dipinto)

https://en.wikipedia.org/wiki/The_Creation_of_Adam

https://en.wikipedia.org/wiki/The_Birth_of_Venus

https://en.wikipedia.org/wiki/Flagellation_of_Christ_(Piero_della_Francesca)

https://en.wikipedia.org/wiki/File:Mona_Lisa,_by_Leonardo_da_Vinci,_from_C2RMF_retouched.jpg

Notes

1: The Pazzi Conspiracy (Congiura dei Pazzi in Italian) was a failed plot by members of the powerful Florentine Pazzi family and others to displace the Medici family as rulers of Renaissance Florence. On 26 April 1478 there was an attempt to assassinate Lorenzo de 'Medici and his brother Giuliano. Lorenzo was wounded but survived; Giuliano was killed.

written by Emiliano Pennisi (Sogang University)

39

University

The world did not know the university's idea and implementation before the Mediterranean region knew it, and it would not be an exaggeration if we said that all universities in the world owe a debt to the Mediterranean region. The first universities known to the world were University of Zaytouna, Al-Azhar University or Al-Azhar Mosque, and, University of Al-Qarawiyyin, in Tunisia, Morocco, and Egypt respectively, established more than a thousand years ago from the Mediterranean region to the world.

Even after the European renaissance era, delegations were sent from the northern Mediterranean to the Arab countries, specifically to Egypt, Morocco, and Syria, to acquire knowledge. Here the university was one of the axes of the European transition of the Arab world for the sake of development. However, Europe was not "copying" the Arab examples of universities literally without interference, but it was more playing the role of developer and improver. It presented the model of the modern civil university. It started with the establishment of the University of Bologna, which was established in Italy in the eleventh century, specifically in the year 1088. Therefore, we can say that both the first university in the world and the first modern university in the world came out from the Mediterranean region.

With the development of relations between the European and Arab Mediterranean sides, the university was a means and a goal at the same time. If we skip several centuries until we reach the nineteenth century, with the beginning of 'Muhammad Ali Pasha's' rule of Egypt, and in the midst of his quest for a renaissance, he had no choice but to intensify the movement of educational missions abroad, and the host country was only one of the countries in the northern Mediterranean region, which started by Italy followed by France and other European countries like Austria and Britain.

The university has always played an enlightening role in the Mediterranean. Enlightenment ideas in Europe were launched from universities. Universities and their professors in Europe played a large and profound role in consolidating the concepts of the state and the philosophical and legal concepts of the state and its function and related concepts such as citizenship, state- people relationship, or civil society.

The southern Mediterranean has provided a lot to the northern Mediterranean and to the world when we talk about founding universities. The Arab world witnessed a large list of ancient universities that were founded since ancient times. Some of these Arab universities have been classified as the oldest universities in the world and have gained great fame at the Arab and international levels. The history of oldest Arab universities dates back to the eighth century AD, which is the University of Zaytouna, which was founded in Tunisia in the year 737 AD under the rule of the Umayyad prince 'Ubaid Allah ibn al-Habhab'. Some sources indicate that Zaytouna University is the oldest university in the Islamic world and the entire world. Several years later, the Zaytouna Mosque was established in the same place. The university offered religious lessons (Maliki jurisprudence, Hadith, and the Qur'an) in addition to literary and scientific studies. The name of Zaytouna University has been associated with many figures, such as Ibn Khaldun.

The University of Al-Qarawiyyin, or the Al-Qarawiyyin Mosque, was founded by Mrs. Fatima Al-Fihri in 245 AH 859 AD. Throughout its history, it underwent a group of changes and expansions as the rulers competed to improve its service, especially the sultans and kings of the Alawite state. A large number of Islamic figures and figures of Arabic literature and philosophy graduated from this university, in addition to many Western scholars who learned from its sciences, such as the student 'Gerbert Aurillac,' who later became (Sylvester II), who held the papacy in 999 AD, and the great Arab scholar (Ibn Khaldun) founder of sociology. Al-Qarawiyyin University has a system of specialized academic chairs that makes it a multi-study university.

Egypt has one of the oldest universities in the world that is still fully operational: Al-Azhar University. It differs from its fellow historical universities in that it maintained the development of its knowledge and roles. It began as a university, then a university for Sharia and Islamic sciences, then expanded to include all religious and modern sciences and fields of knowledge alike. It is considered as the largest religious educational institution in the world to date.

If we look at the beginnings of Al-Azhar University, we will find that it was founded in Egypt in 970 AD during the Fatimid era in Egypt. Al-Azhar University inherited Al-Azhar Mosque, which dates back to the era of the Fatimid state, where 'Jawhar al-Siqilli' laid the foundation stone, by order of the Fatimid Caliph 'al-Muizz Lidin Allah', in the year 359 AH (971 AD). Then studies began in it effectively at the end of the reign of al-Muizz Lidin Allah, in the year 365 AH (October 975 AD), in the first educational scientific seminar. Until today, Alazhar university still providing its services to students from all over the world.

Al-Azhar was originally established as a school to teach students from the primary stages until obtaining the Al-Azhar graduation certificate, which is a certificate specializing in Islamic knowledge sciences in various specializations. But in its modern years, the university has branched out into other fields of science and literature, and business, economics, medicine, engineering, and agriculture can be studied at Al-Azhar University, which received its accreditation as an official academic university in 1961.

Al-Azhar Foundation is unique, compared to other universities, in supervising a chain of schools that includes more than two million students, and there are more than four thousand educational institutions in Egypt linked to Al-Azhar. Al-Azhar is consulted on fatwas and trains preachers who are sent by the Egyptian government to all parts of the world. Al-Azhar Library is considered second in importance after the Egyptian Documentation House. Among its most famous graduates historically are 'Ibn Khaldun', 'Ibn Hajar al-Asqalani', 'al-Sakhawi', 'Musa ibn Maimun', 'al-Hasan ibn al-Haytham',

'Muhammad ibn Yunus al-Masri', 'al-Qalqashandi', and many other scholars who provided humanity with a scientific wealth, the credit for which goes back to their studies at Al-Azhar University.

Throughout history, Al-Azhar University sometimes played a political role, for example, in managing the European competition over Egypt. When the French occupation of Egypt came in 1798, Napoleon Bonaparte, the leader of the campaign, realized the importance of the university and the influence of his sheikhs on the Egyptians, so he started to show great respect for them, hoping to attract their respect and among them he could control on the Egyptian people, but it didn't work at the end.

Generally, the university was only a mirror of the Mediterranean's economic and social progress level. If we look at Egypt, for example, we will find that in the late eighteenth century, it declined to an unprecedented degree, and the state of education and agriculture (the pillars of development and the economy in Egypt in that period) deteriorated as tremendous taxes were imposed. The tragic result was the cultural decline of the Egyptian nation, at a time when Western European countries were transitioning from the Renaissance to the Age of Enlightenment, which had the strongest influence on the path to building modern-day civilization.

Egypt was suffering from Ottoman colonialism, a period of decline in its history that was associated with complete external control over its wealth and resources, which led to a decline in interest in education until it was completely marginalized, which led to a comprehensive decline in all aspects of social, political, intellectual, cultural, artistic, and religious life. This dark image remained until the time of Mohammad Ali Pasha, the founder of models Egypt

Student exchange and educational missions played an important role in the development of modern Egypt. One of the most important purposes of the educational missions was forming a generation of professors and scholars educated in European culture, preparing translators to translate books in various sciences and arts, and among the first to understand history in the nineteenth century in Egypt was 'Othman Nour El-Din', who began the translation movement, translating English naval regulations for use in the navy. In addition to the presence of some envoys who translated books in the arts in which they specialized, the mission was usually divided between one member who specialized in translation, and the rest were prepared to master foreign languages in order to participate in the translation movement later.

The purposes of the scholarship varied from educational, cultural, political and security. Muhammad Ali Pasha tended to send various missions to the kingdoms of Europe in order to create in Egypt a generation of professors and scholars who received European knowledge in Europe and in European languages, so that after their return they would replace the foreign professors, doctors, engineers, officers, and manufacturers. Muhammad Ali succeeded in achieving this goal to a large extent.

The mission from Egypt to Europe was not a temporary or one direction, but it was sustainable. We had the Egyptian School established by Muhammad Ali in Paris to accommodate members of the missions. Then, the 'Al-Alsun' School was established in Egypt to Egyptianize the science of translation and prepare Egyptian cadres who could complete the process of transfer, development, and dissemination of knowledge.

During the reign of Muhammad Ali, seven missions were sent, the first of which was in the year 1809 to Italy, and then numerous missions were sent to Italy, France, England, and Austria to study medicine, engineering, military and nautical arts, translation, law, administration, chemistry, history, mathematical sciences, agriculture, printing, shipbuilding, weaving of all kinds, plumbing, and many others from the areas of knowledge and practical skills. The last of these missions to England was in early 1848, one year before Muhammad Ali's death.

Egypt during the era of Muhammad Ali may not have known the university as we understand it in our modern era, but his era witnessed the emergence of what was known as high schools or colleges that represented the nucleus of major universities in Egypt and the region, including the Al-Alsun School. It is an example of the university's service to the community and meeting its development demands. Here, the history of Al-Alsun College is connected to the history of the modern Egyptian Renaissance. Since its establishment in the early era, Al-Alsun School has fulfilled its assigned hopes, providing the country with skilled translation professionals. The school was established by 'Sheikh Rifa'a Rafi' al-Tahtawi' (1216-1290 AH) (1801-1873 AD) in the year (1351 AH-1835 AD) to form a generation of intellectuals who would be a link between Arab and Western culture, versed in Arabic literature and the literature of foreign languages, capable of Arabizing foreign books, and advancing Government administration in the positions entrusted to them. It later transferred to the Faculty of Al-Alsun at Ain Shams University.

This was the case with the Engineering School, which dates back to the beginning of engineering education in Egypt to the year 1816, when Muhammad Ali established the "Engineer Khana School" in the citadel, which took into account the gradual formation of it and began with preliminary classes in the art of engineering. In 1834, the Engineer Khana School was opened in a regular capacity in Bulaq. Studies continued there, but it was closed in September 1854. Until it was included in the Faculty of Engineering at Cairo University. Therefore, the concept of the university, as presented to the world by the northern Mediterranean, may not have been completely transferred to the south in the modern era immediately after the establishment of higher schools and colleges, but it took some time.

The university or higher schools remained a cornerstone of Egypt's renaissance educational policies, especially during the reign of Muhammad Ali Pasha the Great in the early to mid-nineteenth century AD. Muhammad Ali's educational policy was directed at developing and strengthening the army and preparing employees for his government, but it was a reason for Egypt's openness to Western culture. Here, the student exchange movement between the two parts of the Mediterranean was one of the most important doors to this openness, and the translation movement carried out by these envoys was the door. The second is to complete openness to Western society. Under orders from the Pasha these envoys were personally responsible for collecting and purchasing the most important and most recent books published in each of their specialities. The missions were the best valid and effective tool in transferring Western sciences, arts, and industries to Egypt in knowledge and practice.

By tracking the movement of establishing universities in the southern Mediterranean, we will find a huge gap between the pioneer universities established in the eighth, ninth, and tenth centuries AD and the universities that came after them. We will reach the beginning of the twentieth century until we find an integrated university being established in the southern Mediterranean, and this happened in Egypt through the establishment of Cairo University.

Cairo University is considered the second oldest Egyptian university and among the oldest Arab universities after Al-Zaytouna University, Al-Azhar University, and Al-Qarawiyyin University. It was known as the Egyptian University and was opened as a private university in 1908 AD. Then, in 1917 AD, the government decided to establish a university that would include the existing higher schools in the university. The schools of law and medicine were included in the university in 1923 AD, and it was agreed between the government and the administration of the private university to merge into the new university, with the College of Arts being the nucleus of this university.

In 1925 AD, a decree was issued establishing the public university under the name of the Egyptian University. It compromised four faculties: Arts, Sciences, Medicine, and Law. The School of Pharmacy was included in the Faculty of Medicine in the same year. In 1940 AD, the name of the Egyptian University was changed to Fouad I University until 1953 AD, when the name of the university was changed from Fouad I University to Cairo University.

The university's name has been associated with many prominent political, scientific, and literary figures, including rulers and heads of state such as 'Saddam Hussein', 'Yasser Arafat', and 'Adly Mansour', in addition to Nobel Peace laureates such as 'Mohamed ElBaradei' and 'Naguib Mahfouz', and scholars such as 'Ali Mustafa Mosharafa', 'Magdi Yacoub', and 'Imad Abdel Salam Raouf'.

The Mediterranean countries, both northern and southern, provided the nucleus of universities in the world. We can verify this by examining the list of the ten oldest universities in the Arab world: In the year 1080, the Italian University of Bologna was founded, and today it is the oldest university in the Western world, after which the University of Oxford was founded. This was followed by the establishment of several prestigious universities, such as the University of Cambridge and the University of Padua. Today, all of these universities are considered among the oldest and most prestigious universities in the world, and they were all built following the Islamic university model that Egypt, Morocco, and Tunisia knew years before Europe.

The cities of the southern Mediterranean have known knowledge and enlightenment, and their educational and enlightenment institutions - for thousands of years - have had a great role in scientific exploration. For example, the ancient Library of Alexandria. It is true that it was not the only library in the ancient world, but it was the most famous of them, despite the presence of other libraries that preceded it. Historians disagreed about the true founder of the library, some of whom attributed it to Ptolemy I (Soter), and some attributed it to Ptolemy II. Ptolemy I was widely cultured, so he was credited with founding it. Scientific Complex and Royal Library.

The library contained more than half a million scrolls, and science and mathematics received continuous advances at the hands of the library's scholars and curators, including Aristarchus, who was guided by the Earth's rotation around the sun, and Eratosthenes, who was able to measure the Earth's circumference. In the library, Euclid also composed a writing known as The Elements, 'Heron' invented the steam engine, and the Greek translation of the Old Testament of the Torah was also completed in the library. Regarding the real reasons for the disappearance of the ancient Library of Alexandria, it is historically certain that the legend disappeared due to a fire at the hands of Julius Caesar in 48 BC.

If science is what builds man and man is what builds nations, then universities and student exchange between the two sides throughout history have had a great impact in shaping culture, concepts, and values between the two parts of the Mediterranean. If the culture on the southern and northern sides of the Mediterranean is more homogeneous, we can say that the university created a common culture that resulted from the intensity of interaction and student movement and brought about cultural rapprochement and civilizational understanding between the two culturally different parts of the Mediterranean.

The nature of dependency or interdependence between the South, the Mediterranean, and the North has remained the same with regard to the role of the university or student exchange in general. Until now, we have found that universities on both sides have played the role of "refuge," whether for the sake of education or the sake of survival. So far, we have found that the percentage of Arab students in France is about 29% of the total international students, according to 2022 figures. Although the exchange between the northern Mediterranean countries remains greater, about 55 thousand Syrian students are in Egypt.

The student exchange movement continues between the two sides of the Mediterranean, and university education is still the founding ground for the "Westernization" movement or transfer from the West and its influence. Today, many Arab governments in the southern Mediterranean are adopting the approach of copying European universities in the Arab region or cooperating to open Arab copies of European universities. This also serves a major European economic interest. Rather, this confirms the level of mutual influence and dependence between the two sides and the exchange of roles between the two parts of the Mediterranean, between those who influence and those who are affected, from ancient times until now.

Rightly, the university physically consists of students, professors, and classes. However, historical experiences teach us that material capabilities were not responsible for the renaissance and dissemination of knowledge if they were not combined with another, more important component, which is knowledge. Therefore, we will find that the countries' renaissance on the Mediterranean's banks was linked to the desire to acquire science and learn about the latest achievements in all fields. Here, we must point out that the student exchange movement between the countries of the region began in the southern Mediterranean in the eleventh century and then turned to the north direction, that is, from the Arabs to Europe in the nineteenth century. This is known as educational missions. Students exchange for studying in university remains one of the best-explainingways to describe the relationship between the two sides of the Mediterranean from thousand years ago and till today, and in all cases, "university" was a keyword.

Keywords

Arab, Egypt, Science, Islam, Renaissance

References

https://www.balagh.com/article/%D8%AF%D9%88%D8%B1-%D8%A7%D9%84%D8%AC%D8%A7%D9%85%D8%B9%D8%A9-%D9%81%D9%8A-%D8%A7%D9%84%D8%AA%D9%86%D9%88%D9%8A%D8%B1-%D8%A7%D9%84%D9%81%D9%83%D8%B1%D9%8A

https://www.annajah.net/%D9%86%D8%B8%D8%B1%D8%A9-%D9%81%D9%8A-%D8%AA%D8%A7%D8%B1%D9%8A%D8%AE-%D8%A3%D9%82%D8%AF%D9%85-%D8%A7%D9%84%D8%AC%D8%A7%D7%D9%85%D8%B9%D8%A7%D8%AA-%D8%A7%D9%84%D8%B9%D8%B1%D8%A8%D9%8A%D8%A9-article-26843

https://uaq.ma/index.php/2014-01-08-09-43-58/2014-01-08-09-45-08/jami3-alquaraouiyine

http://www.azhar.edu.eg/

https://www.marefa.org/%D8%AC%D8%A7%D9%85%D8%B9%D8%A9_%D8%A7%D9%84%D8%A3%D8%B2%D9%87%D8%B1#%D8%A7%D9%84%D8%A3

%D8%B2%D9%87%D8%B1_%D9%81%D9%8A_%D8%A7%D9%84%D8%B
9%D8%B5%D8%B1_%D8%A7%D9%84%D8%AD%D8%AF%D9%8A%D8%
AB

https://www.alfaraena.com/8-%D8%AC%D8%B0%D9%88%D8%B1-%D8%A7%D
9%84%D9%81%D8%AC%D9%88%D8%A9-%D8%A7%D9%84%D8%AD%
D8%B6%D8%A7%D8%B1%D9%8A%D8%A9-%D8%B9%D8%B5%D8%B1-
%D8%A7%D9%84%D8%AA%D9%86%D9%88%D9%8A%D8%B1-
%D8%A7%D9%84%D8%A3/

https://alsun.asu.edu.eg/ar/page/1

https://www.asu.edu.eg/ar

https://eng.cu.edu.eg/ar/engineering-education-history/

https://cu.edu.eg/ar/Home

https://m.ahewar.org/s.asp?aid=672748&r=0

https://anamusafer.com/%D8%A3%D9%82%D8%AF%D9%85-10-%D8%A
C%D8%A7%D9%85%D8%B9%D8%A7%D8%AA-%D9%81%D9%8A-
%D8%A7%D9%84%D8%B9%D8%A7%D9%84%D9%85-
%D8%A7%D9%84%D8%B9%D8%B1%D8%A8%D9%8A/

http://www.alexandria.gov.eg/services/tourism/alextourism/culture/%D9%85%D9%8
3%D8%AA%D8%A8%D8%A9-%D8%A7%D9%84%D8%A7%D8%B3%D9%
83%D9%86%D8%AF%D8%B1%D9%8A%D8%A9.html

https://www.skynewsarabia.com/world/1568558-%D8%A7%D9%84%D8%B7%D
9%84%D8%A7%D8%A8-%D8%A7%D9%84%D8%B9%D8%B1%D8%A8-
%D9%81%D8%B1%D9%86%D8%B3%D8%A7-
%D8%A7%D9%94%D8%B9%D8%A8%D8%A7%D8%A1-
%D9%85%D8%B9%D9%8A%D8%B4%D9%8A%D8%A9-
%D9%88%D8%B5%D8%B9%D9%88%D8%A8%D8%A7%D8%AA-
%D9%8A%D9%88%D9%85%D9%8A%D8%A9

written by Nilly Kamal Elamir (Independent researcher)

40

Bell- Ringing

Campanology
The Art of Bell-ringing and Bells

A bell is a hollow metallic object that makes a loud, sonorous sound when struck. The function of a bell is to attract attention by being rung in a variety of ways. Bells range in size from small, portable handbells to massive objects, up to several feet high and weighing several tons, that are suspended in the towers of churches, civic towers, and other structures that serve as gathering points. They can be made either as the familiar mouth bells, which are open on one side, or as crotals, hollow spheres containing a pellet inside. From small, portable handbells to the larger ones suspended in church towers, these artefacts have played a multiplicity of roles in different societies throughout history. Shaped either as mouth bells, of which we are mostly accustomed, they can be rung, if portable, by the swinging of the hand, or if large and non-portable, by it being struck from inside by a clapper or from outside by a hammer. A clapper is a rod, made from soft wrought iron or wood with a metal head, the length of the bell, attached to a hook in the internal top of the artefact, striking the inside when the bell is swung or pulled by a rope while the bell remains still. On the other hand, a hammer is a rod which is affixed to an outer support frame and positioned to strike the bell's rim. A spring keeps the hammer from resting on the bell. There are bells which are rung by hand with a type of hammer called the mallet.

From the large variety of bells of all shapes and sizes, the larger bells in church or communal towers, usually occupying the highest points of the built skyline, have had the most profound effect on society. These bells not only summoned people for divine worship but, before the invention and spread of clocks, provided time and the rhythm of daily life to the community. Conversely, during social conflicts, the pealing of church bells could also voice dissent and accompany protests and riots.

A whole lexis of terms has developed to describe some of the bell's social functions, generally derived from the word Campania, the name of a province of Italy where bronze casting flourished from ancient times. From this name comes the medieval Latin word 'Campana' for "bell" and hence 'Campanile' for "bell tower." The resulting word Campanology' has come to include all matters pertaining to bells, bell-casting, and tolling (ringing) practices. Deriving from this term, 'Campanelismo' describes 'bell tower disputes' occurring at the parish level, expressing a strong sense of localism, usually engendering rivalry between neighbouring communities – as found in most villages and towns of Mediterranean Europe and the islands.

The etymological association with church Latin has helped perpetuate the idea that bells and bell-ringing originated in Europe – a thesis which, however, is not historically substantiated. On the contrary, solid evidence directs us elsewhere as proof which shows that the use of bells predates Christianity by millennia. Both textual evidence and archaeological artefacts indicate the earliest use of bells in China around 1700–2000 b.c.e. Early artefacts which functioned as bells, and which are found exhibited in the museum of Chinese history (Peking), consist of a thick wire frame of a little box and a larger hexagonal pyramid artefact which was struck by a hammer to produce sound. Believing in the transcendental force and universal harmony of sound, the Chinese used bells as ritual instruments, placing them as central artefacts in their Buddhist and Taoist temples. More sporadic evidence also suggests that bells were also employed in India later during this same period. The use of portable bells in the ancient civilizations of Persia and Egypt is also recorded in a rather fragmented manner. Much more solid evidence of the quotidian use of bells comes from the Roman period, depicting small bells hung around the necks of animals and condemned criminals, while larger handbells were used, variously, during rituals of death, in joyous festivals, and for celebrating imperial victories.

Surfacing from this social and cultural historical backdrop, early Christians took over these customary uses of bells. A few of the earliest Christian hand bells, cast around the time when St. Anthony of Egypt – himself being depicted carrying a hand bell in later manuscripts – was alive (c.250-c.355), have been found in a hermit's cave in Egypt and are now in the collection of the Coptic Museum in Cairo. Historians now believe that much of ancient campanological knowledge that made its way to medieval Europe from the Far East came by way of Egypt via the Mediterranean Sea. By the Middle Ages, however, Christians had generated a mythology about the origin of church bells, associating them with Christian personages, martyrs, hermits, and saints. The most popular of these were the above-mentioned Saint Anthony of Egypt and Saint Paulinus of Nola (ca. 353–343), the latter of whom was supposed to have invented the church bell around the year 400. But again, for all these stories, there is no solid historical evidence.

From 610 c.e. another religion important in the history of bells was also spreading: Islam. According to the teachings of Islam, the human voice is the only worthy instrument to call the faithful to worship. This belief, sustained by the conviction that the sound of bells disturbed the souls reposing in the atmosphere, established a negative perception of bellringing among Muslims. Consequently, in Islamic regions, including the South-eastern European Christian countries that formed part of the Ottoman Empire (ca. 1300–1918), bellringing was generally regulated and, in some cases, prohibited.

In Christian Europe, bells started to be listed in church inventories, and bell-ringing practices were recorded in ecclesiastical texts during the Middle Ages. Bells were usually rung in two ways: either by striking the bell with an external hammer (pulsare) or by a rope tied to the internal clapper (nollare), with the bell being in a fixed place. This led to the casting of bells with a loop on top to be hung on a log, usually in a window arch. At this same time, bell-tolling, institutionalized as the voice of a powerful Church, was coming under strict canonical rules. Apart from handbells which were operated inside abbeys and monasteries, the larger bells were gradually installed in the more important churches by the permission of the ecclesiastical authorities. Hence, one finds that in the year 835 C.E., a dozen bells were fixed in the cathedral of Le Mans in France as this practice was spreading throughout the Frankish domains, though it took to the 10th century for large bells to be installed in smaller country churches throughout Western Europe. Bellringing came increasingly to take on a more central role in society. In addition to church bells, civil tower alarm bells or 'campanili' started being built with the intention of guarding the city defences and securing their populations. One of the earliest civic towers was built in Venice around the year 1000, while another one was constructed in Ragusa (Dubrovnik) in 1444. Indeed, the period starting from the 12th to the 14th centuries was one characterised by the spread of civic tower bells in Europe.

Fig 40–1. Church bell tower Noto Sicily

Specific bell-tolls signified meanings: calling people to church or marking the rituals of baptism, marriage, death, and burial. Throughout the year, bell ringing signalled the turning of the season and the start of popular festivities. Church bells also transmitted information and sounded warnings to the people. The sound of the tocsin, with its high-pitched, nervous clangour, was used to raise the alarm; it signalled calamity, ranging from the landing of pirates or the sighting of enemy armies, to an outbreak of fire or approaching thunderstorms. Those daily instances were sounded in different chimes that were immediately understood by the local folk. Habitual bell-tolling evoked a sense of time and place, punctuating the main annual and seasonal events with various outbursts, thus anticipating and calling out people for customary social gatherings, festivities, and community events.

But more profoundly, customary ringing made up the daily routine, regulating the activities of the common people. In 13th-century France, for example, bells were rung to call Christians to prayer at six in the morning (matins), midday (midi), and six in the evening (vespers); later, these ringing sessions came to be known as the Angelus (the term taken from the opening words of the prayer Angelus Domini). Numerous churches came to install a special 'Angelus' bell for this purpose. Thought to have magical powers, bells were also rung to keep away natural disasters and to disperse thunder and evil, as evidenced by the inscriptions and symbolic decorations incised on them. In the ninth century, some outdoor church bells, rung by a rope tied to the clapper, were used in the Greek Levant, although the semantron (Greek term for "sign"), which was a two to five metres long wooden board which was struck by a hammer to make a rhythm, suspended horizontally in the church or carried on one's shoulders, was the normal instrument used to call the faithful for worship in the Greek Church.

From the fall of Constantinople in 1453 to nearly two centuries after, very little information exists on the use of bells in churches. With the Turkish invasion of these territories, very few bells remained except in those islands which came under Genoese or Venetian rule – such as Corfu, the Ionian Islands, and Crete. Throughout this period, the Greek Orthodox churches kept the semantron as the main instrument for the call of worship. With the gaining of Greek independence from the Ottoman empire, and from 1832 onwards, bells came to be installed in churches. From then onwards, church bell ringing came to form part of their religious ritual. When it came to Russia, the first mention of bellringing, fused with the knocking of the semantron, was in Kiev, just after the Orthodox Church had been moved there from Constantinople. Gradually from the 17th to the 19th century, the Russians evolved a unique bell-ringing method known as the 'Zvonit', which was played with a cluster of small and large bells in most of their churches, gradually taking the place of the semantron.

For the Catholic and Greek Orthodox rites, bellringing remained an essential practice down to the twentieth century. Replete with magico-sacred associations, it accompanied most liturgical activities and celebrations, such as Christmas and, especially in the Orthodox tradition, Easter. Creating a complex sonorous language of communication through a variety of sound-producing techniques – chimes, peals, turnings, and half-turnings – which converge into a complex repertoire marking distinct meanings, times, and events, required ample bell tolling skills that were usually transmitted from one generation of bell ringers to the next.

The Protestant Reformation of the 16th century brought about significant changes to campanarian customs and attitudes. While their predecessors had revered the magical powers of church bells, the founders of Protestantism considered the notion blasphemous. Both Lutherans and Calvinists condemned the use of bellringing to dissipate thunderstorms, avert earthquakes, and scare away evil. Martin Luther (1483–1546), for one, abolished such routine rites as the baptism of bells, which he interpreted as a profanation of the sacrament of baptism. In England, the dissolution of monasteries and forfeiture of their treasures to the Crown accompanied the Reformation, and this change diminished the importance of church bells. Consequently, fewer new bells were cast, and some important bell foundries were closed though this did not lead to the destruction of all medieval bells or of bell-ringing customs. Notwithstanding their reaction to church bells and bellringing, it seems that most Protestant churches in Britain and continental Europe did keep a bell to summon people to their own religious services. The continued presence of bells and of interest in bell-tolling in Britain was confirmed by the invention of the art of 'change ringing' as a new bellringing mode in the early 17th century. In the older common method of ringing, introduced in the Middle Ages, and which continued to be used in most churches in Catholic Southern Europe, a person rang the bell by pulling a rope attached to a lever. The lever made the bell swing up 90 degrees to come in contact with a metal clapper hanging inside the bell. On the other hand, 'change ringing' uses several bells, each tuned to a different pitch and rung in a set sequence by a separate player, one player to each bell. It was made possible through the invention of a 360-degrees rotating wheel, which enabled bells to be rung by rotation through a full circle, first in one direction, then in another, with the clapper striking the bell ones on full turn. A rope passes in a groove around the wheel, from where it slides through a slot down through an opening in the floor below. A player holds the end of the rope in one hand and the tufted end (called "the sally") with both hands, pulling it and then letting it free but holding on the end of the rope. This design allowed for precise control of the instant when the clapper struck the bell, and consequently bells could be rung in a series of mathematical patters called 'changes' to produce a harmonic sound not achievable by the traditional fixed bells.

Fig 40–2. Bells exhibited at Sofia centre, Bulgaria

Varied as these bell-ringing methods were, they still employed identically cast bells made out of bronze. A durable alloy of copper and tin, bronze is capable of withstanding heavy strikes and moreover emits a rich, sonorous sound. The process of bell-casting has remained nearly the same for centuries, except that in the present-day, mechanical means and electronic tuning are employed. The traditional knowledge and specialized skills involved in the process, a portion of which remains a zealously guarded family secret, have been transmitted from one generation to the next by an oral tradition. Each bell begins with a separate mould, which was traditionally a "mud pie" made out of a mixture of clay with other material (such as cow dung) for the inner core and the outer cope, this making a bell-shaped case. The gap between these two is filled with a measured amount of melted copper and tin; most bells take 77 percent copper and 23 percent tin and left to cool slowly without cracking. Afterwards, the bell maker breaks the mould and removes the bell, which is now ready to be tuned. Precise tuning to the desired pitch is achieved by the shaving of the bell's metal interior. The final addition is the clapper, which is made from wrought iron. A softer metal than bronze, wrought iron is used to avoid cracking the bell.

It is due to the common alloy of copper and tin that bells have had a seemingly perplexing, but very real, connection with weaponry and warfare, even though as from the second half of the 15th century, cannon contained only 8–12 percent tin as against the 23–26 percent tin used to cast bells. It was not by accident, therefore, that bells were the first objects to be removed from churches and communal towers to be smelted to make cannon and other weaponry during wars, from the 16th century down to the Second World War. During World War II, in Germany and Eastern Europe alone, 33,000 bells were used to make armaments. Church bells were requisitioned and melted for armaments whenever war broke out and on many occasions triggering emotive responses, disgruntlement, and even resistance from the local communities, as happened in the Habsburg lands, in France and Italy during both world wars. With the end of these tremendous conflicts, a number of these bells were recast and returned to their former locations.

Bell-tolling has been used as from the 16th century by monarchs and state authorities in their bid to assert their personal political authority and foster political allegiance. In this way, bell pealing has become an essential element in the staging of public celebrations, such as military victories, and the commemoration of important events, such as coronation days, birthdays, and weddings. Up to the present, church bells and communal bell towers have also helped to represent shared local, community and national identities and generate an emotional sense of collective belonging, gathering village and townsfolk together for celebrations, festivities, and other social events. In contrast, and as much as celebrating power and regulating daily life, bellringing from the local campanile resonated social nervousness and restlessness in the community during riots, rebellions, and revolutions, with bells being rung brusquely, aberrantly, and usually with a broken rhythm.

To be sure, at present, while bells, bell towers, and bellringing do not regulate our lives anymore and, indeed, have had most of their traditional social functions made obsolete by modern technology, they remain important as part of our collective symbolic landscape, shared soundscape, and public memory, especially in Southern Europe.

Keywords

Bellringing; bells; bell-towers (campanili); bell-casting; campanology; campanelismo; civic towers; Angelus Domini; semantron; Catholicism; Orthodox Church; Protestant Reformation; 'change-ringing'; bell-casting.

References

Chircop John, 'From the Pulse of Social Routine to the Subversion of Normality. The multiple use of bell tolling in two colonial sites: the Ionian Islands and Malta 1800–1870s, Journal of Mediterranean Studies, vol. 19 (1), 2010, 1–26.

Cenghiora, G., and Nones, P.G., Nove Secoli di Campane (Piovan Editore, 1986)

Corbin, A., Village Bells. Sound and Meaning in the Nineteenth–Century French Countryside, London, MacMillan Publishers Ltd., 1999.

Cressy, David, Bonfires & Bells. National memory and the Protestant Calendar in Elizabethan and Stuart England, Sutton Publishing, 2004.

Garrioch, David, 'Sounds of the City: The Soundscapes of Early, Modern European Towns,' Urban History, vol.30 (1), May 2003, 5-25.

Price, Percival, Bells and Man, Oxford, Oxford University Press, 1983.

written by John Chircop (Malta University)

41

Ex-Voto
Ex-votive Offerings

Ex-voto (from the Latin 'Ex-voto suscepto') denotes a votive offering made to a deity or saint in fulfilment of a vow for a miracle granted. The votive object being offered was also meant as a sign of gratitude by the vower, usually accompanied by prayer, ritual performances, and other worship practices that involved the use of accessories such as candles, wax tapers, torches, or oil for lamps to light the sanctuary, as well as other small objects intimately associated to the cult of the sacred entity to whom the offering was made.

Candles, incense, and oil burning were a mainstay in these votive offering rituals – in processions, celebration of mass and customary blessings – which transferred the object offered from a common into a sacred space (be it a temple, sanctuary, shrine, or chapel) that was normally dedicated to the deity or saint who interceded the miracle. These kinds of votive ceremonies were themselves meant as an expression of faith and bonding of a devoted person, family, or community, with the supernatural. All such votive cults were an embodiment, and a tangible manifestation, of a deeply engrained, ancient, collective belief which, as cultural anthropologist A.H.J. Prins puts it, "may well be an inbred yearning of mankind."

Votive offerings have certainly existed from the earliest civilizations. Evidence of gifts left in fulfilment of vows in gratitude for a miraculous act or 'divine favour' are found in all regions of the world throughout history and across civilizations and religions. Once transferred, blessed, and displayed with other ex-votos in the sacred spaces of shrines, temples, or sanctuaries – and usually hung on walls, placed near altars or in front of icons – these votive objects were transformed (and elevated) into devotional items of cult, gaining a sense of reverence with the faithful. Certainly, they functioned as tangible evidence of miracles granted by a particular deity or venerated saint – and of the latter's power to intercede with God – in defiance of, or by suspending the laws of nature, purposely to cure, deliver, or save from sure death or grievous harm an individual or a group of believers.

Ancient material objects used as votive offerings ranged from sculptured tablets, plaques, figurines, and statuettes made from stone, marble or clay, mostly illustrating or shaped in anatomical images (heads, arms, ears, eyes, legs, females torsos and breasts, being the more distinct) found in temples or other sacred sites, from Neolithic times through Mesopotamian and Egyptian civilizations to classical Greco-Roman times, where they become more visible.[1] Most importantly, the latter votive material culture of the Roman era left an indelible mark on early forms of Christian worship, and most visibly in the

---

1 One can mention here the eyes/face sculptured votive, dated 4th century Greece, that was found at the Asclepias sanctuary and is now exhibited at the Acropolis Museum, Athens.

votive-supplicatory practices of this religion – with material votive objects remaining a popular Catholic cult till the present. With such origins in early civilization and ancient forms of belief, the culture of votive offerings continued to evolve, taking on Christian motifs and symbols, and the belief in the powers of the intercession of the saints and the Holy Virgin Mary that became principal sacred figures in the worship customs of Catholicism and the Eastern Orthodox Church.

Typology of Ex-votive Offerings[2]

Votive objects constitute one main category of materials offered in the fulfilment of vows. These are of two types, with the first made up of objects of daily use presented as physical evidence of an accident, misfortune, or illness suffered by the supplicant after a miracle was granted. These objects were not created or in any way originally meant to be used as ex-votives, but due to their close link to the miracle granted to a vower, were transformed into devotional items. Often one finds written messages on paper or parchment, press cuttings or photos, testifying to the 'miracle' – or 'extraordinary favour' – granted, being attached to the votive object, explaining the miraculous act. The bulk of these votive-devotional objects are made up of ordinary things, such as a shred of textile, a piece of sailcloth or rope offered as a pledge for being saved from drowning or shipwreck, or else crutches, bandages, orthopaedic and

---

2 This section is mostly based on the author's own-going fieldwork on the collections of ex-votive objects and paintings found in various sanctuaries and churches, mainly in Italy (especially Sicily), the Maltese Islands, Greece and France.

other medical implements offered as part of vows related to the healing of an afflicted or injured organ of the body; or a baby's gown or 'lock of hair' offered as a fulfilment of a vow taken on a complicated pregnancy and childbirth. The more physically intimate to the traumatised, afflicted – and miraculously healed – body, the more powerful, suggestive, and valued the item becomes with the community of the faithful.

A second type of votive object is artefacts made on purpose, ordered, or bought ready-made from artisan shops usually located near the sanctuary. Examples of these artefacts abound, with the most impressive being the elaborate ship models (usually in silver) seen hanging in front of icons in sanctuaries all over southern Europe. Fine artistic examples of these ship models, such as those found in the Notre-Dame-de-la-Garde in Marseilles, were offered as votives by ship captains, crews, or travellers as fulfilment of vows made in perilous circumstances – such as during sea storms – to be saved from drowning or shipwreck. In this category, one finds ready-made artefacts like the popular ex-votive 'Tama' (Greek – plural 'Tamata'). Deposited mainly in Eastern and Greek Orthodox Churches, these are small metal sheet plaques – usually tin but sometimes silver plates– on which an image of a 'miracle-cured' part of the body was embossed and offered in fulfilment of a pledge to a saint, martyr, or the Virgin Blessed Mary. Most of these plaques illustrate the afflicted – and then miraculously healed – body part: breasts, kidneys, eyes, hearts, limbs, and other vital organs. 'Tama' is usually often hung on walls in Orthodox churches, monasteries, and shrines – as, for instance, in the Hilandar Monastery on Mount Athos. Yet, the same type of artefacts is also very popular with Catholic devotees, as seen in many Roman and Orthodox Catholic Churches dotting Mediterranean Europe, such as those in the sacristy of the 'Gesu' Nuovo' Church in Naples or in the shrine of 'Santa Rosalia' in Palermo, Sicily. These types of votive plaques or 'Tamas' are found available to be purchased from shops, ready to be offered as ex-votos for the miraculous cure and the restoration of parts of the body from severe illness or grave injury.

Fig 41–1. Tama votives at Chiesa Maria della Grazia, Catania

Ex-votive paintings form the other main category of votive offerings. One can safely conclude that these votive tablets ('tavolette votive') are the most prevalent in Catholic Southern Europe. Their origin is traced back to the Middle Ages, with the tradition of displaying small votive pictorials in sanctuaries dedicated to saints beginning in Italy, then spreading to various parts of Europe and beyond, from the 1590s, to the 'New World' by the French and Spanish colonisers. Evidently, the culture of painted wooden 'Tavolette' being offered as the fulfilment of a vow, evolved into a popular Catholic expression of faith in Mexico – as in other parts of Latin America – where they came to be known as 'Retablos' (meaning 'Behind the Alter' where they were usually displayed). Hand-painted, these wood 'Retablos' became an immensely popular folk art on its own, covering entire walls of sanctuaries as can be seen at 'The Virgin of Guadalupe and Our Lady of San Juan de Los Lagos', but also in numerous other parish churches, pilgrimage shrines and way-side chapels.[3] On their part, the French transferred the Catholic tradition of ex-votive paintings and their customary rites of offering and installation in churches with their colonisation of Nouvelle-France (today part of Canada), where this votive cult took root, as seen in the collections found at the Basilica of 'Notre-Dame de Quebec' and Saint Joseph's Oratory in Montreal.

As an evolving tradition, ex-votive painting became a unique form of religious folk art, with its own style, expressing a deeply-rooted communal faith in divine intervention – usually through the intercession of a patron saint, martyr, or the Blessed Virgin Mary. As such, they functioned as a tribute, sign

---

3 A significant number of retablos was collected by the famous Mexican painter Diego Rivera. His companion and artist Frida Kahlo herself owned over four hundred of these ex-voto paintings which were a main source of inspiration for her paintings.

of gratitude, and commemoration of miraculous favours granted to individuals and groups in the community delivered from dangerous sure-death events, serious injuries, and illness. Numerous collections of such ex-votive paintings are found all over Catholic Southern Europe, with some of the most popular being the Sanctuary of the 'Madonna del Carmine' in Catania, the shrine of Santa Rosalia in Palermo, the Church of 'San Sebastian Los Caballeros' in Zamora, Spain, or at the sanctuary of 'Madonna Tal-Grazia' in Haz-Zabbar, Malta. All these collections of votive paintings cover a very wide range of life contingencies and adversities, from all sorts of personal misfortunes, accidents, and illnesses to collective natural calamities such as earthquakes or floodings – with the universality of human vulnerability being their fundamental leitmotif.

Structure of ex-votive paintings

Ex-voto paintings are typically small – usually circa 50-55 cm in width – wood panels bearing the letters *V.F.G.A.*, which stand for 'Votum Fecit, Gratiam Acceptit (Vow Made, Grace Received)' and done by amateur painters. The typical spatial configuration of an ex-votive painting is made up of three parts. Firstly, the saint, martyr, or the Blessed Virgin Mary – with whose intercession the vow was granted – is usually posed in the uppermost corner of the composition. Secondly, a short, usually one to two lines of script at the very bottom of the painting, gives thanks to the same interceding saint for the miracle, with the name of the person offering the ex-voto and the date of the extraordinary event clearly indicated. Thirdly, most of the painting is taken by a detailed depiction of the unexpected event, the act of hostility, or the calamity endured by the person portrayed at the very instance he/she made the vow, in kneeling or praying posture or with open arms, for a miraculous intervention. Ex-voto paintings are snapshots of the very instant before a miracle was conceded, and it is therefore only through their being publicly displayed in the sanctuary that testifies to – and commemorates – the granting of a miracle.

The person pledging a vow is usually pictured at the centre stage of the composition, frequently accompanied by others who helped during his/her extreme ordeal and who also witnessed the 'miraculous act.' Examples from these votive paintings depict a handful of courageous individuals swimming out, or throwing rope, to rescue others from drowning; a mother assisted by passers-by to pull an apparently dead child from a well; a midwife helping a complicated childbirth; surgeons during an 'emergency operation' – all scenes which in one way or another acknowledge a measure of human assistance before the realisation of a miraculous act.

While these votive paintings, deposited and displayed in places of worship, immediately express a deeply engrained communal spiritual belief in the powers of the supranatural, for the social historian and anthropologist, they also provide a unique and elaborate picture of the daily life of the people and their world view. Much more than written records, ex-votive paintings provide graphic descriptions of the extensive range of vulnerabilities felt daily by the 'common folk' throughout history – of their not- so- infrequent accidents on work sites; of unexpected mishaps when things seemed to be going well; of sickness and near-death instances – expressing their emotional

Fig 41–2. ex–voto painting offered by Salvatore Pulis in fulfilment of a vow: thankful to the Holy Virgin Mary from being saved from sure drowning. Sanctuary of Our Lady of Graces, Zabbar, Malta.

state: fears, pain, sadness and anguish, but also of anticipation, in specific times and spatial contexts. For the discerning eye, these naïve, colourful, often out- of- perspective, paintings narrate stories through which one can explore the emotional-psychological states of individuals and groups, and the wider, intricate philosophy of life of a whole community.

Subject matter – principal themes

The typical pictorial background found in these (usually dated) ex-voto pictures is one which illustrates scenes taken in real time and geography: a ship going down in a storm; the interior of a bedroom with a doctor trying to stop bleeding from a body; an on-going battle in a field full of corpses of soldiers; buildings falling apart and over a person during an air bombardment or an earthquake. These pictures capture the instant 'Ad Extremis' which the vower experienced, bringing out his/her own emotions of fear, alarm, suffering, call for distress and suspense, in one's histrionic posture but also in the graphic details and exaggerated portrayal of selected items of significance from the background. Taken together, ex-votive paintings make up a visual mosaic of humanity's corporeal and mental suffering – a detailed list of all imaginable adversities, suffering and existential vulnerabilities.

Consequently, the bulk of ex-votive paintings fall under two main distinct themes. The first category deals with personal misfortunes, including the portrayal of 'sure death' events on 'Land and Sea': illustrations of fishermen struggling in rough seas or others being attacked by brigands or pirates; of a girl falling from a high roof before hitting the ground; a boy being knocked down by a bus, or one being thrown under a moving tractor or charged by a ferocious beast. Together with depictions of these personal adversities/ accidents, other paintings portray collective calamities – earthquakes, floodings, bad harvests or an outbreak of disease – with the vower portrayed in praying mode, pledging a vow to a saint or the Virgin Mary if delivered from devastation.

The second set of ex-votive paintings treats all sorts of body health issues, depicting corporeal infirmities, illnesses, injuries, and afflicted parts of the body, but also mental anguish, depression, and madness. Vividly illustrating a vower's own subjective corporeal experience but also of his/her loved ones under physical pain or undergoing surgery, facing life threats, on the streets, on their death bed, or severely subdued by an injury at work, these paintings tell a much more impressive and realistic story than the already discussed anatomical images embossed on metal plated sheets – the 'Tamas'– usually found in the same church and offered to the same saint or sacred figure. Being visibly displayed in an organised manner in churches or sanctuaries, these pictorial ex-votives give testimony to and show gratitude for the graces (miracles) granted, for the restitution of a healthy body or mind, through the intercession of a saint or the Blessed Virgin Mary, to whom that sacred place is usually dedicated. In this way, they are considered devotional items by the faithful, and in turn, they continuously attract devoted pilgrims and more pledges to their extraordinary cult.

Deposited and hung one near each other, in a shrine or sanctuary, the numerous ex-votive paintings constitute a unique material culture which underpins the collective imagination of local communities. They constitute a visual depository of indigenous knowledge and local daily life coping strategies. Collectively and in conjunction, they operate as commemorative tablets, and thus as mnemonic devices, in the intra-generational transmission of shared memories – further engendering a collective sense of belonging to a universally exposed humanity.

Keywords

Ex-votive paintings; votive offerings; vows; ritual; sanctuaries; miracles; anatomical votives; Catholicism, Orthodox Church; *tama*; *tavolette votive*; *retablo*; *Ex-voto suscepto*.

References

Centini, Massimo, *Ex Voto. Gli Oggetti e il Rapporto con il Divino*, La Feltrinelli, 2019.

Didi-Huberman, Georges, *Ex Voto*, Raffaello Cortina Editore, 2007.

Morel, J.P., Ex-Voto par transformation, ex-voto par destinazion (a` propos du depot votif de Fondo Ruozzo a` Teano), in M-H Mactouse, E.Geny, *Melanges Pierre Leveque, VI, Religion*, Les Belles Lettres, 1992, 221-232.

Prins, A.H.J., *In Peril on the Sea. Maritime Votive Paintings in the Maltese Islands*, Said International, Malta, 1989.

Salvatori, Mariolina Rizzi, 'Porque no puedo decir me cuento: Mexican Ex-Votos Iconographic Literacy', in John Trimbur, edit., *Popular Literacy: Studies in Cultural Practices and Poetics*, University of Pittsburgh Press, Pittsburgh, 2001.

written by John Chircop (Malta University)

42

Islamic Medicine
A History of Islamic Medicine

Islamic Medicine, developed between 6th and 14th centuries, originated from Greek sources and expanded with contributions from Persia, Syria, India, and Byzantium. This knowledge was translated into Arabic, then thoroughly assimilated, codified, and 'Islamized.' Both Muslim and non-Muslim physicians enriched it through observation and experimentation, transforming it into a comprehensive and practical science. Islamic medicine's influence spread across the Islamic world and beyond, impacting Europe, Asia and the Far East for nearly a millennium. It established enduring standards in hygiene and preventative care, significantly enhancing public health across diverse regions.

Religious nature

Islamic medicine is fundamentally based on the concept of 'Tawhid', or divine unity, viewing the body as an organic whole. Treatments and techniques are grounded in the belief that both the patient and the physician must recognize Allah as the ultimate healer. The primary source of inspiration in Islamic medicine is the Quran, the word of Allah, with secondary guidance drawn from the Hadith or Sunna, which are the authenticated sayings and traditions of the Prophet Muhammad (570–632).

While the Quran offers limited direct medical guidance, its broader spiritual guidance is crucial for both physicians and patients in the approach to illness and healing. Naturally, early in Islamic history, a body of Hadith literature known as 'Prophetic Medicine' emerged, offering guidance on diet, natural remedies, and the management of simple ailments. It also provided injunctions against contact with contagious diseases, such as leprosy, and advised avoiding areas of epidemics, reflecting an early understanding of disease prevention.

Although 'Prophetic Medicine' was distinct from the more scientific and analytical Islamic medicine, it emphasized the ethical duty of Muslims to care for the sick. The Prophet Muhammad taught that Allah provided a cure for every ailment, and it was a Muslim's duty to care for both the body and spirit. This holistic approach to health, rooted in religious teachings, aimed to improve healthcare quality and ensure access for all, with the Hadiths offering a framework for a comprehensive, ethical approach to medical care.

Theoretical features

Islamic medicine has deep roots in Greek and Roman traditions. In the early days of Islam, there was debate over whether to adopt medical techniques from Greek, Chinese, and Indian sources, as these were seen by some as pagan. However, Islamic physicians were eventually given the freedom to study and incorporate these techniques. Over time, Muslims translated medical literature into Arabic, expanding and refining the knowledge they inherited from other civilizations. They improved upon these traditions while preserving the core principles of medicine, creating a legacy of scientific and cultural renaissance.

Islamic medicine was heavily influenced by the works of Greek and Roman scholars, particularly Galen and Hippocrates. Islamic scholars translated extensive Greek texts into Arabic and built upon them, producing new medical knowledge. To make the Greek tradition more accessible and systematic, they organized this vast body of knowledge into encyclopedias and summaries.

A key theoretical belief in Islamic medicine was that life is not merely a result of the physical body but also the presence of 'Ruh (the soul)', which gives vitality. Treating a disease required considering both the physical and spiritual aspects of the patient.

Islamic medicine also saw the rise of polymaths, or Hakims, who excelled in multiple fields, including medicine, philosophy, law, and theology. Polymaths like Al-Razi, Ibn Sina (Avicenna), and Ibn al-Nafis were central to the development of Islamic science, embodying the unity of the sciences. Their work orchestrated significant advancements in various disciplines. Ibn Sina's 'Canon of Medicine' is a prime example of this intellectual legacy. This 5-volume encyclopedia systematically organized medical knowledge of the time and became the most influential medical text of the Middle Ages. It was later translated into Latin and widely disseminated across Europe, forming the foundation for Western medical education during the 15th and 16th centuries. The Canon of Medicine was published more than 35 times during this period, highlighting its profound impact on the history of medicine.

Chronological features

During the early Caliphates of the Umayyads and Abbasids, Islamic medicine reached its peak, supported by the patronage of the Caliphs. This period saw both Muslim and non-Muslim physicians thrive, accumulating and expanding medical knowledge into what became known as Islamic medicine. The historian Ibn Khaldun noted that "Science thrives only in affluent societies," and indeed, between the 7th and 12th centuries, Islam integrated elements from Egyptian, Persian, Roman, and Near Eastern cultures, becoming the center of a brilliant civilization that excelled in science, philosophy, and the arts.

However, from the 15th century onward, the Islamic world faced significant challenges, including Mongol invasions, natural disasters, loss of trade, and European imperialism. These events led to political and economic decline, which, combined with the rise of the European Renaissance and scientific revolution, eventually challenged Islamic medicine.

The golden age of Islamic medicine, spanning from the 8th to the 14th centuries, was driven by several factors. First, Muslims, following the Prophet's encouragement to seek knowledge, highly respected scholars, leading to strong support from the Caliphs for science, medicine, and philosophy. Caliph al-Ma'mun founded the House of Wisdom in Baghdad, a major academic institution that became the center for translating Greek scientific works into Arabic. This institution played a crucial role in advancing Islamic science, philosophy, art, and architecture, producing some of the greatest thinkers of the Islamic world.

Another key factor was the ease of communication across the vast Islamic Empire, facilitated by the universal use of the Arabic language. This linguistic unity removed language barriers and fostered the exchange of knowledge. The widespread availability of books, supported by the introduction of paper-making from China, led to the establishment of libraries and learning institutions across the Islamic world, from Cairo to Baghdad to Spain. This academic atmosphere not only preserved ancient knowledge but also stimulated new scientific and medical advancements that would later influence European scholars.

Early development (6th to 9th century)

The influence of Greek medicine on Islamic practice was well established before Islam's rise, particularly in Jundishapur, where Khusraw Anushirwan (531-579 AD) founded a renowned medical school and hospital. This center integrated Greco-Syriac and Indian medical knowledge, thriving even after the Islamic invasion. The first recorded Muslim physician, Harith bin Kalada, was educated there, and the school's teachings, influenced by Alexandria and Antioch, became a model for later Islamic medical institutions.

During the Umayyad and Abbasid Caliphates, Jundishapur's influence persisted. Scholars like Sergius of Rasulayn translated the works of Hippocrates and Galen into Syriac, later translated into Arabic, deeply impacting Islamic medicine. Under the Abbasids, Baghdad emerged as a major medical hub.

Caliph al-Mansur invited Jirjis Bukhtyishu, the head of Jundishapur, to treat him, sparking the establishment of numerous hospitals and an Islamic Renaissance in medicine.

Hunayn ibn Ishaq (808–873 AD) was pivotal in this era, translating Greek and Syriac medical texts into Arabic, including works by Galen and Hippocrates. His translations enriched the Arabic medical lexicon, laying the foundation for a sophisticated medical language. Another important figure, Ali ibn Sahl (Al-Tabari), authored 'Paradise of Wisdom', one of the oldest encyclopedias of Islamic medicine, incorporating knowledge from Greek, Syriac, Persian, and Indian sources.

A significant development during this period was the establishment of hospitals funded by charitable donations (Zakat tax). By the 8th century, these hospitals had spread throughout the Islamic world, becoming a cornerstone of Islamic medical contributions. Secular hospitals, known as Bimaristans, also developed throughout the Arab world, offering inpatient and outpatient care without discrimination based on gender, religion, social, or economic status.

Islamic hospitls not only provided care but also served as centers for education and research, sending physicians and midwives to rural areas. The education of physicians was highly structured, often based on tutorship, with meticulous record-keeping to ensure accountability and facilitate knowledge dissemination. Islamic medical studies included rigorous training in basic sciences like alchemy, pharmacognosy, anatomy, and physiology, followed by clinical training in hospitals. Physicians were required to pass oral and practical exams to be licensed. Medicine was seen as both a science and a philosophical practice grounded in religion and ethics.

Islamic scholars also made significant contributions to pharmacology. Early works on pharmacognosy predated the translation of Greek texts, such as those by Dioscorides. By the 9th century, these texts' translation into Arabic laid the groundwork for further developments in Islamic pharmacology. Scholars experimented with herbs, anesthetics, and techniques like distillation and crystallization, introducing new drugs like camphor, senna, and musk. The first pharmacies were established in Baghdad in 754 AD, and by the 12th century, pharmacology had become an independent discipline, separate from medicine and alchemy.

Al-Kindi (800-870 AD), one of the greatest Islamic polymaths, played a crucial role in developing Islamic pharmacy. While heavily influenced by Galen, he made unique contributions through his 'Aqrabadhin (Medical Formulary)', describing preparations from plant, animal, and mineral sources. He incorporated knowledge from India, Persia, and Egypt into the existing corpus. The work of scholars like Al-Kindi marked the first significant division between medicine and pharmacology as distinct sciences in history, laying the foundation for modern pharmaceutical practices.

Islamic Epoch (10th to 13th Century)

During this era, Islamic medicine reached its peak, producing many notable physicians whose works became standard references for centuries. These scholars' contributions also laid the foundation for European Renaissance medicine, where many ancient Greek texts, preserved and expanded upon in

Arabic, were rediscovered.

This era also saw one of the largest and most advanced hospitals, the Mansuri Hospital in Cairo, which was completed in 1248 under the Mameluke ruler Mansur Qalaun. This hospital could accommodate 8,000 patients and featured separate wards for different medical specializations, including surgery, fevers, and eye diseases. It also housed a pharmacy, library, lecture halls, and places of worship for both Muslim and Christian patients, reflecting the inclusive nature of Islamic medical care.

Among the most famous physicians of this period was Muhammad ibn Zakariya al-Razi (865-923 AD), who became the chief of a Baghdad hospital and made significant contributions to medicine. Al-Razi is credited with differentiating smallpox from measles, introducing mercurial ointments, and authoring over 200 books, including 'Al-Hawi', a 30-volume medical encyclopedia that became a cornerstone of Western medical education. His works remained standard texts until much later when figures like al-Majusi and Ibn Sina emerged.

Al-Majusi (died 982-994 AD) was another significant figure, directing the Aduddawlah Hospital and writing 'The Complete Book of the Medical Art', a well-organized and systematic text. Al-Zahrawi (930-1013 AD), known as the father of surgery, introduced tracheotomy, lithotomy, and the use of cotton and catgut in surgery. His 30-volume' Tasrif' became the first illustrated surgical textbook and remained the standard in Western universities for centuries.

Ibn Sina (980-1037 AD), also known as Avicenna, was perhaps the greatest physician of the Islamic era. His Canon of Medicine later served as the standard medical textbook in Europe until the 17th century. Ibn Sina's expertise extended beyond medicine to philosophy, metaphysics, and logic, earning him the title "The chief master" and "the second philosopher after Aristotle." He made significant advances in diagnosing diseases, stressing hygiene, dietetics, and a holistic approach to patient care.

Ibn al-Nafis (1210-1288 AD) was another crucial figure, best known for his discovery of pulmonary circulation. He challenged Galenic physiology, correctly describing the lesser circulation of blood from the heart to the lungs, a concept that was not fully understood in Europe until centuries later. His boldness in questioning established medical theories set him apart as one of the greatest physicians of his time.

In pharmacology, al-Biruni (973-1050 AD) authored 'The Book on Drugs', a comprehensive compendium of drugs and their uses, while Ibn al-Baytar (1197-1248 AD) wrote the 'Compendium on Simple Medicaments and Foods', an extensive alphabetical guide to over 1,400 medicinal items. These works were pivotal in the development of Islamic pharmacology and were widely referenced in both the Islamic world and Europe.

Epilogue

Islamic scholars gathered extensive medical knowledge from around the world, adding their own observations and innovations, laying the foundation for modern medicine. Islamic medicine represents a significant period of advancement in the history of medicine, especially before the technological developments of the 20th century.

Today, Islamic medicine, particularly Unani (Tibb) medicine, continues to be practiced in parts of South Asia, with medical schools in India teaching it alongside modern medicine. Unani medicine is also practiced in rural and urban areas, regulated by the Indian Medical Council, and enjoys popularity in Afghanistan, Malaysia, and parts of the Middle East.

The primary challenge for Islamic medicine today lies not in its practice but in adapting it to modern needs. A dichotomy between Islamic and Western medicine emerged in the late 16th and 17th centuries, raising questions about how Islamic medicine is defined and integrated into contemporary healthcare systems.

Keywords

Islamic medicine, Quran, Prophetic medicine, House of Wisdom, Ibn Sina, *Canon of Medicine*

References

Manfred Ullmann, *Islamic Medicine*, Edinburgh University Press, 1997.

Guy Attewell, "Islamic Medicines: Perspectives on the Greek Legacy in the History of Islamic Medical Traditions in West Asia," In H. Selin (Ed.), *Medicine Across Cultures: History and Practice of Medicine in Non-Western Cultures*, 325–350. Kluwer Academic Publishers, 2003.

Husain F. Nagamia, "Islamic medicine history and current practice," *JISHIM (Journal of the International Society for the History of Islamic Medicine)*. 2003; 2 (4): 19–30.

Peter E. Pormann and Emilie Savage-Smith, *Medieval Islamic Medicine*, Edinburgh University Press, 2007.

written by Min Bae (Busan University of Foreign Studies)

Index

372, 381~383, 388, 391~395, 398,
399, 408, 415, 418~420, 423, 425, 509,
531~533

Mythology 20, 29~31, 36, 38

Dictionary of the Mediterranean
Inter-Civilization Exchanges

초판인쇄 2024년 11월 29일
초판발행 2024년 11월 29일

지은이 Yong Soo YOON
펴낸이 채종준
펴낸곳 한국학술정보(주)
주 소 경기도 파주시 회동길 230(문발동)
전 화 031-908-3181(대표)
팩 스 031-908-3189
홈페이지 http://ebook.kstudy.com
E-mail 출판사업부 publish@kstudy.com
등 록 제일산-115호(2000. 6. 19)

ISBN   979-11-7318-055-2 93920

that in the year 835 C.E., a dozen bells were fixed in the cathedral of Le Mans in France as this practice was spreading throughout the Frankish domains, though it took to the 10th century for large bells to be installed in smaller country churches throughout Western Europe. Bellringing came increasingly to take on a more central role in society. In addition to church bells, civil tower alarm bells or 'campanili' started being built with the intention of guarding the city defences and securing their populations. One of the earliest civic towers was built in Venice around the year 1000, while another one was constructed in Ragusa (Dubrovnik) in 1444. Indeed, the period starting from the 12th to the 14th centuries was one characterised by the spread of civic tower bells in Europe.

Fig 40–1. Church bell tower Noto Sicily

however, Christians had generated a mythology about the origin of church bells, associating them with Christian personages, martyrs, hermits, and saints. The most popular of these were the above-mentioned Saint Anthony of Egypt and Saint Paulinus of Nola (ca. 353–343), the latter of whom was supposed to have invented the church bell around the year 400. But again, for all these stories, there is no solid historical evidence.

From 610 c.e. another religion important in the history of bells was also spreading: Islam. According to the teachings of Islam, the human voice is the only worthy instrument to call the faithful to worship. This belief, sustained by the conviction that the sound of bells disturbed the souls reposing in the atmosphere, established a negative perception of bellringing among Muslims. Consequently, in Islamic regions, including the South-eastern European Christian countries that formed part of the Ottoman Empire (ca. 1300–1918), bellringing was generally regulated and, in some cases, prohibited.

In Christian Europe, bells started to be listed in church inventories, and bell-ringing practices were recorded in ecclesiastical texts during the Middle Ages. Bells were usually rung in two ways: either by striking the bell with an external hammer (pulsare) or by a rope tied to the internal clapper (nollare), with the bell being in a fixed place. This led to the casting of bells with a loop on top to be hung on a log, usually in a window arch. At this same time, bell-tolling, institutionalized as the voice of a powerful Church, was coming under strict canonical rules. Apart from handbells which were operated inside abbeys and monasteries, the larger bells were gradually installed in the more important churches by the permission of the ecclesiastical authorities. Hence, one finds